EATING WELL
WHEN YOU JUST CAN'T EAT THE WAY YOU USED TO

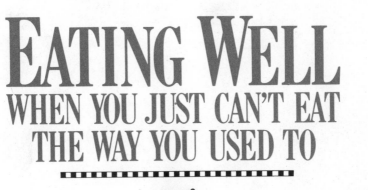

EATING WELL
WHEN YOU JUST CAN'T EAT THE WAY YOU USED TO

BY
JANE WESTON WILSON

ILLUSTRATED BY
G. BRIAN KARAS

WORKMAN PUBLISHING, NEW YORK

Library of Congress Cataloging-in-Publication Data
Wilson, Jane W.
Eating well when you just can't eat the way you used to.

Bibliography: p.
Includes index.
1. Cookery.   2. Aged—Nutrition.   I. Title.
TX715.W74915   1987   641.5′627   85-40525
ISBN 0-89480-943-1 (pbk.)

Cover design by Kathleen Herlihy Paoli
Book design by Kathleen Herlihy Paoli with Margaret Lem
Cover and book art by G. Brian Karas

Workman Publishing Company, Inc.
1 West 39 Street
New York, New York 10018

Manufactured in the United States of America
First printing November 1987

10 9 8 7 6 5 4 3 2 1

We are grateful to those authors and publishers who gave us permission to include recipes that previously appeared in other sources.

p. 201 From *Gourmet Cookery for a Low-Fat Diet* by Elise Cavanna and James Welton. Copyright © 1956. Reprinted by permission of Prentice-Hall, Inc. Englewood Cliffs, N.J.

p. 207 Reprinted from *The Taste of Washington* by Fred Brack and Tina Bell. Copyright © 1986 by Fred Brack and Tina Bell. Published by Evergreen Publishing Co., Seattle, Wash.

pp. 220, 263 From *Simple Food for the Good Life* by Helen Nearing. Copyright © 1982. Published by Delta/Eleanor Friede Books. Reprinted by permission of the author.

p. 238 From *The Northwest Cookbook* by Lila Gault. Reprinted by permission of The Putnam Publishing Group. Copyright © 1978 by Lila Gault.

p. 250 From *Cold Pasta* by James McNair. Copyright © 1985 by James McNair. Published by Chronicle Books. Reprinted by permission of the publisher.

pp. 276, 283 From *Real Food* by Marian Tracy. Copyright © 1978 by Marian Tracy. Reprinted by permission of Viking Penguin, Inc.

p. 280 From *Lifespice Saltfree Cookbook* by Ruth and Hilary Baum. Reprinted by permission of the Putnam Publishing Group. Copyright © 1986 by Footnote Productions Ltd.

p. 352 From *Festive Vegetarian: Recipes and Menus for Every Occasion* by Rose Elliot. Copyright © 1982, 1983 by Rose Elliot. Reprinted by permission of Random House, Inc.

p. 354 Copyright © 1986 by the Center for Science in the Public Interest.

p. 371 This recipe first appeared in *Family Weekly* magazine.

DEDICATION

▲▲▲

To my over-50 compatriots and the burgeoning group on their way to
becoming 50:
May we feast lightly so we can flourish longer.

To my mother, whose early death drew me to the kitchen for comfort and
nurturing.

In sweet memory of
Jeff, Danny, Jerry, Frank, Jean, Marcie, Ceil, Bob.

To my role models, who shower courage, commitment, talent, generosity
and abounding joy on their work and dreams:
*Maggie Kuhn, Eda LeShan, Myrna Lewis, Joan Gussow, Frances Moore
Lappe, Joanne Woodward, Lena Horne, Colin Tudge, Paul Hawken,
Edward Espe Brown, Stephen Levine and Paul Newman.*

To two very new and much loved beings in the world:
Sylvie and Ariana.

ACKNOWLEDGMENTS

▲▲▲

Ceil Gross collaborated with me on this book, taking it on as a full-time job,
organizing voluminous material, and testing endless recipes in those early
months. Her commitment to and belief in the book were with me all the way
through.

Carol Saltus brought her consummate writing talent to this book, in
style, in structure, and in love of language; without her rich and forceful
contribution, the project would not have come to fruition.

Thanks to Laura Torbet for first showing me how to make the book
viable, and to Jane Gilmartin Gilchrist for expertly taking it to the next stage
where it became workable. Many other talented people helped clarify some
of the ideas in this book; they include Gloria Hainline, Rose Mary Mechem
Gordon, Harriet Mason, Kathleen Brady, and Janis Graham.

I'm grateful to two nutritionists, Mae Norris and Jenny Harris, who
helped me grasp the principles of healthy eating. And Dr. Joseph Fennelly
gave of his expertise by reading the health section of this book.

My hat goes off to Elizabeth deUnda, Chef Fedele Panzarino and Madeleine Boulanger, who turned me from an amateur cook into a professional one. My warm appreciation also to the great cooks and fine friends who enhanced the book by sharing their recipes and love of food: Nene Schardt, Hans Hartmann, Leila Melman, Susan Dresner, and Barbara Grogan. The recipe testers, who offered many valuable ideas and suggestions, included: Eleanor Tomic, a gifted caterer and cook who tested and scaled down many of our Party Box recipes and generously shared recipes of her own; DeAnn and Dan Murphy; Chuck Baran; Stella Baran; Sandy Norris; Marion Belcher; Susan Goss; and Arthur Gross.

My thanks to Wayne Hamm for manuscript editing and typing hundreds of recipes over and over again, as well as for his constant support and good cheer. Additional manuscript typing help came from Davidson Lloyd and Dolores Modrell.

I'd like to thank Barbara Plumb for bringing me to Peter Workman's attention; Peter Workman for his enthusiasm for this subject; senior editor Sally Kovalchick for standing in for the reader until this book achieved clarity; Bob Gilbert for his dedication to the book and kindness and patience with me; Kathy Herlihy Paoli and Judy Jones for art and copy; Brian Karas for the illustrations; and Babs McLain, who on the phone and in person always made me feel welcome.

Thanks to my agent, Berenice Hoffman, who stood by me and for this book and never lost faith in either.

Thanks also to the boss ladies who make up my support system and network; to my friends who lovingly and with humor and compassion stayed the course and made this part of the journey worth the long effort; and of course to Vangie Hayes and Hank McGarrity, who got me to take a chance on turning my avocation into a vocation and taking the plunge into my career and business, The Party Box.

There isn't a bouquet large enough to give all the young men and women who came through The Party Box and who made our parties both work and fun. And I would especially like to thank Mary Michaels for seventeen years of unswerving work and care for our parties and Donna Lindemann for getting everything and everyone to the parties with unfailing accuracy and good spirits.

The Time of Our Lives

▼▼▼

I began this book after I discovered that there are no guides to eating well and living well for those of us who are fifty and over. I did discover books that explained very scientifically, very dryly, how to restrict our diets and how to cut back, down, and out. But I found few guides that encouraged us to live and eat more abundantly and enjoyably by adapting the food we've known and loved all our lives to our new lifestyle—a lifestyle that makes it possible for us to move into the second half of our lives with undiminished energy, enthusiasm, and buoyancy.

Although we're increasing in numbers more rapidly than any other age group, we find very little written for us as a group. It is up to us to look after ourselves. We need to share our experience —and experience is one thing we've all got plenty of—to help ourselves and each other.

We have a fresh opportunity to redefine ourselves—our relationships, our health, our future. Front and center in this reassessment is how and what we eat.

The aim of this book is to show you how to feast every day (but lightly), how to entertain often, how to splurge on occasion; and how to do it all in a healthy way.

CONTENTS

▼▼▼

The Time of Our Lives vii
A Fifty-Year Love Affair 1

Chapter I

FEASTING EVERY DAY–5

▼▼▼

New Styles of Eating. 7
Eating Well as a Couple 12
Eating Well as a Single Person . . 18

Chapter II

HEALTH: THE BODY IS THE NEW FRONTIER–22

▼▼▼

Understanding the Body 23
Oops! I Can't Eat the Way I
    Used To 28
One Diet for All 30
Portion and Proportion:
    A Truly Balanced Diet. 34
How to Diet and Not Notice It . 38

Chapter III

SHOPPING SMART: HOW TO SPEND, HOW TO SAVE–45

▼▼▼

The Weekly Supermarket
    Shopping Guide 47
Alternatives to the Supermarket 54

Chapter IV

STREAMLINED PREPARATION–58

▼▼▼

Equipment 59

Saving Time in the Kitchen 61

Chapter V

ENTERTAINING FOR THIS SEASON OF OUR LIVES–73

▼▼▼

Friendly Occasions 77
Summer Entertaining: Light
    and Simple Entertaining 88
Entertaining for a Crowd 96
Holiday Entertaining 103

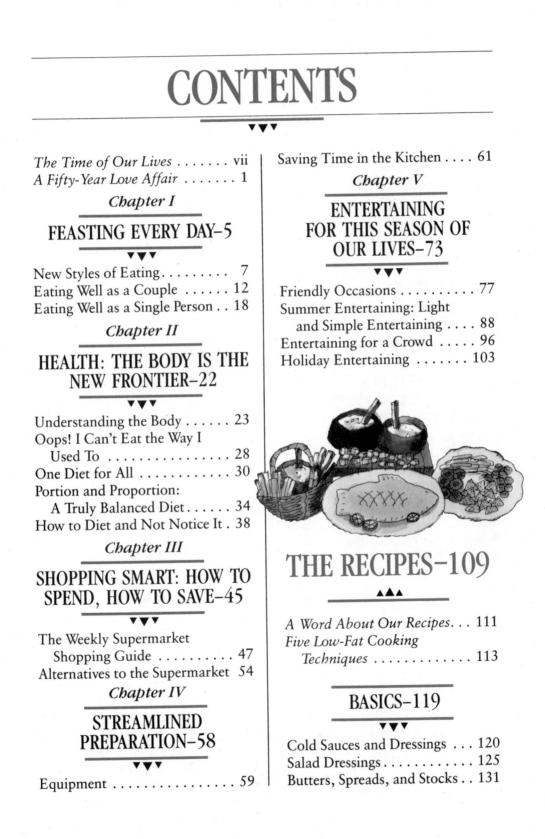

THE RECIPES–109

▲▲▲

A Word About Our Recipes. . . 111
*Five Low-Fat Cooking
    Techniques* 113

BASICS–119

▼▼▼

Cold Sauces and Dressings . . . 120
Salad Dressings 125
Butters, Spreads, and Stocks . . 131

HORS D'OEUVRES/ BUFFET–141
▼▼▼
Hot Hors d'Oeuvres 142
Cold Hors d'Oeuvres 148
Hors d'Oeuvres for a Light Buffet
    or Late Supper 152

SOUPS–161
▼▼▼
Cold Soups 162
Hot or Cold Soups 167
Hot Soups. 173
Entrée Soup-Stews 177

ENTRÉE AND SIDE VEGETABLES–183
▼▼▼
Entrée Vegetables 184
Side Vegetables 194

GRAINS AND BEANS–209
▼▼▼
Rice 210
Bulgur, Couscous, Kasha 217
Beans 223
Impromptu Bean Dishes 227
Lentils and Peas. 230

PASTA–235
▼▼▼
Hot Pasta Dishes. 236
Cold Pasta Dishes 249

THE SALAD SCENE–253
▼▼▼
Entrée Salads 254

Interchangeable Side Salads. . . 267
Satisfying Vegetable Salads . . . 275
Light and Lively Aspics 282
Light and Lively Slaws 284

CASSEROLES–287
▼▼▼
Freeze-Aheads. 294

FISH AND SEAFOOD–305
▼▼▼
Baked Seafood 306
Broiled, Sautéed, and Grilled
    Seafood. 312
Poached and Steamed Seafood 318

POULTRY–321
▼▼▼
The Versatile Chicken 322

MEAT–333
▼▼▼
Beef Dishes 334
Other Meats 338

DESSERTS–343
▼▼▼
Everyday Desserts 344
Muffins and Quick Breads . . . 353
"There, There" Desserts 358
Cookies 361
Special Splurge Desserts 367

Appendix 373
Mail-Order Shopping 374
Bibliography. 376
Index 379

A Fifty-Year Love Affair

▼▼▼

I've been in love with cooking and entertaining since I was a child. The family tradition of festive food probably started with my grandmother, who sometimes acted as hostess for her brother, Will Stephens, when he was governor of California.

I first learned about food during my childhood from the succession of cooks—black, German, and Swedish—who moved through the kitchen in our big house in Los Angeles, helping my father and grandmother bring up two motherless girls. For me, the sunny, five-windowed kitchen looking out on the lovely backyard with its purple and green fig trees and flourishing grape arbor was the heart of the house. Something was always cooking on or in the Old Reliable stove—bubbling soups and stews, fragrant pans of bread and rolls, browning casseroles.

I loved the daily round of kitchen chores—rinsing vegetables, and pushing potatoes through the ricer and meat through the grinder. But the most fun was the special chores we did when we entertained: rolling butter balls between two grooved wooden paddles; polishing little silver nut dishes for the burnished cashew nuts my grandmother oven-roasted for the holidays.

When I was eight, my grandparents celebrated their fiftieth wedding anniversary. We had a caterer for that unforgettable occasion, and the kitchen was full of bustling activity and wonderful smells. People and presents were everywhere; there were trays and trays of dainty hors d'oeuvres, and a huge cake. From that day I still treasure a lovely fruit bowl edged with gold filigree.

Another special day was my thirteenth birthday. We had a delicious chicken salad, with chocolate icebox cookies and whipped cream for my birthday cake. And as a special treat, my father took my twelve teenage friends and me to see the movie *Pinocchio.*

My father, a fanatic Stanford University alumnus and

booster, frequently had friends to Saturday lunch during football season. The women wore huge, feathery chrysanthemums that perfumed the house. My father was a man of immense charm and *joie de vivre*. His first love was music. At parties late at night, I used to sit at the top of the stairs, listening with delight as he played and sang his own songs and the show tunes of the day, while conversation and laughter bubbled around him. The food was an inseparable part of the gaiety. We served big California-style salads—Caesar, chicken with vegetables or fruit, tiny baby shrimp with dill, seafood—and hot and cold roasts, aspics, and homemade sponge or angel food cakes.

After I grew up and moved to New York, I never forgot those wonderful parties and I never let cramped apartments cramp my style. Throughout careers in publishing, advertising copywriting, and theater, entertaining was my greatest pleasure and favorite way to relax.

FROM A PARTY IN A BOX TO COOKING FOR 4,000

▲▲▲

Almost by chance, at the ripe age of forty-two, parties became my profession. An idea for a "Party in a Box"—launched in my seven-by-ten-foot apartment kitchen, with a freezer in the bedroom—led to a whole new career. For two years my little cottage food industry survived nicely in my tiny apartment. Then a write-up by Jean Hewitt in *The New York Times* and a reception I catered for four hundred at Time, Inc. for the Mexican Winter Olympics (I enlisted the help of many friends and *their* apartments) pushed me out into the world to look for a larger space.

I found a little shop a few blocks from my home. It was only fifteen by thirty feet, but compared to my apartment it seemed huge. It became a retail store, where we prepared all the components for a party, from hors d'oeuvres to desserts; customers could either buy the whole meal from us, or just one or two dishes. In those early days, people were drawn into the store by the aroma of pecan chess tarts and lemon-lime chicken, and the stacked florists' boxes packed to the brim with goodies for picnics and concerts in the park—that was the main emphasis then, although I did cater a few large parties.

In 1972 I met Jeff Perlman, an advertising copywriter who was moonlighting as the Underground Chef. Not only was he a great and imaginative cook; he was also a gifted designer who set the stage and created the decor for our festivities. Together we catered parties that served, over the years, more than a quarter-million people.

We had more than our share of glamorous and glittering evenings: a party on Pier 92 for the NAACP, which featured Alvin Ailey and the cast of *Ain't Misbehavin'* and a live disco; a fashion show of Bill Blass' favorite gowns at Bergdorf-Goodman; a cocktail buffet at Bloomingdale's for one of Paul Newman's favorite charities. There were celebrations at the great public places of New York: a fund-raiser at the New York City Opera where Beverly Sills sang and Nureyev danced; a party at the New York Botanical Garden in the Bronx to mark the release of Stevie Wonder's album "The Life of Plants"; and a reception for the King and Queen of Sweden at the Brooklyn Museum, to name only a few.

It all culminated one warm spring night when approximately four thousand celebrated the Brooklyn Bridge Centennial. Under a yellow and white tent by the water's edge, fourteen hundred New York movers and shakers dined on a cold supper of filet mignon with horseradish sauce; gala vegetables; snow pea, mushroom, and daikon salad; and Vienna chocolate cake, amid a spectacular fireworks display. Earlier that same evening, two thousand people wandered through the neighborhoods near the bridge. The streets had been decorated in the style of the New York of 1883—our bartenders wore striped jackets and bowler hats, and some of New York's notables strolled about in period dress. Huge buffet tables lined the streets and displayed the fantastic variety of New York's ethnic foods: Chinese, Italian,

Middle Eastern, among others. Aboard a boat in the East River, four hundred guests of Time, Inc. were served hors d'oeuvres and a huge seafood salad of shrimp, scallops, and red and green peppers, along with chicken sesame, followed by chocolate bursts, lemon squares, and great clusters of grapes and strawberries. A wonderful celebration for New York City's favorite bridge.

Throughout The Party Box's kaleidoscope of festivities, certain ways with food remained constant. We always made a point of using the freshest food, of the highest quality. Our food tasted of itself; we never tried to disguise it with overseasoned sauces. Our clients loved our fresh vegetables, our lighter desserts, our entrées featuring fish and chicken rather than red meat. Elaborate galantines dripping with Madeira, mousselines, and beef Wellington were not our style. Food beautifully presented and tasting of itself was The Party Box style.

After seventeen hectic but wonderful years as a party giver, I retired from the profession, but food and entertaining remain the center of my life.

Chapter 1

FEASTING EVERY DAY

▼▼▼

Coming as I do from the world of feasting and parties, and needing to devise a new, healthier style of eating for this period of my life, I've learned how to reconcile what would appear to be two opposing lifestyles: how to feast every day, yet maintain a healthy and weight-controlling diet.

Feasting every day is a concept that means many things, but above all it encourages abundance rather than settling for deprivation. I don't think it's any fun to count calories, and I don't intend to begin now. "Indulge in moderation," said Albert Camus, and that's an appropriate slogan for this time of our lives. We also need to bring imagination, inventiveness, and a sense of adventure to the way we nourish ourselves every day.

Feasting every day means exploring the world's cuisines for dishes we can adapt to the American kitchen. You'll find recipes in this book from Morocco, China, India, Mexico, and points in between. Many of the foods are peasant dishes that use seasonings and spices to enhance their subtlety. Our healthier cooking uses complementary accompaniments—light sauces, dressings, condiments—to add piquancy and counterpoint to the inherent flavor of the basic ingredients themselves.

Feasting every day does not have to cost a lot. The peasant-based dishes in this book use inexpensive ingredients. Fresh fruit may seem like an extravagance, but it is actually much cheaper than a ready-made cake. Take advantage of what's in season at its precise peak of perfection; husk an ear of corn sweet enough to eat raw, fresh from the farm stand; on a crisp October day, enjoy a fragrant Anjou pear. Every day you can have "party food"—the kind we tend to think of as too expensive and luxurious for daily fare—for much less than you'd pay for commercially prepared "gourmet" entrées: strawberry and pineapple kabobs are every-day food as special as party food—special, not because of its richness, but for its perfect freshness, flavor, and just as impor-tant, its beauty. When you think of memorable party feasts, wasn't it the appearance of the food, the style with which it was presented and served, and the visual harmony of color and form, just as much as the taste, that made it an experience to be savored?

Eating is the most sensuous of all human activity. Food should be prepared with love and joy, and should always remain a central source of nourishment for *all* our senses. It should appeal not only to taste, but also to sight, smell, touch, and even hearing. All the knowledge about the aesthetic appeal of food— the texture, the colors, the feel of the food—that I've accumu-lated over the years as a party giver is yours to explore in the recipes, menus, and suggestions for entertaining that I share with you here.

This time of life brings with it not only the opportunity to eat better than ever before, but also the chance to make mealtime a more rewarding experience in all kinds of ways. Freed from the responsibility of raising a family, we can now take time for ourselves—that can mean either streamlining the preparation and serving of meals, or restoring to mealtime something of its old ceremonial meaning. We can take either more time, or less—and I'll show you how to do both.

New Styles of Eating: We're Ones and Twos Now

▼▼▼

In this time of life we're liberated from many of the constraints of family and work life, and that means we're free to experiment with new patterns of eating, to revitalize our attitudes toward mealtimes, the central events of our day. But so often in my travels I hear people say, "I don't bother when it's only me." "We don't fuss with meals now that it's just the two of us." "We don't entertain much any more."

It makes me sad to hear that, because such statements reflect a denial of self and a refusal to appreciate the simple joy of preparing and eating good food. Of course it's important to know how to keep meals simple when we need and want to. Our free time, our leisure, is truly precious; even though we may have more of it now, we still don't want to waste any of it. On the other hand, we should not seek total escape from the kitchen into the frozen foods section of the nearest supermarket.

One of the best ways to take advantage of our new flexibility, and one you may not have thought of, is to rearrange the schedule of meals. Take the cue from other countries. Try breakfast at midmorning, lunch in midafternoon, and a light supper or *tapas* later in the evening as they do in Spain. Or, take a long siesta after lunch, then dine at eight or nine. Or do as the English do—make "high tea" at four in the afternoon the main meal of the day.

Two Breakfasts

When we rushed the kids to school before rushing off to the office, we usually shoveled a big breakfast into them and ourselves as soon as we woke up. Now we can start the day in a more relaxed way.

Wake yourself up with some light exercise, some easy stretches, or a brisk walk. Get your body going first, then break your fast with fruit. Make it an abundant meal, consisting only of fruit: a whole melon with fresh strawberries in summer, a combination of pears and persimmons in the fall; or two baked apples, or two poached pears. Make it a feast for the eye as well as the palate.

Then an hour or so later, eat a second breakfast. I learned to do this from a nutritionist, Jenny Harris. I had chronic low blood sugar that was exacerbated by the long fast of the night, and when I complained that by midmorning I was ravenous, to the point where I would gobble down our Party Box nut mix by the handful right out of the freezer, Jenny suggested the two-breakfast solution. This is a useful tip for many people; it raises the blood sugar in two stages and maintains it at a high level throughout the morning. Try a handful of nuts and yogurt, or a big helping of cereal and some low-fat cottage cheese for your second breakfast. To help reduce cholesterol and fat in your daily diet, save eggs for the weekend. Then make a special omelet or French toast.

Get a Third of Your Nutrients Early in the Day

Most health authorities recommend eating a third of your daily quotient of nutrients at breakfast. This doesn't mean, however, restricting your breakfast to "breakfast foods." Wherever did that rigid notion come from? Eggs, cereal, bacon, toast, the obligatory orange juice—no law, nutritional or otherwise, dictates such a menu. Over the years I've met many people who breakfast on soup and a salad, vegetables and pasta, or steak and potatoes. Experiment with varying the way you break your fast. In winter, a hearty miso tofu vegetable soup is a good start; in summer, a grain or vegetable salad.

Lunch: The Main Meal

Nutritional experts increasingly advocate making lunch the main meal of the day. You're getting nutrients for the afternoon ahead, and because your metabolism is higher in the middle of the day than toward the end, you burn more of the calories consumed at lunch more efficiently than those consumed at dinner, which means you're less likely to gain weight from lunch than from dinner. Have your meat and dairy foods at lunch; they take longer to digest, and can be better assimilated during the afternoon than at night.

LUNCHES TO GO

Menu 1
Carrot and Pignoli Loaf*

Five-Minute Salmon and White Bean Salad*

Florine Snider's Summer Poached Peaches or Nectarines*

Ginger Icebox Cookies*

Ginger Beer/Herb Tea

*Recipe included

Menu 2
Mainly Meat Meat Loaf with Green Herbs*

White Beans with Lemon*

Magenta and Orange Slaw*

Swedish Sweet Butter Cookies*

Sparkling Waters/Coffee

*Recipe included

I much prefer eating this way now that I'm used to it. I save the lighter foods—the vegetables, pasta, grains, and salad—for dinner. It doesn't make sense to eat heaviest just when we're winding down at the end of the day.

For many of us it makes sense to center our entertaining around lunchtime. This is our peak energy time, and it's a lovely occasion for lingering over a good meal. And at this time of our lives we often prefer not to drive after dark. Cold entrée salads are ideal for lunching in or out of doors, are easy to prepare, and make a bountiful meal, with a good balance of animal protein, and vegetables, pasta, grains, and beans (see Entrée Salads, pages 254–266).

Another lunchtime strategy is to pack a lunch for a daytime lecture, movie, concert, or tour; have it before or after the event. (See Lunches to Go, page 9.)

Dinner: Small Dishes as Entrées

Eating lighter at dinner is easy and fun if you serve a number of small dishes as the entrée. At The Party Box we developed many superb first courses for our fancy sit-down dinners that included salads, soups, fish, pasta, and vegetables. Two or three of these— such as a pasta with one of the pestos or roasted red pepper sauce; a stuffed artichoke or a new potato; walnut and watercress salad—would make a splendid meal. In restaurants I often order as my dinner a combination of all first courses such as soup, risotto, and fish. Such a selection offers a generous variety of flavor and texture, and is more satisfying than one big entrée. In fact, I find I almost always eat less this way, with fewer calories, than if I ordered a conventional three-course dinner.

You'll find in this book many choices for small-dish meals, including salads with grains and beans and half portions of entrée salads—all easy-to-prepare and which can be made ahead and eaten anywhere, anytime.

This new style of eating leaves you feeling satisfied, not stuffed, and ensures an easier, sounder night's sleep.

Many Small Meals a Day

During the year when I was following a special diet for a prediabetic condition, my doctor encouraged me to eat six small meals a day, giving my digestive system less to handle at any one time. This is good advice for most people. In addition to protecting the body from being assaulted with too much food at once, it ensures a steady flow of nutrients to the bloodstream, with fewer ups and downs of the blood sugar.

"The Arts of Eating"

Colin Tudge coined this phrase. *How* we eat in our middle and later years is just as important as when or what we eat. In his book *Future Food,* he says, "Sensuality is one thing and stoking up is another, and the two should not be confused." We Americans tend to rush through our meals, as though time spent at the dinner table is time wasted. That may have been necessary and inevitable when we were feeding growing families, but it is no longer the case. As my friend Elane Finley describes, "When I was raising six kids, I felt as though I were running a filling station. I filled them up, moved them out, and got on to the next meal."

We seldom, except at holidays, think of mealtime as a ceremony worth lingering over for its own sake. Yet in many countries, mealtime is one of the high points of the day, full of ritualistic significance. The Japanese have their tea ceremony. And even in pragmatic England, teatime is a ceremony almost outside time, with its own special traditional foods, elaborate tea-making and serving equipment and dishes, spirit lamps, exquisite china cups and saucers. In India, before food is served it is first placed on a small household shrine to receive a formal blessing from the gods protecting the house. To inaugurate or restore the ceremonial aspect of mealtime, now that we have the leisure to do so, is to bring a measure of order and beauty into our lives.

"Food is naturally beautiful. You want to add to its beauty, not detract from it," designer Paula Schaengold said to me when I visited her home on Long Island. In over thirty years of friendship, every meal I've ever had at Paula's has been composed (and I do mean composed, like a work of art) with beauty in mind. The arrangement at breakfast looks like a Japanese painting: a soft-cooked egg in its pristine white shell, set on a glass plate with a small gray bowl next to it; toast nestled in a snowy white napkin in a bamboo holder, butter in a wooden box; orange juice in squat, heavy French jam glasses. At lunch, two oysters rest on their half-shells on an oblong blue plate, with individual white trays of half an avocado, red peppers, and cucumbers. For dinner, Paula presents small pink crabs on large round wooden plates, cilantro butter in a terracotta pot, slivers of mackerel sashimi on a tiny plate, miso soup with cubed butternut squash in a bowl with a top, and rice with sesame seeds in a lacquered bowl. The art of serving has never been so simply or so profoundly expressed as in these small, perfect feasts.

Paula says, "It's no trouble for me to serve food this way. My mother always took the time to set a tablecloth and fresh napkins at every meal, and I just followed her example. I have a number of simple serving pieces and trays in wood, glass, pottery, and china—they're inexpensive and they lend such visual variety to our simple meals. Sometimes I set out meals on a tray; that saves a step. We can have our trays anywhere in the house—but I still like to arrange them thoughtfully and carefully."

She laughed when she told me about visiting a friend who really believed in saving steps. "She had bought some cold cuts at the deli, and she didn't even remove the paper; just opened the package and set it, paper and all, on a plate. When I offered to arrange it she said, 'Your stomach doesn't know the difference.' Well, I think it does! I think beautifully presented food puts you at ease, and you digest it better. At any rate, I know it *feels* better. It's much more satisfying. And what feels better must in some way be better for you. The Japanese have a saying: 'Food must first feast the eye.' And the Japanese reverence for daily living is an attitude I've adopted at least in the meals I serve."

EATING WELL AS A COUPLE

▲▲▲

Retiring may mean an even more difficult period of adjustment than marriage. For years, each partner was in charge of his or her own particular domain. Now these two "in charge" people are together in one domain, and some concessions may be necessary to make it work—as much in patterns of eating together, or separately, as in anything else. Twenty-four-hour-a-day togetherness can mean you'll be out of sync with each other, and out of sorts. But it was never written in stone that the two of you have to eat breakfast, lunch, and dinner together day in and day out, just because one or both of you has retired.

Times to Be Together

One of the nicest times of the day when you were working was the cocktail hour. It was a chance to relax and unwind from the pressures of the day, to talk things over, to rev up the palate for dinner with snacks and drinks. There's no reason to give that up now. The drinks may be lighter or even nonalcoholic, the snacks less caloric, but it's all in the interest of taking better care of ourselves and each other. The moment shared is what counts.

DELUXE DINING AT HOME

Interchangeable Hot or Cold Menu for Dinner or Later Supper

*Angel Hair with Broccoli Flowerets and Peas**

*Filet Mignon with Sylvia Sherry's Horseradish Sauce**

or

*Gala Vegetables**

Assorted Breadsticks

Raspberry Aspic with Chopped Fresh Lime with Marlu's Chocolate Bursts**

Demitasse Coffee or Decaffeinated Coffee

*Recipe included

On the special once-a-year occasions, New Year's Eve, a birthday, an anniversary, our thoughts automatically turn toward celebrating in a posh restaurant. But these days, making the restaurant scene can be more punishing than pleasurable, both to the person and the pocketbook. These are very special moments of coming together. Why eat out among strangers when you can dine sumptuously at home, with wine and candlelight, for under $25.00 for two? I offer an interchangeable hot or cold menu for deluxe dining that calls for flowers, linen napkins, and your best crystal and silver (page 13).

Times to Be Apart

If one of you whizzes through breakfast and the other likes to dawdle—why not? If lunch for the wife is peaches and cottage cheese or leftovers from the refrigerator—fine; but her husband is used to a substantial meal at lunch. So what's the solution? For a man who has worked all his adult life, the transition is not an easy one. Jules Willing in *The Reality of Retirement* writes, "To some men of the business world, the luncheon meeting is the most important part of the day... It is a meaningful ritual and often an elaborate one... The purpose of lunch at home is to eat—perhaps the least important aim of the business lunch.... One of the reasons the day seems to be longer for the retired person in the early months is that morning and afternoon run together without the lunchtime ritual."

Having lunch out makes a welcome break in the day. One way to do it is by scheduling sports activities at lunchtime: golf, swimming, tennis, a workout at the gym can recharge energy for the rest of the day. Going to a daytime film, taking a university extension or graduate course and using that occasion for a meal in a restaurant afterward or before, lends a fresh perspective, and provides some welcome time apart. "In all relationships," Jules Willing says, "some space is necessary across which partners can reach out to each other."

When Husband Retires First

School administrator Bill Proppe took early retirement, but Phyllis, his wife, continues to work as Director of the Volunteer Bureau of Greater Portland. When they both worked, Phyllis said, "I had an hour after I got home to put dinner together. Now, too often, when I open the door, there is 'Starving Bill' ready to eat right away because he has skipped lunch or just opened a can of his favorite chili. (Unless he has sampled pre-prepared dinner items that sometimes must be labeled *Do not eat!*) Bill and I both welcome ideas for stocking the refrigerator and cupboards with items to make satisfying lunches that are tempting and easy."

You'll find lots of recipes (see below) that will brighten up lunchtime, even for a kitchen novice on his own—and some take as little as ten minutes to prepare.

IMPROMPTU MEALS

These easy soups and salads can be made in 15 minutes or less and are perfect for a quick meal or nosh or a quick get-together.

SOUPS:
Five-Minute Purely Pea Soup
Beet and Cucumber Soup

SALADS:
Five-Minute Salmon and White
    Bean Salad
Green-and-White Tuna Salad

Whether prepared to freeze ahead or as individually packed leftovers, these dishes offer quick and easy meals and make last-minute entertaining a snap.

LOAVES:
Pacific Salmon Loaf
Mainly Meat Meat Loaf with
    Green Herbs
Carrot and Pignoli Loaf
Yellow Split-Pea Loaf with Vege-
    tables, Cheese, or Tofu

**ENTRÉES IN BOILABLE
    BAGS:**
Vegetable Chili
Picadillo
Chickadillo

Eating Lighter and Enjoying It More

Like so many of us, Ann and John Erwin feel that keeping their weight within healthy limits is the key to enjoying this season of their lives, which they've looked forward to for so long. John has semiretired from his real estate business, and the pressure is off. There's time now for traveling together, and a new lifestyle at home.

"When our family was growing up," says Ann, "like most mothers I cooked alone in the kitchen. The evening meal was the hearty one, lots of roasts and loaves and casseroles to fill everyone up. Now John likes to come into the kitchen and cook our small dinners, and I help him. We're company for each other—it's the best time of the day."

"I can't eat the way I did when I was forty," John says, "I simply can't. And I don't want to get fat. It's taken a bit of doing, I can tell you, to switch over. Cooking the way we do now has made it possible, but it didn't happen overnight."

Ann and I go back to junior high school days. When I visited them recently in Los Angeles, they told me, "We're going to treat you like family. This is the way we eat now." We had Chicken Piccata, Moroccan carrots, and fruit and cheese for dessert. There was wine for dinner, followed by decaffeinated espresso. Even though the meal was simple, none of the amenities of dining were sacrificed. Food was brought to the table on lovely serving dishes, there were candles, and coffee was served in one-of-a-kind demitasse cups from Ann's mother's collection.

This is Ann's and John's daily eating pattern, as Ann explains: "Breakfast is cereal and lots of fresh fruit. When we're home for lunch, we have cottage cheese, fruit, nuts, yogurt. We keep dinner simple, like the one we served you, Jane. We 'traded' the wine for starch, and we usually have fruit for dessert. We never feel stuffed, and the calories we save at home we can spend when we entertain and travel."

Ann and John Erwin's solution may not suit everyone; it takes some experimenting, some trial and error to learn which eating patterns work best for each of us. But this kind of experimentation is taking creative responsibility for your life and your health.

Different Waistlines

Matters can become complicated when one person tends to gain weight and has to curb his or her intake, while the other may have no difficulty maintaining a healthy weight. While Ross Hainline hasn't gained a pound in forty years, Gloria has been "edging up" a little and she's decided to get that extra weight off. Gloria points out, "When I want to maintain my weight, I serve myself a third less of what I give Ross. If I want to lose a pound or two, my portion is half of what I serve him."

Nene and Bernie Schardt ate the same amounts of food until Bernie retired. Nene, at five feet, ten inches, has always had to fight to keep her weight up to 104. Bernie, whose life had become more sedentary and less pressured, still liked his big portions, followed by a rich dessert. She knew that a sweet "Don't you think you've had too much, dear?" was definitely not the way to handle the problem.

"I just increased more of my own in-between-meal snacks and served less at regular meals. At the same time I encouraged Bernie to have a dessert of homemade plain or fruit bread and fresh jam, or one of my fruit aspics. This worked most of the time. When we ate out or entertained, Bernie could afford to let go a little since our daily eating pattern had become so much lighter for him."

For Will and June Stonier, forming new eating habits meant cutting out almost all butter and salt in cooking and substituting wine or lemon juice and fresh herbs. You don't miss the salt when food is flavorful enough either on its own or with good herb seasonings.

"We've even found," June says, "that the muffins I whip up for breakfast or lunch, with a bit of jam or preserves, also make a most satisfying dessert. It seems that when we gave up salt and butter, we were rewarded by a reduced craving for sweets."

Different Diets

Sometimes basic diets may differ. If one partner is on a restricted diet, such as no-salt, low-fat, or no dairy products, it is not necessary to cook two separate meals. Many of the foods in this book are prepared with little salt or other seasonings, and are cooked using methods requiring no fat, such as poaching, broiling, pan broiling, steaming, and baking. The dishes for each person can be prepared together, and then seasoned according to individual needs.

EATING WELL AS A SINGLE PERSON

▲▲▲

The attitude too many of us bring to eating alone is simple and bleak: "Why bother?" Why bother, that is, with anything more than getting the food inside us as expeditiously as possible. Some of us don't even take the trouble to sit down. We gulp our meals—if they can be called that—standing over the kitchen sink. Why do we treat ourselves this way? We would never dream of treating so thoughtlessly even a remote acquaintance who happened to drop in.

"When we're alone, we tend to put ourselves on 'ignore,'" is the way Edana Evans describes it. Edana raised four children as a single parent. Now they've all flown the coop. "At first, it was actually frightening to eat alone," she told me. "What I do now is fix myself a nice dinner—the kind of dinner I'd serve someone else—and set a place for myself, but not at the dining-room table. I fix a tray, I even put a flower on it, then I cozy up with a good book or in front of the TV."

Facing an empty chair across a table can make anyone feel lonely. A tray or a comfortable wooden cutting board permits you to eat wherever you want. And using pretty serving pieces and attractive settings, such as a little pottery dish to hold fresh lemon for tea, a nice pitcher for cream, a separate plate for salad, and pleasant utensils enhance your sense of occasion. These attentions do for yourself what they would do for a guest: they make you feel special.

Cooking for One at Home

Some of us don't feel like preparing elaborate meals or spending a lot of time in the kitchen; some of us are new to the kitchen. Yet we'd like to eat well. This book will help you to simplify meal planning and shopping in order to spend less time in the kitchen. It will offer advice on how to stock the freezer, and give you recipes for soups and salads for any-time-of-day eating. There are recipes for one-pot cooking with almost no cleanup, and for delicious entrées in a package (pages 307, 340).

Cooking for Two When You Are One

Sharing meals can be as casual as potluck. "I've got a casserole, you bring the salad greens." My neighbor Sam Assaid and I put together a Palm Sunday meal on fifteen minutes' notice, and we invited two other neighbors to share it with us (page 232).

Another time I stopped at a gourmet grocery take-out and found the delicacies irresistible. I was about to head for home when I realized I was just a few blocks from my friend Sandy Norris. I called and found she'd just come back from an early evening class. "This is better than if we'd planned it!" Sandy said. "When Bernie comes home we'll have this as a first-course antipasto, and all I'll have to do is heat up the chicken and peas from last night." We had a wonderful visit together, and sharing the food gave it an extra warmth.

Cooking together is a great antidote to loneliness. Too often, though, we tend to hold back, sure that no one else feels as we do. Don't hesitate to take the initiative. If shyness is in your way, get over it—it's now or never. This is no time to be inhibited in reaching out to others.

Cooking for Barter

"The Vegetable Chili is in the container with the blue lid on the bottom right-hand shelf of the refrigerator." I often leave some such message on my friend Del Gordon's answering machine. It's one of the ways I look after others, and get taken care of myself. So many of us, when we have no one to cook and care for, suffer a crippling lowering of self-esteem, which may even damage our health. This is true for both men and women.

Cooking for my young friends in our New York brownstone and for friends scattered around town gives me a sense of extended family. I usually make dinner for my working chums once or twice a week—it nurtures all of us. And in return, I get the kind of help I need. My neighbor Sam and I share a car and an urban garden, and take turns tending them. My exercise teacher Ellen Lederman gives me massages in exchange for heat-up dinners. Del solves any electrical or mechanical problems, whether it's my typewriter, phonograph, or living-room lamp.

All of us have particular skills. Mine is cooking; maybe yours is gardening, or doing handyman chores around the house or yard. When I visited my friend Nene on Cape Cod, she asked me to help her plant her garden. Plant we did, twenty-four geraniums and twenty-four yellow-orange marigolds, while sheltering under our sou'westers in the pouring rain. In exchange, that evening I got Nene's Classic New England Fish Chowder, my favorite.

Families of Choice

A new design for living is emerging in this country, in response to big changes in family patterns and to certain economic realities. And it's a design that can lead to countless new opportunities for enriching our later years. Maggie Kuhn, founder of the Gray Panthers, calls it the "family of choice," and as a result of her personal experience with shared living, Maggie has helped to organize the National Shared Housing Resource Center, and serves as chair of the board.

When Maggie's brother died and left her alone in a big house in Philadelphia, instead of selling it, she adopted her own family of choice: friends of all different ages who came to live with her. They all love it, and the person who is home least is Maggie, because she's on the road all the time promoting her ideas.

Maggie's solution is a vital option for the increasing number of retired single people who want an alternative to living alone. Two- or four-family houses which four or five people buy jointly is another option. Or there are the planned communities funded by insurance companies, hospitals, churches, or private investors. These offer a variety of living arrangements: houses, single rooms, apartments, or simple community dining rooms. What they have in common is a style of living that allows us to make new friends, and share the breaking of bread.

All these arrangements center around the kitchen, which we so often remember from our childhood as the gathering place, the heart of the house. Eating—our first joy, our first communion with the outer world—should remain always a fundamental pleasure, linking us all our lives long with our earliest memories of love.

Chapter II

HEALTH: THE BODY IS THE NEW FRONTIER

Until recently, health was defined simply as freedom from disease. But we have always felt that there was a great gulf between the fact of not being actually ill and buoyant well-being. Today we're reluctant to settle for anything less than living at the peak of our powers, whatever our age. And we're increasingly aware that this in turn depends to a large extent on the way we take care of our bodies in our middle and later years.

Many of us, as we approach these years, suffer more from a vague but pervasive anxiety about the body deteriorating, than from any actual physical problem. This anxiety, in turn, prevents us from facing the facts about aging—although here, as in every other area of life, knowledge is power. In the meantime, we continue to ignore our bodies as much as possible, until something goes awry. As comedian-activist Dick Gregory says, "We take better care of our cars than our bodies. We're always looking for the ideal fuel, we're careful to give them a checkup every 5,000 miles. . . ." We rarely give our bodies this kind of attention until they send out signals of distress.

Often the signals are simply the result of years of stress, lack of exercise, and poor eating habits. So when we hit fifty or so, we're entering what my friend Jane Gilchrist calls "the catch-up years"—when we face the payoff for previous years of neglect.

What doesn't help our anxiety at all is the polysyllabic words that seem to have been coined for the express purpose of striking terror into the heart of medical laypeople: osteoporosis, diverticulitis, atherosclerosis. If you're like me—or rather, the way I used to be—whenever you hear them, you simply shudder and quickly turn your mind to something else, praying that you don't ever have to find out what they mean. The only trouble is that this attitude is likely to result in a familiarity with them in the future.

UNDERSTANDING THE BODY

▲▲▲

Each of us has to take responsibility for keeping our body in optimum good health. This is a necessary price we must pay; what we once could be thoughtless about, we now need to pay some attention to. It's not a heavy price; it simply means that we can't take good health as much for granted as we once could.

Taking responsibility means, first of all, looking at some of the facts of aging, which, let me remind you, doesn't begin at the age of fifty, or thereabouts, but starts, in fact, when we are born. And the onset of some age-related conditions can begin as early as thirty, or in some cases even in the twenties.

An important fact to keep in mind is that our metabolism slows down as we get older. This is universal, and it's not any kind of ailment. All it means is that our bodies don't require as much fuel, or calories, for repair and maintenance as they did when we were younger. The problem is that our appetite remains the same. If we continue to eat the same amount while our metabolism slows down, we will inevitably gain weight.

This slower metabolism makes it more important than ever that we combine healthy eating habits, including reducing our intake of calories, with a regular program of exercise. It needn't be violent or strenuous, but exercise should become a daily habit. Exercise increases metabolism so that the body "burns" calories at a faster rate for hours afterward, making it easier to maintain or lose weight. It seems that exercise also normalizes the appetite, reduces cravings or the impulse to "binge." Exercise—the right kind—is more, not less, important for us over-fifties than it is for any other age group. It keeps our joints flexible, gives tone to our muscles, strengthens our bones, and helps maintain a high level of strength and endurance.

We also need to pay attention to the latest medical wisdom about the way our bodies work. Once it was thought that a high-protein diet was the ideal diet for weight loss. Now we've come to understand that for maximum health, energy, and longevity—as well as for maintaining and losing weight—the food family to emphasize is complex carbohydrates, the vegetable kingdom of whole grains, fresh fruits and vegetables, and legumes.

A diet high in complex carbohydrates also provides a great deal of fiber. Fiber is the indigestible residue, the outer husks of grains, the cellulose of vegetables and fruits. It moves all the way through the digestive system, and is now recognized to be a prime element in keeping the intestines healthy.

Increasing your intake of complex carbohydrates *automatically* reduces the intake of fats and sugars. The more vegetables, fruits, legumes, and grains you add to your diet, the fewer concentrated calories you'll be consuming in the form of animal fats and refined sugars. The reason for this is that complex carbohydrates, for the most part, have a higher ratio of bulk to calories than animal products. It's this greater bulk that satisfies hunger more cheaply, calorically speaking.

The complex carbohydrates, in other words, have it all: they're satisfying, lower in calories, and far more healthful than the animal fats and proteins. We shouldn't eliminate these last two from our diet entirely. Rather, we need to make sure that two-thirds of the foods in our diet come from the vegetable kingdom, and one-third from the animal. Many recipes and menus in this book have been devised to help you do just that.

Reducing our caloric intake is only half of the battle in dealing with a slower metabolism. We also need to increase "outgo" or exercise. At the beginning of the recent aerobic exercise craze, running and high-intensity aerobics involving a lot of jumping were considered just the ticket for fitter bodies. Since then, such strenuous exercise has been linked with joint injuries. It's now clear that the benefits of aerobic exercise can be achieved with far less violent forms such as: low-intensity aerobic dancing that involves no jumping; race walking, with a brisk arm swing; and even just ordinary brisk walking.

Perhaps the best all-around exercise, beneficial even for injured or arthritic joints, is swimming.

Tai Chi, an ancient Chinese discipline of meditative movements practiced as exercise and often called "swimming in the air," is also excellent for promoting flexibility, and tranquility, as is yoga. Any and all of these forms of exercise increase resilience, strength, and stamina, and their low-intensity character makes them easier to sustain as a lifelong program than the more strenuous high-intensity exercises.

One of the fearsome words associated with aging, which many of us had never even heard until a few years ago, is osteoporosis. It means literally "porous bones," and refers to a loss of calcium from our bones. Bones become more fragile and the spine begins to compress. This process begins in the mid-thirties, and is most common among post-menopausal women. Calcium, a component of all bodily fluids, is vitally connected to the heartbeat, nerve impulses, muscle contraction, enzymes and hormone regulation. If we're not getting enough calcium from our food, then our bodies take it from the bones. Women, whose skeletons are lighter than men's, are particularly susceptible to osteoporosis. There seems to be a link with the estrogen levels in women, which begin to slowly drop in the early thirties, and then accelerate through menopause.

I was fortunate enough to be part of a hospital study that measured bone density, the only reliable test for the presence of osteoporosis. For my age, my bone density was 10 percent below normal. The doctors advised exercise. My friend Ellen, who teaches exercise to the over-fifties, explained that exercise promotes tension in the skeletal system through skeletal muscle activity, and this in turn keeps bone mass high—yet another reason for stepping up our exercise. We also need to make sure there is plenty of calcium in our diet. We have to be careful here. Dairy products are a good source for calcium, but many are high in animal fats. Fortunately there are plenty of non-dairy sources of calcium available to us from the bountiful vegetable kingdom, as well as low-fat dairy products such as skim milk.

Another word whose meaning most of us are fuzzy about is diverticulosis. This is a condition in which little pouches pop through the inner lining of the colon, creating pockets that can harbor bacteria. It is widely believed that the pouches occur because our low-fiber diet does not provide enough bulk passing through the colon to keep it active.

If these little pouches become infected and rupture, we then have the disease called diverticulitis, whose symptoms are pain, chills, fever, constipation, and bleeding from the rectum. If it becomes serious enough, it may require surgery. Says Dr. Martin E. Plaut, author of *The Doctor's Guide to You and Your Colon,* "... half of the American population older than sixty years have diverticulosis. Can we prevent these troublesome complications? A diet high in fiber may be a valuable preventive measure. More fiber or bulk widens the colon and as a result lowers the pressure inside it [which prevents the formation of the little bacteria-harboring pockets]." It is recommended that if we have this condition, we avoid eating nuts and the seeds in cucumbers, tomatoes, and berries, which can get caught in the pockets and possibly cause inflammation. Cucumbers and tomatoes can be seeded before eating, and berries can be eaten as conserves, which can be strained first.

Atherosclerosis, a term more of us may be familiar with, is the clogging of arteries with a kind of plaque of which a major component is cholesterol. Animal (saturated) fats—those that are solid at room temperature—contain high levels of cholesterol, and dietary cholesterol is in turn implicated in the laying down of this plaque. If the arteries become totally blocked, usually from a bit of plaque breaking off and momentarily closing off the passageway for the blood, we suffer a heart attack or stroke.

Heredity can be a factor here, and although we can do nothing about heredity, we can watch our weight, live a less stressful life, and reduce the amount of saturated fat in our diet. The recipes in this book cut back on saturated fats.

A hereditary predisposition to a health problem needn't be the end of the line. Being conscious of the predisposition enables you to take evasive action against it. Myrna Lewis, an authority on the problems of older women, says, "Hypertension runs in our family, and when it began to show up in me in my mid-forties, I realized that I wanted to do whatever I could to allay it. Diet and exercise were what I could do, and since I've started attacking the problem on those two fronts, I've been feeling much better in every way. And there's no sign now of hypertension."

Adult-onset diabetes, another inherited tendency, can be combatted in the same way. When confronted with it myself in my mid-forties, I reduced stress, changed my diet, and increased exercise. I'm still free of it fifteen years later.

Need I mention that stopping smoking is probably the greatest health gift we can give ourselves? The earlier we stop, the better chance the body has to recover.

The body's capacity for renewal is nothing short of miraculous. I'm a natural optimist. I always like to look on the positive side, and I don't relish the prospect of living in a chronic state of fear of the aging process. Why should our new leisure merely mean exchanging one stress—the stress of pursuing a career and raising a family—for another: the terrors of aging? That's why I resisted my impulse to bury my head in the sand, and instead set about informing myself as to what those big words meant. Now I know what to do about them, and I do it, and it hasn't been a chore at all—on the contrary, I'm living better than I ever have. So can you.

OOPS! I CAN'T EAT THE WAY I USED TO!

▲▲▲

Difficulty with digestion is one of the most common problems in our middle and later years, and one with a wide range of consequences that can directly and indirectly affect our well-being. Most of us didn't know what it was to have a digestive system when we were younger, aside from a dim memory of the time we ate too many green apples or chocolates and "paid for it" a few hours later. Usually we could and did eat anything and everything with blithe indifference.

When I taught a class in how to open your own restaurant some years ago, I took the class members to a new type of restaurant for dinner every week. I thought nothing of sampling five different appetizers, entrées, and desserts, besides eating my own generous portions. Today I'd feel zonked afterward, glutted and sluggish. My body can't handle that much heavy food anymore. Is this a blessing in disguise? I think so. My body was signaling me to stop overloading it with rich and heavy food.

"My stomach didn't forgive me for two days," was how my friend Margaret Medgard put it, telling me about a weekend family reunion. "I ate gobs and gobs of food—my sister's shrimp salad, my cousin's coleslaw. Everybody in my family has some dish they're proud of, and I had to try them all—roast pork, chocolate devil's food cake, apple pie—and did I pay for it later!"

Perhaps only a few years ago we were able to get away with being "good" during the week, saving up to splurge on the weekend. No more. "If your stomach can't handle a flood of butter, eggs, and heavy cream during the week, why should it be able to on weekends?" as my friend Gloria Hainline sensibly pointed out. If we splurge every weekend, we'll spend half the following week recovering, and that's too hard on our system.

"Indulge in moderation" is our best solution. If we eat moderately 85 percent of the time and save the splurging for truly special occasions—traveling, treating ourselves to an exceptional meal in our favorite restaurant, weddings, anniversaries—we'll be doing our bodies a great favor, for which they will repay us gratefully with enhanced well-being.

Before we can get on this new track, though, it may be necessary to dismiss some of our most deep-rooted eating habits and establish new ones. If we've followed a typical American eating pattern, our diet has consisted of a high proportion of animal fats—meat, cheese, butter, cream, and eggs; overly processed foods (meaning excessively high in salt and sugar) such as frozen TV or "gourmet" dinners and frozen vegetables with overseasoned sauces; refined flour (meaning all starch and no fiber) in breads, cookies, and cakes; sugar, sugar, sugar in soft drinks and commercial desserts. Some of these habits are so entrenched, we may feel all but addicted to our overconsumption of fat, sugar, and salt. What's habitual with us, though, is no more than that—the result of years of conditioning. And what has once been conditioned can be reconditioned; we can form new habits, learn to follow new patterns. Even what tastes good to us can be changed, for taste is acquired, and once we've established a habit of eating lighter, our former taste for rich, heavy food will come to seem like an aberration. However, it does take patience with ourselves and a sense of humor—and a reasonable tolerance toward the inevitable occasional lapse.

For there will be some backsliding; the habits of a lifetime aren't dismissed overnight. You *will* splurge sometimes; there will be times when you can't help it. Don't berate yourself when you do; just get back on the track. The whole point of this new way of living is to be kind to yourself; so show this kindness in both the long *and* the short run.

The best advice for forming new habits is found in the government dietary guidelines, a set of seven nutritional recommendations.

ONE DIET FOR ALL

▲▲▲

The guidelines apply for everyone, across the board, regardless of age. They have a special application to our age group, however, because they're more urgent for us. That's why I'm listing and discussing each of them specifically. Most of the recipes and menus in this book have been adapted to conform with the guidelines; they're lower in fats, both animal and vegetable, salt, and sugar, and higher in fiber. So even if you just use the recipes and menus and ignore the guidelines, you'll be following them without even having to think about them. But in line with my convictions about taking creative responsibility for your own well-being, I'd like to review them here, however briefly, from our particular perspective.

Eat a Variety of Foods

Making a point of eating a broad selection of fruits, vegetables, grains, legumes, dairy products, meat, fish, and poultry will ensure that you get the whole spectrum of nutrients you need for optimum health: protein (from both animal and vegetable sources), carbohydrates, fats, vitamins, and minerals. If you find it hard to digest raw fruits and vegetables, as some of us do, you'll find many delicious ways to cook them described in this book.

Maintain Ideal Weight

We need to pay special attention to this (as I'm sure you don't need to be told), for it becomes more difficult on the other side of fifty—first, because our metabolism slows down, as I've discussed, so that we burn calories at a reduced rate, and second, because we're usually less physically active than we used to be. A program of regular exercise is imperative when we're over fifty— daily if possible, if not at least three times a week.

A balanced way of eating is essential here too; you'll find some specific weight-loss advice later in the chapter. Simply following the seven government nutritional guidelines, however, will usually do the trick.

Reduce Consumption of Fat, Especially Saturated Fat

Because fat is fat is fat; it puts pounds on you faster than anything else (ounce for ounce, fat has twice as many calories as sugar). This is all the reason you need for cutting back on *every* form of dietary fat, whether it's animal or vegetable. Even olive oil and fish oils that have recently been shown to be beneficial in lowering blood cholesterol levels will still, used in excess, make you fat. (There are trade-offs in diet as in everything else.)

We also should cut back on animal fats for the reasons I've already gone into—the increased risk of atherosclerosis that is associated with high levels of animal fats in the diet.

See the section on cooking techniques (pages 113–118) for low- or no-fat preparation of meat, chicken, and fish that makes it full of flavor and preserves its freshness and texture. You can almost always reduce by half the amount of fat called for in the preparation of practically any dish. The recipes in this book show you many ways of using only the leaner cuts of meat and less of it, while getting most of your volume from vegetables (see also Portion and Proportion, page 34).

Eat Foods That Are High in Fiber

Again, there's a double advantage here. First, fiber in itself helps to prevent or alleviate such disorders as diverticulosis and adult-onset diabetes. Milder cases of diabetes have been successfully treated by diet alone—usually a high-fiber, low-sugar diet. (Do not of course attempt this on your own without consulting your physician.)

A high-fiber diet can benefit all of us for the same reason it helps diabetics: complex carbohydrates release sugar into the bloodstream gradually, ensuring that energy is delivered over a longer period of time and more evenly, without any abrupt ups and downs. Simple or refined sugars cause blood sugar to zoom up, then plunge back down.

It's only the diets of affluent societies, and recently affluent at that, that can afford to feature great slabs of meat as the centerpiece of a meal, with the vegetable products as an after-thought. Virtually all primitive and agrarian societies have con-centrated on the vegetable kingdom for most of their sustenance, using meat as only one ingredient among many. In the early 1900s, the American diet was still of this type. Whole foods such as whole grains, cereals, vegetables, and fruits, were the stan-dard. People ate local produce, and meat was a special, not even a daily, event. Then industrialization and affluence both took their toll. It came to be mistakenly believed, even by the medical profession, that a diet high in animal protein was the most desirable. Meat became a daily or even thrice daily event. The subsequent rapid rise in diseases such as atherosclerosis, adult-onset diabetes, and diverticulosis is now seen to be in part a direct consequence of this drastic change in our eating patterns.

We've recently come to understand that the way to reverse this lethal trend is to increase fiber and cut back on meat, and that the two need to go hand in hand. If you increase your intake of high-fiber foods, using the techniques and recipes in this book, you'll learn innumerable ways of treating meat as a minor ingredient, but one that still imparts flavor. (See for example the recipes for Steak Salad Niçoise, page 255, and almost all the casseroles.) You'll get the full flavor of the meat with only a small fraction of the fat, and most of your protein will come from vegetable sources.

Avoid Too Much Sugar

Sugar, unlike animal fat, isn't believed to be responsible in itself for life-threatening illness, but it is high in calories without contributing anything nutritionally. Refined sugars tend to send the blood sugar into a jagged pattern of abrupt highs and lows, and they've been implicated in tooth decay.

Many people over fifty, however, seem to develop a craving for sugar they haven't had before, and the suspicion is that this may be both a cause and a signal of malnutrition. If your habitual response to hunger between meals is to reach for the candy box, take a close and honest look at your other eating habits. The chances are there's some entire category of nutrient you're omitting. Try substituting fresh fruit when you're hungry for sugar between meals—a baked apple, poached pears, a bunch of grapes. And see the Everyday Desserts recipes (pages 344–352) in this book—there are lots that don't overload your system with refined sugar. In almost every conventional dessert recipe, you can cut the sugar called for by half without sacrificing flavor or sweetness.

Avoid Too Much Sodium

Excessive sodium seems to increase the risk of hypertension in those who are genetically susceptible to it, and is dangerous to those who already suffer from it. Most of us tend to oversalt our food to such a ridiculous extent that apart from the health risk, it masks every other flavor and makes our meals monotonous. My own pet peeve is the people who dowse their food with salt before even tasting it.

Even if hypertension is not a problem for you, try replacing most of your salt with herb or spice seasonings and wine or lemon juice—you'll be surprised how much better your food will taste.

Drink Only in Moderation

You scarcely need to be told this. But we're also told that a glass or two of wine at dinner may actually be beneficial to our health and increase longevity.

You may not find it easy at first, or even possible, to incorporate these seven guidelines all at once into your daily eating pattern. *Gradually* should be your watchword; don't try or expect to overthrow the habits of a lifetime overnight.

There's another reason for taking your time. If you've been eating very little fiber (what we used to call roughage) for a long time, you may already be suffering from sluggish bowels, or even the early stages of diverticulosis, and have trouble digesting raw fruits and vegetables. Suddenly changing to a high-fiber diet can cause digestive upset. So don't try to do it all at once. And please don't try to dose yourself with pure bran—get it naturally, in your food. Start with adding fibrous foods a little at a time—perhaps in just one meal a day.

An easy and delicious way to make the transition is with vegetable soups. Also try cooked vegetables—puréed or steamed —and poached fruits. When you've become accustomed to this new style of eating, then gradually start adding raw fruits and vegetables to your meals.

PORTION AND PROPORTION: A TRULY BALANCED DIET

▲▲▲

The changeover from a diet high in animal products to one that features the vegetable kingdom can be almost completely painless—in fact, you'll find that you're eating a richer variety of foods, and in even greater quantity. You won't be depriving yourself; you'll be eating more abundantly than ever. How? By using meat as one ingredient only, among an assortment of others: meat in small quantities (you need only four ounces a day of meat, seafood, or chicken) in a casserole, or as a component in one of the entrée salads that were such favorites at The Party Box, such as Steak Salad Niçoise, or Fusilli and Scallop, in which meat and vegetables are featured in the proportion of one-third to two-thirds.

The federal guidelines suggest that we consume sixty percent of our calories in the form of complex carbohydrates, twenty-five to thirty percent in protein (your current diet probably reverses those proportions), and ten to fifteen percent in fat. If you eat a variety of foods that includes grains and beans, pasta and potatoes, orange and green fruits, and vegetables, you'll have no trouble getting your sixty percent complex carbohydrates. Your twenty-five to thirty percent protein can be either animal or vegetable, but you don't need more than four ounces of fish, meat, or dairy products a day. It's actually even simpler than that. Think of your daily diet as a plate divided into thirds. Don't worry about percentages or ounces; just remember, "two-thirds, one-third"—two-thirds vegetables, one-third meat and dairy products.

Some of your daily food intake will automatically be fat, even in the leanest cuts of meat. The rest of your ten to fifteen percent of fat can come from the oil in salad dressing, a small handful of nuts, or half an avocado. Since the bulk of your food will come from vegetables, the protein and fat components of your diet will occupy a much smaller portion of your daily plate.

This does not, however, mean that the portions have to be paltry. On the contrary, you'll be adding more to your plate. But with this new style of eating, instead of a chunk of meat, a heap of mashed potatoes, and a dollop of vegetables, you'll be able to have as many as three different vegetables on your plate, in addition to grains, beans, pasta, or potatoes, with your four ounces of meat, fish, or chicken. I always like to have one or two hot and perhaps one cold vegetable; such combinations as a Skillet Skirt Steak served with Marinated Carrots with Red Peppers; Chicken Piccata served with Baked Onions with Balsamic Vinegar, Zucchini Italienne, and Rice Pilaf with Pignoli and Italian Parsley; or Shrimp Seviche with Kohlrabi and Bosc Pears. Such combinations give you a range and variety of color, flavor, and texture that will make your palate sing. Nutritional experts recommend that we have at least one vegetable in each of the orange and green families every day for our best chance at optimum health. Orange vegetables give us Vitamins C, A, and D; greens, the darker the better, supply calcium and minerals, see facing page). And if you include orange, green, purple, red, and yellow vegetables every day, you'll be getting the full range of nutrients you need—naturally.

The Whole Story

"Devitalized, denatured, tasteless" are the unflattering terms that best describe the modern American diet, especially if we rely heavily on ready-prepared foods, and shop exclusively in the supermarket. We've tampered with our food, stripped it of its natural goodness, impoverished it in order to enrich stockholders of the giant food companies. "Shelf life" is longer for refined, heavily processed food, treated with chemicals so it won't spoil. What's good for the shelf is bad for us.

Now at last we're becoming aware of how harmful to our health this practice is, and this new awareness is one of the sources of the prevalent nostalgia for the "good old days." "An agriculture that is whole nurtures the whole person, body and soul," Masanobu Fukoda, the Japanese authority of farming, tells us in *The One Straw Revolution*. We're becoming sophisticated enough to realize that a return to the old-fashioned wholeness of "natural" food can help to save us from technologically caused malnutrition, in which health is sacrificed to the convenience of the marketplace.

Whole means unrefined, unprocessed, unpeeled, and unhulled; whole grains, cereals, and flours. When we over-process wheat, we throw away the wheat germ, which contains most of the nourishment, and the bran—then buy them back separately, to restore to our diet the nutrients we need. Processing food this way eliminates much of its nutritive value.

Fruits and vegetables with their skins on are valuable sources of fiber, as well as rich in vitamins and minerals, many of which are in the skin. (I recommend that you don't peel your vegetables. Scrub them well, but leave the skin on—for both aesthetics and health.) Leaving the tops on such vegetables as beets provides a double-health bonus—those greens contain more nutrients than the beets themselves. Nuts should be eaten unbleached, unsalted, not blanched, and dry roasted. If you like them roasted, roast them yourself in the oven (page 137).

One unequivocal improvement in life today has been the return of the bakery that sells whole-grain and dark European breads; some breads even proudly announce themselves as containing seven or eight different grains. No longer are we compelled to bake our own, or settle for cellophane-wrapped damp white cotton.

Taking advantage of this new emphasis does require some planning. It means doing some of your shopping in the old style, at the greengrocers, the fishmonger, the butcher, the baker. That's why I've included advice on shopping (pages 45–57). It's an integral part of eating well, and deserves a chapter to itself.

ORANGE AND GREENS—HAVE ONE EVERY DAY

IN SOUPS:
Carrot Vichyssoise
Beet and Cucumber Soup
Fiery Pumpkin Soup
Emerald Broccoli Soup

IN SALADS:
Slaws: Magenta and Orange Slaw
  (Beet and Carrot)
Minnie Levy's Vegetable-Rich
  Slaw
Salads: Three-Green Salad with
  Grapefruit and Olives

AS A MAIN COURSE:
Spaghetti Squash with Garden
  Tomato Sauce
Acorn Squash with Pears
Vegetable Couscous
Carrot and Pignoli Loaf
Gala Vegetables
Mexican Fiesta Vegetables

IN SIDE DISHES:
Chinese Emerald Brown Rice
Zucchini Italienne
Stir-Fry Broccoli with Garlic,
  Ginger, and Soy
Stir-Fry Asparagus with Ginger
  and Soy
Brussels Sprouts with Vermont
  Cheddar Cheese
Brussels Sprouts with Vinaigrette
Purée of Parsnips and Carrots
Marinated Carrots with Red
  Peppers
Red or Green Swiss Chard,
  Italian Style
Interchangeable Greens with
  Nene's Lemon-Garlic Dressing
Watercress Raita
Carrot Raita

HOW TO DIET AND NOT NOTICE IT

▲▲▲

Is it really possible? To diet and not notice it? We're all so used to psyching ourselves up for one big effort, The Diet That Will Do It All. We throw all the goodies out of the refrigerator, gear ourselves up to a drastic weight-loss push—all the while keeping one eye cocked on the calendar for the day it will all end, so we can go right back to the eating habits that put the weight on in the first place. Like a teeter-totter, we're always either up or down, and the diet "works," as they all work, only temporarily. The Emerald City of Oz is still a distant dream.

I've kept a copy of one of the tabloids that bore the headline THREE SUPER CRASH DIETS. On page three it told how to "mix and match" them. There are thousands of these diets, and they still keep coming—because all of us tend to put on our "green glasses" when it comes to losing weight. It's so tempting to suspend our common sense, and succumb to the promise of losing ten pounds in a week. Our rational mind knows it can't be true, but our fantasy is stronger.

To achieve such quick weight loss, the balance of nutrition must be radically interfered with. Even so, the body is not long fooled; it plateaus, to save us from ourselves, protect itself from starvation. Nevertheless, it can be dangerous to play around with the radical regimes, and it gets more dangerous as our bodies reach the fifty mark and don't bounce back from abuse quite as quickly as they once did.

What I'm after in this book is combining feasting with sound nutritional principles. It's as simple as that. But it means giving up the binge-and-bust syndrome, and it probably means eating less of what we're used to eating most of—meat and dairy products. That's not so easy to do, no doubt about it. I love a pat of butter on a cracker, my cream cheese-and-chive butter on rye bread. I enjoyed making sauces with flour and butter, and then adding the final touch of sweet butter that gives a silken sheen.

But as I'll show you in the menus and recipes to come, satisfaction can come from more than meat, butter, and sugar. As my friend Natalie Ramondi discovered, "There really *is* life after chocolate and butter." The eye and the mind will learn to experience pleasure in a different form, and the body will too. It may take awhile, but once it has learned this, you won't feel hungry between meals, or stressed from all that fat.

So forget about specific weight-loss diets. The rationale of this book is to show you how to form new eating habits *for life;* the right kind of feasting as a new way of life. How to eat in a way that is delicious and satisfying, yet enables you to control your weight. Most of the menus I've included supply ample nutrition, while keeping the calories from escalating (except for special splurges)—yet you'll feel hungry only at mealtime.

How can I promise that? By ensuring that the basis of every meal is drawn from the great world of complex carbohydrates. These foods combine bulk (from which the fiber comes) with low calories—or rather, they're low in calories relative to their bulk. That means that you can fill up on them without putting on pounds. This is the new style of dieting. We've realized that the high-protein, low-carbohydrate weight-loss diet that was fashionable a few years ago not only doesn't work over the long haul (no one could stay on it for longer than a few weeks at a time), but it actually can be dangerous. Excessive amounts of protein can be harmful, and it was also a diet excessively high in saturated fat.

The style of eating I'm proposing will help maintain your weight over a lifetime. These recipes and menus are all (unless specified otherwise) low in fat, salt, and sugar, yet high in sensual pleasure. Experiment with them, mixing and matching the recipes, and experiment with portion sizes. You won't feel deprived, in any of your senses, with the menus I suggest. You'll be eating well-balanced meals every day, maintaining or losing weight, and you'll feel as if you're feasting.

Vegetables: The Natural Way to Diet

The members of this kingdom, from aristocrats to commoners, are the stars of the new nutrition. Perhaps the greatest novelty of

the way of eating I'm proposing to you is the emphasis on vegetables—so many of us grew up calling them "rabbit food," convinced that the only "serious" food is meat. Most of the vegetables we remember from our formative years were boiled for forty-five minutes to an hour, resulting in uniform sogginess and lackluster color.

The vegetables in this book are prepared raw, steamed, poached, baked, and pickled. In combination with other ingredients in entrées, salads, and casseroles they can become our greatest allies in our campaign for fitness. And they come in such an astonishing variety of tastes and textures, we'll never tire of them. They're beautiful to look at, too, and they contain not one speck of cholesterol. Could you ask for anything more?

In the box opposite are ten vegetables, all extremely low in calories and high in water content, that lend themselves elegantly to a great variety of dishes. In the chart I suggest three different dishes for each vegetable. Keep in mind that salad dressings make wonderful marinades for vegetables.

Appetite Versus Hunger: Snacks

When we're hungry, our bodies send out very clear signals. The stomach growls, we salivate, we may even feel fatigued. That

TEN GREAT LOW-CALORIE VEGETABLES— AND THIRTY WAYS TO FIX THEM

VEGETABLE	HOT	COLD	MARINATED
Artichoke . . .	Steamed with Tamari-Lime Dressing	Stuffed with Bulgur and Golden Raisins	Vegetable Salad Niçoise
Broccoli	Stir-Fry Broccoli with Garlic, Ginger, and Soy	Emerald Broccoli Soup	Nene's Lemon-Garlic Dressing
Carrots	Carrot Vichyssoise	Purée of Parsnips and Carrots	With Red Peppers
Cauliflower . .	Steamed with Fennel and Cumin	Lemon Zest Cauliflower Soup	With Curry Dressing
Cucumber . . .	Curried Cucumber	Beet and Cucumber Soup	Hans' Cucumber and Fresh Bean Salad
Fennel	Sautéed in Tarragon Butter	Raw with Lime Juice	Julienne with Vinaigrette
Mushrooms .	Stuffed with Spinach and Feta	Snow Pea, Mushroom, and Daikon Salad	In Lemon and Oil
Onions	Baked with Balsamic Vinegar	Green Beans and Red Onion in Lemon Dressing	Mandarin Orange, Scallion, and Red Onion Salad
Peppers	Quick Black Beans and Red Peppers	Robusto Pasta and Chicken Salad with Red and Green Peppers	Esther's Roasted Red Peppers
Zucchini	Zucchini Italienne	Nene's Zucchini-Apple Soup	Spring Green-and-White Rice Salad

means the body is running out of fuel.

Appetite, on the other hand, is the greedy kid who says, "Gimme, gimme, gimme." "Boy, that hot dog looks good." "I think I'll have a double scoop of strawberry vanilla." "Chocolate icebox cookies? I haven't had those in years." Appetite is association. It's awakened by memories of good times from the past—summers at the ballpark, on the boardwalk, at the circus; winters, after sledding or skating. We may think that little kid doesn't live in us any more. Forget it—he or she is always there, fighting to get out. We need someone more grown-up to take him in hand and say, "You're not hungry, honey. You just want to be reminded of happy times."

Emotional hunger is more immediate. We eat to cheer ourselves up when we feel bad, to give ourselves love when we feel we're not getting it from outside, to stave off loneliness and anxiety. Too often, though, the rewards we give ourselves are self-punishing—rich, heavy food; liquor; cigarettes.

"We crave snacks when the mouth needs a little something and the spirits need a lift," says my friend Harriet Mason. This craving has nothing to do with actual hunger—it always comes between meals. We rummage around in the refrigerator or rush out to the supermarket for a bag of potato chips or a quart of ice cream. We've learned from experience that eating lots of sugar or fat all at once may make us feel bad in the end, but first we'll feel good.

You won't hear me saying, "Don't ever do that." I do it sometimes, as we all do; I love ice cream whenever I have a sore throat, even though I know it's not good for me. And mashed potatoes or macaroni and cheese are just as comforting now as they were when I was little. And remember those six-decker sandwiches Dagwood would console himself with—whenever Blondie or Mr. Dithers got to be too much for him?

Then there's the perennial favorite of compulsive midnight eaters: a pint of ice cream and a frozen cake. That's a combination that will put you to sleep like a log. And when you wake up, you'll still feel drugged, and drag around until noon.

For midnight snacking or any other time, there are so many

other delicious and more healthful things for us to treat ourselves with. What you're looking for in a munchie is snap, crackle, and crunch. These will provide those enticing sounds without the fat of potato chips, and with a seductive range of flavors.

MUNCHIES

Popcorn with seasoning, but no butter

Oven-roasted nuts

Crudités (raw vegetables) served with fresh lime juice

Oriental vegetables served with fresh lime juice

Crunchy dry cereals with no sugar

Miniature rice cakes

Puffed wheat or rice

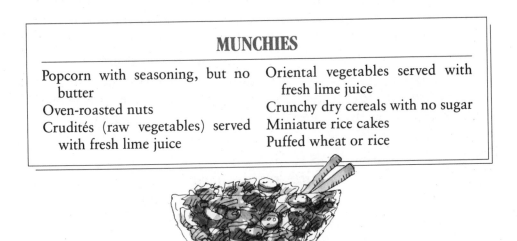

Guilt-Free Treats

The sweet has always been the treat, and the way to get it was to make your way stoically through the rest of your meal first. Then you were rewarded with Mom's apple pie, or, in restaurants, with chocolate decadence.

Well, none of this computes any more in terms of real fitness. It's hard for us even to digest rich desserts now—and yet we don't want to give them up. So I've included some desserts that carry no penalty—neither now nor later. They're made without milk, butter, or cream, without sugar, wheat, or eggs. And they're just as good for breakfast as they are for a snack.

I was introduced to these desserts when I was baby-sitting with a friend on a farm outside of Toronto. Elane has eleven grandchildren, four of whom are allergic to eggs, wheat, and sugar. Her daughter Betsy Speck, their mother, and Elane developed for them such dessert recipes as Elane's Hearty Apple-and-

Oat Muffins and Pure Fresh Fruit "Ice Creams." You'll find them in the dessert section. At any age, it's a boon to be able to cut these things out if we want or need to. I've been eating and enjoying these desserts ever since I first tasted them. It's great to be able to eat something sweet and not feel hungry soon afterward. There's no plunge in the blood sugar after its initial steep rise, as with refined sugar. No urge to rush out and buy another candy bar right after you've eaten one. See if you don't agree.

Perhaps by now you're beginning to realize that nothing dire need happen to our eating habits to ensure that we take our over-fifty years in stride. There's no need to become a nutritional expert either, if your interest doesn't incline that way. Just a few simple principles, such as reducing intake of fats, sugar, and salt, and the one-third–two-thirds ratio of meat to vegetable products (which almost by itself will take care of the fat-sugar-salt cutback), are all you need to remember. Better eating and better health will become a matter of course. We can look forward to making the changes necessary for a balanced diet without fearing that from now on, eating has to be dull. All the food in this book is delicious.

Chapter III

SHOPPING SMART: HOW TO SPEND, HOW TO SAVE

▼▼▼

Taking creative responsibility—taking charge, really—of our own well-being begins not at the dinner table or even in the kitchen, but in the supermarket. And it means, first of all, becoming aware of exactly what it is we're buying.

There is a government requirement we should all be familiar with and make use of: the mandatory list of ingredients that appears on every can and every package. And here's where our creative responsibility comes into play. We can't afford to leave our glasses at home when we go to the supermarket—or even to the health food store, for that matter.

Consider these examples: A salad dressing mix touts "low cholesterol." If you stop there and buy it, thinking that it will be "healthy" in every other respect, think again. It's loaded with added salt and sugar as well as numerous stabilizers and preservatives. The label on a chocolate candy bar at the health-food store reads "No chocolate, no caffeine!" Great. But read on—it does contain a great deal of sugar and palm oil. Palm oil, as you should know, along with coconut oil is one of the few vegetable oils that is saturated and high in cholesterol. It's used because its "shelf life" is longer than that of other vegetable oils. You might even find wax listed among the ingredients!

Forewarned is forearmed. *Take the time to read the labels.* They're our only protection against advertising hype. Consider, for instance, that innocent word "natural." If it's natural it's *got* to be good, right? Wrong. Sugar is natural, salt is natural, and so are arsenic and lead. "Natural" is a legally meaningless word that tells you nothing about what you're getting. Very often its only purpose is to arrest the shopper's thinking. A handy thing to keep in mind is that ingredients are listed in their order of prominence. On a can of canned tomatoes, for instance, the list of ingredients leads off (one hopes) with tomatoes. If sugar appears next, that means that there is more sugar in the canned tomatoes than anything else except tomatoes. And so on. The further down the list sugar and salt appear, the better.

It's not enough to study the labels; ask questions, too, and don't be afraid to challenge the store manager. Where do the apples come from? Which fruit is waxed? Are the oranges dyed? How long has that bag of flour been sitting there? Ask, badger, make a pest of yourself if necessary. Joan Gussow, professor of nutrition at Columbia University, spells it out this way. "It's important to realize that you do have clout. There are over 12,000 separate items on the supermarket shelves, and each one of them has to earn its place there. If you don't buy it, out it goes!"

The front line in the campaign for optimum health isn't the kitchen, it's the supermarket. That's where you start taking creative responsibility for your well-being.

THE WEEKLY SUPERMARKET SHOPPING GUIDE

▲▲▲

Try shopping my way, and I'll guarantee you three benefits: 1) a lowering of your food bill by one-third; 2) less time spent in the store; and 3) a healthier diet. Simply by reorganizing the sequence in which you shop for food, you will achieve the two-thirds–one-third ratio of carbohydrates to protein that gives you the healthiest balance.

My six-category guide, therefore, is organized by the sequence in which foods should be purchased. It will probably reverse your usual shopping pattern, but there's a reason for doing it this way. When we shop, most of us head first for the meat department, then speed through the frozen food section for side dishes, the produce department for salad items, and then to baked goods for dessert. In other words, what we start with is what we consider most important—we spend most of our time, thought, and money choosing that. Everything else is an afterthought.

What I'm asking you to do instead is choose the items from the vegetable and plant kingdoms first. Only after you've selected your fresh vegetables, fruits, grains, beans, and pasta should you turn to the animal kingdom. Meat and dairy products are high in undesirables like fat, cholesterol, and calories; hence we want to make them secondary to the vegetable products—buying them, in other words, in order of their importance in our diet.

The other category of purchase we want to cut back on is processed foods. Of course, frozen fruits and juices and vegetables, canned fish and beans and soups are useful in emergencies or as components of recipes when we need to save time or cut corners. So we'll continue to buy them, but only in moderation.

On the other hand, super-convenience foods, such as ready-prepared frozen meals—TV dinners, entrées in boilable bags, gourmet "diet" dinners, and so forth—can and should be totally eliminated. Most are super-high in cost, loaded with additives, and sky-high in sodium. The "flex cooking" techniques I describe in the next chapter show you how to put together a far more delicious and healthful meal in not much more time than it takes to boil a commercial frozen entrée bag; in fact, your freezer will be stocked with your *own* entrées in boilable bags, and they'll contain only what you put in them.

Following are the categories I've set up for organizing this new way of shopping. Once you see how it pays off in time saved and better eating, you'll do it automatically.

Category I: Produce

You should always have on hand the basics: yellow onions, garlic, celery, peppers, potatoes, carrots; salad greens—you may want to shop for these more often than once a week, especially if you have a good neighborhood greengrocer; other vegetables in season, such as squash, Brussels sprouts, fresh peas and green beans; citrus fruits, bananas, and apples; and other fruits in season, such as pears, grapes, cherries, apricots, melons, berries.

One sometimes hears protests that fresh vegetables cost more per pound than do canned or frozen. They sometimes do, but you'll usually find that they're well worth it.

Five pounds of vegetables can serve as components for as many as twenty different dishes. You can use the flowerets of broccoli, for example, for sautéing, and the stems for salads and soups. Beets can be used in salads, for pickling, and for aspics. Beet greens make a nourishing and delicious side dish. From a bunch or two of carrots you can produce vichyssoise, a loaf, a slaw, and a raita, and eat them raw. A pound of zucchini can give you a substantial soup, and a quick sautéed vegetable.

Vegetables can be eaten raw, sautéed, baked, poached, steamed, and stir-fried; served in soups, casseroles, salads, side dishes, and desserts. Fruits go into sorbets, cobblers, soups, and salads. And if you eat them with the skins on, they'll give you additional fiber and a wealth of vitamins and minerals that have not been diminished or destroyed by heat or processing.

Category II: Grains, Beans, and Pasta

For years we were conditioned to cut down on these "starches" in the belief that they were fattening. Now that we realize that the source of the excess calories in complex carbohydrates is the butter or heavy sauces accompanying them, and that these low-cost, high-energy, "clean" (without fat) sources of fuel are one of our most valuable foods, they are being restored to center stage at mealtime. Most supermarkets carry a good selection of all these items. Buy at least a pound each of a grain, a bean, and a pasta, every week. (In the next chapter you'll see how extremely versatile they are, with new ways of preparing them.) Each pound will give you as many as eight servings, at pennies a serving.

GRAINS: At the supermarket you'll find long-grain, brown, and converted rice, as well as kasha and couscous. Avoid instant rice and rice mixes that contain vegetables and rice, or wild rice and long-grain rice. They all contain added salt and sugar, and are ridiculously expensive when compared with the cost of making your own combinations. Kasha and couscous are especially good in casseroles during the cold winter months. For other non-doctored varieties, try the health-food stores; most of them carry an amazing assortment that will make you want to experiment. The ethnic markets, especially the Indian stores, are an excellent source, too.

BEANS: Now that so many cuisines are emphasizing regional, ethnic, and peasant food for healthier eating, beans are moving off the supermarket shelves into great hearty dishes: black beans for feijoada and soups, pinto and kidney beans for Tex-Mex dishes, black-eyed peas for Southern cooking, lima and navy beans for New England baked beans, split peas and lentils for soups, loaves, and dahls. Great nutrition here, for pennies.

PASTA: The supermarkets have always featured a good selection of pasta. Thanks to its elevation to the status of number one complex carbohydrate for endurance and energy (it's what the marathon runners choose to stoke up on before their ordeal), pasta should be a regular feature on the menu, as well as appearing in several side dishes through the week. Try the various shapes, and spinach pasta and noodles too. You can get whole-wheat and tomato pasta, even pumpkin, at some specialty shops.

Category III: Meat, Chicken, Fish, and Dairy Products

This category, which most of us shop for first, has now moved down to third place in my shopping scheme, for it is going to constitute only a third of our daily diet. Federal guidelines recommend that we cut our consumption of meat by half (assuming that you currently eat about what the average American does), with red meat being used only occasionally instead of daily as the main course for dinner, as well as for breakfast and lunch.

Fish and chicken are superior choices for protein, especially when we choose lean fish and remove the skin from chicken (see the low- or no-fat ways of preparing them, pages 113–118).

There are ways to buy high-quality protein economically, too. Just because we're ones and twos now does not mean we should buy small quantities of the higher priced cuts of meat—lamb chops, pork chops, chicken in pieces. Continue to buy in quantity, as you did when shopping for a big family; buy roasts instead of chops, whole chickens. The supermarkets now offer small, two- to four-pound roasts. If your market doesn't, ask your manager to supply them. One of these roasts will give you enough for several main meals, with plenty left over for casseroles and sandwiches. Do the same when you buy ground meat; buy several pounds so you can make not only hamburgers, but a pasta meat sauce, a meat loaf, and a casserole.

Buy a whole roasting chicken or the family pack, even though there's only one or two of you. It costs much less per pound, and the number of meat-stretching soups, salads, and snacks it provides makes it even more economical.

Buy fish in a store that keeps it on ice for freshness. Too often fish at the supermarket looks as if it's been on the road for a while. The best choice, if you must buy your fish in a supermarket, might be frozen fish or canned fish packed in water. Or, if you know the buying habits of your local store, make sure you buy your fish the first day it's available—you might plan to make your supermarket run on that day.

Cut back on dairy products, and you automatically cut back on fat, cholesterol, and calories. For special-occasion recipes we can still use butter, rich cheeses, and heavy cream, but for your daily diet, use low-fat milk and low-fat cottage cheese, skim-milk mozzarella and part-skim ricotta, and low-fat yogurt. Use olive oil or small amounts of vegetable oils for cooking; cut back on the amount suggested in the recipe, if you're using an old-style cookbook. (Most recipes in this book use very small amounts of fat or none at all.) And try nonstick pans; there are some good-quality ones available now that are more durable than they were in the early years of Teflon®. Their advantage is that they can often make it possible to eliminate fat when preparing many dishes that required it.

Have eggs on weekends—they're a valuable source of protein. But don't eat eggs every day; they're very high in cholesterol.

Category IV: Necessities

Necessity items include the things we should always have on hand, whether we buy them every week, like bread and cereals, or only twice a month, like oil and vinegar, or rarely, as needed, like spices and herbs.

There are great differences among breads, so read the labels carefully. Even if they say whole grain or enriched wheat, check for sweeteners and additives; the same goes for pitas, English muffins, and rolls. If there's a baker in your town who provides whole-grain breads and rolls, by all means go out of your way to patronize him—you will be generously repaid for the extra time and trouble.

Cereals range from almost 100 percent sugar to none. Pure cereals are more expensive—we now pay to have things left out.

Try cooking grains, such as rice, kasha, bulgur, couscous, or granola, for homemade cereals.

When buying oils, avoid those that combine different oils or contain added ingredients, such as garlic; the oil is probably of inferior quality and flavoring has been added to disguise this fact. If you want garlic in your oil add it yourself, at home.

Rice wine vinegar is less acidic, only four percent to the usual five percent. I use it in most of my salad dressings. It is now available in supermarkets and I've even found brown rice vinegar in my local market. You can buy fancy herb vinegars in gourmet food shops, but they're easy to make at home, and infinitely cheaper (page 129).

Whenever possible, buy your herbs fresh, or grow your own. And always, if you can, buy your spices in ethnic markets, where they're sold by weight; you'll be amazed by the difference in price—and freshness.

I prefer to use superfine sugar for baking cookies—it gives a smoother texture. From a health standpoint, there isn't much difference between brown and white sugar, so use whichever flavor you prefer. Just remember to cut back on sugar in most dessert recipes. Always buy unbleached white or whole-wheat flour, available at the supermarket. Other flours—rye, buckwheat, barley, graham—are found in health-food stores.

Category V: Convenience Foods

Convenience foods are the big trap in our food budget. It's where many of us spend the most, rather than the least.

Regular convenience foods, canned or frozen whole foods, are among our compromises-that-work. It's not necessary to prepare everything from scratch every day for every meal. So don't throw out the tomato paste or the can of kidney beans—take advantage of them. Most of these convenience foods are reasonably priced. But restrict their use, so you don't make a habit of trading health for convenience, and rinse them well where possible to eliminate excess salt or oil.

Super-convenience foods are super-silly in terms of cost, time, and health. The number of these items is staggering—the more familiar include food extenders, instant mashed potatoes, bottled salad dressings or mixes, packaged bread stuffing, sandwich spreads, frozen mixed vegetables such as peas or rice and mushrooms in butter sauce, vegetables in pastry, cheese with salami or garlic, low-cal cheese (usually with lots of additives), spinach in butter or cream sauce, and TV dinners.

The spinach in butter sauce is more than double the cost of frozen leaf spinach. You could buy a quarter pound of butter with the difference, melt two tablespoons for the spinach, and have six tablespoons left for buttering toast or making cookies or a sauce. And *imitation* butter flavor is more expensive than the real thing! As for the creamed spinach, it's advertised as "creamed spinach with *real cream*." How about that—real cream in creamed spinach! How much do you get for that extra eighty cents? A half cup? I doubt it. What's the yield? You can cook that plain ten ounces of frozen spinach as is and serve it hot as a side dish, or combine it with rice and fresh ginger to make a great Chinese side dish that serves six.

It's easy to read the bold-type advertising claims the super-convenience foods make about their ingredients: butter flavor and real cream. To discover more, you have to read the fine print: they often contain sugar, corn syrup, molasses, and other sweeteners. These at least are familiar. Then there are the multisyllable chemical additives, whose effect on our bodies is speculative at best. Yet another reason, and perhaps the best, for avoiding as much prepackaged food as possible.

Category VI: Treats and Luxuries for the Pantry

Natural treats such as nuts, raisins, dried fruit and popcorn make good snacks, and when used as ingredients, they can make cookies, cakes, and quick breads more nutritious. Avoid store-bought cookies, cakes, doughnuts, soft drinks, and potato chips with their excess salt, fat, and sugar.

Luxuries for the pantry—from appetizers to desserts—are not necessities, but they can dress up an ordinary meal and ensure that you're not caught empty-handed when unexpected company shows up. Stock an assortment of your favorites. They can be accumulated over a period of time and kept for weeks, even months. Some of these items, such as hearts of palm and kumquats, make it easy to prepare interesting impromptu meals, adding fancy touches to simple fare.

Be sure to have on hand some pantry items of your own making. The Basics recipe section offers a variety of homemade luxuries and treats that will add interest and spark to your meals: the sauces; the special salad dressings (you should keep several different ones on hand in the refrigerator at all times—they can transform a simple salad); the herb butters and spreads; the chutneys and fruit jams; the herb vinegars; and the home oven-roasted nut mix.

You might also want to keep on hand a good selection of crackers, rusks, and biscuits; tins of salmon or shad roe (if you can still find it) and antipastos. Roasted red peppers, olives, and artichoke hearts in jars or cans are good standbys, and marrons and brandied fruits are wonderful splurges.

ALTERNATIVES TO THE SUPERMARKET

▲▲▲

With one-stop supermarket shopping you can shop wisely and well. But now that we have more time and only ourselves to cook for, why not take advantage of all the other markets, which offer so much in the way of quality, variety, and economy?

Independent Markets

How many of us learned the ABCs of cooking from our neighborhood butcher, who taught us the different cuts of meat, how to prepare them—often giving detailed recipes—and then slipped us a bone for the dog or a kidney for the cat? The fishmonger, if you were lucky enough to have one, knew just which fish bones and heads made the finest sauces and stocks. And the greengrocer let us choose our own fruit. They taught us how to tell when a melon was ripe, and introduced us to some of the newer fruits and vegetables. Put yourself in their capable hands again. If you've been long accustomed to supermarket shopping, the range and variety of what the specialty shop offers will astonish you. Choose just what you want, in the exact quantities you need, from freshly watered and carefully handled produce. We should all support these neighborhood specialty shops. If they should disappear—and they're hard pressed by the giant supermarket chains—we'll all be the poorer for it.

Local Farmers

City dwellers used to have to go to the country if they wanted produce fresh from the farm. But these days, in many areas, farmers truck their produce into the city two or three times a week and set up shop in designated "greenmarkets" from early spring, and often remain through late fall. The changing seasons continually offer new selections—early peas and lettuce, squash, beans, broccoli, cherries and nectarines, kale, beets, sweet potatoes, turnips, sweet yellow, red, green, and even chocolate-colored peppers, and Bosc pears.

Sometimes the farmers offer fresh grape juice side by side with Concord grapes. Winemakers, cheesemakers, and bakers are there, too, with homemade and often irresistible products.

If you live in a warmer climate than I do, you can enjoy this windfall all year round. At Pike Place Market in Seattle, Washington, the local farmers bring in every kind of fresh vegetable and fruit imaginable 365 days a year. And in the summer, roadside stands entice you to pull over and choose from field-fresh produce.

Ethnic Markets

Shopping in these markets is like entering another country, each one a world in itself. And they offer marvels: silken homemade ricotta, a dozen different kinds of olives and olive oils, wild onions in barrels. A treasury of spices and nuts can be found in Indian shops, at prices that will astound you.

Because I love ethnic foods and found many of them where I live, I've included a number of recipes featuring them in this book. If some of the ingredients are not available where you live, consult the mail-order sources listed in the appendix.

Today health-food stores are everywhere, in resorts, cities, small towns. Though some of the more common health-food items are becoming available in supermarkets, such as sprouts, tofu, and whole-grain breads, health-food stores offer a far greater variety of grains such as millet, wheat berries, basmati and wild rice; soy, potato, and rice flours; nuts, nut butters, dried fruits, maple, rice or barley syrups.

WHAT TO BUY IN ETHNIC MARKETS

ORIENTAL MARKETS (CHINESE AND JAPANESE):
agar-agar, bamboo shoots, tofu (bean curd), buckwheat noodles, dried day lilies, five-spice powder, kuzu, litchee nuts, miso, dried mushrooms, Oriental sesame oil, rice vinegar, seaweed, tamari, water chestnuts

ITALIAN:
coppa, mozzarella, olive oils, pasta, prosciutto, pignoli, ricotta

MIDDLE EASTERN:
bulgur, couscous, baby eggplant, feta cheese, grape leaves—stuffed and unstuffed, assorted olives, string cheese, tahini, taramasalata

INDIAN:
almond essence, basmati rice, cashews, cilantro, lentils, pickled limes, orange water, rose water, spices, garam masala, curry powder, yellow split peas

MEXICAN:
green chiles, jícama, tomatillos, tortillas—flour and corn

Co-op Shopping

My New York City friend and neighbor, Susan Dresner, and I pool our time and resources to go shopping at the big greenmarket in Union Square. Along with the rows and rows of herbs, bushels of vegetables, and pails of flowers, there are meats, fish, cheeses, breads, and homemade jams and conserves. We often split huge bunches of fresh dill, rosemary, basil, oregano, and tarragon, as well as pots of three or four different kinds of herbs, which I keep in the kitchen.

In the fall we'll split a pork roast or a slab of bacon, a pound of Vermont Cheddar cheese, or one of those big, fragrant loaves of rye or pumpernickel, or a half-gallon jug of fresh pear or grape juice. If you go for the big bunches, the huge squashes, the whole loaves, the slab of bacon, and divide it among your friends and neighbors, you'll never eat better, and with less waste!

Shopping Every Day

I consider shopping at the supermarket a way of laying in supplies once a week, just as they did in those western movies I grew up on—settlers came into town to stock up on basics at the general store. I shop for those foods that will be used throughout the week—the meat and dairy products, the frozen and canned goods. All these play a part in cooking ahead, in stocking the freezer and the larder.

But if you like to shop, and have the opportunity to shop every day or every few days for fresh produce, by all means do so. Get to know your local fishmonger, greengrocer, and butcher. If you're growing your own and shopping at farmers' markets and the local greengrocer, you can eat the way we did when I was young—we bought our vegetables from the vegetable man who came to the door, we picked up chicken and fresh eggs on a Sunday drive in the country, and we drove to our favorite Italian and Chinese neighborhood grocers to buy cheese and litchee nuts.

Chapter IV

STREAMLINED PREPARATION

▼▼▼

As a caterer, I quickly became expert in preparing the components of a meal ahead of time—and often in a place far distant from where it was to be eaten—and assembling the components at the last minute. I had to know down to the second how long each ingredient needed to cook using which technique, how to hold ingredients in readiness for the next stage without sacrificing flavor, texture, or appearance, and in what order to assemble the elements of a dish for the final presentation to the guests.

Here is where my seventeen years of catering experience can pay off for you: the techniques for saving time and steps, and with superior results. That's the goal for this time of our lives: to eat splendidly without spending hours in the kitchen.

Let's begin with our tools; every workman is dependent first of all on the tools of his trade.

EQUIPMENT

▲▲▲

The first step in streamlining your kitchen operations is to take inventory. You've probably accumulated over the years a large and random assortment of equipment: an electric frying pan, a Crockpot, a toaster oven, blenders and processors and dozens of other electric gadgets. If your kitchen space is limited, you don't have the room to store, let alone use, all this paraphernalia.

For my kind of cooking—steaming, baking, poaching, broiling, and low-fat sautéing—you need only a few basics: two-, four-, and six-quart saucepans; a six- to eight-quart kettle; a four-or six-quart casserole; small, medium, and large frying pans; and a double boiler. A wok and a steamer are also very useful.

In my small apartment kitchen—the same seven-by-ten-foot one in which I started my business—I've cut out all the extras and work with just a few basics. For years I never owned a food processor, and I can still do very well without one. On the other hand, I never relegated my blender to the second shelf in the back. I use it all the time. It makes margaritas, soups, and mousses; it makes spreads and dips; it chops nuts and parsley. I prefer an electric hand mixer too, which I can use in any bowl, to a big clunky countertop machine. And though a food processor is wonderful for shredding carrots and cheese, a $4.00 hand shredder from the hardware store will do just fine.

In addition, I like to always have on hand a number of simple, practical instruments, in quantity, without which I couldn't run my kitchen (see Everyday Equipment and Utensils, page 60).

I find a small kitchen scale indispensable, and it takes up very little space. If you are restricting certain things in your diet, you usually need to weigh out exact amounts. Some recipes, especially those for bread and other baked items, often give ingredients by weight. And a scale can improve your overall eating habits by making you more conscious of just how much you are eating—judging amounts by volume alone can sometimes be deceptive.

EVERYDAY EQUIPMENT AND UTENSILS

• A good set of knives (I prefer carbon steel because you can sharpen them).

• Five sets of measuring spoons.

• Three or four wooden paddles and spoons.

• Three or four rubber spatulas.

• Glass and metal measuring cups in different sizes.

• Stainless steel, pottery, and glass mixing bowls in various sizes.

• Assorted open and closed stoneware or pottery crocks and jars for storing in the refrigerator or setting out on shelves.

A new piece of equipment that's appearing in more and more kitchens is a microwave oven. Some are so tiny they will easily fit under a kitchen cabinet. There are many books now available on microwave cooking, so I will not explore it in any detail here, except to note just how quickly it does cook some foods: a baked potato in seven minutes, an apple in five, and frozen dishes heated in what seems like seconds.

Plan your kitchen strategy and, for maximum efficiency, keep at hand only what you use often, and store the rest. A kitchen is a workshop. Having just the right equipment—no less, and no more—and using it to its fullest extent will help your workshop to function smoothly.

Mise en place

Mise en place is a French phrase which means "putting in place." In a restaurant, everything that is going to be used in a recipe is prepared and set out ahead. Then as the chef proceeds through the recipe, what's needed is right at hand, even in the most complicated recipe.

Too often I have seen cooks trailing back and forth from sink to refrigerator to cupboard to cutting board, taking out one ingredient at a time, one piece of equipment at a time, even cutting green beans or scallions one at a time. Take a tip from a professional: organize. Organization is essential, as you will see, in component cooking, when all four burners are busy. Planning and forethought will enable you to make the most economical use of your time and energy and will help you achieve outstanding results with the least effort. And you'll spend less time in the kitchen.

SAVING TIME IN THE KITCHEN

▲▲▲

Rethinking our shopping habits is an essential step, as we've seen in the preceding chapter, in reshaping our eating habits to meet our new priorities. And streamlining our time in the kitchen is no less essential if we're to eat more healthfully, abundantly, and pleasurably than ever before, without becoming a slave to the stove.

Streamlining makes possible what I call "flex cooking," which includes several ways of preparing food ahead so that you'll always have a well-stocked refrigerator, providing you with varied and interesting choices. You won't have to spend time preparing meals from scratch, and using your own homemade ingredients guarantees health, economy, and enjoyment because you're not relying on commercially frozen or canned dishes. Flex cooking provides components of entrées, or luncheons or snacks, buys lots of time out of the kitchen, and gives you an array every day of different fresh entrées from which to choose.

One thing our new lifestyle means is that we're no longer tethered to producing meals on schedule for a growing family. We can eat when we like: have two breakfasts, the main meal at lunchtime, a light early or late supper, or even six small meals a day. Our days are freer and more fluid, and that means we may even want our meals to be portable. The flexibility of our time invites a flexibility in our approach to cooking as well.

My catering techniques are very handy for our new lifestyle. You may already have used some of these approaches, while others you've probably never applied systematically.

Freeze-Aheads

If you were in the habit of cooking ahead and freezing food to have on hand to feed the family, you already know how efficient this technique can be. Now that we've become ones and twos, there's no reason to change that habit. Quantity shopping, as I recommended in Chapter 3—buying whole roasting chickens, several pounds of ground meat, generous amounts of fresh produce, pasta, grains, and beans—saves money and allows you to prepare several meals at once.

Coordinate your shopping with a cooking session in which you prepare several dishes at once to freeze and have on hand to heat up. If quartered chickens are on sale, make Lemon-Lime Chicken, or Mitz Perlman's Chicken Dinner in a Pot. With ground beef, you can make a simple meat loaf, Picadillo, and little Mini Dijon Burgers. Cube chicken breasts, prepare four different marinades, and freeze a batch of raw chicken in its own marinade. Or take it a step further and cook the breast in its marinade for a few minutes and then freeze it. The chicken will only need to be cooked for a few more minutes after you've thawed it.

Pasta sauces can be made ahead and kept ready in the freezer for a meal in ten minutes, the time it takes to cook the pasta. These sauces also go well with many of the fish and chicken recipes—especially the Thick Chunky Pesto, the Quick-Roasted Red Pepper Sauce, and the Garden Tomato Sauce. Even the Saté Dipping Sauce freezes beautifully and can be thinned out with a little chicken broth for a tasty dish of cold sesame noodles. Keeping an assortment of frozen sauces on hand expands almost to infinity your repertoire of quickly prepared, interesting meals.

Always prepare a full recipe—whether meat loaf, a casserole, chicken breasts, muffins, whatever—then freeze what's left in individual serving packages to have on hand for a quick meal any time. Or even better, prepare two loaves at a time, while you're at it—it doesn't take that much more time. Slice one loaf and freeze in individual packages, and freeze the other whole to have on hand for company. Do this with all the loaves, not only meat loaf, but also the salmon, carrot, yellow split-pea—they're all good for either lunch or dinner. Men love them and they can easily reheat a slice or two for lunch.

Freezing is a lifesaver when you're cooking for a crowd for a summer weekend or winter holidays. Some of the less expensive casseroles that feed the multitudes include Chicken and Lamb Couscous, Picadillo, and Chickadillo. All of these, and many others, freeze well. And the loaves I mentioned earlier make grand casual fare, hot or cold, and are especially nice for summer picnics or as portable lunches. Always make extra when you're preparing any favorite dish—you eat now and freeze for later. Get into the habit of preparing a dish with the freezer in mind.

Never fill up your own freezer with commercially frozen food. Remember, you can make your own "gourmet" entrées that will be more delicious and healthful.

Component Cooking: Prepare Ahead, Assemble at the Last Minute

This is the definition of a caterer's life—prepare everything ahead up to a point, then assemble it all quickly, just before it's eaten. This method is not only a great time and energy saver, but it allows you to have on hand the elements for richly varied snacks, quick meals, pick-me-ups, as well as for more elaborate luncheons and dinners, and feasts for entertaining.

Component cooking means, first of all, having on hand in the refrigerator or freezer a good assortment of the basics that keep well: the cold sauces, such as Saté Dipping Sauce; Party Box Sauce Niçoise and a variety of salad dressings—Curry, Nene's Lemon-Garlic and Citrus Vinaigrette; mayonnaise; chicken and vegetable stocks; clarified butter; and fruit jams.

Make a habit of always having several kinds of vegetables and greens in the crisper, so you can quickly assemble an interesting "salad of the moment." In the recipe section on salads, you'll see how adventurous you can be in combining elements to make unusual salad combinations: Bosc pears, golden raisins, and green cabbage; watercress, new potatoes, and walnuts; oranges, cucumbers, and radishes. Improvise your own combinations; learn to trust your sense of what will taste good with what, and don't be afraid to experiment.

Component cooking also means preparing a quantity of one ingredient so it is used in a variety of ways. For instance, if you've just bought a couple of pounds of green beans, you can use half of them for chicken in the pot, and marinate the other half in a dressing with dillseed, red onions, and Nene's Lemon-Garlic Dressing and serve as a salad. If you've poached some chicken breasts, you can serve them cold in Chicken Salad Niçoise and Curried Chicken Salad, or hot in Chickadillo and Chicken Chili.

I always keep an assortment of marinated vegetables in the refrigerator (they keep almost as well as if they were pickled). I always have several slaws (shredded vegetable combinations), some cold pasta or grains, such as cold rice or bulgur or beans, to use as the basis for any number of dishes (see Cook Once, Eat Twice, page 66). The same goes for fruit; you can use it for salads or combine various kinds to make lovely compotes.

What component cooking means for entertaining is the difference between a hostess who can only muster the energy for a once-a-year extravaganza because she gets so exhausted from the stress of preparation, and a hostess for whom it's so easy that she has friends over at least twice a month. Entertaining is made easy when it's done with a strategy and careful planning. Freezing can be done days or weeks ahead; marinating, two or three days ahead. Many casseroles actually taste better when made a day ahead, so that the flavors have time to blend.

Here's an example of a big party buffet using the method of component cooking. An impromptu sixty-first birthday party that started with a few friends and grew to twenty, became an opportunity to use some of my favorite Middle Eastern recipes. (See the menu on the opposite page.)

The Lamb Balls and the pastries were prepared days in advance, and frozen. The Persian Chicken Balls were made in the morning. The fruit was plumped and the yogurt left to thicken overnight, with the cucumber added the next morning and left to

BIRTHDAY MENU

*Baba Ganouch, string cheese, Marinated Olives**

*Minted Lamb Balls with Pignoli**

*Persian Chicken Balls**

*Vegetable Couscous**

*Yogurt and Cucumbers in the Middle Eastern Style**

Steamed Kale

Fruit and Finger Pastries

marinate that day. The Vegetable Couscous was prepared early in the day and heated just before serving; the lamb balls and the pastries defrosted overnight in the refrigerator. This left only the steamed kale to be prepared and the heating of the Persian Chicken Balls and Lamb Balls just before the party.

The buffet was rich and varied, yet quite manageable; and I had plenty of time and energy to enjoy my guests.

Both of the Supper-by-the-Bite menus (pages 98–99) include many components that can be prepared ahead. Ham and turkey can be cooked the day before. Gravlax can be marinated three days ahead. Filet can be cooked in the morning. Many of the hors d'oeuvres can be frozen days in advance. The sauces for the crudités can be prepared a day in advance. All you need to do near serving time is cut up the vegetables and prepare the fruit.

A party of some size isn't quite as easy as falling off a log; it does take some effort and energy and planning. But you can pull it off, by making it as simple as possible for yourself—and certainly these techniques will do that for you.

Cook Once, Eat Twice

These "cook once, eat twice" components are a tremendous timesaver, and an easy way to vary your menus. It's almost like eating out all the time—you can have your basic ingredient hot or cold, dressed or sauced, or seasoned any way you like. Another advantage is you're less likely to rely on commercially frozen vegetable dishes, for which you pay an outrageous price for a little mediocre butter or cheese sauce.

For these components, I've concentrated on the complex carbohydrates—the rice, grains, beans, pasta, and vegetables—that should comprise the greater part of our daily menus. Remember that you should always have on hand at least a pound of dried beans or lentils, a pound of rice, and pasta. Unlike when you were raising a family, you're going to use each pound for as many as three or four meals. The charts on the next few pages show you how to use each component—whether it's rice, or a grain, or vegetables—both hot and cold; hot immediately after you've cooked it, and cold a day or two later as a component in a salad, sandwich, antipasto, or loaf.

The reward for your efficiency is that instead of having to cook each meal from scratch, or having an array of less-than-thrilling leftovers that depresses your spirits every time you open the refrigerator door, you'll have at least two dishes from each cooking session, dishes highly individual in flavor and texture because they've been dressed up in ways that enhance the main ingredient differently. White beans, for instance, can be used in a White Satin Bean Soup, White Beans with Lemon that makes a lovely cold side dish, or as part of an antipasto (see Cook Once, Eat Twice Beans, Lentils, and Peas, page 69). If your basic ingredient is rice (see Cook Once, Eat Twice Grains, page 69), you can serve it hot in Rice Pilaf with Pignoli and Italian Parsley, and the remainder will make a delicious cold rice salad with black olives, raw corn, and scallions. (And incidentally, if you serve two complementary incomplete protein sources such as rice and beans in the same meal, either hot or cold, you get a complete protein as well.)

A large quantity of pasta can be halved and served hot as a first course or light entrée, and then used in a cold side dish or entrée salad (see Cook Once, Eat Twice Pasta, page 68); for instance, hot Fusilli with Henry Grossi's Tomato Sauce Picante with Eggplant, and cold Fusilli Salad with Roasted Red Peppers, Artichoke Hearts, and Black Olives.

The versatility of vegetables is nothing short of miraculous. We had ten vegetables in Chapter 2, served thirty ways. And here we have ten more vegetables from which you can make twenty more hot and cold recipes (Cook Once, Eat Twice Vegetables, below), using those several pounds of vegetables you pick up at

COOK ONCE, EAT TWICE VEGETABLES

VEGETABLE	HOT	COLD
Asparagus......	Stir-Fry with Ginger and Soy	Crudité
Beets.........	Buttered Beets	Scandinavian Pickled Beets
Brussels Sprouts .	with Vermont Cheddar Cheese	with Vinaigrette
Cabbage.......	Skillet Slaw with Peppers, Peas, and Golden Raisins	Bosc Pears, Golden Raisins, and Green Cabbage Slaw
Celery.........	Vegetable Chili	Curried Chicken Salad
Corn..........	Grilled in Husks	Black, Yellow, and Green Rice Salad
Eggplant.......	Baked Eggplant with Nutmeg and Ginger	Baba Ganouch
Sweet Potato/ Yam	Mexican Fiesta Vegetables	Ruth and Hilary Baum's Yam and Apple Salad
White Potatoes ..	Elise Cavanna's Cucumber Potatoes with Fresh Dill	Mediterranean Potato Salad
Turnips........	Ceil's Turnip Soufflé	Gado Gado Salad with Saté Dipping Sauce

the supermarket or your greengrocer each week: hot Brussels Sprouts with Vermont Cheddar Cheese; cold Brussels Sprouts with Vinaigrette; hot Elise Cavanna's Cucumber Potatoes with Fresh Dill; cold Mediterranean Potato Salad; hot Stir-Fry Asparagus with Ginger and Soy; cold asparagus in crudités; and so on.

But that's only the beginning. When you have your refrigerator stocked with five or six cold starches—cold beans, rice, pasta, potatoes, and vegetables—you can have, as I do, a selection of three or four ingredients for breakfast, lunch, and dinner. And I've always found that when I have a variety of small dishes, rather than one or two big ones, I always eat less and feel that I'm getting more.

COOK ONCE, EAT TWICE PASTA

PASTA	HOT	COLD
Angel Hair	with Garden Tomato Sauce	with Broccoli Flowerets and Peas
Farfalle	with Caribbean Rouge Sauce	with Endive and Pink Dressing
Fusilli	with Henry Grossi's Tomato Sauce Picante with Eggplant	with Roasted Red Peppers, Artichoke Hearts, and Black Olives
Linguine	Pasta Paella	Straw and Hay
Buckwheat Noodles	with Asparagus, Ginger, and Soy	with Scallions and Smoked Oysters
Green Noodles . .	with Skillet Slaw	Apricot Kugel
Penne	with Pesto Sauce without Cheese	with Ratatouille
Ruote	with Thick Chunky Pesto	with Chicken Gascony
Small Shells	with Quick Roasted Red Pepper Sauce	with Scallop Seviche
Ziti	with Chicken Moroccan with Cilantro Sauce	with Red Cabbage and Pimiento-Stuffed Olives

COOK ONCE, EAT TWICE BEANS, LENTILS, AND PEAS

BEANS	HOT	COLD
Black Beans	Black Bean Chili	Black Bean and Vegetable Salad
White Beans	Tuscany Beans	White Beans with Lemon

LENTILS AND PEAS	HOT	COLD
Lentils.	Sam's Aunt Fanny's Lentils and Rice	Lentil-Rice Salad with Red Onion
Yellow Split Peas .	Dahl with Scallions, Tomatoes, and Lemon	Yellow Split-Pea Loaf with Vegetables, Cheese, or Tofu

COOK ONCE, EAT TWICE GRAINS

GRAINS	HOT	COLD
Brown Rice.	Chinese Emerald Brown Rice	Brown Rice with Seasonal Vegetables
Bulgur	Eleanor Tomic's Rice-Bulgar Pilaf with Walnuts	Bulgur Salad in Cucumber Boats
Couscous	Couscous with Carrots, Almonds, and Currants	Fruited Couscous Salad
Kasha	"Kashaed" Mushrooms	Kasha with Crisp Green and Yellow Vegetables
White Rice	Rice Pilaf with Pignoli and Italian Parsley	Black, Yellow, and Green Rice Salad; Spring Green-and-White Rice Salad
Wild Rice	Wild Rice with Shiitake Mushrooms	Wild Rice with Tri-Color Peppers

Cook Once, Eat All Week

If you like to concentrate your time in the kitchen, getting a lot done in one big marathon session, this is the approach for you.

You can do cook-aheads for regular menus, for entertaining, or for special diet menus. These cook-aheads can be practically anything, including a roast, a casserole, soups, side dishes, desserts, and even munchies. In a single two-hour session you can prepare all of these, thus saving several hours of cooking throughout the week, and cutting down enormously on your expenditure of fuel and energy.

This technique was perfected during my years as a caterer. In essence, it's preparing ahead, assembling at the last minute. Cook in the oven and on top of the stove, freeze, blend, and marinate, all at once. The rest of the week, whether it's a roast night or a dinner party for friends, the only thing left to do is to boil water for pasta or prepare a fresh salad.

Choose a time to try a cook-ahead when your energy is high, and you've got plenty of leisure. Don't attempt your first one when you're tired, under pressure, or busy with company. It will require your full attention for the time it takes—but the results will be well worth it.

If you find this procedure works for you, you may want to make your own chart. Start with a selection of recipes. Decide which ones require pre-preparation: cutting up, soaking, marinating, and so forth. Divide the recipes into what goes into the oven and what you can cook on top of the stove; decide, too, which you may want to freeze.

I used my cook-ahead approach when visiting some recently retired friends, Rose Mary and Doug Gordon, who now live in Seattle. Both Doug and Rose Mary had acted professionally, and Doug had had a serious bout of diverticulitis. To stay trim, Doug swims every morning. Rose Mary, who still has a twenty-five-inch waist, has always cooked simply and well, but she was eager, now that she at last had some leisure, not to find herself trapped in the kitchen. Yet she wanted to be sure she and Doug were eating in a balanced way.

Rosie and I made up our shopping list (below) from the categories in Chapter 3. Though Doug and she usually stick to fish and chicken, one of her young nieces was coming to spend a few days, and she had decided to make a roast with enough leftovers to last the visit.

Here's the way to get it all done.

First, put the lamb into a preheated 475° oven. Vegetables get added to the roasting pan when the heat is reduced to 350°.

While the lamb is in the oven, cook on top of the stove. Start with the longest-cooking food first, the beans. For the bean soup, cook presoaked beans in water in a medium-size saucepan, using a ratio of 4 cups of water to 1 cup of beans. In another medium-size saucepan, cook beans and water in a ratio of 1 cup of beans to 3 cups of water for the bean salad. On the third burner, cook 2 cups of rice with 3¾ cups of water. This will yield 6 cups of rice, which is enough for the rice pilaf and the rice salad.

SHOPPING LIST FOR SPRING COOKING MARATHON

PRODUCE:
Italian flat-leaf parsley, carrots, celery, cucumbers, lemons, mushrooms, sweet red and green peppers, potatoes, yellow squash, zucchini

GRAINS, BEANS, PASTA:
1 pound small white beans
1 pound rice

MEAT, FISH, CHICKEN:
1 leg of lamb (about 3 to 4 pounds), 1 pound boneless, skinned chicken breasts, 1 pound fresh salmon steak or 1 15-ounce can red salmon

DAIRY:
½ pound unsalted butter, ½ dozen eggs, 1 quart milk

CONVENIENCE:
canned salmon if fresh not available

NECESSITIES:
dried apricots, baking powder, capers, corn oil, dillseed, unbleached all-purpose flour, whole-wheat pastry flour, lemon extract, pimiento-stuffed olives, pepita nuts, rice vinegar, dried rosemary, sugar, brown sugar, 1 can (16 ounces) whole peeled tomatoes

COOK-AHEAD PLAN

PREP	ON TOP OF THE STOVE	IN THE OVEN	FOR THE FREEZER
Presoak beans Marinate roast Prep vegetables Marinate cu- cumbers Presoak apri- cots	White-Satin Bean Soup White Beans with Lemon Rice Pilaf with Pignoli and Italian Pars- ley/Rice Salad Chickadillo	Roast Leg of Lamb El Greco with pan vegeta- bles Apricot Loaf Pacific Salmon Loaf	Apricot Loaf Pacific Salmon Loaf Chickadillo

One burner is free, on which you can cook up a simple casserole for freezing. Chickadillo is an easy one—it takes less than 45 minutes to prepare and cook.

While the roast is in the oven and the presoaked beans, rice, and casserole are cooking on top of the stove, your hands are free, except for occasional stirring and poking. Use this free time to assemble a loaf and a quick bread, which will go into the oven an hour after the roast or at the same time depending on the size of the roast.

When all of this is completed, you will have stocked your freezer with a salmon loaf, a quick bread, and a party casserole. You will have cooked ahead for the entire week, including a roast, vegetables, bean soup and salad, rice pilaf and salad—and you'll even have dishes for entertaining. If you're a cookaholic like me, you'll also use this time to make a cucumber condiment and salad dressing.

This is a concentrated effort. But as Rose Mary said after doing this cook-ahead, "It really works! When my niece came, I had loads of things to feed her. And two weeks later I still had the Apricot Loaf for munchies for Doug and me. It really did give me a lot more time out of the kitchen."

Chapter V

ENTERTAINING FOR THIS SEASON OF OUR LIVES

▼▼▼

In more ways than we perhaps imagine, our lives in our middle and later years can become richer, more expansive than ever—and nowhere is this more true than with entertaining. And yet I too often hear people say, "We don't entertain any more," as though they no longer had any reason to! When I hear that, I flinch. To give up entertaining is to impoverish ourselves in ways that have nothing to do with money or the lack of it. Like love, entertaining is a conduit, a connection, and this is the time of our lives, more than any other, to move out toward others. We're not so preoccupied now with our own narrow goals—career, children, getting ourselves established in life—that necessarily took most of our time and attention when we were younger. We don't have to think any longer of entertaining as a status maneuver or as a means of establishing social identity—if we don't know who we are and what we stand for by now, we never will. We can now connect with others more freely and generously than ever before.

When you think about it, some form of feasting accompanies every important occasion of our lives. People gathering to break bread together has always had a deep social meaning. The celebration of almost all religious sacraments, in practically every religion, is accompanied by the partaking of food. Of all the many kinds of parties we did at The Party Box, the ones whose memories I cherish most are those that commemorated the landmark moments: weddings and anniversaries; birthdays and bar mitzvahs; births and deaths.

My most poignant memory is of a memorial luncheon. The

menu, which was glorious, featured dishes from The Party Box's most glamorous parties. It had been chosen by my partner, Jeff Perlman, shortly before he died at thirty-seven of Hodgkin's Disease, and I followed it in every detail. He wanted it to be a joyous occasion, recalling the pleasures of the past. He had left a letter to be read aloud to all his friends who were gathered. We wept and laughed, toasted and feasted, and departed with a feeling of joy and fulfillment. That experience deepened my love of celebration; it made me understand that we can celebrate the life that was lived even at the moment of saying good-bye.

But of course, it's the hope of this book that entertaining not be reserved just for the momentous occasions. Entertaining should be easy, casual, and above all frequent. Sometimes the impetus can come from starting a new life in a new place. My friends Nene and Bernie built a second home on Cape Cod, where they had summered for years. After Bernie sold his business and Nene quit teaching, they moved up there to live year-round.

"We entertained even more than we did in New York," Nene told me. "We always had too much to do in the city; there was never enough time. But when we lived on the Cape year-round, entertaining was the way we saw our friends." Nene can always find some excuse for a party—like her party to celebrate the blossoming of Montauk daisies. "When they come into bloom late in September, the bushes look like giant snow balls. They're a spectacular sight, and it's about the latest time in the year we can sit outside in the evenings.... After Bernie died, I thought for a while I just wouldn't be able to manage entertaining by myself. But I solved that problem by enlisting some of the young people who work in the restaurants around here. They helped me do a sit-down candlelight dinner in my studio, and my big eightieth birthday bash this September."

My own favorite style of entertaining will always be the kind we do as a group—the church supper, the neighborhood block party, the urban garden picnic—to which everyone comes carrying a covered dish, often made from a family heirloom recipe handed down through generations. This book, too, has been a community effort. Many of the recipes have been collected over the years from friends and from the many people who cooked and served for us at The Party Box.

If you've been restricting your entertaining to those once- or twice-a-year events you just can't avoid, perhaps you'll change your mind when you glance over these twenty-two menu plans for any occasion, special or casual. They're designed to make it all as easy as possible. None of them involves putting on the ritz or cooking to impress, only good conversation over simple and delicious food and drink—just the recipe for making spirits soar.

If I've persuaded you this far, don't start looking for excuses: "I gave my china to the kids." "I don't have enough chairs." "We don't have a dining room in our new apartment." "There's a hole in the rug." "I've forgotten how to cook for so many." Just about everybody you know is in the same boat—so press on!

Wherever you're living now, and whatever you've got on hand, will do just fine. If I were to walk in your door right now, I'd probably find within ten minutes almost everything you'd need to give any of the parties suggested in this section. Wall hangings can double as throws or runners for the table, the coffee table, the floor (yes, you *can* eat off the floor!), or the ground outdoors. Or you can use rugs, madras bedspreads, or quilts. You can press into service copper pots, the Art Deco vase on the mantel, old silver platters, pewter pitchers, glass dessert dishes—any and every style works in this casual kind of mix.

Table Settings

No matter where I travel about the country, teaching at gourmet food shops and on television, I always present the foods I've prepared in serving pieces bought or borrowed locally. I like to do this because it proves that beautiful serving pieces are available everywhere, in every price range, from many sources—from the inexpensive cost-plus bazaar type of import-export shops where I get wine glasses, napkins, throws, and baskets, to one-of-a-kind pieces of pottery from local artisans, to beautiful art nouveau trays from an antique or secondhand store, to good stoneware and oven-to-table casseroles from department stores or the cookware sections of gourmet shops. There's an infinite number of ways to set a mood, create a style, and make a feast visually beautiful without great expense.

Don't be afraid to mix silver, china, lucite, wood, and stainless steel serving utensils; who says they have to match? In fact, you create a much more individual and interesting look when you mix them than if you use matched sets of Lenox, Baccarat, and Wallace.

Disposables

You can choose from a huge variety of paper and plastic utensils. It's become quite acceptable to use plastic glasses for drinks at parties, since most people simply don't have enough of their own to go around. The same is true for paper or plastic plates. Just be sure to buy the extra-thick laminated kind—they come in all sorts of sizes, colors, and patterns. A beautiful supper can be ruined by a soggy, disintegrating paper plate.

Unless you are doing a sit-down dinner, you can mix paper, plastic, silver, and china. They don't have to match; no one is going to sit and compare silver patterns, and you can borrow some. Since it's almost impossible to juggle both a cup and saucer and a dinner plate while standing, use a glass or pottery mug for coffee or tea, or possibly good-quality plastic.

Centerpieces

We tend to think of centerpieces as necessarily flowers. But really, a huge bunch of gladioli plunked down in the middle of the table at a buffet overpowers the food. Many of the menus will show you how to think differently about decor. For instance, the centerpiece can be an element of the food itself—fresh and dried chilies make a great centerpiece for the Mexican Fiesta or Spanish Supper on the Grill.

And for that matter, why restrict yourself to the dining room table? Create an outdoor French country buffet; an environmental dinner party on your living room floor; a box supper you can eat anywhere in the house. Or how about a do-it-yourself kitchen party, where the guests help make their own dinner?

About Our Menus

Any of the recipes in these menus can be used elsewhere. Those included in this book are asterisked. Each dish will stand on its own, and can easily be incorporated into your own menus. My menus here are only suggestions, to fire you up and get you excited about party-giving. Mix and match them as much as you like. My heartfelt desire is to make you so excited about the idea of entertaining that your own imagination will take over.

Friendly Occasions

▼▼▼

A relaxed and casual style of entertaining simply becomes a way of seeing our friends as often as we like, with no fuss and a minimum of expense and effort.

Interchangeable brunches and suppers are ideal for our more leisurely lifestyle, and they can be served with equal aplomb at noon or at 7:00 P.M. The food can be prepared easily in advance. And since off-hour meals are usually lighter, a party for four to six can be served for $4 or less per person.

Luncheons can play a more important role in our entertaining. In this time of our lives, the middle of the day is more leisurely—no dashing back to the office. And we have more energy midday for entertaining.

And then there's the one-pot approach to entertaining, whether with soups, stews, entrée vegetables, or stove-to-table-top casseroles. All you need to go with them is a crusty bread with one of our herb butters, a greens-of-the-season salad, and either a light or a heavenly rich dessert, depending on the entrée. This is where I splurge on durable six-quart oven-to-table casseroles from gourmet cookware shops or ethnic shops that carry big cooking pots. I get them in a variety of colors so I can mix and match them, or follow a seasonal or ethnic theme.

INTERCHANGEABLE BRUNCHES AND SUPPERS

▲▲▲

Two of the easiest and most popular ways to entertain at home are with brunch and supper. Both call for lighter, less formal menus, with foods that can be prepared inexpensively and in advance. They are easy to serve and easy to eat—and best of all, they're totally interchangeable.

French Country Brunch or Supper

Wherever I've served this menu, it's always been a runaway favorite. I remember in particular a benefit party we did with a fashion show by the designer Cacharel at Bloomingdale's. They wanted a country-fresh feeling, so we chose green and white

FRENCH COUNTRY BRUNCH OR SUPPER

*Salmon Quiche**

*Chicken Gascony**

*Ratatouille**

Grapes and Strawberries

Finger Cookies

gingham tablecloths, and for serving pieces, crocks and baskets and wooden cutting boards.

French provincial cooking is increasingly popular these days. We've fallen out of love with *haute cuisine*—overly rich, heavily sauced food. This French country menu shares many of the Mediterranean flavors of Italy and Spain. Ratatouille, for instance, a great Provençal dish, has its Spanish counterpart, Pisto.

The Chicken Gascony in this menu is our interpretation of a duck recipe from a French chef. Shallots and garlic and a great deal of chopped parsley make the dish both pungent and colorful. The density of the salmon allows the quiche to hold up beautifully when cold. Quiches very often get "weepy," causing soggy crusts; not this one.

You can make everything in this menu a day or two ahead, and you may freeze the quiche and chicken. The marinade for the chicken is usually made twenty-four hours ahead, and ratatouille always tastes better at least a day after it's made.

The only thing left is to rinse the fruit and place the dainty cookies on a plate (these also can come from the freezer).

Flowers and serving ware can pick up the pinks and purples of the Ratatouille and the Salmon Quiche, and the green and white of the chicken. Serve ratatouille in a stoneware crock, the chicken on a green-leaf-lined flat basket-tray or plate, the quiche in a colorful ceramic plate, and the fruit in baskets or on terracotta saucers.

Hearty Portuguese Brunch or Supper

This hearty meal, good any time of year, is not for the faint-hearted for the flavors as well as the colors are strong—salted cod, spicy black olives, rosy-red linguiça, and dark green kale. And the make-ahead casserole just needs last-minute heating.

Here's another chance to use your orange-brown pottery serving dishes. Try the bread on a wooden board, the butter in a ceramic pot, and for a gorgeous contrast, the oranges with port on a black plate.

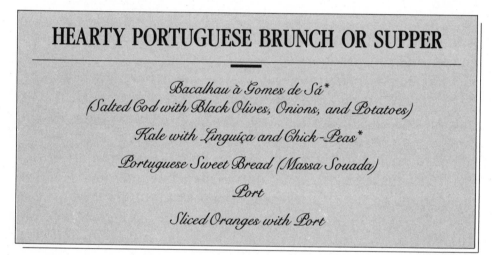

HEARTY PORTUGUESE BRUNCH OR SUPPER

Bacalhau à Gomes de Sá*
(Salted Cod with Black Olives, Onions, and Potatoes)

Kale with Linguiça and Chick-Peas*

Portuguese Sweet Bread (Massa Souada)

Port

Sliced Oranges with Port

STOVE-TOP TO TABLE-TOP CASSEROLES

▲▲▲

I love anything that's good *and* easy, and these top-of-the-stove, quick-to-fix, all-in-one-pot main courses have been a favorite for years—but now they really come into their own at this time of our lives.

The casserole dinner, like the church supper, goes back to frontier days, along with barn raising and "putting by" food. It's an old-fashioned, let's-all-pitch-in style of entertaining that's wonderfully companionable and perfectly suited for low-budget feasts and get-togethers.

Organize your own casserole group, whether you're single or a couple. If you've moved to a new town, or into a new apartment like newlyweds, a shared casserole dinner is the perfect way to start making new friends.

Jeff's Cassoulet Dinner

This interpretation of cassoulet cuts back on the heavier meats and speeds up the cooking process by using canned beans—it can be done in about 35 minutes, from start to finish.

When we did a series of television programs of holiday entertaining ideas, this is the menu we chose for between Christmas and New Year's, the "drop over for a bite of supper" kind of occasion. When you've just about done yourself in with holiday cooking, this one is simple.

Since cassoulet is French, I suggest accompanying it with French bread and an herb butter, a sharp, pungent green salad, and a light but elegant dessert. Cassoulet is good anytime, but it's especially comforting during the winter months.

Use whatever flowers are in season in your region. You might serve the bread on a wooden board, the salad in a crockery salad bowl, and of course the cassoulet directly from the pot it cooked in. This is where those great six- or eight-quart enameled cast-iron casserole pots in orange, blue, or yellow make a pretty statement for the main course.

JEFF'S CASSOULET DINNER

*Jeff's Cassoulet**
*French Bread with Tarragon Butter**
Watercress and Arugula Salad
*Cassis Mousse**
*Swedish Sweet Butter Cookies**

Mitz Perlman's Chicken Dinner in a Pot

When my partner Jeff's parents, Mitz and Ray Perlman, sold their house in a Chicago suburb and moved to Sun City, Arizona, they eventually learned a new way to cook and entertain friends. As Mitz explained to me, "Like everyone else who first moves here, we went on entertaining just the way we used to in Illinois, with lots of courses, one or two entrées. Then all of a sudden we realized that was just too much! Nobody ate like that anymore. The other day we had dinner at the home of one of our most elaborate party-givers, and she had pared the menu down to cheese and crackers, broiled flank steak, spinach casserole, garlic bread, and ice cream. And believe me, it was plenty!

"When I cook now, I always try to make it one dish, whether it's Brunswick stew, fish chowder, Hungarian goulash, or country chicken. Besides that, I have at most maybe a fruit cup as a first course, a green salad, some sort of bread, and a dessert I make or buy."

"I like to use my big, colorful Mexican cups for soups and soup-stews, with big plates in other colors, and some kind of pretty throw on the table. I often start with flowers on the table, and then remove them after the first course and put the tureen or pot in the center, and serve from there."

MITZ PERLMAN'S CHICKEN DINNER

Mitz Perlman's Chicken Dinner in a Pot*

Bagel Chips

Seasonal Greens with Basil Vinaigrette*

Seasonal Fruit

THE CHEF HERALDS THE SOUP

▲▲▲

Soups have comforted humans since we learned to make fire. The fundamentals have remained essentially the same: water from a stream, root vegetables from the forest, grain from the field, meat on the bone. Every country has its particular versions and refinements. Soup can be simple and pure, or very complex and multilayered.

There are some soup dinners I shall long remember. My sister Gerry served a rich Russian vegetable borscht, with a cucumber and dillseed salad and for dessert fresh strawberries with whipped cream. My friend Nene made a vegetable-beef soup-stew at her house on Cape Cod. She had picked every vegetable just hours earlier from her garden. To go with it there was fresh chard, slightly warm, served with a lemon, oil, and garlic dressing, glistening like gold on the dark green leaves; and for dessert a blueberry cobbler. And Jeff made a cioppino soup stew for a very elegant party for a designer in a sleek triplex apartment. Everybody had to dig in to crack the shellfish, which helped break the ice.

I like to bring my soup directly to the table in an earthy pottery tureen with a large pottery ladle. Feel free to use oven- and stove-top casseroles, and mix and match individual glass, enamel, or pottery bowls. Finish with a colorful garnish. Enjoy soups for Saturday or Sunday supper, or for a long, lazy Saturday afternoon lunch.

Beef-and-Vegetable Stew

At least once or twice during the fall or winter, serve this wonderful old-fashioned soup for a friendly get-together. It's the perfect rendering of the one-third–two-thirds balance of protein to carbohydrates.

This menu, like the fish chowder that follows, is fashioned after Nene's and my sister Gerry's style of eating with friends: a simple salad, crusty bread, and a simple dessert.

Serve the stew in a stove-to-table pot, the Swiss chard in a bowl, and the apples in whatever you cooked them in. A big, colorful napkin in the bread basket, a good herb butter, some late garden flowers, and you've got it.

BEEF-AND-VEGETABLE STEW

---

*Beef-and-Vegetable Stew**

*Italian Bread with Rosemary Butter**

*Red or Green Swiss chard, Italian Style**

Baked Apples

Classic New England Dinner

A fish stew is a chowder in the North, a gumbo in the South, and a cioppino in the West. The best of them always include fresh-caught fish, sometimes mixed with shellfish, or even chicken or other meats as in gumbos.

Use for the most part less expensive fish and shellfish, splurging with one special bit of lobster, crab, or shrimp.

This menu features the quintessential New England fish chowder, which is made without cream or milk, and I think is the better for it. It is rich, and yet so simple.

A pretty, tart salad of greens with grapefruit and black olives adds a flash of freshness that balances nicely with the richness of the soup.

The cobbler made with pears and apples is the perfect ending to this classic meal.

I love this soup in a big, colorful pot on a table covered with a crisp white tablecloth, with a vase of fresh flowers for color.

CLASSIC NEW ENGLAND DINNER

*Classic New England Fish Chowder**
*Bread with Cilantro Butter**
*Three-Green Salad with Grapefruit and Olives**
*Pear and Apple Cobbler**

VEGETABLE ENTRÉES

▲▲▲

"I know I should be eating more vegetables," a friend of mine said over lunch, "but how do you make a plateful of vegetables interesting?"

I knew that vegetables could be not only interesting, but lavish party fare, and I decided to prove it by experimenting with the great peasant dishes—couscous, feijoada, curries, chili. In nearly every country but ours, meat has always been expensive, and sometimes not available at all. Many peasant dishes combine vegetables, beans, and rice, to provide complete vegetable protein that is every bit as nourishing as animal protein, and without the cost of meat—either to your purse or your heart.

I've taken some liberties with the classic recipes, omitting meat and adding other vegetables not usually included to enhance flavor in the absence of meat. And I've garnished the dishes with whole peppers, tomatoes, apples, and oranges.

I'd recommend that at least the first time you make these menus, you follow the seasonings suggested for each dish. It's the seasoning that defines these national dishes, even more so than the basic ingredients. Once you've familiarized yourself with the basic recipes, feel free to experiment and improvise. Let the ingredients and your imagination be your inspiration.

Brazilian Vegetable Feijoada

The classic version of Feijoada, the great national dish of Brazil, is usually made with a number of meats and pork sausages, which seem too heavy and fatty for today's lighter eating. The version found here is all vegetable and very flavorful. For the grain, sometimes I use couscous, bulgur, or brown or white rice. If you're pressed for time, canned black beans may be used to produce a quickly made entrée casserole. For a heartier first course, serve the Scallop Seviche with pasta shells.

What makes this dish festive is the choice of accompaniments: chopped hard-cooked eggs, a circle of fresh corn, and limes and lemons.

When I served a similar but simpler menu to friends for an early weeknight dinner, I started with Scallop Seviche, which I had marinated ahead, followed by the Vegetable Feijoada I had cooked in the morning and just reheated, and a flan which went in the oven as we sat down to dinner. Although the main course was substantial, none of us felt stuffed. Since I had omitted the grain that night, the beans were combined with more vegetables, many with high water content, which I find makes the dish easier to digest.

The hot-from-the-oven flan added just the right note for the ending, simple and elegant—gliding down the throat with the lingering flavor of oranges.

BRAZILIAN VEGETABLE FEIJOADA

*Scallop Seviche**

*Brazilian Vegetable Feijoada**

*Flan with Orange Curaçao or Amaretto**

Mexican Fiesta

Mexican Fiesta, or Mexican pot-au-feu, is an adaptation of a recipe from *The Book of Latin American Cooking* by Elisabeth Ortiz. Her classic version uses meats and chicken along with vegetables and fruit.

I turned it into a Mexican pot-au-feu, all vegetables without the meat in a hearty entrée that combines, as Mexican cooking traditionally does, both potatoes and sweet potatoes, squash, peppers, beans, and green chiles and cilantro for seasoning. Circles of corn, and garnishes of avocado and peaches make this a spectacular entrée.

With such a rich entrée, a light first course of seviche, using shrimp, kohlrabi, and Bosc pears is a wonderful start. And since there is a great variety of fruits and vegetables in the main course, you can skip the salad, if you prefer. Flan, guavas, and cheese, or the Mexican Bread Pudding make a very nice dessert.

My favorite serving piece for large peasant dishes is a warm, earthy orangy-brown fired clay pot about sixteen inches around. The first course can be skewered or served on small glass plates. My friend Susan Goss has a great collection of heavy blue Mexican glassware she likes to use with this, and I have some rough-cut glass Mexican dishes I use. A centerpiece of dried chiles or a grouping of pots of flowers is nice with this. Use brilliantly colored serving dishes and napkins.

MEXICAN FIESTA

*Shrimp Seviche with Kohlrabi and Bosc Pears**

*Mexican Fiesta Vegetables**

*Mexican Bread Pudding (Capriotado)**

Summer Entertaining: Light and Simple Entertaining

▼▼▼

Whatever the scale and style of your summer entertaining, make it easy on yourself. A two-hour cook-ahead, like the one Rose Mary Gordon did when her niece was coming to visit, allows you to be relaxed and sociable rather than a slave to the kitchen. Don't even think about separately planning and preparing three meals a day. Choose a combination of foods that works for casual entertaining.

For breakfast, lay out a help-yourself buffet with cold cereals, yogurt, a bounty of fresh fruits, assorted cheeses and rusks, and a basket of quick breads that you've cooked ahead of time and kept in the freezer. Brunch, lunch, and supper can easily be assembled from a supply of frozen loaves, casseroles, quick breads, impromptu meals of soups, side dishes, and salads; our mix-and-match dishes can be eaten at room temperature indoors, outdoors, or as picnic fare at any time of day.

Whether it's a hibachi on the terrace or a full-scale cookout in the backyard, this is the time to enjoy a barbecue. Don't restrict yourself to the usual summer fare of hot dogs or hamburgers for the kids and steaks for the neighbors. Included here are two of my favorite barbecues: Luau on the Grill and Spanish Supper on the Grill. These menus use fish and chicken, which offer a lighter, more healthful, and, I think you'll find, welcome change from the usual barbecue.

PICNICS
▲▲▲

Who can resist a picnic? From the first vagrant breeze of spring to the last glow of Indian summer, we'll seize on any excuse to go off to the woods or the beach. A gingham cloth to throw over a wooden picnic table, a blanket at the beach; then opening up the hamper, sharing and passing the food.

Holidays are meant for picnics, of course, but you don't have to wait for the calendar. All sorts of events can be an opportunity to make the perfect picnic. What about an environmental picnic at the summer solstice to celebrate the arrival of summer, with everything in edible containers? Or the many wonderful plays, ballets, and day events around the country? Or even a Chinese-American picnic to commemorate the inventors of fireworks as well as Independence Day?

Enjoy them all. It's the most relaxed way of entertaining, because all the work is done ahead. And it can be as casual or as elegant as you choose.

Summer Solstice Environmental Buffet

This is a perfect party for environmentalists (may our numbers become legion!) because virtually no debris is left over to litter the landscape. All the food is served in edible containers, and the décor and serving pieces are of natural substances.

SUMMER SOLSTICE ENVIRONMENTAL BUFFET

Carrot Vichyssoise* in Summer Melons

Vegetable Salad Niçoise* in Savoy Cabbage Leaves

Bulgur Salad in Cucumber Boats*

Finger Fruit in Lettuce Cups

Marlu's Chocolate Bursts*

For the tablecloth: a cotton bedspread to spread over a picnic table or on the grass. I use one that cost $14.95 and has broad yellow, orange, chartreuse, and turquoise stripes. For plates: woven mats or flat baskets with leaves. For serving pieces: wooden forks, chopsticks, or tongs. You'll find many attractive natural serving pieces at import-export, cookware, and artisan-oriented stores. Napkins? Don't chicken out in favor of paper, use cloth napkins or bandannas. A coconut makes a fine communal finger bowl. Halve the coconut, fill it with water, and float petals or lime or lemon slices in the water. For an exquisite fragrance, add orange or rose water.

The serving holders for the food can be melons for the Carrot Vichyssoise; ruffly savoy cabbage leaves for the Vegetable Salad Niçoise; cucumber boats for the side salad; lettuce cups for the fresh fruits.

Chinese-American Fourth of July Picnic

What's the Fourth of July without fireworks? This year, plan a picnic to celebrate our own Independence Day as well as the Chinese invention of fireworks.

In planning your picnic, aim for the essence and spirit of both Chinese and American foods that include a cross section of tastes, colors, and textures.

This menu was created for the visit to America by the table tennis team from the People's Republic of China. Asked by *Sports Illustrated* magazine to cater the event, we were sworn to secrecy. When the time came, CIA agents rifled through each of the picnic boxes before they were given to the players. Later we heard that the team liked our meal best of any they had on the tour.

The same menu was later adapted for a feature in *The New York Times Sunday Magazine*. It's one of our favorite picnic box combinations; we've served it a hundred times. I think you'll like it, too.

CHINESE-AMERICAN FOURTH OF JULY PICNIC

*Lemon-Lime Chicken**

*Steak Salad Niçoise**

*Black, Yellow, and Green Rice Salad**

*Stir-Fry Asparagus with Ginger and Soy**

*Kumquats, Mandarin Oranges, and Litchee Nuts on Skewers**

*Ginger Icebox Cookies**

BARBECUES

"Entertaining outdoors is more convivial," says my friend Gloria Hainline. "There isn't the confined feeling you get around a dining room table. Summer is when I do most of my entertaining, just for that reason." Whether on the terrace or in the backyard, at the beach or on a campground, a barbecue is the essence of summer.

My two favorite barbecues are those that follow: a Spanish Supper on the Grill and a Luau on the Grill. Chicken and fish, which offer alternatives to fatter meats, are beautifully suited to the grill. Packaged meals (see chicken and fish in a package, page 307) and all manner of vegetables and fruits also lend themselves perfectly to barbecue. Skewers of vegetables or fish, chicken, beef, and lamb, marinated ahead of time, are a quick-cooking way to enjoy rich flavor with less fat and fewer calories.

Spanish Supper on the Grill

This simple Spanish barbecue menu, a whooping bargain for feeding a crowd, is likely to make you popular in barbecue circles. I first came up with the idea when I was visiting my niece and nephew, Rona and Dick Dorn, in Spring, Texas. Like many young couples with children (they have four girls), they don't have a big budget—and Rona loves to entertain. My solution was this supper. It costs around $3.50 to $4.00 a person, including beer and sangria, and we got everything at the supermarket. And we spent most of the day *not* preparing this dinner.

The chicken needs to marinate for four hours in the refrigerator before it goes on the grill. The Gazpacho made in the blender requires only the roughest chopping of vegetables; the Cold Bean and Pea Salad takes about ten minutes. The Mexican Wedding Cookies can be made the night before, or weeks before and frozen. The garlic bread goes on the grill when you're ready to turn the chicken.

This menu particularly lends itself to colorful and inexpensive paperware. Use summer colors or orange, yellow, and green in the napkins, plates, and forks. Arrange summer flowers, such as zinnias and marigolds, in a copper kettle or earthenware jar. Serve the Gazpacho in mugs. Line a platter with fresh collard greens or lemon leaves and pile the chicken high. Serve the salad in a glass bowl and the garlic bread in a basket lined with a blue cloth napkin.

SPANISH SUPPER ON THE GRILL

*Gazpacho**

*Chicken Achiote**

*Cold Bean and Pea Salad**

Garlic Bread

*Mexican Wedding Cookies**

Luau on the Grill

This menu can be prepared on a small terrace in the city sixteen floors up, or in your backyard. I've done it in both places.

In Hawaii, a luau means a pit, a pig, and an all-day affair. Our luau means fish or chicken, a big salad, grilled corn, peppers, and pineapple.

The marinades for both the chicken and the fish are light, but flavorful and can be made ahead. The Gado Gado Salad lets guests make their own. And the other vegetables and fruits grill at the same time as the fish or chicken.

Use woven mats, colorful plates and napkins, and tropical flowers to create a Hawaiian mood.

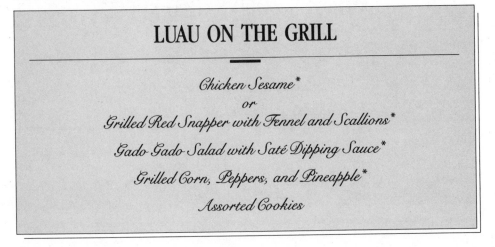

LUAU ON THE GRILL

*Chicken Sesame**
or
*Grilled Red Snapper with Fennel and Scallions**

*Gado-Gado Salad with Saté Dipping Sauce**

*Grilled Corn, Peppers, and Pineapple**

Assorted Cookies

SERVE EVERYTHING COLD

▲▲▲

Growing up in California, I've always eaten and enjoyed cold entrées, such as salads and roasts. Since many of us now live in warm climates the year round, here are two very special menus, one featuring a shrimp curry salad, the other a cold pork tenderloin roast and two colorful and flavorful grain salads.

I've often heard that "men don't like cold entrées," except on picnics. But many of The Party Box's most glamorous creations were cold suppers served after the theater, opera, or ballet—and they were devoured!

These two menus are as elegant as any, and my hunch is that the plates will all come back empty.

Glamorous Cold Salad Supper

This is a breathtakingly beautiful menu, like a Matisse still life: the pink, green, and chartreuse of the shrimp, apples, and curry dressing; the red, green, and yellow peppers against the deep

---

GLAMOROUS COLD SALAD SUPPER

Beet and Cucumber Soup*

Curried Shrimp Salad*

Wild Rice Salad with Tri-Color Peppers*

Carrot Raita*

Pure Fresh Fruit "Ice Cream"*

Ginger Icebox Cookies*

brown of the wild rice; the bright orange of the Carrot Raita and the more pastel shades of the Pure Fresh Fruit "Ice Cream" served in goblets.

To show off the food as it deserves, I would set a very dressy table. Glass serving pieces and plates would be perfect, catching the flicker of the candles and acting as a shining backdrop for the vivid colors. Serve the cookies in a flat basket lined with an attractive napkin.

Elegant Cold Roast Pork Supper

The small, perfect pork tenderloin roast is the centerpiece of this meal. Because of the way it is marinated and allowed to cool completely before it is sliced, the meat comes out a pristine white, fragrant with allspice, peppercorns, and sage.

An apricot aspic with rosemary, pickled beets, and couscous salad add an array of vibrant colors and textures to this unusual menu. And one of my all-time favorite desserts, Frank Pimentel's Raisin-Bread Pudding, is as elegant a finale as one could ask for.

ELEGANT COLD ROAST PORK SUPPER

*"Spirited" Cold Roast Pork Tenderloin**

*Rosemary-Scented Apricot Aspic**

*Fruited Couscous Salad**

*Scandinavian Pickled Beets**

*Frank Pimentel's Raisin-Bread Pudding**

Entertaining for a Crowd

Special occasion entertaining for a crowd can be birthdays or anniversaries, teenagers' parties, or planning-the-project committee meetings. They can be formal or informal, cost very little, or be a once- or twice-a-year occasion for really splurging. They can be for ten people, or twenty, or fifty. There are two ways that I use to tackle crowds.

One is the "supper by the bite" approach. I invite people for cocktails and serve a light supper, which may be nothing more than a variety of finger foods. It's bountiful entertaining, which, with a little planning, can be easy. Getting a week or a day or two head start means cooking ahead, assembling at the last minute, and using techniques that include freezing and marinating. Then on the day of the party there are only a few small tasks left, and instead of frantically cooking up to the last minute, you can relax a bit and be ready to enjoy your guests.

For this cocktail-party approach, I've given you two menus. One is a standard but extremely popular buffet that we served for every conceivable kind of occasion. The second is a very elegant spread, the kind we would do for glittering fashion benefits in department stores. Everyone loved those luscious finger foods, which neither dripped down the front of gowns nor resembled the usual cocktail-party circuit fare—bite-size filet mignon and gravlax, breath-taking antipastos, and clusters of grapes and strawberries, all shown off against a mix of terra-cotta, black lacquer, wooden boards, and baskets.

Surprisingly, these extravagant menus are not as expensive as they may seem. Half a seven- or eight-pound salmon filet, which we cured to make gravlax, can be stretched to serve forty people, and a whole filet mignon from thirty-five to fifty when you are serving a variety of other things.

My second method for entertaining a crowd involves food a bit more substantial, handled in a way similar to the "friendly occasion" suppers. I sometimes serve one of the great peasant one-pot dinners, such as couscous, chili, curry, or picadillo, along with a green salad, bread, and finger pastries. The type of menu works especially well for a planning meeting, a late light supper after a big event, or a teenage party.

Or, you may want to use these ethnic "soul foods" for a theme party. Each recipe lends itself to a number of variations: the chili can be made with chicken, or black beans, or vegetables as well as with the usual ground meat. The same goes for the curries and couscous and even the picadillo, which can become "chickadillo" by changing the ground meat to chicken. The seasoning defines the dish; the ingredients can be as varied as your imagination. Select a first course, condiments, salad, and dessert that reflect the country you've chosen for your theme. Colorful serving pieces lend a festive touch.

Holiday entertaining is a special category all its own usually involving a crowd and the traditional foods we remember from childhood. Hams and turkeys, compotes, sweet-potato soufflé, and special holiday desserts—they all have heartwarming appeal. My strategy is to make a buffet party a holiday gift to my friends, whether it's an old-fashioned buffet or a formal one with filet mignon and wild rice.

SUPPER-BY-THE-BITE

▲▲▲

I n my seventeen years on the party circuit, the party we were asked to do most often was, of course, The Cocktail Party. And coincidentally, just as my career as a caterer was getting underway, those traditional silver trays of canapés—indistinguishable dabs of meat garnished with mayonnaise and cream cheese on soggy rounds of white bread—were vanishing from the scene. Our clients asked for more vegetables, hearty and forthright meats—big baked hams, whole filets of beef, whole roast turkeys—and hors d'oeuvres of more heft and substance.

Party locations were changing, too. Hotels were still favored spots, but more often parties were being held in public places that had never known a chafing dish—department stores, discos, skating rinks, museums, libraries. And these new spaces demanded an entirely different approach to the presentation of food. Flat silver trays in a grand nineteenth-century palace like the New York Public Library would have made the food look insignificant. In such a theater, the food needed to become a

ELEGANT COCKTAIL BUFFET

Oriental Vegetables with Saté Dipping Sauce*

Cubed Filet Mignon with Sylvia Sherry's Horseradish Sauce*
served on Whole-Wheat Baguettes

Gravlax* on Pumpernickel with Pommery Mustard with Green
Peppercorns

Chicken or Lamb Moroccan*

Italian Antipasto*

Strawberries and Grapes

Finger Pastries

STANDARD COCKTAIL BUFFET

*Crudités with Sauce Niçoise**

*Whole Standing Baked Ham**
With Pommery Mustard Sauce and
Raisin-Pumpernickel Bread

*Potted Cheddar with Port and Walnuts**

*Mousse of Salmon**

Assorted Crackers and Rusks

Strawberries and Grapes

Finger Cookies

dramatic spectacle that drew the eye. The food had to become the show, and it had to stand up to the vastness of its surroundings.

My partner Jeff knew instinctively how to rise to this challenge. Our first big department store party was in Bloomingdale's model room, with seven hundred guests. "Everything must be big, Jane," Jeff said to me. "Big baskets, big trays, lots of *height*—that's what we need to show off the food."

In all his food designs, Jeff applied two basic principles. The first, to maintain a sense of balance and proportion by integrating the three elements of Sky, Earth, and Man (this is a Japanese concept), which give height, breadth, and dimension to the buffet. This rule of proportion applies whether you're using huge tables to serve 800, or a 48-inch round table in your living room.

The second principle he called "Like things with like things." The bread stays with bread, the meat is by itself, crudités are the vegetable statement, and the strawberries and grapes are yet another grouping.

Supper-by-the-Bite serves as a light dinner of finger food, and for me, it is the "supper" solution to the bigger party. But for those guests who may want to go on to dinner afterward, they can eat as much as they want of the lighter things without feeling they've already had a full meal.

The foods for a Supper-by-the-Bite should be various and luxurious: roast turkey and ham; filet mignon or gravlax; crudités or Oriental vegetables; potted cheese; Mousse of Salmon or Sole; Chicken Sesame, or Moroccan, or Gascony; Italian or Middle Eastern Antipasto; an assortment of fresh fruits.

This approach to entertaining allows us to "indulge in moderation" with the foods we shouldn't have often. The quantities are small so we needn't worry about overdoing it. It's adaptable to practically any occasion, year round. And since the party is at "cocktail time," it ensures an early evening for your guests.

Use anything and everything for the presentation: baskets, wooden boards and bowls, lucite, enamel, lacquer, terra-cotta and, of course, china and glass.

Whenever and however you choose to serve your Supper-by-the-Bite, keep in mind Jeff's two principles: balance height, breadth, and dimension, and keep like things with like things.

COOKING FOR A CROWD: VARIATIONS ON A THEME

▲▲▲

The easiest and surest way to success when you're cooking for a crowd is one-pot casserole cooking. Not only is it quick and inexpensive, but it's enormously popular.

I can't tell you how many requests we had during The Party Box years for Picadillo. It's nothing more than basically a ground-meat stew, which is native to Mexico, Cuba, and most of South America. Once we served it as part of a huge buffet at Sotheby's, with a South American theme. The menu included banana and strawberry daiquiris, and margaritas made from every conceivable fruit, Picadillo, hams, and South American antipasto.

Picadillo can become Chickadillo simply by replacing the meat with chicken, and the kidney beans with chick-peas. To maintain the Mexican theme, serve Brown Rice with Pepita Nuts and Italian Parsley and a simple salad, with rum-flavored mousse or a flan for dessert. I like to serve this menu on vivid Mexican earthenware crockery, with Mexican accents that include serapes and colorful plates and napkins.

The chicken curry recipe Madeleine Boulanger shared with me became one of our standbys for big parties—one of the biggest, a party for 1,000 at the original Studio 54. For this party we had huge displays of crudités, great pots of curry, and tables full of delicious condiments.

When you're making a curry at home you can show off your own versatility with the variety of accompaniments that make this dish so special, or you can ask each of your guests to bring a condiment. The golds and chartreuses in the curry can be picked up in brass trays, Indian runners, and small lacquered and enamel dishes for the condiments.

Couscous is another enormously popular one-dish casserole. We served it at a luncheon at *Sports Illustrated* during a week of luncheons planned for a film presentation. I had thought it might be a little exotic for that company, but when the luncheons were extended for another two weeks, this menu was requested.

And finally, chili. Oh my, the times we've served chili! At the New York Public Library, at Bloomingdale's, at the New York State Opera. And it was always a miracle we didn't run out,

VARIATIONS ON A THEME

Chicken and Lamb Couscous or
Vegetable Couscous* or
Couscous with Carrots, Almonds, and Currants**

Yogurt and Cucumbers in the Middle Eastern Style*

Henry's Cucumber, Radish, and Orange Salad*

Pecan Chess Tarts*

VARIATIONS ON A THEME

*Picadillo or Chickadillo**

*Brown Rice with Pepita Nuts and Italian Parsley**

Seasonal Green Salad

*Mousse with Rum**

VARIATIONS ON A THEME

*Madeleine Boulanger's Shrimp Curry with Apples and Peaches**
or
*Madeleine Boulanger's Chicken Curry with Apples and Peaches**

*Carrot or Watercress Raita**

*Curried Cucumbers**

Lemon Mousse

VARIATIONS ON A THEME

Chicken Chili or*
Black-Bean Chili or*
*Vegetable Chili**

*Gazpacho**

*Salsa**

*Rice or Bulgur**

*Mexican Bread Pudding (Capriotado)**

*Mexican Wedding Cookies**

because *everybody* wanted seconds. Sometimes we overlook these great classic ethnic "soul foods," thinking that they're not fancy enough for parties. Well, I can assure you that almost all the socialites and celebrities to whom we served these dishes over the years would take any of them any day over a galantine or a stroganoff.

Each of these three basic dishes lends itself perfectly to the "variations on a theme" approach, and I've included several variations of each, with an expandable menu that allows you to keep it as simple as possible or to include a variety of introductory and side dishes. So pick and choose among these suggestions, or mix them with your own or others in this book, depending on your mood.

In the decor and serving pieces, use the most brilliant colors; the countries of origin of all these dishes are hot and sunny, and you can afford to go all out in vividness.

Even a tiny apartment (believe me, I know from experience!) can accommodate up to twenty people when you serve one of these one-dish casseroles, with finger pastries for dessert, both on paper plates. So don't hesitate—have a crowd over several times a year, whether it's friends or colleagues or the neighborhood. Everyone loves a party, and when it costs no more than three to five dollars a person, you can afford it. It's a gift to others and to yourself!

Holiday Entertaining

▼▼▼

The great holidays—Christmas and Chanukah, Easter and Passover, Thanksgiving—are what remain of the ancient religious rituals and feasts. These are the seasons for both the big family get-togethers and the more casual socializing with neighbors, friends, and acquaintances. And most of us have happy recollections of these holidays that go back as far as earliest childhood.

Many families have one special dish that is traditional: oyster stew on Christmas Eve; the special chestnut stuffing for the turkey, whose recipe Aunt Dot would never part with. For me it was the roasted cashews my grandmother made only for such festive occasions.

This is the season, too, for bringing homemade gifts of food for the table: spiced fruit, chutney, brandy-soaked fruit cake, or a scrumptious dessert such as Cranberry Jubilee.

We celebrate holidays with food in overflowing abundance. We're bound to overindulge a little, but it's worth it to renew happy memories. You'll find a mix of rich and not so rich recipes for holiday feasting in this book. Partake of either, or both, and enjoy it all!

Traditional Holiday Buffet

This menu was our perennially popular holiday buffet for office and home parties because it incorporates all the old favorites of the season, along with year-round favorites: turkey or ham (or both); a lasagna (I chose Zucchini Lasagna in case some of the guests were vegetarian); Cold Bean and Pea Salad with Fresh Herb Vinaigrette; and of course, the luscious compotes and chutneys that spice up this kind of buffet—cranberry chutney, peach chutney, or my very special compote of dried fruits with fresh lime and pears. You might also want to include fruit breads along with regular breads with Party Box Chive Butter.

Continue a traditional look with red and green tablecloths and napkins and any combination of serving pieces—china, pottery, glass, baskets. Red tablecloths with pots of paper white narcissus are lovely.

For a dessert table, you might want to try what we once did. Cover a styrofoam Christmas tree (you can get them at party stores during the holidays) with heady balsam branches, and attach big red and green apples with wooden picks. Then surround the centerpiece with all sorts of delicious finger pastries and clusters of fruit.

Happy holidays!

TRADITIONAL HOLIDAY BUFFET

Whole Standing Baked Ham* and/or Roast Turkey Breast

Zucchini Lasagna*

Winter/Summer Fruit Compote*

Peach Chutney, Cranberry Chutney

Cold Bean and Pea Salad with Fresh Herb Vinaigrette*

Assorted Cheeses, Breads, Party Box Chive Butter*

Finger Pastries

Finger Fruit

Late Christmas Eve Supper

This is a marvelous menu to serve, buffet style, to ten or twelve special friends or your family on Christmas Eve. Everything is do-ahead, and because it's a cold presentation, you can go out Christmas caroling or to a special midnight service and return to this super-elegant, already-prepared buffet with plenty of energy left to devote to your guests.

Although some of the ingredients are costly—filet mignon, wild rice—served as they are in this buffet they go a very long way and satisfy a hungry crowd.

Use silver, glass, and lucite serving pieces to add shine and gleam to the table. And don't forget colorful cloths and napkins for the table.

Serve the Cranberry Jubilee in a chafing dish and ignite with brandy before spooning it over ice cream. This spectacular dessert is a sure-fire way to end a special holiday meal.

LATE CHRISTMAS EVE SUPPER

Filet Mignon* with Sylvia Sherry's Horseradish Sauce*

Wild Rice with Tri-Color Peppers*

Green Beans and Red Onion in Lemon Dressing*

Gazpacho Aspic*

Cranberry Jubilee*

Just Before Midnight New Year's Eve Buffet

Ham and/or turkey can make one last appearance at a New Year's Eve buffet, in a most unexpected role as part of Paella Salad. Surrounded by black mussels, pink shrimp, rosy-red lobster, green peas, scarlet pimiento, ruddy sausages, and a touch of yellow saffron, it's an unusual and beautiful entrée. And there are a number of other very special dishes that can make a "Just Before Midnight" New Year's Eve supper colorful, light, and yet satisfying, with a Spanish flavor: black beans with red peppers; orange sweet potatoes; rosy new potatoes; fluffy Kale with Linguiça and Chick-Peas; cucumber, radish, and orange salads.

End the meal with a Spanish trifle in a huge punch bowl. I like to use the flan with orange Curaçao as the base, then a store-bought or home-baked pound cake soaked in orange Curaçao, with—yes!—whipped cream, just this once. The rest of the meal is so perfectly balanced that the extra calories in the dessert are easily affordable for this last splurge of the Old Year.

A South American-Spanish-Mexican assortment of pottery, earthenware, and baskets can point up all the vivid colors of the meal. Go formal with matching colored napkins and plates, or informal with a whole bouquet of colors. Big, gaudy Mexican paper flowers in woven baskets and multicolored runners set a gay mood for this exuberant evening.

JUST BEFORE MIDNIGHT NEW YEAR'S EVE BUFFET

*Gazpacho**

*Paella Salad**

*Quick Black Beans and Red Peppers**

*Kale with Linguiça and Chick-Peas**

*Henry's Cucumber, Radish, and Orange Salad**

Sweet Potatoes and New Potatoes

Spanish Trifle

THE RECIPES

▼▼▼

A WORD ABOUT OUR RECIPES

▼▼▼

Throughout my fifty years of cooking, beginning with the first sponge cake I baked when I was ten, I have been fascinated by recipes, those mysterious formulas for producing delicious things to eat, often with what seem to be the most improbable combinations of ingredients. I've read probably thousands of cookbooks in my time, own at least seven hundred, and have tried many hundreds of recipes. Some of my favorites among them have never been written down or even verbalized, but simply demonstrated.

When I started my business I tested many more recipes, and by trial and error I learned that "creative" cooking didn't mean making changes just for the sake of being original. Sometimes it meant being inspired by the beauty, fragrance, and flavor of the ingredients so as to combine them in new ways that would have never occurred to me, but seemed, when I tried them, to heighten the individuality of each. Other times the "inspiration" was as mundane as not having on hand a certain ingredient called for in the recipe and needing to substitute another. Often an ordinary dish was transformed into an extraordinary one.

What also evolved in my cooking was a versatility achieved through variations on a theme—using a relatively small number of ingredients to produce a broad range of effects. It's the seasonings that define the dishes in my repertoire, whether the country of origin is France, China, Morocco, Spain, or Italy; whether the basis is chicken, lamb, beef, beans, or vegetables.

More than anything else, I like to use foods in their natural state, whenever possible; it always results in the brightest, clearest, most sensuous flavors and colors: the brilliant orange of parsnips and carrots, the lush green of "purely" pea soup, the intense fuchsia of raw beets and cucumbers combined with yogurt, the subtle chartreuse of a curried shrimp salad.

For this book I tested recipes from many sources: The Party Box, from restaurants, cookbooks, friends, and from people in their fifties to their eighties from across the country who have shared their creative solutions for cutting back on calories and fat. This doesn't mean to say that I intend to cut out two favorite categories of foods—breads and desserts—as a part of our everyday feasting. In this book I've compromised by including two delicious fruit breads and two very healthy muffins along with selected desserts.

Ethnic restaurants all over the country are teaching us new ways to enjoy vegetables, grains, and beans from cultures that for generations have known how to make the most of them. Inventive young men and women chefs have turned to the bounty of the vegetable kingdom and explored the pleasures of regional cooking to offer us a stunning array of appetizers, entrées, and salads. In bookstores and libraries everywhere, more and more shelfspace is being given to books that feature the joys of lighter, healthier, and festive eating (see the bibliography at the end of the book for further reading).

Wherever possible, I've tried to give proper credit for recipes received, whether in person or in print. Wherever I've failed to do so, the failure was unintentional. I've sometimes received recipes that their donors truly believed were family heirlooms, only to find them in existing cookbooks. Many of our Party Box recipes were sent to clients for their own entertaining, and some have appeared in national magazines or my newspaper food columns. I've sometimes been startled to see one of our recipes appear word for word in another cookbook without credit, but I'm glad they've found a wider audience. Cooking is the most social and communal of all the arts. Almost all the recipes in existence are variations on a few basic, often centuries-old themes. Recipes are meant to be passed around; I hope you'll do so with the ones you enjoy in this book.

Five Low-Fat Cooking Techniques

▼▼▼

My philosophy of food is to start with the freshest ingredients of the highest quality, then prepare them in the way that will most enhance their intrinsic taste.

There are five cooking techniques particularly well suited for underscoring the flavors of food—and they also happen to use very little fat, adding few calories and little cholesterol. I've cut back on the fat even further in adapting them for use here and in my home kitchen. Three use little oil, and two use none at all. These techniques are: low-fat sautéing, poaching, steaming, baking in parchment paper, and quick-broiling.

Except perhaps for baking in parchment paper, all of these methods are probably familiar to you. They're slightly revised versions of techniques you've undoubtedly used often before, and they can be easily adapted to suit most recipes.

The only seasonings used with these techniques are spices, herbs (fresh, if possible), the juice of lemons, limes, or oranges, and wine. Whether you cook chicken, fish, or red meat, vegetables, or fruit, they will have delicate texture and a lovely, clear, distinct flavor.

LOW-FAT SAUTÉING

▲▲▲

Many cooks have fallen into the habit of sautéing everything in lots of butter or oil, and they're encouraged to do so by recipes that use double the necessary amount of fat. But you don't need all, or any of that fat, if you sauté in a preheated heavy pan at high heat—this is also known as "pan broiling." The intense heat immediately draws out juices that lubricate the pan, then sears the food, locking in the remaining juices and giving it a nice burnished look.

Nonstick skillets work well for this kind of sautéing, making it virtually foolproof. These skillets are now available in a much heavier-gauge metal than when they were first on the market, and are even easier to use. You can also use stainless steel or cast iron, but then you'll need a little lemon juice or a scant teaspoon of olive oil, sesame oil, or butter to prevent sticking.

The secret of sautéing over a high heat with little or no fat is to keep the pan moving around on the burner so that it never sits still on the heat. You want to keep the food "jumping"—which is what "sautéing" means—so it can't stick to the bottom of the pan.

I use this method mainly to cook firm fish filets or steaks, such as salmon, scrod, sea bass, and halibut, boneless chicken

LIGHT-IN-CALORIE RECIPES

LOW-OIL SAUTÉING
Shell Steak Paillard with Thyme
Skillet Skirt Steak
Chicken Piccata
Skillet Fish Steak on a Bed of Peppers and Onions

POACHING
Poached Filet of Sole with Fresh Mushrooms
Poached Chicken Breasts
Florine Snider's Summer Poached Peaches

STEAMING
Lemon-Sweet Steamed Scrod
Steamed Scallops with Shades of Jade Vegetables
Steamed Chayote
Steamed Cauliflower with Fennel and Cumin

Interchangeable Greens
Red or Green Swiss Chard, Italian Style
Steamed Potatoes with Yogurt and Fresh Chives

BAKING WITH PARCHMENT
Fork-Tender Baked Chicken Breasts
Package Baked Dinners: Meal-in-a-Package—Fish Filet with Vegetables; Kay Meserve's Lamb Chop Dinner with Vegetables
Baked Onions with Balsamic Vinegar
Flaky Baked Salmon Steak

QUICK-BROILING
Barbara Grogan's "Under-the-Broiler" Gingered Shrimp
Broiled Scrod with Chunky Pesto

breasts, and beef or veal that's been sliced and pounded thin. It's not an ideal technique when you're cooking for a number of dinner guests—it's too difficult to keep several pans going at once. But because it's so quick and easy, it's perfect when you cook for one or two. Try Chicken Piccata this way, and see recipes for Shell Steak Paillard with Thyme, and Skillet Fish Steak on a Bed of Peppers and Onions.

POACHING

▲▲▲

Poaching is cooking in water or other liquid that is held below the boiling point, at a steady, gentle simmer. It requires no fat at all, and the food stays moist and tender. The poaching liquid is also an ideal medium through which to impart subtle flavors to delicate foods such as fish filets, chicken, fruit, and eggs. These are my favorite foods for poaching, although I do occasionally poach scallops and shrimp with water flavored with wine, and lemon, sometimes a bay leaf and spices. I've also poached whole small fish in a large pot. (Fish poachers are expensive and awkward to store, and I find they're not really necessary.)

Choose a pot which will snugly hold the food you're poaching; don't overcrowd the pot, or the food won't cook evenly. Then simply cover the food with liquid—water, stock, wine, whatever the recipe calls for. Fish filets, small (half pound) whole fish, and boneless chicken breasts usually take only about ten to twelve minutes to poach. Underripe fruit will take a little longer. (Poaching is the perfect way to enjoy fresh peaches, which usually arrive underripe in our markets, and stay that way—they spoil before they ripen, as a rule. Poaching them, with the skins on for extra fiber, makes them tender, delicate, and flavorful.)

The liquid in the pot should never reach a rolling boil. Boiling overcooks the food and toughens it. This is especially true for chicken, so be particularly careful when you're cooking chicken breasts to keep the heat at a gentle, slow simmer throughout.

Recipes I'm especially fond of that use this technique include

Poached Filet of Sole with Fresh Mushrooms, Poached Chicken Breasts, and Florine Snider's Summer Poached Peaches.

STEAMING
▲▲▲

Steaming means cooking food over, not in, a small amount of boiling water, on or in some kind of rack with a hole or holes that allow steam to rise and cook the food. It ensures absolute purity because the water never touches the ingredients. If you add seasonings to the water, their aroma infuses the food, but the seasonings themselves never touch the food, which is a boon if you're cooking for someone on a rigidly restricted diet.

You can steam most vegetables such as cauliflower or broccoli, combinations of vegetables such as carrots, parsnips, and chayote, or entrées such as scallops with broccoli and scallions.

I've experimented with a number of steaming utensils and have found that the cheapest and easiest to use is the stainless steel basket steamer available for a few dollars at any housewares store. The wooden three-story steamer available in Oriental shops in gourmet departments in department stores is excellent. There is also a pottery steamer shaped like an angel-food cake pan, which is particularly good for capturing the juices of the food you're steaming.

If you are a two-diet family, steaming is a way to ensure absolute purity, as well as extremely tender results. Once the food is steamed, it can be seasoned or sauced for individual diet needs.

BAKING WITH PARCHMENT PAPER
▲▲▲

Parchment paper seals in heat and moisture, so the food steams and cooks in its own juices. This method is not only the surest way to get absolutely fork-tender chicken breasts and fish, it's also wonderfully easy, since you can prepare all the ingredients ahead of time and you don't need to keep close watch while they're cooking.

I use parchment in two ways. First, I cook fish or chicken by itself, unsealed, between two sheets.

Preheat the oven to 325°F, then line the bottom of a baking pan that's large enought to hold the filets in a single layer with parchment paper. Arrange the chicken breasts, which should be boned and lightly pounded, or the fish filets in the pan. Sprinkle them with a little lemon juice, salt, and pepper, then cover everything with another sheet of parchment. The chicken should take about 15 to 18 minutes, half-inch-thick fish filets about 10 to 12 minutes. To check for doneness, simply lift up the parchment. Poultry is done when the juices run clear when pricked with a fork, and fish is cooked when it flakes easily with a fork.

The second way I use parchment is to cook a whole meal in a parchment package—the only trick is to choose ingredients that all require about the same amount of time to cook. Thin flounder filets, for instance, would be ready long before large pieces of broccoli. The rule of thumb to remember is: Equal weights cook equally. In a package with a whole lamb chop, for example, chunks of potatoes, carrots, and celery would be perfect. For packages of quick-cooking fish or poultry, simply cut those vegetables into smaller pieces, or use faster-cooking vegetables such as squash, snow peas, or sliced mushrooms. You may also cook vegetables or fruits this way.

Remember that whatever is on the bottom of the package cooks faster, so layer your ingredients accordingly.

To make the envelope for the meal, start by folding a large rectangular piece of parchment (approximately 11x15 inches) in half. Open the paper, and layer your meat or fish, potatoes, and vegetables slightly off center, a little to the right or left of the fold. Fold the paper over the food, then crimp and flatten and pleat the edges together until the package is closed. The parchment should be sealed tightly so that none of the steam and aroma escape. Sealing it airtight makes the parchment brown beautifully and puff up, so that it's pretty enough to serve in the envelope—guests can open their own.

Recipes that lend themselves to cooking in parchment include Kay Meserve's Lamb Chop Dinner with Vegetables and Fish Filet with Vegetables.

QUICK-BROILING

▲▲▲

Instead of sticking a big steak or half a chicken under the broiler, try broiling lighter fish filets or steaks, chicken in parts, or skewers of meat. If you let them marinate for as little as half an hour, you can have an almost infinite variety of flavors that let you eat around the world.

Preheat the broiler for about 5 minutes before you begin cooking. I broil fish and seafood about 6 inches from the flame, and I generally choose firm-fleshed fish such as swordfish, salmon, scrod, halibut, and shrimp because they don't break apart when you turn them.

Chicken—both breasts and cubes on a skewer—as well as skewered meats should be broiled about 6 inches from the flame.

BASICS

▼▼▼

Homemade fancy butters, vegetable and chicken stocks, sauces, seasonal salad dressings, herb vinegars and oils, chutneys—how nice to have these on hand to add a spontaneous sparkle to your cooking and entertaining.

Chicken or beef broth in cans (bouillon cubes have too much salt) are convenient, but better still are your own homemade chicken and vegetable stocks. Making stocks yourself also means that you control the amount of salt. When they're well flavored with herbs, you often need no salt at all.

Salad dressings such as Nene's Lemon-Garlic Dressing and the vinaigrettes can be made well ahead to dress any cold vegetable or impromptu salad. Our favorite Party Box sauces—Niçoise, Saté Dipping Sauce, Russian Dressing—hold up well for a good week in the refrigerator without losing any flavor.

I like to make up many of the basics, such as the salad dressings or some of the sauces or stocks, while I'm doing a "cook once, eat twice" session.

And don't forget the seasonal offerings—the jams, chutneys, and compotes—that must catch the fruits of summer and autumn at their brief moment of perfection.

Cold Sauces and Dressings

▼▼▼

THE PARTY BOX SAUCE NIÇOISE

▲▲▲

At hundreds of cocktail parties, I would overhear party-goers trying to guess what was in the Sauce Niçoise we served with crudités. As with most of our recipes, it contains only a few ingredients. Refrigerate for up to five days.

1½ cups Hellmann's Mayonnaise or Angie's
    Mayonnaise (page 121)
1 can (6½ ounces) large pitted black olives, drained
    and rinsed
2 cloves garlic, peeled and coarsely chopped
2 tablespoons capers, drained and thoroughly rinsed

YIELD
2 cups

1. In a blender or a food processor fitted with a metal blade, combine ½ cup of the mayonnaise, olives, garlic, and capers. Whirl until blended but with small pieces of olives still visible.

2. In a medium-size mixing bowl, whisk together the sauce and the remaining mayonnaise. Refrigerate, covered.

SATÉ DIPPING SAUCE

▲▲▲

For a change of pace, serve Oriental vegetables instead of crudités with this sauce for dipping. You will also find the sauce served with the Gado Gado Salad (page 265). It can be refrigerated for three to five days or frozen for one month.

1 canned mild whole green chile, rinsed, seeded, and
    coarsely chopped
2 large cloves garlic, peeled and coarsely chopped
3 tablespoons freshly squeezed lime juice
3 large scallions, trimmed and cut into sixths
½ cup heated Chicken Stock or All-Vegetable Soup
    Stock (pages 138–139)
¾ cup smooth or chunky peanut butter (no salt added)
1 teaspoon coarsely chopped peeled fresh gingerroot

YIELD
1 ⅔ cups

1. In a blender, combine all the ingredients and whirl until smooth, but still with flecks of scallions. The mixture should be thick; it will thicken as it stands.

2. Cool and refrigerate, covered, or freeze. If sauce separates, stir until smooth consistency.

ANGIE'S MAYONNAISE

▲▲▲

This is a good basic alternative mayonnaise, which uses only one egg. Add your own combinations of fresh herbs or seasonings. Refrigerate for up to four days.

YIELD
1 cup

1 egg
2 tablespoons freshly squeezed lemon juice
½ teaspoon Dijon-style mustard
1 cup corn oil

1. In a blender, combine the egg, lemon juice, and mustard. Whirl just to mix. Add ¼ cup of the oil and whirl on high speed until blended.

2. As you continue to blend, pour in the remaining oil in a thin, steady stream until blended.

3. Pour into a glass bottle or jar, cover, and refrigerate.

SYLVIA SHERRY'S HORSERADISH SAUCE

▲▲▲

Serve this sauce with hot or cold filet mignon. The sauce keeps a week in the refrigerator.

1 pint sour cream
½ cup Hellmann's Mayonnaise or Angie's Mayonnaise
    (page 121)
1 bottle (6 ounces) prepared white horseradish, undrained
½ tablespoon freshly ground white pepper

YIELD
1 ½ pints

1. In a medium-size mixing bowl, combine all the ingredients until well blended.

2. Pour the sauce into a quart glass jar, cover, and chill until ready to use.

YOGURT CHEESE

▲▲▲

Yogurt has become a staple in the American diet. In this recipe, yogurt is drained to create a low-fat alternative to cream cheese. If you don't have cheesecloth on hand, use paper toweling. The cheese keeps for three days. Serve with roasted sesame seeds (page 137).

YIELD
1 ¾ cups

1 container (32 ounces) plain yogurt
¼ cup finely chopped fresh herbs

1. Line a colander or large sieve or basket with 2 layers of cheesecloth. Place it over a large bowl to catch the drippings.

2. Scoop the yogurt onto the cheesecloth, cover, and let drain 4 to 5 hours at room temperature. After 2 hours, using a spatula, flip the yogurt over.

3. The yogurt should reach the consistency of ricotta-type cheese in 5 hours. For a firmer cream cheese-type texture, continue to drain another hour or two.

4. When the cheese has reached the desired consistency, place in a bowl or container, cover, and refrigerate. At this point you may combine the cheese with the finely chopped fresh herbs for a spread.

For Horseradish-Yogurt Cheese Spread with Strawberries

Combine 1 cup Yogurt Cheese with 4 teaspoons prepared white horseradish, undrained, and mix well. Pour into an attractive bowl and serve with 2 pints rinsed and hulled strawberries.

RUSSIAN DRESSING

▲▲▲

Arthur Gross, one of the recipe tasters for this book, says, "That Russian Dressing is great! I've been putting it on everything!" The fresh herbs and fresh lime juice are what make the difference. It goes very well with turkey breast. Refrigerate for up to three weeks—but it probably won't last that long.

¼ cup sweet relish, drained

2 tablespoons grated yellow onion

1 tablespoon freshly squeezed lime juice

3 tablespoons finely chopped fresh parsley or 1½ tablespoons dried

1 quart Hellmann's Mayonnaise or Angie's Mayonnaise (page 121)

¾ cup chili sauce

¼ teaspoon Tabasco sauce

½ teaspoon dried chervil

½ teaspoon freshly ground white pepper

½ teaspoon salt

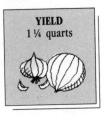

YIELD
1¼ quarts

1. In a large bowl, combine the relish, onion, lime juice, and parsley. Mix well.

2. Add the remaining ingredients and blend thoroughly.

3. Pour the dressing into a glass bottle or jar, cover, and refrigerate.

CILANTRO SAUCE WITH YOGURT AND GREEN CHILES

▲▲▲

The Indian Cafe, a small restaurant a few blocks from my apartment, does the kind of cooking I like best—home cooking. In this instance it's Indian—pakoras and samosas with cilantro sauce, curries, dahls, raitas. As many times as I go there the specials are always special, the sauces always fresh and pungent, the desserts simple yet memorable. My favorite is fig ice cream.

After swooning over the cilantro sauce a number of times, I went around the corner to an Indian grocery store where I buy all my Indian spices, nuts, rice, lentils. When I told the owner how I loved the sauce, he reached into the refrigerator and said, "Here. Make it with these tiny green chiles, garlic, yogurt, and cilantro." And he pressed a huge bunch of cilantro into my hand.

Enjoy this sauce with shrimp, pasta, with any kind of fritter, and as a stunning first course over hearts of palm.

3 large cloves garlic, peeled and thinly sliced
2 canned green chiles, drained, seeded, and finely chopped
½ cup finely chopped fresh cilantro
½ cup plain yogurt

YIELD
1 cup

1. In a blender or food processor fitted with a metal blade, combine all the ingredients. Pulse on and off, about 30 seconds, until creamy but still with flecks of cilantro and chile. Do not overpurée the ingredients.

2. Transfer the sauce to a serving bowl and refrigerate, covered (it will thicken), until serving time.

Salad Dressings

▼▼▼

VINAIGRETTE

▲▲▲

There are as many versions of vinaigrette as there are cooks. The classic vinaigrette has a three-to-one ratio of oil to vinegar, and *fines herbes*. Here I've mixed the oil and vinegar one-to-one to cut back on oil. Chef Fedele Panzarino introduced me to the idea of adding the whites of hard-cooked eggs.

⅓ cup corn oil
⅓ cup distilled white vinegar
1 teaspoon water
1 tablespoon finely chopped parsley
1 tablespoon finely chopped fresh dill
1 teaspoon dried tarragon
1 teaspoon dried chervil
1 teaspoon Dijon-style mustard
Salt and freshly ground pepper, to taste
2 tablespoons chopped hard-cooked egg whites (optional)

YIELD
¾ cup

1. In a small bowl, whisk together the oil, vinegar, and water until well blended. Whisk in the parsley, dill, tarragon, chervil, mustard, and salt and pepper to taste.

2. Pour into a glass jar or bottle, cover, and refrigerate for up to 1 week.

Note: The chopped egg white can be added at serving time. Transfer the dressing to a small bowl and whisk in the chopped whites.

MANGETOUT CRANBERRY VINAIGRETTE

▲▲▲

Here is a delightful seasonal vinaigrette from Mangetout, a catering establishment in Seattle run by two charming and talented cooks, Jane Hummer and Kristi Pangrazio. Since they enjoy sharing good recipes, let me pass this one on to you. This is a slightly creamy dressing flecked with gold and ruby red. It is particularly appealing on fall fruit salads with pears, apples, grapes, persimmons, and pomegranates. Jane and Kristi say it's great on Bosc pears and endive—and on fish and chicken too. Make it up once a week and keep refrigerated.

⅓ cup cranberries, picked over, rinsed and patted dry
1 tablespoon parsley leaves or cilantro leaves, wiped
　　clean with damp paper toweling
1½ to 2 teaspoons Dijon-style mustard
½ cup corn oil
¼ cup red wine vinegar or rice vinegar
1 tablespoon sugar, or more depending on tartness of cranberries
Salt and freshly ground pepper, to taste

YIELD
1 cup

1. In a food processor fitted with a metal blade, finely chop the cranberries and parsley by pulsing on and off about 30 seconds.

2. Add the remaining ingredients and whirl until smooth and creamy, but with flecks of cranberries still visible. Do not overpurée the ingredients.

3. Transfer to a glass jar or bottle, cover, and refrigerate until ready to use.

CITRUS VINAIGRETTE

▲▲▲

I use this refreshingly tart vinaigrette on salads that combine vegetables and fruit with rice or couscous (page 219). Refrigerate seven to ten days.

YIELD
1 cup

2 tablespoons rice vinegar
1 tablespoon water
3 tablespoons freshly squeezed orange juice
3 tablespoons freshly squeezed lemon juice
3 tablespoons freshly squeezed lime juice
1 teaspoon Dijon-style mustard
2 tablespoons corn oil
2 tablespoons snipped fresh chives or dill
Salt and freshly ground white pepper, to taste

1. In a small stainless steel bowl, combine all the ingredients and whisk until well blended.

2. Refrigerate in a covered glass jar or bottle.

OILS

The assortment of vinegars available today enhances our enjoyment of salads, as does the wide variety of oils of different flavors, weights, and textures—heady walnut and hazelnut oils, cold-press sesame, corn and safflower oils, apricot kernel and avocado oils, dark, strongly flavored Oriental sesame oils, and fine olive oils. If your supermarket does not carry a full line of oils, look for them in gourmet and health-food stores and Oriental markets.

Experiment with oils in your salad dressings and use them to make your own herb-flavored oils.

In her book *Salads*, Amy Nathan suggests a ratio of ¼ cup of freshly chopped herbs to 2 cups oil. Steep in clean, sterilized, and covered bottles for ten days, shaking from time to time. Strain through cheesecloth and re-cork with sprigs of fresh herbs, just as you do the vinegars (page 129). Herb-flavored oils will keep three months in the refrigerator.

NENE'S LEMON-GARLIC DRESSING

▲▲▲

What is pleasant about this do-ahead dressing is how it complements many types of salad. It also adds bright flavor to vegetables, especially steamed greens served hot, warm, or cold. The dressing keeps in the refrigerator seven to ten days.

½ to ¾ cup safflower oil, corn oil, or good-quality Italian olive oil
6 tablespoons freshly squeezed lemon juice (about 3 lemons)
4 medium-size cloves garlic, peeled and finely chopped
¼ teaspoon salt
¼ teaspoon dried chervil
½ teaspoon snipped fresh dill

YIELD
1 ½ cups

1. Combine all the ingredients in a blender and whirl on high speed for 1 to 2 minutes or until the garlic is puréed.
2. Pour into a glass jar or bottle, cover, and refrigerate.

BASIL OR FRESH HERB VINAIGRETTE

▲▲▲

Here's a vinaigrette that capitalizes on any fresh herbs you may be growing and on herb vinegars you may have made. Use basil or any two complementary herbs such as tarragon and dill, marjoram and sage, cilantro and mint with the other ingredients to make a variety of herb dressings. Any variation of this basic vinaigrette goes well with many of the salads found in the salad and grains and beans sections of this book. Refrigerate up to seven days.

¼ cup finely chopped fresh basil or other fresh herbs
2 to 3 tablespoons corn oil or corn and olive oil mixed
2 tablespoons freshly squeezed lime juice
2 tablespoons rice vinegar or any homemade
    herb vinegar

YIELD
½ cup

1. In a small bowl, whisk together all the ingredients.

2. Refrigerate in a covered glass jar or bottle until ready to use.

HERBAL VINEGARS

For a time a while back, I think we got carried away with fancy vinegars. "Nouvelle cuisine" encouraged such combinations as blueberry vinegar with chicken and raspberry vinegar with fish. But herbal vinegars do bring the garden indoors and into our food, and their occasional use is well worth the effort to make them.

A mixture of one or two complementary herbs in season—such as tarragon and dill, marjoram and sage, cilantro and mint—is a good way to start. The ratio is ⅔ cup lightly packed fresh herbs to 1 cup of vinegar, which can be red wine, distilled white, or rice. The better the quality, the better the result. These recipes are by courtesy of my friend Teri Fischer, who has a whole assortment of vinegars she puts up in unusual modern and antique bottles, and even in small decanters.

Her procedure is as follows:

1. Pick the herbs before they go to flower. Bruise them slightly with the flat side of a knife or meat cleaver.

2. Place the herbs in clean, sterilized quart jars with non-metal tight-fitting lids. Add the vinegar of your choice and cover.

3. Steep 2 weeks in a warm dark place, shaking the vinegar from time to time.

4. For final bottling and corking, strain the vinegar through cheesecloth. Discard the herb mixture.

5. Add sprigs of fresh herbs to clean sterilized bottles (see Canning Instructions, page 135), add the strained vinegar, cork for storage, and store in a cool place.

CURRY DRESSING

▲▲▲

This dressing keeps in the refrigerator longer than any freshly made dressing I know. Its perfect balance of ingredients offers a unique flavor and rich color. You'll find it used in several recipes in the salad section. Enjoy it all summer long on fresh vegetables and boiled potatoes. Refrigerate for up to a month.

⅔ cup corn oil
3 tablespoons distilled white vinegar
1 tablespoon curry powder
¼ teaspoon freshly ground white pepper
¼ teaspoon ground cumin or ground coriander
    (optional)

YIELD
¾ cup

1. In a bowl, whisk together all the ingredients until smooth.

2. Store in a glass container or jar, covered, in the refrigerator.

Butters, Spreads, and Stocks

▼▼▼

CLARIFIED BUTTER

▲▲▲

Clarified butter is less apt to burn since all the impurities have been removed. Although we are eschewing the use of butter in quantity, butter in this form is best for our health and most convenient to cook with. It will keep up to one month, covered, in the refrigerator. You will need a strainer, a double thickness of cheesecloth, and a container with a top for storing.

—

½ pound (2 sticks) unsalted butter, cut into thirds

YIELD
¾ cup

—

1. In a double boiler over hot water or in a heavy small saucepan over the lowest possible heat, allow the butter to melt completely. Do not stir it at any time.

2. The clear butter that rises to the top is clarified. Remove the froth from the top with a skimmer. Milk solids will remain in the bottom of the pan.

3. Place a cheesecloth-lined strainer over a storage container. Carefully pour the clear butter into the strainer, leaving the white solids in the saucepan.

4. Cover and refrigerate to use as needed.

COMPOUND BUTTERS

▲▲▲

"Hotel butters," or compound butters, have always been part of French cooking. They are used for hors d'oeuvres, and as a final accent for fish and chicken, or in soups. They are "creamed" butters combined with other flavoring ingredients such as herbs, smoked fish, nuts, mustard, and fruit. If using sweet red pepper, caviar, or smoked fish to flavor the butter, start with a smaller amount than the herbs because they are more intense. Experiment for the balance you like, adding more to taste. Since butter is to be used in moderation, even tiny amounts of these are a splurge. Spread pumpernickel rounds with a delicate lemon butter before adding thinly sliced cucumbers for cucumber sandwiches. Cilantro butter is good over bland fish or chicken breasts. Compound butters should be used the same day they are made unless frozen for future use.

Experiment and enjoy!

For Herb Butters:

2 tablespoons softened unsalted
    butter
1 tablespoon finely chopped
    fresh herbs

For Lemon and Lime Butters:

1 tablespoon softened unsalted
    butter
1 tablespoon freshly squeezed
    lemon or lime juice

HANS' STRAWBERRY FRUIT JAM

▲▲▲

This fruit jam is a happy invention. It satisfies our love for jams but with much less sweetener than usual. Strawberries, or almost any fruit in season, can become a delightful spread with less than a half hour cooking time. Two or three 8-ounce jars in the refrigerator promise much pleasure for desserts and snacks, and they'll make wonderful gifts when you visit friends. Hans' approach to canning for ones and twos is using the 8-ounce jar size, and his method of canning is quick and doesn't require a big kitchen or special equipment. Since strawberry is such a favorite, I'll give the recipe for it as the "basic jam," and depending on the season or where you live, adapt it for other fruits. The fruit jam keeps three weeks in the refrigerator after opening.

---

3 cups fresh strawberries, rinsed, hulled, and lightly
     crushed with a potato masher until broken but
     still retaining their shape
4 tablespoons honey
2 tablespoons freshly squeezed lemon juice
1 package (1¾ ounces) Sure Jell

YIELD
3 8-ounce glass
jars

---

1. In a 4-quart stainless steel or enamel pot, combine the strawberries, honey, and lemon juice. Place the pot over medium heat and, stirring constantly, bring to a boil, about 5 minutes.

2. Add the Sure Jell in a slow, steady stream, stirring constantly to keep the mixture from getting lumpy. Return to a boil and boil 1 minute. The strawberry mixture should roll off a spoon.

3. Remove the pot from the stove and follow the Canning Instructions (page 135).

For Quince or Other Fruit Jams

Substitute for the strawberries, 3 cups prepared quince or other fruit. Apples and quince do not require Sure Jell because of the pectin in the fruit, which gives them the right "jam" consistency.

PARTY BOX CHIVE BUTTER

▲▲▲

We served this smooth cream "butter" with all our breads. It works so much better than the hard pats of butter usually presented at buffets. It's most elegant served in an earthenware crock or glass bowl with snipped chives (dried or fresh) on top. It keeps in the refrigerator three to four days.

YIELD
2 ½ cups

½ pound (2 sticks) unsalted butter, softened
6 ounces cream cheese, softened
1 tablespoon snipped fresh chives or 1 teaspoon frozen
    or dried

1. In a food processor fitted with a metal blade, place the butter and cream cheese and half of the chives. Pulse on and off until smooth and fluffy.

2. Remove the mixture from the food processor and put in a crock or glass bowl. Sprinkle the remaining chives over the top.

3. Refrigerate, covered, until ready to use. Bring to room temperature for smooth spreading.

WINTER/SUMMER FRUIT COMPOTE

▲▲▲

This combination came about when I used some dried fruit I had on hand. Feel free to substitute. The compote is prettiest when the fruit has texture. It goes with poultry or pork and can become an aspic dessert.

YIELD
4 servings

1 cup mixed dried fruit in equal amounts, such as
    apricots, dates or figs, golden raisins, apples,
    peaches or pears, finely chopped
2 cups fruit juice, such as pineapple, apple or peach nectar
2 tablespoons freshly squeezed lime juice

2 slices (each ½-inch thick) fresh unpeeled lime, cut
   into very small dice
½ Bosc pear, unpeeled, cored, and finely chopped

1. In a medium-size saucepan over medium heat, combine the dried fruit, the fruit juice, lime juice, and diced lime, and cook at a simmer about 15 minutes or until almost all the liquid except for 1 or 2 tablespoons has been absorbed by the fruit mixture.

2. Transfer to a bowl and add the finely chopped pear. Serve warm.

For Fruit Aspic Dessert

At this point, if you want to make an aspic, remove the liquid from the pot, combine it with 2 teaspoons gelatin or agar-agar (page 283), return it to the pot, and continue cooking for another 5 minutes. Pour into a 1-quart mold sprayed with nonstick vegetable cooking spray and chill 2 hours or until firm.

CANNING INSTRUCTIONS

These instructions are for all the canning recipes in this book, including the fruit jams, pickles, and chutneys.

On a rack in a very deep, wide-bottomed kettle (at least 8-quart size), place clean, new, or ready-to-use-again 8-ounce canning jars and their lids. (Although jars and rings can be reused, always use new lids.) Pour enough boiling water into the kettle to cover the tops of the jars by 2 inches. Boil 10 minutes. With metal tongs, remove the jars from the kettle and wipe them off with a clean cloth. Fill the jars with whatever canning mixture you are preparing, to just below the rim. Wipe around the rim so no seeds or liquid prevent sealing. Screw on the tops, finger-tight; do not try to wrench them closed. Place the filled jars on a rack in boiling water to cover the tops of jars by 2 inches for 10 minutes. This process will tighten the seals. Remove the jars from the kettle, wipe dry, and cool on a wire rack. Test seals. Store in the pantry or refrigerator.

Sugar in large amounts acts as a preservative in standard canning. When less sugar is used or honey is substituted, the preserving agent is reduced and mixtures made from less sweet and more delicate fruits need to be refrigerated.

HOLIDAY SPICED FRUIT

▲▲▲

This fruit is a wonderful condiment for a holiday buffet or any buffet throughout the year, and is perfect for gift giving. Fill either 8- or 16-ounce jars with the mixture. It can be refrigerated for weeks or frozen for months. You may substitute various dried fruits for those used here.

1½ tablespoons finely chopped candied ginger
1 pound dried pears, halved
1 pound dried apricots, halved
½ pound golden raisins
2 cans (16 ounces each) fruit cocktail with juice,
    maraschino cherries removed
2 cups apple cider or apple juice
¼ cup brandy (optional)
2½ teaspoons ground allspice
2½ teaspoons ground cardamom
1 tablespoon curry powder
1 pound apples, cored and sliced, but not peeled
6 ounces fresh cranberries, rinsed and picked over

YIELD
2 ½ quarts
Oven
350°F

1. In a large casserole or kettle, place all the ingredients except the apples and cranberries. Bake, covered, in the preheated 350°F oven, stirring frequently, for about 30 to 45 minutes or until the fruit softens but still retains its shape.

2. Add the apples and cranberries and bake until the apples become crisp-tender and the cranberries pop and soften slightly, about 10 minutes more.

3. Remove the casserole from the oven and transfer the fruit mixture to a container with a lid. Cool and refrigerate, covered, for several weeks or freeze. Or follow the Canning Instructions (page 135), and store.

Note: You can also cook the spiced fruit on top of the stove over a very low heat. Be sure to stir constantly to prevent burning.

PARTY BOX NUT MIX

▲▲▲

I was once served a bowl of salted peanuts with tiny cubes of candied ginger in a small farmhouse in Kyoto, Japan.

Delighted with this new twist on a nosh, I added things to it. The result was a colorful mix that combined pepita nuts, golden raisins, ginger, pecans, almonds, and peanuts. We served this at most of our parties, and probably landed some of our biggest parties when it was taken as a gift to a prospective client.

1 pound each of salted or unsalted peanuts, almonds (unsalted Spanish are the best), pecans, and golden raisins
½ pound pepita nuts
½ pound candied ginger, coarsely chopped

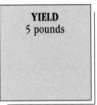

YIELD
5 pounds

1. In a large bowl, combine the nuts, raisins, and ginger. Mix thoroughly.

2. Place in containers with tight-fitting covers for freezing or storing briefly in the refrigerator.

OVEN-ROASTED NUTS AND SEEDS

To control the salt and oil, buy raw nuts and roast and toast them yourself in the oven. You may want to add seasonings such as coarse salt and a drizzle of oil—but this way you control the amount. To roast nuts, spread them evenly on a flat baking pan sprayed with nonstick vegetable cooking spray or lined with parchment paper. Bake at 275°F about 10 minutes. Remove the nuts from the oven and shake them in brown paper bags to absorb some of the oil. Cool and transfer to a container with a lid.

Buy your nuts from specialty nut stores or mail-order houses that specialize in nuts (see Mail-Order Shopping, page 374). Keep them on hand for salads, pilafs, desserts, for guests, and, yes, for yourself.

Almonds   *Pignoli (Pine Nuts)*
Spanish Peanuts *Pepita Nuts*
Pecans   *Sunflower*
Cashews   *Seeds*
Walnuts   *Sesame Seeds*

CHICKEN STOCK

▲▲▲

The tastiest chicken stock will come from older stewing hens. If you can buy from a butcher who stocks free-range chicken, do so. What you want in a chicken stock is bright color, deep flavor, and clarity with as little salt as necessary.

You will need a double thickness of cheesecloth, a large strainer, and storage containers with tops.

YIELD
2 quarts

10 to 12 cups of water
3 pounds chicken pieces, including backs or 1 large
    hen, cut into pieces
4 medium-size carrots, peeled and cut into quarters
1 onion, peeled, halved and stuck with 2 cloves
2 leeks, white parts only, thoroughly rinsed
4 stalks celery, stringed and cut into thirds
Bouquet Garni: 1 bay leaf, 8 white peppercorns slightly cracked, 1 clove
    unpeeled garlic, 3 sprigs of parsley, and 2 sprigs each of thyme,
    marjoram, rosemary, or tarragon, all wrapped in a cheesecloth
    bag and tied

1. In a large kettle, bring the water to a boil over high heat.

2. Lower the heat and add the chicken. Then raise the heat and let the water return to a rolling boil.

3. Boil the chicken 5 to 10 minutes until the impurities rise to the top. Skim off the froth and discard.

4. Add the carrots, onion, leeks, celery, and bouquet garni. Lower the heat and simmer the stock about 2 hours, continuing to skim the froth from the top. Be sure the chicken remains covered with water. Add more if necessary.

5. Remove the kettle from heat. Using a soup ladle or a 4-cup measuring utensil, ladle the chicken stock into a cheesecloth-lined strainer held over a large bowl or other container. With a spatula or wooden spoon, press out the liquid from the chicken and vegetables. Discard the bouquet garni.

6. Let the stock cool (see Cooling Soups, page 176). Refrigerate the stock until the fat rises to the top. Remove the fat.

7. Ladle the stock into storage containers. Cover and refrigerate for 3 to 4 days, or freeze.

ALL-VEGETABLE SOUP STOCK

▲▲▲

Here is a full-bodied vegetable stock. In *The Greens Cookbook,* Deborah Madison and Edward Espe Brown offer a number of other delicious and unusual vegetable stocks.

YIELD
1 quart

1 tablespoon corn or olive oil
1 tablespoon unsalted butter
4 celery stalks, cut into ½-inch pieces
1 medium-size yellow squash, rinsed and cut into
     ½-inch pieces
1 medium-size leek, white parts only, thoroughly
     rinsed and cut into ½-inch pieces
1 medium-size yellow onion, cut into ½-inch pieces
6 medium-size mushrooms, wiped clean with damp paper toweling and
     halved
6 cups cold water
1 onion, peeled, halved, and studded with 2 cloves
4 medium-size carrots, peeled and cut into ½-inch pieces
Bouquet Garni: 8 sprigs Italian flat-leaf parsley, rinsed and patted dry; 2
     sprigs each of fresh bay leaves, fresh marjoram, fresh thyme; 6 slightly
     bruised white or black peppercorns; and 2 leaf tops of celery, all
     wrapped in a cheesecloth bag and tied

1. In a medium-size saucepan over low heat, heat the oil and butter. Add the celery, squash, leek, onion pieces, and mushrooms and cook until translucent, about 3 to 4 minutes.

2. In a large 8-quart soup kettle over medium-high heat, bring the water to a boil. Add the cooked vegetables, onion halves, carrots, and bouquet garni. Return to a boil, then lower the heat and simmer 30 to 45 minutes or until the broth attains a full-bodied flavor.

3. Cool the stock (see Cooling Soups, page 176).

4. Using a soup ladle or a 4-cup measuring utensil, ladle the stock into a strainer lined with a double thickness of cheesecloth held over a large bowl or other storage container. Discard the vegetables and bouquet garni. Cover and refrigerate the stock for 3 to 4 days. Or freeze for up to 6 months.

SUMMER/WINTER CHUTNEY

▲▲▲

This delicious chutney was first made for me with a ripe, luscious mango by my friend Hans one late summer day. When I visited him in Wilmington, Delaware, later in the fall, he asked me to bring a mango so he could make it again. Alas, no mango anywhere, so instead he bought a big crookneck squash and made a "winter" chutney that sported the same rich orange color and blended beautifully with the other flavors of the chutney.

1 cup firmly packed light brown sugar
1½ cups vinegar
1 tablespoon salt
3 large cloves garlic, peeled and finely chopped
1 large mango, peeled, flesh removed from the pit and
    cut into ¾-inch cubes or ½-inch slices or 2 cups
    peeled cubed crookneck squash (cut into 1-inch cubes)
1 tablespoon Dijon-style mustard or 1 teaspoon mustard seeds
1 tablespoon chopped peeled fresh gingerroot
1 cup golden raisins
2 teaspoons curry powder
½ teaspoon ground coriander
1 teaspoon finely chopped, rinsed, seeded canned green chile
8 drops Tabasco sauce or ⅛ teaspoon cayenne pepper

> **YIELD**
> 3 8-ounce glass
> jars

1. In a medium-size saucepan over medium heat, dissolve the sugar in 1 cup of the vinegar. Add the salt and the garlic.

2. Add the mango or squash and simmer in the vinegar solution until the edges soften, about 10 to 15 minutes.

3. Add the mustard, gingerroot, raisins, curry, coriander, green chile, and Tabasco. Simmer for 10 minutes, stirring often.

4. Add the remaining ½ cup vinegar and simmer until the mixture reaches the desired jam-like consistency.

5. Remove the saucepan from the stove and follow the Canning Instructions (page 135).

HORS D'OEUVRES/BUFFET

▼▼▼

Every country has its own hors d'oeuvres: the meezze of the Middle East, the zakushki of Russia, the entremets of France, the tapas of Spain. Whatever your choice, hors d'oeuvres are ideally suited for all kinds of entertaining, for a few friends to a crowd.

Many of these hot and cold hors d'oeuvres—Artichoke Soufflé Squares, Mini Dijon Burgers, Minted Lamb Balls with Pignoli, Cheddar Pennies—freeze well. Make up a big batch, freeze either in small packages, enough for one or two, or by the dozen when you're preparing for a big party. Others can be prepared a day or two in advance and kept in the refrigerator until serving time. This way you can stagger your kitchen time, saving the final effort for those hot hors d'oeuvres that can only be prepared at the last moment and served piping hot, straight from the oven. Don't attempt to serve more than one or two of these at a party you're doing by yourself, or you'll have your head in the oven half the time. But even for a big party you need only a couple of hot hors d'oeuvres.

The recipes for cold hors d'oeuvres—the one- or two-bite pickup kind served on leaf-lined platters—are few, but very special. The salmon mousse can be made way ahead, frozen, and defrosted, as can the cheese spread. That leaves only preparing the vegetables, whether for crudités or Oriental Vegetables, and assembling the antipasto. The important thing, always, is to enjoy your party, which means feeling fresh, not exhausted.

The point is that you can entertain as elaborately or as simply as you like, depending on how you combine the elements. Bringing lots of your friends together at a big party is a special pleasure. These recipes should help make it easy for you.

Hot Hors d'Oeuvres

▼▼▼

MINI DIJON BURGERS

▲▲▲

Everyone likes hamburgers. This cocktail-sized version is perfect for a party. Peppers, onions, and Dijon mustard are a super combination, good with large hamburgers as well. They can be frozen raw for three to five days and baked, unthawed, for eight to ten minutes.

1 pound ground top sirloin
2 tablespoons finely chopped sweet green pepper
2 tablespoons finely chopped scallion
1½ tablespoons Dijon-style mustard
¼ teaspoon salt
⅛ teaspoon freshly ground black pepper
8 slices firm white sandwich bread, crusts removed

| YIELD |
| 3 dozen |
| **OVEN** |
| 425°F |

    1. In a medium-size bowl, lightly blend together all the ingredients, except the bread, with a fork.

2. With a 1½-inch cookie cutter, cut out 36 rounds of bread (about 5 rounds per slice).

3. Using a standard measuring tablespoon, shape 36 balls of the meat mixture.

4. Place each hamburger on a round of bread and arrange the rounds 1 inch apart on a baking sheet sprayed with nonstick vegetable cooking spray or lined with parchment paper.

5. Bake the hamburgers in the preheated 425°F oven for 6 to 8 minutes or until slightly pink in the center. Transfer to a serving tray. Serve hot.

CHEDDAR PENNIES

▲▲▲

These rich Cheddar morsels are a crispy accompaniment with cocktails or soup. Like the ginger cookies (page 364), you can make the batter ahead, shape it into small logs, and freeze.

¼ pound (1 stick) unsalted butter, softened
¼ pound sharp Cheddar cheese, shredded on a hand grater, then very finely chopped
3 dashes Tabasco sauce
¼ teaspoon salt
1 teaspoon chopped fresh dill or rosemary or ½ teaspoon dried dillweed
1⅓ cups unbleached all-purpose flour

YIELD
2 to 3 dozen depending on size

OVEN
325°F

1. In a medium-size bowl with an electric beater or a hand mixer, combine the butter and Cheddar, Tabasco, and seasonings and blend until creamy.

2. On low speed, add the flour, a third at a time. The dough will be soft.

3. Gather together the dough, remove from the bowl, and place it on wax paper. If it is too soft to shape into logs, refrigerate it until firm. Shape into 2 logs about 1½ inches in diameter.

4. Refrigerate until firm, about 2 hours, or freeze the dough in plastic freezer bags for future use.

5. When ready to bake, remove the logs from the refrigerator and cut into ¼-inch- to ½-inch-thick slices.

6. On a cookie sheet sprayed with nonstick vegetable cooking spray or lined with parchment pa-

per, arrange the Cheddar pennies 2 inches apart.

7. Bake in the preheated 325°F oven for about 15 minutes or until slightly brown and almost crisp. The center can be a tiny bit soft. Cook a little longer if necessary. Remove the cookie sheet from the oven and immediately remove the Cheddar pennies to a serving tray and serve hot. Or cool on a rack and store in an airtight container. You may freeze at this point in the airtight container. To reheat, thaw on a cookie sheet and heat in a 325°F oven for 1 to 2 minutes.

ARTICHOKE SOUFFLÉ SQUARES

▲▲▲

This is without a doubt one of the all-time favorite Party Box hors d'oeuvres. It goes with everything. Serve it hot or cold in a basket lined with collard greens or as part of an antipasto. Freeze it, or refrigerate, covered, for three days.

2 large cloves garlic, peeled
6 large scallions, trimmed and chopped into thirds
2 jars (6 ounces each) marinated artichoke hearts, thoroughly rinsed and drained
6 large eggs
½ teaspoon dried oregano, crushed, or ½ teaspoon freshly grated nutmeg
¼ teaspoon freshly ground black pepper
Dash Tabasco sauce
2 cups (about 8 ounces) shredded Cheddar cheese

YIELD
64 1-inch squares
OVEN
350°F

1. Spray an 8x8-inch baking pan with nonstick vegetable cooking spray, or line it with parchment paper and spray the parchment.

2. In a food processor fitted with a metal blade, add the garlic and whirl until chopped. Add the scallions and whirl until finely chopped. Add the artichoke hearts and whirl briefly to coarsely chop.

3. In a medium-size bowl, with an electric beater or a hand mixer, beat the eggs for 3 minutes.

4. Add the beaten eggs to the artichoke mixture along with the seasonings and pulse on and off just to blend. Add the cheese and pulse on and off until smooth but tex-

tured. The mixture will be thick.

5. Spread the mixture evenly in the prepared pan.

6. Bake in the preheated 350°F oven for 20 to 25 minutes or until a tester inserted into the center comes out clean. Transfer to a rack and cool slightly.

7. With paper toweling, pat the surface to remove excess "fat" from the cheese.

8. Turn the soufflé out onto a cutting board and cut into squares for serving. Or cool the soufflé squares on a tray and freeze in plastic freezer bags. Thaw soufflé squares on a baking tray before reheating to avoid overcooking.

SPINACH AND FETA STUFFED MUSHROOMS

▲▲▲

The spinach, feta, and mushrooms create an elegant deep green, white, and beige color combination. The filling also works beautifully when combined with Yogurt Cheese (page 122) and served in hollowed-out breads as part of a buffet selection.

2 tablespoons olive oil
¼ cup chopped shallots
1 scallion, trimmed and finely chopped
1 package (10 ounces) frozen chopped spinach, thawed and squeezed dry
⅓ cup parsley sprigs
¼ cup snipped fresh dill
¼ pound feta cheese, crumbled
1 egg yolk, lightly stirred with a fork
30 mushroom caps, 1½ to 2 inches in diameter, stems removed and caps wiped clean with damp paper toweling

YIELD
2 ½ dozen mushrooms or 1¾ cup filling
OVEN
400°F

1. In a medium-size skillet over medium heat, heat the oil. Add the shallots and scallion and sauté until softened, about 4 minutes. Add the spinach and cook until all the moisture has evaporated.

2. Transfer the spinach mixture to a food processor fitted with

a metal blade. Add the parsley, dill, feta, and egg yolk, and whirl. The mixture should remain textured.

3. Fill each mushroom cap with about 2 level teaspoons of spinach filling, mounding it neatly. Arrange the filled mushrooms in a shallow baking pan sprayed with nonstick vegetable cooking spray or lined with parchment paper.

4. Bake in the preheated 400°F oven for 5 to 7 minutes. The mushrooms must remain crunchy. Let cool slightly, for 2 minutes, and serve hot on a serving tray or an earthenware platter.

MINTED LAMB BALLS WITH PIGNOLI

▲▲▲

Most caterers are always on the lookout for one of those one- or two-bite morsels that can be eaten with ease. These minted lamb balls are small enough to pop in the mouth without causing an awkward mouthful.

1 pound freshly ground lean lamb
¼ cup whole-wheat bread crumbs
¼ cup pignoli (pine nuts), finely chopped
1 large egg
2 tablespoons chopped fresh mint
½ teaspoon coarse (kosher) salt
½ teaspoon freshly ground pepper

YIELD
40 1-inch balls
OVEN
375°F

1. In a medium-size bowl, combine the lamb, bread crumbs, pignoli, and egg. Add the mint, salt, and pepper and mix.

2. Spray a baking tray with nonstick vegetable cooking spray or line it with parchment paper.

3. Pinch off walnut-size pieces of the lamb mixture and roll into round balls. Arrange 1 inch apart on the baking sheet.

4. Bake in the preheated 375°F oven for 4 minutes. (Do not overcook. You want them just slightly pink inside.)

5. Remove the lamb balls from the oven and let cool slightly. Pat them with paper toweling to remove excess fat.

6. Transfer the balls to a platter and serve with small wooden picks for an hors d'oeuvre or, if they are to be a part of a buffet, arrange on a platter with some fresh mint garnish. Or freeze and reheat at 250°F until warmed through.

PERSIAN CHICKEN BALLS

▲▲▲

I developed this recipe for a class I was teaching that featured all-vegetable dishes except for a small selection of hors d'oeuvres made with meat. These colorful Chicken Balls are one of those hors d'oeuvres. To serve as a dinner entrée, shape into balls two to three inches in diameter.

4 ounces dried peaches
4 ounces dried apricots
2 ounces golden raisins
½ cup sherry
1 cup cubed poached chicken breast (page 322)
1 teaspoon unsweetened coconut flakes
1 tablespoon peanut oil or cold-press sesame oil
2 teaspoons curry powder
1 teaspoon ground cumin
1 teaspoon ground allspice

YIELD
40 1-inch balls
OVEN
325°F

1. In a medium-size bowl, soak the dried fruit in sherry for 30 minutes. Drain and cut into ½-inch slices.

2. In a food processor fitted with a metal blade, in 2 batches, whirl the chicken and fruit mixture until the consistency of oatmeal.

3. Transfer the mixture to a medium-size bowl and combine with the coconut flakes.

4. In a medium-size skillet over medium heat, heat the peanut or sesame oil and spices for about 1 minute. Add to the chicken and fruit mixture and blend well.

5. Spray a baking sheet with nonstick vegetable cooking spray or line with parchment paper.

6. Pinch off large walnut-size pieces of the chicken mixture, roll into round balls and arrange 1 inch apart on the baking sheet.

7. Bake the chicken balls in the preheated 325°F oven until just heated through, about 5 to 7 minutes.

8. Transfer the balls to a platter and serve at room temperature.

Cold Hors d'Oeuvres

▼▼▼

SKEWERED SCALLOPS WITH ZUCCHINI AND SUMMER SQUASH

▲▲▲

Shrimp and scallops are always a favorite at parties. One way to make them go further is to thread them on skewers with vegetables, then pass them on an attractive platter rather than placing them out on a buffet where one or two people can devour them all.

—

1 pound sea scallops (about 30 to 32), rinsed
½ cup dry white wine (optional)
2 cups water or as needed
¼ cup freshly squeezed lemon juice
¼ cup freshly squeezed lime juice
2 tablespoons corn oil
2 tablespoons snipped fresh dill or chives or 1 teaspoon dried
1 small dried red pepper
Salt and freshly ground black pepper, to taste

YIELD
6 to 8 servings
PREP
Marinate scallops 2 hours; zucchini, squash, 1 hour

¼ pound zucchini and ¼ pound yellow squash, or ½ pound zucchini scrubbed, cut lengthwise into quarters, then crosswise into ½-inch-thick slices

1. In a medium-size saucepan over low heat, poach the scallops in gently simmering wine and water to cover until they turn opaque, about 3 to 5 minutes. Drain.

2. In a stainless steel bowl, whisk together the lemon and lime juices, oil, dill, dried red pepper, and salt and pepper to taste. Pour half the marinade into another bowl, add the scallops and let marinate 2 hours. Put the zucchini in the other bowl and let marinate 1 hour.

3. Drain the scallops and squash thoroughly and pat dry on paper toweling. Then thread on skewers, alternating them. Arrange the skewers on a platter.

For Marinated Shrimp and Snow Pea Kabobs

Substitute 1 pound shrimp (about 30 to 32), peeled and deveined, for the scallops and ¼ pound snow peas, trimmed, stringed, and cut into thirds for the zucchini. Do not marinate the snow peas. Thread on skewers, alternating them.

CHERRY TOMATOES WITH SALMON CREAM

▲▲▲

Cherry tomatoes filled with this wonderful salmon cream-cheese mixture are an elegant hors d'oeuvre. Serve them in baskets lined with lemon leaves or lovely green-and-white-ribbed collard greens.

1 pint cherry tomatoes (about 20), rinsed and stemmed
¼ pound smoked salmon or lox
4 ounces cream cheese
2 teaspoons snipped fresh dill

YIELD
10 servings

1. Cut a very thin slice off the *bottom* of each tomato (this will make it sit flat rather than wobble). Slice off tops of tomatoes, and with

the end of a teaspoon, remove the seeds and membrane. Place the tomatoes open side down on paper toweling to drain.

2. In a food processor fitted with a metal blade, place the salmon, cream cheese, and dill. Pulse on and off until smooth; do not overpurée.

3. Fill a pastry bag fitted with a decorative tip with the salmon mixture and fill the tomato shells. Or with a ½ teaspoon measure, spoon the mixture into the tomatoes.

4. Chill, covered, until ready to serve.

SHRIMP SEVICHE WITH KOHLRABI AND BOSC PEARS

▲▲▲

I first used this recipe for a luncheon of vegetable chili and chicken, cheese, and vegetable enchiladas I prepared at my cousin Laurie Davis' house outside of Santa Fe. One of the guests was Denise Kusel, the style editor for the *Santa Fe Reporter,* and it was through her I began writing a bi-monthly food column for the *Reporter.* Serve this seviche as part of a buffet or as a delicious first course. You may substitute Jerusalem artichokes, jícama, or water chestnuts for the kohlrabi.

———

¼ cup freshly squeezed orange juice

2 tablespoons freshly squeezed lemon or lime juice

¼ cup corn oil

6 crushed white or green peppercorns

1 tablespoon finely chopped cilantro or Italian flat-
leaf parsley

1 pound poached large shrimp (page 257), sliced in half

2 Bosc pears, unpeeled, sliced into ½-inch slices, then cut in half

½ pound kohlrabi, peeled and sliced lengthwise into ¼-inch-thick slices, then cut in half

Garnish: cilantro or parsley sprigs

| YIELD |
| 6 servings |
| PREP |
| Marinate 2 hours |

1. In a medium-size stainless steel or glass bowl, combine the orange juice, lemon or lime juice, oil, peppercorns, and cilantro. Add the poached shrimp and stir to mix well. Cover and marinate at room temperature for 2 hours.

2. On 6 skewers, alternate the shrimps, kohlrabi, and pears. Serve on an attractive platter. Garnish with cilantro or parsley sprigs.

For a First Course:

Sprinkle paper-thin slices of unpeeled pear with lemon juice. Slice peeled kohlrabi into paper-thin slices. Arrange 2 pear slices, 2 kohlrabi slices, and 6 shrimp on individual plates. Garnish with cilantro or parsley sprigs.

GUACAMOLE WITH TOFU

▲▲▲

A friend, Rain Parrish, who knows both Mexican and vegetarian food, suggested this combination. Tofu adds protein to the dip and makes the guacamole an even brighter emerald green.

3 scallions, trimmed and coarsely chopped
2 ripe avocados, peeled, halved, pitted, and coarsely chopped
1 small tomato, peeled and diced
1 can (4 ounces) mild green chiles, drained and seeded
2 ounces tofu, cubed
1 tablespoon freshly squeezed lime juice
½ teaspoon ground cumin
Dash cayenne pepper
Salt and freshly ground black pepper, to taste

YIELD
6 servings

1. In a food processor fitted with a metal blade, chop the scallions.

2. Add the avocados, tomato, chiles, tofu, lime juice, and seasonings. With quick on and off pulses, whirl the mixture just until blended but not puréed; it is important to retain some texture.

3. Spoon into a serving bowl, correct seasonings and serve with tortilla chips for dipping.

Hors d'Oeuvres for a Light Buffet or Late Supper

▼▼▼

MARINATED OLIVES

▲▲▲

Most commercial olives either have no taste or are bitter. Drain them thoroughly and try making your own marinade. Once you do, you'll want to have these olives on hand all the time. The marinade lasts a couple of weeks. You may treat Spanish pimiento-stuffed green olives the same way.

¼ cup corn oil
¼ cup chopped parsley, dill, or cilantro
1 tablespoon dried chervil
2 large cloves garlic, peeled and very finely chopped
1½ cups large pitted black olives (about 6 ounces),
    drained and thoroughly rinsed

YIELD
1 ½ cups

PREP
Marinate 2 to 6
hours

1. In a medium-size bowl, combine the oil, herbs, and garlic. Mix thoroughly.

2. Add the olives and mix.

3. Marinate, covered, 2 hours at room temperature or 6 hours in the refrigerator.

4. Transfer to a 1-quart container. Refrigerate, covered, until serving time.

BABA GANOUCH

▲▲▲

Baba ganouch is a Middle Eastern way of balancing vegetables, seeds, and nuts that's both nutritious and delicious. It's good with either walnuts or sesame paste. Include it in your repertoire of dips or serve in halved pitas as a part of an antipasto.

———

2 eggplants (about 1 pound each), washed, stemmed, and patted dry
3 tablespoons freshly squeezed lemon juice
1 tablespoon finely chopped scallion
1 clove garlic, peeled and finely chopped
1 tablespoon olive oil
1 tablespoon sesame paste (tahini) or 1 tablespoon walnuts, finely chopped
1 tablespoon finely chopped cilantro or parsley
Salt and freshly ground black pepper, to taste
Garnish: cilantro or parsley sprigs

YIELD
2 cups
OVEN
400°F

———

1. Place the eggplants in a shallow baking pan with ½ cup of water. Prick each two or three times with a fork.

2. Bake in the preheated 400°F oven for 40 to 60 minutes or until the eggplants are soft when pierced with a fork.

3. When the eggplants are cool enough to handle, peel and cut into chunks. Sprinkle with 2 tablespoons of the lemon juice.

4. In a food processor fitted with a metal blade, or by hand, chop the eggplant to a coarse pulp. Transfer it to a medium-size bowl. Stir in the scallion, garlic, oil, sesame paste, remaining lemon juice, chopped cilantro or parsley, and salt and pepper.

5. Refrigerate the spread, covered, until serving time, or serve it at once in a bowl with the cilantro or parsley sprigs as garnish.

MOUSSE OF SALMON

▲▲▲

Since salmon is very rich, I've eliminated the heavy cream in this mousse, and as a result have cut back on fat and calories without diminishing the flavor.

½ pound baked salmon (page 306)
2 large eggs, separated
3 dashes Tabasco sauce
¼ cup coarsely chopped yellow onion
½ cup Hellmann's Mayonnaise or Angie's Mayonnaise (page 121)
1 tablespoon snipped fresh dill
3 tablespoons freshly squeezed lemon juice
1 envelope unflavored gelatin
1½ tablespoons dry vermouth or sherry
½ cup Chicken Stock (page 138) or canned chicken broth
Salt and freshly ground pepper, to taste
Garnish: lemon leaves or lime slices

YIELD
12 servings

PREP
Refrigerate 1 hour

1. In a medium-size bowl, combine the salmon, egg yolks, Tabasco, onion, mayonnaise, dill, and lemon juice until well mixed.

2. In a small bowl, beat the egg whites until they form soft peaks.

3. In a bowl, soften the gelatin in the vermouth for 3 minutes.

4. In a small saucepan over medium heat, heat the stock. Add the gelatin and vermouth and cook, stirring, until the gelatin is dissolved, about 3 minutes.

5. Pour the chicken stock mixture into a blender and blend for 30 seconds. Add the salmon mixture,

salt and pepper and pulse on and off until the mixture is smooth and thick, but still with some texture.

6. Transfer the mousse to a bowl and quickly fold in the egg whites with a spatula.

7. Spray a 1-quart mold (a copper one in the shape of a fish is pretty) with nonstick vegetable cooking spray. Pour the mixture into the mold and refrigerate until firm, about 1 hour. You may freeze the mousse at this point wrapped tightly in plastic wrap. To serve, thaw overnight in the refrigerator.

8. Unmold on a leaf-lined platter and garnish with lime slices.

For Mousse of Sole
An excellent and very inexpensive "supper-by-the-bite" item: substitute for the salmon ¼ pound poached sole. Decrease the lemon juice to 2 tablespoons and add ½ cup heavy cream in step 5. Follow the rest of the recipe exactly.

CRUDITÉS WITH SAUCE NIÇOISE

Crudités are ideal for our time of life. In small amounts, served with fresh lime juice and seasonings, they can grace your daily table. For parties add seasonal vegetables such as asparagus in spring and yellow wax beans in fall and serve with Sauce Niçoise, the most requested dip of The Party Box.

YIELD
10 servings

1 bunch celery, separated into stalks, washed, stringed, and leaf tops removed
5 to 6 scallions, trimmed
5 to 6 carrots, rinsed, peeled, and cut lengthwise into ½-inch-wide strips
½ pound green beans, trimmed
1 medium-size zucchini, scrubbed and cut lengthwise into ½-inch-wide strips
1 bunch broccoli, stems removed and cut into flowerets
1 cauliflower, base removed and cut into flowerets
½ pint cherry tomatoes (about 10 to 12), rinsed and stemmed
10 whole mushrooms, wiped clean with damp paper toweling
1 recipe Party Box Sauce Niçoise (page 120)

Fill the bottom of a basket, about 6 to 7 inches in diameter and 4 to 5 inches deep, with heavy paper (I use brown shopping bags) so that at least half the basket is filled. Cover the paper with colorful cloth napkins. Place the tall vegetables first, in the back: the celery, scallions, carrots, green beans, and zucchini. Then arrange the broccoli, cauliflower, cherry tomatoes, and mushrooms. Pour the Sauce Niçoise into a pretty glass or white china bowl and serve with the crudités.

POTTED CHEDDAR WITH PORT AND WALNUTS

▲▲▲

Tawny port and walnuts give a distinctive flavor to this cheese-and-butter spread. A definite favorite of the English, it goes along on any picnic. It is especially handsome when served in a hollowed-out dark pumpernickel bread. Round or oval-shaped loaves of bread are available from most bakeries or the gourmet section of supermarkets. To make a container for the potted cheese, cut a circle 3 inches in diameter and 3 inches deep in the top of the loaf. Gently lift out the bread top and reserve, covered, until serving time. Fill with the cheese mixture at room temperature and garnish with chopped walnuts.

1 cup (2 sticks) unsalted butter, softened
½ pound Cheddar cheese, broken into chunks
2 tablespoons port wine
½ tablespoon Worcestershire sauce
1- to 2-pound loaf of round bread, hollowed out (optional)
¼ cup walnuts, coarsely chopped

YIELD
20 servings

1. In a food processor fitted with a metal blade, combine the butter and Cheddar cheese. Whirl until smooth. Add the port and Worcestershire sauce and blend again.

2. With a rubber spatula, remove the mixture from the processor, scraping it out thoroughly, to a sheet of wax paper and gently shape into a ball. Wrap in wax paper and refrigerate, 30 minutes to firm.

3. Spoon the mixture into the hollowed-out bread. Sprinkle with the walnuts.

4. Serve with assorted crackers, small slices of bread and a wooden spreader.

GRAVLAX

▲▲▲

My introduction to gravlax was when The Party Box catered the cocktail party celebrating *The Cooking of Scandinavia,* the first book in the Time Inc. Foods of the World series. In the late Sixties gravlax was relatively new to most Americans. Now it is one of the more popular ways to serve salmon. You'll find it offered as part of the Elegant Cocktail Buffet (page 98). Although 48 hours is the recommended time for curing, 24 to 36 hours will be sufficient. Serve on a cutting board surrounded with sliced lemons and limes, a good Pommery mustard and thinly sliced dark pumpernickel bread.

3 to 4 pounds fresh salmon, center cut, cleaned,
    boned, and split in half

¾ cup coarse (kosher) salt

⅓ cup sugar

2 tablespoons whole white peppercorns, crushed in a
    mortar and pestle

2 bunches fresh dill, rinsed and wiped with damp paper toweling

YIELD
10 to 12 servings
Prep
Marinate 24 to 36 hours

1. Place half of the salmon, skin side down, in a glass or pottery bowl large enough to hold both pieces on top of each other.

2. In a small bowl, mix the salt, sugar, and pepper.

3. Sprinkle a small amount of this mixture evenly over the fish in the bowl and press it in slightly. Add one-third of the dill, laying it lightly on the fish.

4. Repeat with the salt mixture and dill, until the mixture and dill are used up.

5. Place the other half of the salmon on top, skin side up. Cover the salmon with plastic wrap and place a plate weighted with heavy cans on it; refrigerate. Turn the fish every 12 hours. It will release liquid, which is part of the curing. Spoon the liquid over the salmon. When the curing is complete, remove the fish from the marinade and scrape off the dill and seasonings. Pat dry. Serve the gravlax on a cutting board and slice as necessary.

ITALIAN ANTIPASTO

▲▲▲

Antipasto is a year-round favorite. Most popular is melon wrapped with prosciutto. Also use pears or apples.

YIELD
8 to 10 servings

1 cantaloupe or honeydew melon, peeled, seeded, and
    cut into 1-inch cubes or 3 each green and purple
    figs, rinsed, and cut lengthwise into quarters
¼ pound thinly sliced prosciutto
2 jars (6¼ ounces each) marinated artichoke hearts,
    rinsed, drained, and quartered
1¼ pounds smoked fontina or smoked mozzarella, cut into 1-inch cubes
¼ pound small size (2-inch diameter) Genoa salami, thinly sliced
1 package (12 ounces) Italian bread sticks
1 recipe Marinated Olives (page 152)

1. Wrap the melon cubes with the thin slices of prosciutto and fasten with wooden skewers or picks.

2. Arrange all the ingredients in separate groupings on a large platter.

HUMMUS

▲▲▲

Hummus is perhaps the most popular of all Middle Eastern dips. This recipe comes from my Lebanese friend Elizabeth Matta. It is quick to make and freezes well.

YIELD
2 cups

1 can (19 ounces) chick-peas, liquid reserved
½ jar (4 ounces) sesame paste (tahini)
¼ cup freshly squeezed lemon juice
¼ cup freshly squeezed lime juice
3 large cloves garlic, peeled and finely chopped
Salt and freshly ground pepper, to taste
Garnish: finely chopped, Italian flat-leaf parsley, or pomegranate seeds

1. In a blender or food processor fitted with a metal blade, combine the chick-peas with half of their reserved liquid, the sesame paste, lemon and lime juices, and garlic. Whirl until a smooth purée, about 2 to 3 minutes; do not liquefy. Season with salt and pepper. You may freeze the hummus at this point in a tightly sealed container.

2. Serve the hummus in a bowl and garnish with Italian parsley or pomegranate seeds. Serve with vegetables and pita bread wedges.

MIDDLE EASTERN ANTIPASTO

▲▲▲

The Party Box served this antipasto at a party for Stevie Wonder at The New York Botanical Garden. The emphasis was on vegetarian food and this fit the bill perfectly.

1 can (6 ounces) pitted black olives, drained
1 bottle (7¾ ounces) pimiento-stuffed Spanish olives, drained
2 cans (15 ounces each) stuffed grape leaves (also called dolmas), drained
8 ounces feta cheese, cut into 1-inch cubes
8 small pita breads, halved
Hummus (opposite)
Baba Ganouch (page 153)
Garnish: thin lemon slices

YIELD
10 servings

PREP
Marinate 2 hours

1. Marinate the olives according to instructions on page 152 for 2 hours.

2. On a large platter, arrange the stuffed grape leaves, feta, and olives in sections, reserving space for the pita bread.

3. Fill each pita half with 1 tablespoon of the Hummus or Baba Ganouch and arrange them on the platter.

4. Garnish with the lemon slices and serve.

FRUIT FOR THE BUFFET

▲▲▲

Fresh whole strawberries and clusters of seedless grapes, served in baskets and huge terra-cotta flowerpots covered with colorful napkins, were a Party Box signature; they were both beautiful and practical—no bother with seeds, pits, and peels.

Fruits refresh the palate after intensely flavored cocktail fare. Or they can be served with finger pastries for pick-up-and-eat desserts, for Supper-by-the-Bite, or for a buffet dinner.

ORIENTAL VEGETABLES WITH SATÉ DIPPING SAUCE

▲▲▲

Oriental vegetables—daikon, Chinese cabbage, snow peas—are a welcome addition to our old favorites.

YIELD
12 servings

1 head Chinese celery cabbage (Napa cabbage), end trimmed and leaves separated; cut triangular pieces from the thickest portion of each leaf base, reserve remainder

2 large daikon radishes, peeled and cut into 1-inch-thick slices

4 sweet red peppers, rinsed, seeded, and cut lengthwise into 2-inch-wide strips, then halved

4 small to medium-size yellow squash, rinsed, trimmed, cut lengthwise into 2-inch-wide strips, then halved

4 small to medium-size zucchini, scrubbed, trimmed, cut into 2-inch-wide strips, then halved

½ pound snow peas, rinsed, trimmed, and stringed

1 recipe Saté Dipping Sauce (page 121)

---

1. Arrange the vegetables in their own separate bunches around the perimeter of a flat basket or platter.

2. In the center of the basket or platter, place a wooden or glass bowl or crock filled with the Saté Dipping Sauce.

SOUPS

▼▼▼

Here you'll find soup in many roles—the overture to a meal, a complete hearty lunch, the centerpiece of a friendly get-together, or even dessert. And soups can be one of the best time-savers when frozen in boilable plastic freezer bags for a quick pick-up meal.

A delicious fruit soup such as Arthur Cafiero's Hungarian Plum Soup makes an equally good first or dessert course. The Gazpacho brightens everyday summer meals as well as parties. Some of the quick vegetable soups are especially colorful, such as the dazzling Beet and Cucumber Soup and the Five-Minute Purely Pea Soup.

You'll also find a section of soups that can be served either hot or cold. These are all-vegetable soups that contain no cream, milk, butter, or eggs, but are as rich and creamy tasting as you could hope for; it's the special blend of vegetables that does the trick. And they're so satisfying, you can't believe how low they are in calories. Once you've tasted these rich vegetable soups, you may never want to return to the heavier cream soups.

The full-bodied hot and hearty soups make wonderful meals in themselves. They include the great classic regional soups—Beef-and-Vegetable Stew, Classic New England Fish Chowder, and Texas-Style Shrimp-Chicken Gumbo. They're perfect for a simple come-on-over-for supper—just add a salad, crusty bread, and a light dessert.

I can't think of a more pleasant way to welcome friends for dinner than with a generous tureen of steaming soup.

Cold Soups

▼▼▼

BEET AND CUCUMBER SOUP

▲▲▲

This is a light first course or "pick-me-up" soup. It's quick to make, brilliant in color, and subtle in flavor.

2 medium-size beets, peeled and shredded with a hand grater (about 1 cup)

2 medium-size cucumbers, peeled, seeded, shredded with a hand grater, and squeezed to remove the liquid (about 1 cup)

2 cups plain yogurt

¼ teaspoon sugar

1 tablespoon freshly squeezed lime juice

2 tablespoons chopped fresh dill

YIELD
3 cups

1. Combine the beets, cucumber, 1 cup of the yogurt, sugar, lime juice, dill, and the remaining 1 cup of yogurt in a blender. (The last cup of yogurt is added on top to ensure proper blending of the ingredients.)

2. Pulse on and off until puréed but still with small pieces of beets and cucumber visible, about 15 seconds for a chewy soup, 30 seconds for a smooth one.

3. Pour the soup from the blender into a bowl. Chill in the refrigerator for about ½ hour before serving.

For Beet and Carrot Soup

Replace the cucumbers with 3 large peeled and shredded carrots. Add 2 tablespoons tangerine or orange juice concentrate. Follow the remainder of the recipe exactly.

FIVE-MINUTE PURELY PEA SOUP

▲▲▲

A soup in five minutes is a boon and frozen peas make it possible. The thawed peas are heated for only two or three minutes to keep their vibrant green color. Fresh mint gives the soup bright flavor.

YIELD
2 ½ cups

1 package (10 ounces) frozen peas, thawed
3 scallions, trimmed and coarsely chopped
2 Boston or romaine lettuce leaves, rinsed and patted dry
3 sprigs of fresh mint or 1 teaspoon dried
1 teaspoon dried basil
1¼ cups water
Garnish: fresh mint or lime slice

1. In a small casserole or saucepan, combine the thawed peas, scallions, lettuce leaves, mint, basil, and ¼ cup of the water. Heat over low heat until the peas are slightly cooked, about 3 minutes. Do not overcook as the peas will lose their bright green color. Cool slightly.

2. Pour the soup into a blender along with the remaining cup of water. Whirl until a very smooth purée, about 2 minutes.

3. Transfer to a medium-size glass bowl. Refrigerate, covered. Serve chilled, garnished with the mint or lime.

For Pea Soup with Watercress

In Step 1, add ½ bunch watercress, stemmed, rinsed, and patted dry, to the peas and cook for 3 minutes.

ARTHUR CAFIERO'S HUNGARIAN PLUM SOUP

▲▲▲

This soup graced many a feast at Concerts in the Park in New York. Arthur made these occasions wonderfully festive, spreading tablecloths on the grass and even including candelabras. He thought nothing of preparing three- or four-course dinners that might include salmon coulibiac, fruited pork tenderloin, and cream cheese cake. His recipe for this soup was very rich and included wine, brandy, and sour cream. I've made this version lighter in calories, but it's just as beautiful and flavorful.

1 can (16 ounces) plums, drained, stoned, and
    coarsely chopped, with juice reserved
1 cup water
¼ cup freshly squeezed orange juice
1 tablespoon Grand Marnier
1 teaspoon orange water
1 teaspoon grated orange rind
1 teaspoon ground cinnamon
1 pinch salt
1 tablespoon arrowroot or kuzu (page 293)
½ cup water
½ cup plain yogurt
½ cup sour cream
Garnish: plain yogurt or sour cream

YIELD
4 cups

PREP
Refrigerate overnight

1. In a medium-size saucepan over medium heat, combine the plums and their liquid, 1 cup water, orange juice, Grand Marnier, orange water, orange rind, cinnamon, and salt and cook for about 5 minutes.

2. In a 1-cup measuring cup, combine the arrowroot or kuzu with the ½ cup water. Mix thoroughly and add to the soup, stirring briskly until the soup begins to thicken, about 5 minutes.

3. Remove from the heat and cool.

4. Pour the cooled soup into a blender or food processor fitted with a metal blade in two batches

and pulse on and off. You want the soup thick and flecked with bits of plum.

5. Remove the soup from the container and place in a large bowl. Whisk in the ½ cup each yogurt and sour cream. The soup will be frothy. Place the soup in the refrigerator overnight so it will thicken and become creamy.

6. Serve cold with a dollop of yogurt or sour cream.

GAZPACHO

▲▲▲

At The Party Box, we made literally hundreds of gallons of this gazpacho in the summer. Gazpacho aspic was my partner Jeff's idea, and it was stunning on a buffet, not only in the summer but for winter holidays, too. When served with an elegant filet, wild rice salad, and green beans, it adds both shimmer and lightness to a rich meal. It also makes a wonderful salad accompaniment when used as a filling for an avocado.

1 can (18 ounces) tomato juice (low-salt, if possible)
3 small yellow onions, peeled and quartered
2 large cucumbers, peeled, seeded, and cut into 1-inch chunks
2 medium-size sweet green peppers, seeded and cut into 1-inch chunks
2 large tomatoes, peeled and cut into 1-inch chunks or 1 can (16 ounces) whole peeled tomatoes, drained
¼ cup olive oil
2 tablespoons tomato paste
2 tablespoons tomato purée
2 tablespoons red wine vinegar
2 teaspoons coarse (kosher) salt
⅛ teaspoon Tabasco sauce
Freshly ground black pepper, to taste
1 canned green chile, seeded (optional)

YIELD
8 servings

PREP
Chill 1 hour

1. In a blender in 2 or 3 batches, blend the tomato juice and vegetables. Pulse the blender on and off for 2 or 3 seconds, until a chunky consistency rather than a real purée.

2. In a large bowl, whisk together the balance of the ingredients and add the mixture from the blender. Whisk until well blended.

3. Refrigerate, covered, 1 hour. Serve cold.

For Gazpacho Aspic

Prepare the gazpacho reserving ½ cup tomato juice. In a small saucepan, sprinkle 2 envelopes of gelatin or 2 tablespoons agar-agar (page 283) over the ½ cup tomato juice and let soften. Over low heat, stir to dissolve the gelatin, about 3 minutes. Remove the pan from the heat and cool slightly. When all the steps for the soup are completed, add the gelatin mixture, stirring to incorporate. Pour into a 2-quart mold sprayed with nonstick vegetable cooking spray. Refrigerate until firm, about 4 hours. To unmold, place a serving platter upside down on top of mold and carefully invert. Gently lift off mold.

CREAMY SOUPS WITH NO CREAM

White-Satin Bean Soup
Mellow Yellow Split-Pea Soup
  with Vegetables
Five-Minute Purely Pea Soup
Lemon-Zest Cauliflower Soup
Carrot Vichyssoise
Nene's Zucchini-Apple Soup
Corn-Potato-Mushroom Chowder
Classic New England Fish
  Chowder

These creamy soups are not thickened with a roux (flour and butter) or with eggs or cream—the very things we're encouraged to cut down on. In these recipes, I've used "nut milk," potatoes, rice or pasta, beans or peas, tofu, arrowroot, or kuzu. You can experiment not only with these thickeners, but with a number of others as well. In his excellent book *A Celebration of Soups,* Robert Ackart offers suggestions with their ratios to liquid. Here are some of them:

Barley: 1 teaspoon to 1 cup liquid
Cornstarch: 1 teaspoon to 1 cup liquid
Oatmeal (quick cooking): 1 teaspoon to 1 cup liquid
Tapioca: ½ teaspoon to 1 cup liquid
Rice: 1 teaspoon to 1 cup liquid
Potato: ½ cup to 4 cups liquid

Hot or Cold Soups

▼▼▼

NENE'S ZUCCHINI-APPLE SOUP

▲▲▲

My friend Nene makes this soup by the gallon and freezes it. It became one of our standbys for the Guggenheim Museum Café luncheons. The apples were an afterthought, but a happy one. Serve either hot or cold.

1 tablespoon unsalted butter
1 tablespoon corn oil
1 teaspoon curry powder
1 teaspoon ground cumin
¼ teaspoon ground allspice
1 cup coarsely chopped scallions, white parts only
　　(about 6 large scallions)
3 medium-size zucchini, scrubbed, trimmed, and cut into large cubes
4 cups Chicken Stock (page 138) or canned chicken broth
3 green apples, unpeeled, cored, and sliced lengthwise into ½-inch slices
Salt and freshly ground black pepper, to taste
Garnish: chopped fresh parsley or thin lime or orange slices

YIELD
4 cups

1. In a large casserole or kettle over medium heat, heat the butter and the oil. Add the spices and sauté for 2 minutes.

2. Add the scallions and sauté until translucent, about 2 minutes. Add the zucchini and sauté until lightly brown, about 3 minutes.

3. Add the stock and bring to a boil. Reduce the heat and simmer, covered, for 20 minutes or until the vegetables are soft. Add the apples and cook another 5 minutes. Let cool slightly.

4. Pour the soup into a blender in two batches, and whirl at low speed for 2 minutes per batch or until the soup is very smooth.

5. Season with salt and pepper. Transfer to a serving bowl and serve hot with garnish. Or cool and refrigerate, covered, until serving time. You may freeze the soup at this point. Garnish as desired.

LEMON-ZEST CAULIFLOWER SOUP

▲▲▲

This is a good, easy-to-digest soup to serve cold in the summer or warm in the winter. It freezes well. Nut milk, a smooth purée of nuts and water, thickens the soup and adds flavor.

YIELD
6 cups

2 tablespoons unsalted butter

1 medium-size leek, white part only, thoroughly rinsed, cut in half lengthwise, then crosswise into thin slices

1 medium-size yellow onion, peeled and coarsely chopped

½ teaspoon turmeric

¼ teaspoon ground allspice

3 white whole peppercorns

¼ cup unsalted cashews

1 cup water

3 cups All-Vegetable Soup Stock or Chicken Stock (pages 138–139)

1 small to medium-size cauliflower, rinsed, heart removed, and cut into large flowerets

1 teaspoon grated lemon zest

¼ cup freshly squeezed lemon juice

1. In a small saucepan over medium heat, melt the butter. Add the leek, onion, and turmeric and sauté for 3 minutes. Add the allspice and peppercorns. Remove from the heat and set aside.

2. In a blender, finely chop the cashews. Add the water and whirl until a smooth purée.

3. In a large saucepan, bring the stock to a boil. Add the cauliflower, sautéed vegetables, lemon zest and juice, and the nut milk.

4. Cook the soup until the cauliflower is very tender, about 10 to 15 minutes. Remove from the heat and cool slightly.

5. Transfer 1 cup of the soup to a blender and whirl until a fine purée. Stir the purée back into the soup.

6. Transfer the soup to a serving bowl and serve hot. Or cool and refrigerate, covered, and serve cold. You may freeze the soup at this point.

EMERALD BROCCOLI SOUP

▲▲▲

Here is "good-for-you" soup that also freezes well. Freeze it in individual portions in boilable plastic freezer bags. When you want a quick-to-fix soup, simply toss the bag into boiling water. Or defrost it and serve cold.

6 cups All-Vegetable Soup Stock or Chicken Stock
    (pages 138–139) or canned chicken broth
1½ pounds broccoli, trimmed, divided into flowerets,
    and stems cut into 1-inch pieces
3 tablespoons unsalted butter
2 cloves garlic, peeled and thinly sliced
1 tablespoon dried chervil or summer savory
½ large yellow onion, peeled and thinly sliced
3 scallions, trimmed and coarsely chopped
2 celery stalks, stringed and cut on the diagonal into ½-inch-thick slices
1 medium-size potato, peeled, cut in half, and then lengthwise into ½-inch-
    thick slices
2 tablespoons snipped fresh dill
Salt and freshly ground pepper, to taste
Garnish: fresh dill sprigs

YIELD
6 cups

1. In a large casserole or kettle over medium heat, heat the stock. Add the broccoli stems and reserve the flowerets. Reduce the heat and simmer about 20 minutes.

2. In a large skillet over medium heat, melt the butter. Add the garlic and chervil and sauté about 3 minutes. Add the onion, scallions, celery, and potato and cook, covered, about 7 minutes.

3. Transfer vegetables to the casserole and cook 10 minutes.

4. Add the broccoli flowerets and cook 2 minutes.

5. Remove the soup from the heat and cool slightly.

6. Pour the soup into a blender or food processor fitted with a metal blade in 2 batches. Add the dill. Whirl the soup until it is smooth, but still with some texture and flecks of broccoli.

7. Season with salt and pepper. Transfer the soup to a serving bowl and serve warm. Or cool and refrigerate, covered, and serve chilled. You may freeze the soup at this point. Garnish with fresh dill sprigs.

FIERY PUMPKIN SOUP

▲▲▲

This pumpkin soup is seasoned with fresh gingerroot, green chile, peppercorns, a dried red pepper, and Tabasco. The tofu or yogurt keeps the fat and calorie count low and makes the orange color of the soup even more brilliant. Substitute any firm squash, such as crookneck or banana, for the pumpkin and enjoy this soup throughout the fall and winter seasons. For a festive Halloween party, serve cold in a medium-size pumpkin shell.

7 cups Chicken Stock or All-Vegetable Soup Stock
    (pages 138–139)
2 pounds pumpkin or any firm squash, peeled and cut
    into 1-inch cubes
1 medium-size yellow onion, peeled and thinly sliced
1 leek, white part only, thoroughly rinsed and cut into
    1-inch pieces
2 teaspoons finely chopped peeled fresh gingerroot
1 canned mild green chile, thoroughly rinsed, seeded, and cut
    into small dice

YIELD
6 cups

1 dried red chile
4 crushed white or green peppercorns
1 to 2 dashes Tabasco sauce
3 or 4 cilantro or parsley stems, rinsed
4 ounces tofu, rinsed and cut into 1-inch cubes, or ½ cup plain yogurt
Salt, to taste
Garnish: slices of sweet red pepper and/or cilantro or Italian flat-leaf
    parsley sprigs

———

1. In a large casserole or kettle over medium heat, bring the stock to a boil and boil for 3 to 4 minutes.

2. Add the pumpkin or squash, onion, leek, gingerroot, green and red chiles, peppercorns, Tabasco, cilantro or parsley stems, and return to a boil. Reduce the heat, cover partially and simmer for 30 to 40 minutes or until the pumpkin or squash is soft. Remove from the heat and cool slightly. Remove the dried red chile. Add the tofu or yogurt.

3. Pour the soup into a blender in 2 batches and whirl the mixture at low speed, about 1 minute each or until the soup is very smooth. It will be a thick purée.

4. Season with salt to taste. Transfer to a serving bowl and serve hot. Or cool and refrigerate, covered, and serve cold. Garnish with sweet red pepper slices and/or cilantro or parsley sprigs.

IMPROMPTU SOUPS

These soups take from five to fifteen minutes to prepare. Perfect for quick pick-up meals or to make and serve to unexpected guests, they're also ideal for the kitchen "novice."

<u>Cold</u>

Beet and Cucumber Soup

Five-Minute Purely Pea Soup

Gazpacho

<u>Hot</u>

Miso Soup with Vegetables

CARROT VICHYSSOISE

▲▲▲

This soup can be served either hot or cold. It tastes even better if made one or two days in advance so the flavors can develop.

YIELD
6 cups

2 tablespoons unsalted butter
½ cup coarsely chopped scallions (about 4 scallions),
    white part only
⅛ teaspoon ground allspice
⅛ teaspoon ground cinnamon
¼ teaspoon freshly ground white pepper
1 tablespoon finely chopped peeled fresh gingerroot
5 cups Chicken Stock or All-Vegetable Soup Stock (pages 138–139) or
    canned chicken broth
1 pound carrots (about 5), peeled and cut into 1-inch-thick slices
2 small new potatoes, peeled and quartered
1 leek, white part only, thoroughly rinsed and cut into 1-inch pieces, or 1
    small yellow onion, peeled and quartered
Salt, to taste
Garnish: 2 strips of sweet red pepper, chopped Italian flat-leaf parsley, or
    thin orange slices

1. In a small skillet over medium heat, melt the butter. Add the scallions, spices, and chopped gingerroot and sauté about 3 minutes. Remove from heat.

2. In a large casserole or kettle over medium heat, bring the stock to a boil.

3. Add the carrots, potatoes, leek or onion, and the sautéed spices to the stock and return to a boil. Reduce heat, cover, and simmer for 20 to 25 minutes or until the carrots are soft. Remove from the heat and cool slightly.

4. Pour the soup into a blender in 2 batches, and whirl the mixture at low speed for 2 minutes per batch or until the soup is very smooth.

5. Season with the salt. Transfer to a serving bowl and serve hot with the garnish. Or cool and refrigerate, covered, and serve cold. You may freeze the soup at this point.

Hot Soups

▼▼▼

CORN-POTATO MUSHROOM CHOWDER

▲▲▲

This is a hearty soup that doesn't call for cream or milk. It's a good thermos soup for trips or picnics, and with the addition of more vegetables—red and green peppers, zucchini, and summer squash—it becomes a robust soup-stew.

YIELD
6 cups

4 tablespoons unsalted butter

2 large yellow onions, chopped

3 cups water

3 large potatoes, peeled and cut into 1-inch cubes

Kernels scraped from 3 ears of corn, or 1 package (10 ounces) frozen corn kernels, thawed

3 cups Chicken Stock or All-Vegetable Soup Stock (pages 138–139)

½ pound mushrooms, trimmed, cleaned with damp paper toweling, and cut lengthwise into ½-inch-thick pieces

¼ cup finely chopped fresh parsley or dill

Salt and freshly ground pepper, to taste

1. In a large casserole or kettle over medium heat, melt 2 tablespoons of the butter. Add the onions and sauté until translucent, about 5 minutes.

2. Add the water and potatoes and bring to a boil. Reduce the heat, cover, and simmer until the potatoes are just tender, about 10 minutes.

3. Stir in the corn and stock and remove the pan from the heat.

4. In a medium-size skillet over high heat, melt the remaining butter. Add the mushrooms and sauté quickly, stirring constantly, until brown, about 4 minutes. Add to the soup, along with the parsley or dill, and heat through.

5. Season to taste. Transfer the soup to a serving bowl and serve hot. Or cool and refrigerate, covered. You may freeze the soup at this point. Reheat to serve.

MELLOW YELLOW SPLIT-PEA SOUP WITH VEGETABLES

▲▲▲

Here's a great vegetable combination featuring split peas. It can be a whole meal, or part of a meal.

1 tablespoon unsalted butter
1 tablespoon corn oil
2 teaspoons curry powder
1 teaspoon turmeric
1 teaspoon ground allspice
1 teaspoon ground cumin
2 celery stalks, stringed and coarsely chopped
2 carrots, peeled and coarsely chopped
1 large yellow onion, coarsely chopped
1 cup yellow split peas, picked over, thoroughly rinsed, and presoaked overnight
6 cups water
Salt and freshly ground pepper, to taste

YIELD
4 cups

PREP
Presoak split peas overnight

1. In a medium-size saucepan over medium heat, heat the butter and oil. Add the spices and sauté

for 30 seconds.

2. Add the celery, carrots, and onion and cook until lightly brown,

about 5 minutes.

3. In a large casserole or kettle over medium heat, combine the split peas and water and bring to a boil. Skim off the scum or froth. Add the seasonings and vegetables from the saucepan. Reduce the heat to a simmer and cook about 40 minutes or until the peas can be mashed with a spoon. Skim occa-sionally as needed.

4. Pour 1 cup of the soup into a blender or food processor fitted with a metal blade. Whirl until pu-réed and return to the soup.

5. Season to taste and transfer to a serving bowl and serve hot. Or cool and refrigerate, covered. You may freeze the soup at this point. Reheat to serve.

WHITE-SATIN BEAN SOUP

▲▲▲

Smooth and creamy without cream. Navy beans have always been popular in soups. This is a special favorite of mine.

1½ cups dried small white beans, picked over,
    thoroughly rinsed, and presoaked overnight

10 cups water

1 teaspoon corn oil

1 bay leaf

1 tablespoon unsalted butter

1 medium-size yellow onion, coarsely chopped

1 teaspoon dried thyme

Salt and freshly ground white pepper, to taste

> **YIELD**
> 6 cups
> **PREP**
> Presoak beans
> overnight

1. In a large kettle, combine the beans and water and bring to a boil. Add the oil and bay leaf. Skim off any scum or froth.

2. In a small saucepan over medium heat, melt the butter. Add the chopped onion and sauté until translucent, about 3 to 4 minutes. Add the thyme. Then add to the bean mixture.

3. Bring the soup to a simmer. Cook for 45 minutes until the beans are soft but unbroken. The soup will reduce by one-half.

4. Remove 1 cup of the beans and place in a blender or food pro-cessor fitted with a metal blade. Whirl until puréed and return to the soup.

5. Season to taste. Transfer to a serving bowl and serve hot. Or cool and refrigerate, covered. You may freeze the soup at this point. Reheat to serve.

MISO SOUP WITH VEGETABLES

▲▲▲

Miso, a paste made from fermented soybeans, is a major component in traditional Japanese cooking. It is a rich source of protein, has a hearty deep flavor, and lasts indefinitely in your refrigerator. Serve this soup at home as a first course or a quick pick-me-up. I love it for breakfast on cold mornings.

1 tablespoon corn oil
1 carrot, peeled and shredded with a hand grater
1 small zucchini, scrubbed and shredded with a hand grater
¼ bunch watercress, rinsed, patted dry, and stems removed
1 sweet red or green pepper, rinsed, seeded, and cut
　　lengthwise into ¼-inch-thick slices
4 cups water
1 tablespoon miso
4 ounces tofu, cut into ¼-inch cubes

YIELD
5 cups

1. In a medium-size saucepan or casserole over medium heat, heat the oil. Add the carrot, zucchini, watercress, and green pepper and toss for 1 minute.

2. Stir in the water and cook for 5 minutes. Turn off the heat.

3. Remove 1 cup of the broth from the soup and combine with the miso in a small bowl, stirring to dissolve. Stir the miso back into the soup. Do not reheat.

4. To serve, add the tofu. Serve in individual bowls with the vegetables divided equally among them.

COOLING SOUPS

Whether you're puréeing a soup or making one to store in the refrigerator for future use, you first need to cool it slightly. The best way to bring a soup to room temperature is to place the soup kettle or casserole in cold water up to one-fourth or one-third the height of the container. I use my kitchen sink, filled about one-third of the way up with cold water.

This cooling technique is especially important for a soup made with chicken stock: if it's refrigerated without first being allowed to cool, the stock will sour.

Entrée Soup-Stews

▼▼▼

CLASSIC NEW ENGLAND FISH CHOWDER

▲▲▲

Make this chowder ahead to give the flavors a chance to blend. Do not let it boil when reheating. This freezes beautifully.

2 pounds haddock filet
10 cups water
1 teaspoon dried leaf thyme
1 bay leaf
6 whole white peppercorns
2 tablespoons unsalted butter
3 medium-size yellow onions, peeled and sliced lengthwise into ½-inch-thick slices
5 medium-size potatoes, peeled and cut into 1-inch cubes

YIELD
6 to 8 cups

1. In a large kettle or casserole over medium heat, combine the fish, 6 cups of the water, the thyme, bay leaf, and peppercorns. Heat over medium heat until the water comes to a boil. Stop cooking. Remove the fish and reserve the stock in the kettle over very low heat.

2. In a medium-size saucepan over medium heat, melt the butter. Add the onions and sauté until translucent, about 10 minutes.

3. Add the potatoes to the saucepan with the remaining 4 cups of water. Simmer until the potatoes are tender yet firm, about 15 minutes.

4. Return the fish to the kettle.

Add the vegetables and enough reserved stock for the fish to float, about 6 cups. Turn off heat. The fish and potatoes should remain chunky and firm.

5. Transfer to a serving bowl and serve immediately. Or cool and refrigerate, covered. You may freeze the soup at this point. Gently reheat the soup to serve, without boiling.

BEEF-AND-VEGETABLE STEW

▲▲▲

Here is a simple stew to make for a "friendly occasions" dinner. Or make it ahead and freeze some of it in boilable plastic freezer bags for future dinners. You can purée one of the potatoes to thicken the stew. But if you plan to freeze the stew, omit the potatoes and use a turnip, butternut squash, or similar vegetables and kuzu (page 293).

In this recipe we use the fatless approach to browning the meat (page 115), which cuts back on calories and fat.

YIELD
4 servings

2 teaspoons freshly ground black pepper

1 pound beef stewing meat, rinsed, patted dry, fat trimmed, and cut into 1-inch cubes

¼ cup red wine or dry vermouth

4 cups canned beef broth

2 tablespoons unsalted butter

1 tablespoon dried marjoram or summer savory

1 bay leaf

1 dried red pepper

½ pound carrots, peeled and cut on the diagonal into ½-inch-thick slices

4 celery stalks, stringed, cut in half lengthwise, then crosswise into ½-inch-thick slices

1 small white turnip, peeled, cut into thirds, and thirds cut in half

2 small potatoes, peeled, cut into thirds, and thirds cut in half

½ small butternut squash, peeled, seeded, and cut into 1-inch cubes

½ large yellow onion, peeled and cut lengthwise into ½-inch-thick slices
1 large zucchini, scrubbed, trimmed, halved lengthwise, and cut into
    ½-inch-thick slices
1 tablespoon kuzu dissolved in ½ cup water (optional)

1. Heat a large casserole or kettle over high heat for 2 minutes until the pot is extremely hot.

2. Rub pepper into the meat and add it to the casserole. Stir with a wooden spoon so the meat is seared and turns brown, about 5 minutes. Remove meat. Add the wine to deglaze casserole.

3. Return the meat to the casserole. Add the broth and reduce the heat to medium. Cover the pot and let it simmer briskly, about 20 minutes.

4. In a large skillet or saucepan, melt the butter and add seasonings. Sauté 1 minute. Add the carrots, celery, turnip, potatoes, and butternut squash and cook, covered, over low heat until the vegetables start to become crisp-tender, about 15 minutes.

5. Add the onion and zucchini and cook, covered, an additional 5 minutes.

6. Transfer the vegetables to the casserole with the meat. Cook another 10 minutes. At this point you can thicken the stew by removing pieces of potato equal to 1 potato and placing them in a blender along with 1 cup of the broth. Whirl until thick, about 2 minutes. Return to the stew. Or add kuzu and ½ cup water, if using.

7. Let the mixture cook 5 minutes longer until it reaches the right consistency. The meat should be tender and the vegetables crisp-tender.

8. Transfer to a serving bowl and remove the red pepper. Serve hot. Or cool and refrigerate, covered. You may freeze the soup at this point. Reheat to serve.

"SOUP'S ON"

These welcoming words herald the beginning of a meal or the entrée itself. When soup is the main course, how it is served makes a difference in its presentation.

Soup Tureens. My favorite is still the old-fashioned, white pottery tureen. If you have one stored away, bring it out to use. Or look for one at a local thrift store or artisan's shop.

Casseroles. When soup is the main course, an old Dutch oven or a sleek, colorful enamel casserole can grace your table.

Glass and Pottery Bowls. Cold soups look beautiful in clear glass bowls of every size and shape. Pottery serving bowls make a dramatic presentation.

DICK DORN'S TEXAS-STYLE SHRIMP-CHICKEN GUMBO

▲▲▲

In this version, my nephew-in-law cuts back on the large amount of butter called for in most gumbo recipes. If you can't find the filé powder in your supermarket or specialty gourmet shop, see Mail-Order Shopping (page 375) for where to send for it. Filé is made from sassafras, and no upstanding gumbo would be without it. I add the shrimp and chicken just at serving time so they remain tender.

YIELD
6 cups

2 tablespoons corn oil
1 cup coarsely chopped celery
1 medium-size onion, coarsely chopped
2 tablespoons unsalted butter
3 tablespoons unbleached all-purpose flour
1 can (16 ounces) stewed tomatoes, undrained
4 cups Chicken Stock (page 138) or canned chicken broth
1 bay leaf
1 teaspoon freshly ground white pepper
Dash Tabasco sauce
1 teaspoon filé powder
1½ cups thinly sliced fresh okra or 1½ cups frozen sliced okra, thawed
1 pound chicken breast, poached and cubed (page 322)
1 pound large shrimp, poached (page 257)
Coarse (kosher) salt, to taste
Cooked rice (optional)

1. In a large skillet over medium heat, heat the oil. Add the celery and onion and sauté about 7 minutes or until softened. Remove to a small bowl and reserve.
2. Melt the butter in the skillet. Stir in the flour to make a roux, stirring briskly to incorporate. Cook for 1 minute, stirring.
3. Add the tomatoes with their liquid and cook 5 minutes.
4. In a large casserole or kettle over medium heat, heat the stock until it boils. Add the celery and onion mixture, seasonings, filé, and okra and cook about 10 minutes.

5. Add the roux and tomatoes and heat until the soup thickens and reduces by one quarter, about 10 minutes. Remove from heat.

6. Add the poached chicken and shrimp and let them heat through about 2 minutes. Season with salt to taste. Transfer the soup to a serving bowl and serve hot. Add rice to each serving, if desired.

RUBY-RED CRANBERRY BORSCHT

▲▲▲

You don't have to wait until Thanksgiving to make this rich, claret-colored cranberry borscht. Cranberries are in season throughout the fall and into the winter. This soup recipe is quick and easy to prepare, gorgeous to look at, and makes a hearty meal in itself. It's a perfect meal for a late fall day.

8 cups water
2 bags (12 ounces each) cranberries, picked over, rinsed, drained, and stems removed
4 tablespoons unsalted butter
3 medium-size red onions, sliced lengthwise into ½-inch-thick slices
3 cups red cabbage (about ½ medium-size head), cored and finely sliced by hand or shredded in a food processor fitted with a shredder disk
1 can (16 ounces) small whole beets, undrained
6 tablespoons orange juice concentrate
2 tablespoons red wine vinegar
Salt and freshly ground pepper, to taste
Garnish: dollop sour cream or plain yogurt, or 1 orange, thinly sliced

YIELD
8 cups

1. In a large casserole or kettle over medium heat, bring the water to a boil. Add the cranberries and cook until they pop and turn shiny.

2. In a large skillet over medium heat, melt 2 tablespoons of the butter. Add the onions and sauté until translucent, about 5 to 7 minutes. Add to the cranberries.

3. Heat the remaining butter in the skillet. Add the cabbage and sauté until limp. Add to the cranberry mixture.

4. Stir in the beets with their juice, orange juice concentrate, and vinegar.

5. Cook until thick and the cabbage and onions are incorporated into the soup, about 15 minutes.

6. Season with salt and pepper. Transfer the soup to a tureen. Serve hot and garnish with sour cream, yogurt, or orange slices. Or cool and refrigerate, covered. Reheat to serve and garnish.

ENTRÉE AND SIDE VEGETABLES

▼▼▼

Something very serendipitous is happening. Just as we're all being encouraged to eat more vegetables, the vegetables themselves are becoming more delicious, abundant, and varied. Not long ago supermarket vegetables were a meager lot: onions, beets, potatoes, carrots, and iceberg lettuce, with another four or five seasonally appearing only in the summer. Now we have vegetables of every imaginable kind, from every corner of the world, and in a whole range of colors: creamy white eggplants, as well as the usual purple; lemon cucumbers; purple string beans, and yellow tomatoes and sweet peppers. And the formerly exotic or strictly regional has become familiar everywhere: chayote, jícama, fennel, mâche, radicchio.

Inventive chefs now use the same imagination in the preparation of their vegetable dishes that was once reserved only for meat, fish, or chicken dishes. There are literally hundreds of wonderfully satisfying vegetable entrées, including the vegetable entrée casseroles from the great ethnic cuisines of Mexico, India, South America, and Morocco that have always made the most of vegetables.

Occasionally I hear the complaint, "Fresh vegetables are too much trouble. It takes too long to cut them up." Not true! Even the most complicated vegetable dishes in this book take no more than fifteen or twenty minutes.

And for me, cutting up vegetables is not a chore, but a real sensual pleasure: I love snapping green beans, slicing carrots or turnips, watching the shape of a red pepper as I cut it lengthwise, following its curve. Perhaps more than anything, I love shelling peas. These simple tasks are serenely satisfying—they help one reach down to the deep rhythms of life.

Entrée Vegetables

▼▼▼

CARROT AND PIGNOLI LOAF

▲▲▲

Serve this vibrantly colorful loaf hot as an entrée with the Gazpacho Aspic (page 166), or cold for lunch or a snack. Pignoli (pine nuts) add protein and crunch. The loaf also freezes well.

1 egg plus 1 egg white
2 medium-size carrots, trimmed and coarsely shredded
¼ teaspoon ground allspice
⅓ cup milk
1 tablespoon corn oil
1 small scallion, trimmed and finely diced
½ sweet red pepper, seeded and finely diced
6 tablespoons fresh whole-wheat bread crumbs
½ cup pignoli, finely chopped
Salt and freshly ground white pepper, to taste

YIELD
4 to 6 servings
OVEN
350°F

1. In a medium-size bowl, beat the eggs and egg white lightly. Add the carrots, allspice, milk, and corn oil and mix thoroughly.

2. Add the scallion, red pepper, bread crumbs, pignoli, and salt and pepper and mix until well blended.

3. Spray a 9x5x3-inch loaf pan with nonstick vegetable cooking spray and line with parchment paper. Add the loaf mixture. Shake the pan so the batter is evenly spread and bang on the counter to remove air bubbles.

4. Bake in the preheated 350°F oven for about 1 hour. The loaf should be firm to the touch. Turn the loaf out onto a cooling rack. Let cool about 20 minutes and remove the parchment paper. Serve at room temperature or refrigerate, covered, and serve chilled. It slices best when cold.

KALE WITH LINGUIÇA AND CHICK-PEAS

▲▲▲

This is a Portuguese dish that my brother-in-law liked to serve for Sunday brunch. I've served it often as part of a lavish buffet. The meat is a minor ingredient, but its flavor permeates the dish. This also makes a delicious entrée when served with Scallop Seviche (page 250) or any marinated fish as a first course, along with steamed new potatoes and crookneck squash.

½ pound linguiça or chorizo, cut into 1-inch-thick slices, and then halved

6 cups kale (1 large bunch), thoroughly rinsed, trimmed, and cut crosswise into 1-inch-wide pieces

2 cloves garlic, peeled and finely sliced

1 can (16 ounces) chick-peas, thoroughly rinsed and drained

Salt and freshly ground pepper, to taste

YIELD
6 servings

1. In a small skillet, sauté the linguiça or chorizo until it renders its fat and turns a bright color. Drain and reserve the sausage.

2. In a large kettle, place the kale, with water clinging to it, in layers. Scatter the garlic throughout the layered kale.

3. Over medium heat, and tightly covered, steam kale about 4 to 5 minutes or just until tender, but still vibrant green.

4. Add the linguiça or chorizo and drained chick-peas. Cover and heat until the sausage and chick-peas are heated through, about 2 to 3 minutes. Season with salt and pepper.

5. Transfer to a serving dish and serve immediately.

BRAZILIAN VEGETABLE FEIJOADA

▲▲▲

This version of feijoada looks beautiful served in a large earthenware bowl or casserole. You may serve the beans with the feijoada spooned over them, or have them in a separate dish. Garnishes may also be served separately. Brown or white rice or couscous make good accompaniments.

YIELD
4 to 6 servings

3 tablespoons corn oil
3 tablespoons unsalted butter
2 whole dried red peppers (remove before serving) or
　¼ teaspoon crushed red pepper flakes
1 teaspoon ground cumin
2 teaspoons dried leaf thyme
2 medium-size sweet potatoes, peeled, cut lengthwise into quarters, and
　then into ¼-inch-thick slices
1 large leek or 2 medium-size leeks, white parts only, thoroughly rinsed and
　cut into ½-inch-thick slices
1 sweet red pepper, seeded and cut lengthwise into ½-inch-wide slices
1 sweet green pepper, seeded and cut lengthwise into ½-inch-wide slices
1 medium-size yellow onion, peeled and cut lengthwise into ½-inch-thick
　slices
1 zucchini, trimmed, halved lengthwise, and then cut crosswise into
　½-inch-thick slices
2 tablespoons dark rum
2 tablespoons freshly squeezed lime juice
1 large tomato, cut lengthwise into ¼-inch-thick slices
2 cans (16 ounces each) black beans, drained and thoroughly rinsed
¼ cup vermouth
Garnish: thin lime or orange slices and cilantro sprigs

1. In a large kettle over medium heat, heat the oil and butter. Add the dried red peppers, cumin, and thyme, lower the heat, and cook for 1 minute. Add the sweet potatoes and cook for 5 minutes.

2. Add the leek and cook another 5 minutes. Stir in the peppers and onion and cook for 5 minutes. Add the zucchini, rum, and lime juice. Combine well, and cook 5 minutes more. Add the tomato.

3. In a saucepan over low heat, heat the beans in the vermouth, stirring occasionally, until hot.

4. Place the beans in a casserole or serving bowl and add the vegetables. Garnish with the lime or orange slices and cilantro sprigs and serve at once.

STIR-FRY VEGETABLES WITH APPLES

▲▲▲

This is one of the first vegetable combinations I came up with when I started experimenting with wok cooking. Serve on rice, or use as a stuffing for sweet red and green peppers.

YIELD
4 servings

1½ tablespoons cold-press sesame oil

1½ tablespoons peanut oil

1 sweet red pepper, seeded and cut lengthwise into ¼-inch-wide strips

1 sweet green pepper, seeded and cut lengthwise into ¼-inch-wide strips

1 zucchini, trimmed, cut lengthwise into thirds, and then crosswise into ½-inch-thick slices

1 yellow squash, trimmed, cut lengthwise into thirds, and then crosswise into ¼-inch-thick slices

1 Golden Delicious apple, cored, unpeeled, and cut lengthwise into ¼-inch-thick slices

1. In a wok or skillet over medium heat, heat the oils. Add the peppers and sauté until crisp-tender, about 3 to 5 minutes.

2. Add the zucchini and yellow squash and sauté until lightly brown, about 3 minutes.

3. Add the sliced apple and cook until crisp-tender, about 2 minutes.

4. Remove the wok from the heat and serve immediately.

SPAGHETTI SQUASH WITH PASTA SAUCE

▲▲▲

This large yellow squash takes on the form and texture of spaghetti when cooked. It's both "pasta" and a vegetable, and you can serve it as either one. If it's available in your markets, try it—it makes a very versatile, inexpensive main dish or side vegetable.

—

1 small spaghetti squash (about 2 pounds), cut in half
   and seeds removed
2 tablespoons Clarified Butter (page 131) (optional)
2 tablespoons freshly grated Romano or Parmesan
   cheese

YIELD
2 servings

OVEN
375°F

1. On a cookie sheet lined with parchment paper or aluminum foil, place the squash halves, cut-sides up.

2. Bake in the preheated 375°F oven until a fork easily pierces the flesh, about 40 minutes.

3. With a fork, gently pull out the strands of squash. They will resemble spaghetti.

4. Place the squash in a medium-size bowl or casserole.

5. If using the clarified butter, melt in a small saucepan over medium heat. Pour over the squash.

6. Add the grated cheese, or use Garden Tomato Sauce (page 241), Quick Roasted Red Pepper Sauce (page 246), or Pesto Sauce Without Cheese (page 248).

RATATOUILLE

▲▲▲

A batch of ratatouille can easily be cooked up once or twice a month, year round. This simple vegetable combination—a classic of Provençale cuisine—goes with meats, fish, chicken, or by itself, hot, warm, or cold. It is delicious, too, as a hearty sauce for pasta or rice. Nor is it time-consuming to prepare; everything goes into one dish and bakes in the oven for no more than forty-five minutes. As in all the vegetable recipes in this book, the vegetables retain their shape, texture, and firmness. For most of the year the tomatoes available in your local supermarket do not yield enough juice for the vegetables to cook in. Therefore, I prefer to use mostly canned tomatoes, with a fresh tomato or two added for the flavor. If you're lucky enough to have access to fresh ripe, juicy tomatoes, by all means use them.

1 small eggplant, trimmed, unpeeled, and cut into 1-inch cubes

2 medium-size yellow onions, peeled and cut lengthwise into eighths

2 large leeks, white parts only, thoroughly rinsed, halved lengthwise, and sliced crosswise into ½-inch slices

1 summer squash, trimmed, cut lengthwise into thirds, and then into ½-inch cubes

1 zucchini, trimmed, cut lengthwise into thirds, and then into ½-inch cubes

1 sweet green pepper, seeded and cut into ¼-inch-thick rings

1 sweet red pepper, seeded and cut into ¼-inch-thick rings

1 can (16 ounces) whole tomatoes, with half the juice reserved

1 fresh tomato, chopped

4 tablespoons olive oil or corn oil

4 cloves garlic, finely chopped

3 tablespoons chopped fresh basil or 1 tablespoon dried basil

1½ tablespoons dried oregano

½ teaspoon dried leaf thyme

½ teaspoon fennel seeds

Salt and freshly ground pepper, to taste

YIELD
6 servings

OVEN
350°F

1. In a large baking dish or casserole, combine the vegetables and pour over the oil and seasonings. Mix thoroughly until all vegetables are well coated.

2. Cover and bake in the preheated 350°F oven for 35 to 45 minutes until tender, but the vegetables should retain their shape. Stir often. The vegetables will release a lot of liquid.

3. Remove from the oven, cool slightly, and serve. Or refrigerate, covered, and serve cold, or at room temperature.

For a Middle-Eastern flavor, add 1 tablespoon of plain yogurt to each serving of cold ratatouille.

ACORN SQUASH WITH FRUIT

▲▲▲

This bottle-green squash makes a wonderful container to fill with fruit, rice, or vegetables. I like to bake it in the oven, along with some sweet and white potatoes, to make the most efficient use of time, energy, and oven space. If you use the fruit filling, it is sweet enough to serve as a dessert. And if you add the fruit in the last ten minutes of cooking, it will retain its crispness, making a nice contrast with the softness of the squash. It can be reheated, but if you do, add more juice and keep it covered, otherwise it will dry out. This is an entrée if you use a whole squash, a side dish if you use half.

---

1 medium-size acorn squash, cut in half and seeds removed
1 teaspoon ground cinnamon
¼ teaspoon ground allspice or nutmeg
¼ teaspoon honey
Juice of ½ lemon
1 apple or pear, unpeeled, cored, and chopped
Garnish: coarsely chopped roasted almonds or finely chopped parsley

YIELD
1 to 2 servings
OVEN
400°F

---

1. On a cookie sheet lined with aluminum foil or in a baking pan, place the squash halves, cut side up. Prick the halves all over with a fork.
2. In a small bowl, mix together the seasonings, honey, and lemon juice. Pour half the liquid into each squash half.
3. Bake the squash in the preheated 400°F oven for 30 minutes. Lower the heat to 350°F and bake another 20 to 30 minutes.
4. About 10 minutes before the squash is done, remove from the oven. Add the chopped apple or pear to each squash half. Return the squash to the oven and bake for the final 10 minutes.
5. Garnish with almonds or parsley. Serve immediately, or at room temperature.

For Acorn Squash with Pilaf

Cook the squash, covered, in the preheated 400°F oven for 30 minutes. Remove from the oven and add any cooked grain pilaf. Return to the oven and bake 10 to 20 minutes or until heated through and the squash is tender.

GALA VEGETABLES

▲▲▲

We've been conditioned to eating our vegetables one at a time—carrots, peas, or broccoli alone, in splendid isolation. But in combination, vegetables offer a range of flavor and a stunning riot of color. This particular combination of vegetables is gorgeous. The Party Box served it at many festive sit-down dinners at New York City's museums, the New York State Opera at Lincoln Center, and the New York Public Library. It was, in fact, our most popular vegetable dish, and its beauty was a big part of its success.

1 carrot, trimmed, peeled, and cut into ½-inch
   matchstick strips 2 inches long
1 yellow squash, trimmed and cut into ½-inch
   matchstick strips 2 inches long
1 zucchini, trimmed and cut into ½-inch matchstick
   strips 2 inches long
1 sweet red pepper, seeded and cut into ½-inch matchstick
   strips 2 inches long
1 sweet green pepper, seeded and cut into ½-inch matchstick
   strips 2 inches long
1 tablespoon unsalted butter
1 tablespoon chopped fresh dill

YIELD
4 servings

OVEN
350°F

1. In a small saucepan over medium heat, blanch the carrots in boiling water 3 to 5 minutes.
2. Place all the vegetables in a medium-size baking dish or aluminum-foil tin and toss. Dot with the butter and sprinkle with the dill. Cover with foil.
3. Bake in the preheated 350°F oven until crisp yet tender, about 15 minutes.
4. Serve hot.

For Chilled Gala Vegetables
To serve cold, blanch the carrots. Combine with the other vegetables and chill (omit steps 3 and 4). Serve with ¼ cup Citrus Vinaigrette (page 127) or Basil Vinaigrette (page 128).

MEXICAN FIESTA VEGETABLES

▲▲▲

A fiesta, indeed, of flavor and color. Serve this in Mexican earthenware or other colorful pottery bowls.

1 tablespoon unsalted butter

2 tablespoons corn oil

1 teaspoon ground cumin

1 teaspoon dried oregano

½ teaspoon crushed red pepper flakes or 1 whole dried red pepper (remove before serving) (optional)

¼ teaspoon fennel seeds, crushed with mortar and pestle

2 medium-size white potatoes, halved, cut into 1-inch-thick half circles, and then halved again

¼ pound green or wax beans, trimmed and cut into thirds

1 small sweet potato, halved, cut into 1-inch-thick half circles, and then halved again

2 medium-size yellow onions, peeled and sliced lengthwise into ½-inch-thick slices

2 sweet red or green peppers, seeded, cut lengthwise into ½-inch-wide strips, and halved

1 zucchini, cut lengthwise into thirds, and then crosswise into ¼-inch-thick slices

1 yellow squash, cut lengthwise into thirds, and then crosswise into ¼-inch-thick slices

1 cup All-Vegetable Soup Stock (page 139)

1 ear of corn, cut into 1-inch circles

2 tablespoons freshly squeezed lime juice

Garnish: ½ bunch cilantro or Italian flat-leaf parsley, finely chopped

YIELD
4 to 6 servings

1. In a heavy kettle over medium-low heat, heat the butter and oil until hot. Add the cumin, oregano, red pepper flakes, if using, and fennel and cook for 1 minute, stirring so they do not burn.

2. Add the white potatoes, beans, and sweet potato and cook, covered, for about 10 minutes.

3. Uncover and stir gently. Add the onions and peppers and cook, covered, for 5 minutes.

4. Add the zucchini and yellow squash and cook, covered, another 5 minutes.

5. Add the stock, corn, and

lime juice and cook 5 minutes.
6. Ladle the vegetables into a

serving bowl. Garnish with the cilantro or parsley, and serve.

SKILLET SLAW WITH PEAS, PEPPERS, AND GOLDEN RAISINS

▲▲▲

This dish is quickly made and can be doubled for a crowd. Serve hot or at room temperature.

YIELD
6 to 8 servings

3 tablespoons corn oil or safflower oil
3 cups shredded green cabbage (about ½ medium-size head)
3 sweet green or red peppers, seeded, sliced lengthwise into ½-inch-wide slices, and then in half
1 package (10 ounces) frozen peas, thawed
1 cup golden raisins

1. In a large skillet over medium heat, heat the oil. Add the cabbage and sauté until it becomes translucent, about 5 minutes. Don't overcook.

2. Add the peppers. Cook and stir until tender, about 2 to 3 minutes.

3. Add the peas and raisins and cook another 3 minutes. Serve immediately, or refrigerate, covered. Serve at room temperature.

For Green Noodles with Skillet Slaw

Cook 16 ounces spinach fettuccine until *al dente* and drain in a colander. Place equal amounts of fettuccine on 4 plates. Divide one-half recipe Skillet Slaw among the four plates of pasta and toss lightly. Serve warm.

Side Vegetables

▼▼▼

STIR-FRY ASPARAGUS WITH GINGER AND SOY

▲▲▲

Pencil-thin stir-fry asparagus were part of the picnic sponsored by *Sports Illustrated* for the People's Republic of China table tennis team. When asparagus is in season, the Chinese use it in every kind of dish imaginable—beef, lamb, pork, chicken, and fish. I particularly like asparagus cooked this way—just barely. When it's not in season, make the same recipe using broccoli.

---

1 tablespoon peanut oil
2 teaspoons Oriental sesame oil
1 tablespoon finely chopped peeled fresh gingerroot
1 pound pencil-thin asparagus spears, trimmed and
    cut into 2-inch lengths
1 tablespoon good-quality soy sauce or tamari

YIELD
4 servings

1. In a large heavy skillet over medium heat, heat the oils. Add the gingerroot and sauté about 1 minute.

2. Add the asparagus and stir quickly, just until crisp-tender, about 2 minutes.

3. Stir in the soy sauce.

4. Transfer to a serving platter and serve immediately, or refrigerate, covered.

For Stir-Fry Broccoli with Garlic, Ginger, and Soy

Substitute 1 medium-size broccoli, flowerets cut from stems (reserve stems for salads) for the asparagus. Follow the directions for asparagus except add 1 teaspoon thinly sliced garlic and sauté with gingerroot.

SCANDINAVIAN PICKLED BEETS

▲▲▲

Beets have usually received a mixed press. The ones we remember from childhood were probably overcooked and oversauced; later we may have learned to love them in borscht. But beets will stand very nicely on their own when simply boiled or baked, peeled, and served hot with a dab of butter or freshly ground black pepper. They're delicious when nothing masks their vibrant color and flavor, and they're good for us. A popular way of serving them is pickled.

1 large bunch beets (4 to 5 beets), stems and leaves removed (reserve beet tops for other use)
½ cup white wine or rice vinegar
1 small yellow onion, diced
½ teaspoon white peppercorns
½ teaspoon whole allspice or ¼ teaspoon ground allspice
⅓ stick cinnamon or ¼ teaspoon ground cinnamon
Sugar, to taste

YIELD
4 servings

1. In a large saucepan over medium heat, cook the beets in boiling water to cover. Partially cover the pan and keep at a rolling boil, but check frequently as beets have a tendency to burn. Add more boiling water if necessary. Cook until tender, about 1 hour.

2. Drain the beets, reserving ½ cup of the liquid. Cool. Peel the beets and cut them into very thin slices.

3. In a medium-size bowl, combine the beet slices with the reserved liquid, vinegar, onion, seasonings and sugar. Stir thoroughly.

4. Refrigerate, covered, until ready to serve.

ESTHER'S ROASTED RED PEPPERS

▲▲▲

This recipe came from my friend Susan Dresner's mother, and Susan says it's as good for you as Jewish chicken soup. It's as robust and full-bodied as meat, and has lots of vitamins A and C, and no fat whatsoever. The marinade, which is simply equal parts of vinegar and water, makes it possible to keep the peppers in your refrigerator almost indefinitely. When red peppers are at their cheapest and most abundant, do what I do: buy a quantity of them, prepare them in one big batch, and store them in jars in your refrigerator.

You may serve them with the garlic alone, or you can add a few drops of fine olive oil and garnish them with chopped fresh parsley. They're wonderful as an antipasto, an appetizer, a side dish, a garnish, or even as a sandwich. They also make a thoughtful gift.

8 sweet red peppers, left whole
12 large cloves garlic, thinly sliced
Water
Cider vinegar

YIELD
1 ½ quarts
BROILER
Preheat
PREP
Marinate overnight

1. Preheat the broiler. Cover a flat cookie sheet with aluminum foil. Place the peppers on the tray. You may want to broil them in 2 batches. Slide the tray under the broiler and broil the peppers, turning constantly, until the skins are extremely wrinkled and beginning to turn black. This should take about 15 minutes.

2. Put the peppers into brown paper bags and close the tops securely. Let stand in the bags for 10 minutes.

3. Dampen your hands with cold water. Remove the peppers from the bags. Slip the skins off. Core and seed the peppers. Cut them lengthwise into ½-inch-wide slices.

4. In a half-gallon jar, alternate layers of the pepper with layers of garlic, ending with a layer of pepper. Cover with equal parts of water and vinegar. Cap the jar and marinate in the refrigerator overnight. Serve chilled or at room temperature.

NOTE: The best way to get the true smokey flavor is to roast the peppers on top of a gas stove. Turn the burner to the highest heat and set the pepper right over the flame. As each side blackens, turn the pepper until all sides are charred. Remove the pepper with wooden tongs so as not to pierce it. Run the peppers under cold water, scraping off the charred skin with a serrated knife. Slit the peppers lengthwise on one side and remove the seeds and stem. Proceed with step 4 above.

FENNEL SAUTÉED IN TARRAGON BUTTER

▲▲▲

Fennel, or finocchio, is now available in many supermarkets as well as in Italian greengrocers. It makes a wonderful hors d'oeuvre, which I like to serve together with peas in their jackets and Yogurt Cheese (page 122) with sesame seeds.

2 tablespoons Compound Butter made with tarragon (page 132) or unsalted butter
2 large fennel bulbs, trimmed and cut into ½-inch pieces
Garnish: 2 tablespoons coarsely chopped fresh tarragon, or 2 teaspoons dried

YIELD
4 servings

1. In a medium-size saucepan over medium heat, melt the butter.

2. Add the fennel and reduce the heat to low. Sauté about 5 minutes, stirring occasionally, until the fennel becomes slightly translucent.

3. Remove from the heat and transfer to a serving dish.

4. Garnish with tarragon and serve immediately.

CEIL'S TURNIP SOUFFLÉ

▲▲▲

Every time I serve this dish, people who haven't had it before will say, "Well, I don't like turnips, but I'll try it." Their next remark is usually, "May I have the recipe?"

1 medium-size yellow turnip or 2 white turnips, peeled
   and chopped
1 egg yolk, well beaten
2 tablespoons unsalted butter
3 egg whites
2 tablespoons light or dark brown sugar (optional)

YIELD
2 servings

OVEN
400°F

1. In a large saucepan over medium heat, cook the turnips in enough boiling salted water to cover until tender. Drain.

2. In a medium-size casserole or soufflé dish, mash the turnips. Stir in the egg yolk and butter until blended.

3. In a medium-size bowl, beat the egg whites with an electric mixer on high speed until they form stiff peaks. Slowly and carefully fold the egg whites into the turnip-egg mixture. At this point, the dish can be refrigerated for 20 to 30 minutes before baking.

4. If you wish a crusty surface, sprinkle brown sugar over the turnip mixture.

5. Bake in the preheated 400°F oven for 15 to 20 minutes or until puffed up slightly and lightly browned.

6. Serve immediately.

BRUSSELS SPROUTS WITH VERMONT CHEDDAR CHEESE

▲▲▲

We all remember only too well those over-boiled Brussels sprouts of our childhood. We've learned since to steam them gently so that they retain their bright green color and their delicate flavor. Around Thanksgiving, Brussels sprouts can be bought on their cone and used in an autumn cornucopia.

½ cup water

1 tablespoon corn oil margarine

1 pint fresh Brussels sprouts, cleaned, bottoms
    removed, and halved

⅓ cup shredded Vermont white Cheddar cheese,
    shredded with a hand grater

YIELD
4 servings
OVEN
350°F

1. In a medium-size saucepan over low-medium heat, bring the water and margarine to a boil. Add the Brussels sprouts and steam for about 8 minutes, covering the saucepan after 2 minutes.

2. Continue cooking until the water is absorbed and the sprouts are a bright green color.

3. Transfer the sprouts to a 1-quart baking dish. Sprinkle the cheese over the sprouts.

4. Bake in the preheated 350°F oven until the cheese has melted, about 7 minutes.

5. Serve hot.

For Brussels Sprouts with Vinaigrette

In a medium-size bowl, combine the cooked Brussels sprouts with ¼ cup Vinaigrette (page 125). Refrigerate, covered, 1 hour and serve chilled.

CURRIED CUCUMBERS

▲▲▲

It seldom occurs to us to serve cucumbers hot, but cooked this way they make an interesting side vegetable or a condiment to serve with curries. The cucumbers become translucent and will keep in the refrigerator for about three days.

1 tablespoon unsalted butter

1 teaspoon ground cumin

1 teaspoon curry powder

1 large cucumber, trimmed, ribbed with a peeler, and
    sliced into ¼-inch-thick slices

YIELD
2 servings

1. In a medium-size skillet over medium heat, melt the butter.

Add the seasonings and the cucumber and cook, stirring, for 2 minutes. The cucumber will yield its liquid but the mixture will appear dry.

2. Cover and let the mixture cook over low heat for 5 minutes.

3. Remove from the heat and serve hot, or refrigerate and serve cold as a condiment.

ZUCCHINI ITALIENNE

▲▲▲

Zucchini is available year round, although it can be expensive off season. It has an all-purpose flavor you can serve with almost anything. Garlic and oil enhance it in this quickly prepared side dish.

——

1 tablespoon plus 1 teaspoon safflower or olive oil
4 cloves garlic, finely chopped
1 large or 2 medium-size zucchini, scrubbed, trimmed,
    and sliced into ½-inch-thick rounds

YIELD
2 servings

1. In a large skillet over medium heat, heat the oil. Add the garlic and sauté for 1 or 2 minutes.

2. Add the zucchini carefully in a single layer.

3. Over medium heat, sauté the zucchini until it turns a golden brown, about 3 minutes per side.

4. Transfer to a platter and serve warm.

GREEK LEMON POTATOES

▲▲▲

Lots of olive oil and lemon, oregano, and pepper are the basis of much fine Greek cooking. They're delicious combined with potatoes that are baked in the oven until crisp-tender. Serve with Roast Leg of Lamb El Greco (page 338), or a seasonal green salad.

3 tablespoons plus 1 teaspoon olive oil
2 large red potatoes, peeled and cut into eighths
1 large clove garlic, finely chopped
1 tablespoon dried oregano
3 tablespoons freshly squeezed lemon juice
Freshly ground pepper, to taste

YIELD
4 to 6 servings

OVEN
375°F

1. In a baking dish brushed with 1 teaspoon olive oil, place the potatoes. Add the remaining ingredients and toss lightly.

2. Bake the potatoes in the preheated 375°F oven until the potatoes are tender yet firm, about 1 hour.

3. Serve hot. Or cool and refrigerate, covered.

ELISE CAVANNA'S CUCUMBER POTATOES WITH FRESH DILL

▲▲▲

This delightful recipe comes from *Gourmet Cooking for a Low-Fat Diet* by Elise Cavanna, published in 1961, which makes it perhaps one of the first gourmet approaches to low-fat cooking.

3 medium-size new or red potatoes, scrubbed
½ bunch fresh dill, plus 2 tablespoons finely chopped
1 small cucumber, peeled, halved lengthwise, seeded, and cut into ¼-inch cubes
¼ teaspoon coarse (kosher) salt
¼ teaspoon freshly ground black pepper

YIELD
2 servings

1. In a medium-size saucepan over medium heat, place the potatoes with ½ bunch fresh dill and enough water to cover and cook about 15 to 20 minutes or until tender.

2. Drain the potatoes and cool slightly. Cut into ½-inch cubes. Discard the cooked dill.

3. In a small bowl, combine the potatoes and cucumber with the salt, pepper, and 2 tablespoons chopped dill.

4. Serve at room temperature.

PURÉE OF PARSNIPS AND CARROTS

▲▲▲

Our first chef at The Party Box, 21-year-old Leila Melman, gave us this recipe. Since parsnips do not seem to have generated a big fan club, we don't tell anyone what's in this dish, and no one is the wiser—unless they ask us, as many do, for the recipe. Serve as part of a meal, a quick pick-me-up, or a side dish. It tastes almost like ice cream when served cold. The brilliant orange has great eye appeal.

4 cups water
2 large parsnips, peeled and cut into 1-inch pieces
2 large carrots, peeled and cut into 1-inch pieces
1 teaspoon unsalted butter (optional)
¼ teaspoon ground nutmeg or cinnamon

YIELD
2 servings

1. In a large saucepan over high heat, bring the water to a boil. Add the parsnips and carrots. Reduce the heat and cook at a simmer until tender, about 20 to 25 minutes. Some water will be absorbed in the cooking. Do not drain.

2. Remove from the heat and cool slightly.

3. In a blender in 2 batches, saving some cooking water for the second batch, combine the parsnips, carrots, butter, nutmeg or cinnamon, and water. Whirl until smooth.

4. Pour into a medium-size bowl, cover, and refrigerate.

5. Serve chilled.

STEAMED CHAYOTE

▲▲▲

When combined with other vegetables, chayote contributes a distinct crisp texture and a lovely pale green color. The flavor is delicate, so don't overwhelm it with seasonings. An unusual and delightful combination is chayote with parsnips and carrots or sautéed with circles of red peppers and white eggplant.

1 chayote, peeled, cored, cut lengthwise into ¼-inch-
thick strips, and then cut into thirds

YIELD
2 servings

1. In a medium-size saucepan with ½ inch water, place a metal steamer containing the chayote.

2. Cover the saucepan and bring the water to a boil. Steam 12 to 14 minutes until crisp-tender.

3. Serve hot.

GRILLED CORN, PEPPERS, AND PINEAPPLE

▲▲▲

Grilled corn in the husk is great any time with any barbecue. Try it with the Luau on the Grill (page 93).

2 ears of corn, opened, silk removed, husks pulled
    back over ears, and soaked in water
2 sweet red peppers, seeded and cut lengthwise into
    ½-inch-wide slices
2 sweet green peppers, seeded and cut lengthwise into
    ½-inch-wide slices
3 tablespoons unsalted butter
Snipped fresh dill (optional)
1 pineapple, peeled, cored, and cut lengthwise into ½-inch-thick strips
Dark rum, as needed

YIELD
4 servings
GRILL
Prepare coals

1. Prepare the grill 1 hour in advance.

2. Grill the corn in the husks for 15 to 20 minutes, turning occasionally.

3. Place the peppers on a large piece of aluminum foil, dab with the butter, and sprinkle with dill, if desired. Seal the foil tightly, allowing for some air space inside.

4. Grill for 10 minutes, or until crisp-tender.

5. Place the pineapple strips on a large piece of aluminum foil. Brush with rum to taste. Wrap securely in the foil and grill for about 10 minutes or until they are heated through and slightly brown.

MARINATED CARROTS WITH RED PEPPERS

▲▲▲

Here is an easy way to enjoy vitamin-rich vegetables. Serve as an accompaniment with any meal or as a small side dish for a small "pick-me-up" meal.

Boiling water, to cover
½ pound carrots, peeled and cut into 1x2-inch finger slices
½ pound sweet red peppers, peeled, seeded, and cut into 1x2-inch finger slices
Juice of 1 medium-size orange
2 tablespoons olive oil

YIELD
4 servings
PREP
Marinate 1 hour

1. In a medium-size saucepan over medium heat, pour boiling water over the carrots and return to a boil. Reduce the heat and simmer about 4 to 5 minutes so the carrots remain very crisp. Do not overcook. You want the carrots to have a firm texture. Drain the carrots in a colander.

2. In a medium-size bowl, combine the carrots and peppers.

3. In a small bowl, whisk together the freshly squeezed orange juice and olive oil.

4. Pour the marinade over the carrots and peppers and marinate for 1 hour at room temperature. Serve at room temperature.

MUSHROOMS IN LEMON AND OIL

▲▲▲

Marinated mushrooms is another of those dishes to have on hand for a between-meals nosh, or to serve as a cold dish, as part of an antipasto, or as a condiment with meats. They take almost no time at all to prepare. When mushrooms are reasonably priced, make up a batch every week. It will keep two to three days in the refrigerator.

¼ pound mushrooms
2 tablespoons olive oil
2 tablespoons freshly squeezed lemon juice
2 teaspoons chopped Italian flat-leaf parsley

YIELD
1 ½ cups
PREP
Marinate
overnight

1. Wipe the mushrooms clean with damp paper toweling. If the mushrooms are small, leave them whole; if they are large, slice them lengthwise into thirds.
2. Combine all the ingredients in a refrigerator container with a cover. Shake it to make sure all the mushrooms are coated with the marinade and refrigerate, covered, overnight. Serve chilled or at room temperature.

BAKED EGGPLANT WITH NUTMEG AND GINGER

▲▲▲

Many eggplant recipes call for deep frying—they may taste good, but the eggplant can absorb too much fat. This light, "no-fat" baked version is a delicious and healthy alternative. Try using some of the colorful new varieties of eggplant now available.

1 large egg
1 teaspoon freshly grated nutmeg
1 teaspoon shredded peeled fresh gingerroot
Salt and freshly ground black pepper, to taste
1 medium-size eggplant, trimmed and cut into
    ¾-inch-thick slices

YIELD
4 servings
OVEN
400°F

1. In a shallow bowl, beat together the egg and the seasonings.
2. Dip the eggplant slices into the mixture, shaking off any excess. Arrange them on a baking sheet sprayed with nonstick vegetable cooking spray.
3. Bake in the preheated 400°F oven for about 5 minutes or until softened. Turn the slices and bake for 5 minutes more.
4. Serve hot or at room temperature.

STEAMING VEGETABLES

Steaming vegetables as briefly as possible helps retain the nutrients that leach out during the longer boiling or simmering process. For successful steaming, don't overcrowd the vegetables; whatever kind of steamer you use, be sure not to let the water touch them; be sure you have a tight-fitting cover; and add any desired seasonings to the water to enhance the flavor.

As a rule, the lighter (that is, higher in water content) the vegetable, the less time it takes to steam. Zucchini, summer squash, mushrooms, onions, and peppers cook much more quickly than green beans, carrots, or potatoes. When combining vegetables, cook like weights with like so they will come out evenly. Cut the vegetables in equal-size pieces.

STEAMED CAULIFLOWER WITH FENNEL AND CUMIN

▲▲▲

Cauliflower is a graceful and undervalued vegetable. As with so many of the vegetables we remember from our childhood, it was usually overcooked, mushy, and tasteless. Try steaming it; you will find that it tastes as lovely as it looks. The seasonings used here impart a subtle but distinctive flavor.

1 medium-size cauliflower
1 teaspoon curry powder
1 teaspoon fennel seeds
1 teaspoon ground cumin
¼ cup dry white wine or dry vermouth

YIELD
4 to 6 servings

1. Trim any blemishes from the white part of the cauliflower. Remove the outer leaves. Cut off the stem but leave the cauliflower whole.

2. Fill a large saucepan 1 inch deep with water. Add the seasonings and wine to the water. Set the cauliflower in a metal steamer and lower it into the water.

3. Bring the water to a boil. Cover and reduce the heat to a sim-

mer. Steam for about 25 minutes or until the cauliflower is tender when tested with a fork. Add more water to the steamer if necessary.

4. Place the cauliflower on a platter. Pour the remaining cooking liquid over the cauliflower and serve immediately.

BAKED ONIONS WITH BALSAMIC VINEGAR

▲▲▲

This idea came from an article by Tina Bell and Fred Brack, who write and publish widely on food and dining in the Northwest. The onions they use are the famous Walla Walla Washington Sweets, one of the loveliest flavors in the whole vegetable kingdom. Although we can't get them in the East, any fresh onions become sweet as can be when baked—red onions are sweeter than yellow. When you add either balsamic or rice vinegar, the acidity of the vinegar marries well with the sweetness of the baked onions. They are particularly good served with any roast, hot or cold. Remove the peels before serving.

4 medium-size to large white or red onions
Olive oil, walnut oil, or corn oil
Coarse (kosher) salt
4 tablespoons balsamic vinegar or rice vinegar

YIELD
4 servings

OVEN
350°F

1. Carefully remove a thin slice from both ends of the onions. Do not peel. Quarter the onions lengthwise.

2. Oil an 8x8-inch baking pan with the oil of your choice and sprinkle lightly with coarse salt.

3. Place the onions in the pan and cover with parchment paper.

4. Bake in the preheated 350°F oven until tender, about 30 minutes.

5. Remove the onions from the oven and brush again with oil. Sprinkle about 1 tablespoon of the vinegar over each onion. Return to the oven and bake 30 minutes longer or until crisp-tender, turning the onions several times and basting with pan oil.

6. Remove the onions from the oven. Carefully peel and serve hot.

INTERCHANGEABLE GREENS

▲▲▲

In this recipe you may substitute beet greens, escarole, kale, or mustard greens for the spinach, or try combining spinach and beet greens. Escarole is a little too tart to mix with spinach. Greens may be served hot, at room temperature, or cold. They may be cooked the day before, but dress and garnish them just before serving, with finely chopped hard-cooked egg white and one teaspoon roasted sesame seeds.

1 pound spinach or 2 bags (10 ounces each) spinach,
    thoroughly rinsed and stems removed
2 cloves garlic, finely chopped
1 to 2 tablespoons corn oil
Salt and freshly ground pepper, to taste
¼ cup Nene's Lemon-Garlic Dressing (page 128)

> **YIELD**
> 4 to 6 servings

1. When the spinach is thoroughly rinsed, lift it carefully without shaking water off and place it in a large pot. Sprinkle with garlic.

2. Add 1 or 2 tablespoons oil. Cover tightly. Steam until the spinach just wilts, about 3 to 5 minutes. Stir once or twice. Add salt and pepper to taste.

3. Just before serving, toss with the dressing.

For Red or Green Swiss Chard, Italian Style

Substitute for the spinach 1 bunch red or green Swiss chard, trimmed, cut into ½-inch-wide slices, and thoroughly rinsed. Cook the chard according to the directions above until it softens but still retains its crunch. Season with the dressing to taste.

GRAINS AND BEANS

▼▼▼

G rains and beans have been the basic nourishment of humankind for thousands of years—ever since we first found grasses growing in the wild and planted seeds. They've been the foundation of every cuisine throughout the world. Only in this country—and only in this century—have they been relegated to second place, behind the animal proteins and fats. The health hazards of this regime have now become so generally acknowledged that grains and beans have resumed their leading role. For those of us who grew up under the dominance of the standing rib roast and the three-inch sirloin steak, it's time to revise our eating habits. It's becoming clearer every day that meat and meat products should play a lesser, indeed a minor role in our daily diet.

Here are pilafs and rice salads that can be served hot or cold. Mixed with a whole palette of vegetables, they are all colorful as well as delicious and can be easily varied according to the season or the meal. Enjoy these salads, as well as those made with couscous, bulgur, and kasha—delicious grains that are increasingly available in supermarkets.

Beans make good down-to-earth eating year-round. Here you'll find them in crisp colorful salads with vegetables, in an antipasto or side dish, or in a tasty entrée dish such as Tuscany Beans.

I encourage you to make beans from scratch most of the time. With the "cook once, eat twice" approach, you can get two or even three uses from a pound of dried beans. I've also included recipes using canned beans for quick impromptu dishes. But even when you thoroughly rinse the canned variety, they still retain some salt, and they cannot approach the flavor, texture, and nutritional value of beans cooked from scratch.

Rice

▼▼▼

OVEN-BAKED BROWN RICE OR CONVERTED WHITE RICE

▲▲▲

I prefer this failproof oven-baked method of preparing rice. There's no chance of burning the rice and each grain remains separate.

1 teaspoon corn or safflower oil
1 cup raw brown rice or converted white rice
1¾ cups boiling water
1 clove garlic, peeled

YIELD
3 cups cooked rice

OVEN
375°F

    1. In a medium-size saucepan or ovenproof dish over medium heat, heat the oil.
    2. Add the rice and remove from heat. Stir until the rice is well coated with the oil.

    3. Add the boiling water and garlic and bring to a boil again.
    4. Place the rice in the preheated 375°F oven. Bake, covered, without stirring, until all the liquid is absorbed, about 35 to 40 min-

utes. Remove garlic before serving.

5. Divide for use. Refrigerate leftovers, covered.

For Top-of-the-Stove Cooked Brown Rice or Converted White Rice

Follow the recipe directions above through Step 3. Reduce the heat to a simmer and cook, partially covered, 35 to 40 minutes, without stirring, until all the liquid is absorbed. Remove the garlic before serving.

CHINESE EMERALD BROWN RICE

▲▲▲

Combining spinach and rice with lots of fresh ginger makes a fine addition to the repertoire of low-fat, low-calorie Chinese dishes. The Chinese, incidentally, do not peel their gingerroot, but simply shred it. Remember, "skins" are a source of fiber. Here add it to the rice as it cooks.

1 teaspoon peanut oil
1 cup raw brown rice
1¾ cups boiling water
2 cloves garlic, finely chopped
2 tablespoons finely shredded unpeeled fresh
    gingerroot (hand grated)
½ of 10-ounce package frozen chopped spinach

| YIELD |
| 4 servings |
| **OVEN** |
| 375°F |

1. In a medium-size casserole over medium heat, warm the oil. Add the rice and turn off the heat. Stir until all the grains are coated with oil.

2. Add the boiling water, garlic, and gingerroot.

3. Cover and bake, without stirring, in the preheated 375°F oven for 35 to 40 minutes or until all the liquid is absorbed.

4. While the rice is baking, cook the spinach, according to the directions on the package. Drain in a sieve, pressing on the spinach to extract all the water.

5. In a medium-size bowl, combine the spinach with the cooked rice. Toss lightly but thoroughly. Serve immediately.

RICE PILAF WITH PIGNOLI AND ITALIAN PARSLEY

▲▲▲

Pignoli (pine nuts) are very high in protein, and add crunch and flavor, while the parsley contributes pungent flavor and loads of vitamin C.

2 cups hot cooked rice, white or brown (page 210)
¼ cup finely chopped Italian flat-leaf parsley
¼ cup pignoli
1 teaspoon unsalted butter

YIELD
2 servings

In a medium-size bowl, combine the rice, parsley, pignoli, and butter and mix until the butter has melted. Serve hot.

For Brown Rice with Pepita Nuts and Italian Parsley
Substitute ¼ cup pepita nuts for the pignoli.

ELEANOR TOMIC'S RICE-BULGUR PILAF WITH WALNUTS

▲▲▲

This makes a lovely, unusual pilaf to go with fish, chicken, or meat, or as an accompaniment to casseroles. It's also good as a stuffing for roast chicken and baked fish.

2 tablespoons unsalted butter
½ cup chopped walnuts
4 scallions, trimmed and thinly sliced
2 cups cooked bulgur (page 217)
2 cups cooked brown rice (page 210)
Garnish: freshly chopped Italian flat-leaf parsley

YIELD
4 servings

1. In a medium-size skillet over medium heat, melt the butter. Add the walnuts and scallions and sauté, stirring, for 2 minutes.

2. Stir in the cooked bulgur and brown rice and cook until all the ingredients are heated through, about 5 minutes. Transfer to a serving dish. Garnish with parsley and serve.

RICE SALADS

▲▲▲

The vegetable combinations you can use in cold rice salads are endless. Try using both cooked and raw vegetables and any leftover chicken or meat you may have on hand. Any of the vinaigrettes found in the Basics chapter go nicely with rice salads. Here are some colorful ones.

COLD BROWN RICE SALAD WITH SEASONAL VEGETABLES

▲▲▲

What's in the crisper today? If you used our weekly shopping guide (page 48) to provide yourself with in-season vegetables, you'll have several kinds to choose from for color, texture, and flavor. The vegetables in this recipe are just the ones I happened to have on hand when I tested this recipe.

2 cups cooked brown rice (page 210), cooled
2 cups vegetables made up from:
   ½ cucumber, peeled, seeded, and cut into fine dice
   6 radishes, cut into fine dice
   ½ zucchini, scrubbed, ends removed, and cut into fine dice
   1 summer squash, trimmed and cut into fine dice
3 tablespoons Fresh Herb Vinaigrette (page 128), made with cilantro and mint

YIELD
4 servings

1. In a medium-size bowl, combine the rice and vegetables.

2. In a small bowl, whisk the Fresh Herb Vinaigrette and pour over the salad. Toss to mix thoroughly.

3. Serve immediately or refrigerate, covered, until serving time.

BLACK, YELLOW, AND GREEN RICE SALAD

▲▲▲

2 cups cooked converted white rice (page 210), cooled
¾ cup finely chopped scallions
¾ cup corn kernels, from the ear or frozen, thawed
½ cup pitted black olives, drained and thoroughly rinsed
¼ cup Fresh Herb Vinaigrette (page 128)

YIELD
4 servings

1. In a medium-size bowl, combine the rice, scallions, corn, and olives.

2. In a small bowl whisk the Fresh Herb Vinaigrette and pour over the salad ingredients. Toss to mix thoroughly.

3. Serve immediately or refrigerate, covered, until serving time.

SPRING GREEN-AND-WHITE RICE SALAD

▲▲▲

2 cups cooked converted white rice (page 210), cooled
½ cup diced sweet green pepper
½ cup diced zucchini
½ cup diced summer squash
⅓ cup finely chopped mushrooms
¼ cup Vinaigrette (page 125)

YIELD
4 servings

1. In a medium-size bowl, combine the rice and vegetables.

2. In a small bowl, whisk together the Vinaigrette and pour

over the salad ingredients and blend thoroughly.

3. Serve immediately or refrigerate, covered, until serving time.

WILD RICE

▲▲▲

Wild rice is actually a grass, and unless you live in Minnesota or California, where it is grown, it can run as high as $12.00 a pound.

1 cup raw wild rice
2½ cups Chicken Stock or All-Vegetable Soup Stock (pages 138–139) or water
1 teaspoon corn oil

YIELD
2½ cups cooked rice

1. Rinse the rice thoroughly in at least 4 changes of cold water.
2. In a large saucepan over medium heat, bring the rice, stock, and oil to a boil.

3. Reduce the heat, partially cover, and simmer about 40 minutes or until the water is absorbed.
4. Divide for use. Refrigerate leftovers, covered.

WILD RICE WITH SHIITAKE MUSHROOMS

▲▲▲

Both of the following combinations, one served hot and the other served cold, are extraordinarily beautiful!

1 ounce (⅓ cup) shiitake mushrooms
2 tablespoons corn oil
5 medium-size scallions, trimmed and cut into ½-inch pieces
1½ cups hot cooked wild rice

YIELD
4 to 6 servings

1. Soak the mushrooms in a small bowl of warm water for 30 minutes. Drain. Squeeze the mushrooms dry in paper toweling. Dice.

2. In a small saucepan over medium heat, heat the oil. Add the mushrooms and sauté 4 minutes or until slightly cooked.

3. Remove the mushrooms with a slotted spoon and reserve. Add the scallions and sauté until translucent, about 3 to 5 minutes.

4. In a medium-size bowl, mix the rice with the mushrooms and scallions. Transfer to a serving dish and serve.

WILD RICE WITH TRI-COLOR PEPPERS

▲▲▲

Because wild rice is expensive, I stretch it by combining it with vegetables in equal proportions. Since the yield is 7 cups cooked rice per pound, it is not as expensive as you might think. Combined with seven cups of vegetables, a pound serves 12 to 14 people.

1½ cups cooked wild rice, cooled
⅓ cup diced sweet green pepper
⅓ cup diced sweet red pepper
⅓ cup diced sweet yellow pepper
⅓ cup diced scallions

YIELD
4 to 6 servings

Dressing:
3 tablespoons rice vinegar
1 tablespoon hazelnut oil
1 tablespoon freshly squeezed lime juice
Salt and freshly ground white pepper, to taste

1. In a medium-size bowl, combine the rice and vegetables.

2. In a small bowl, whisk together the dressing ingredients. Add the dressing to the rice mixture and mix thoroughly.

3. Serve immediately or refrigerate, covered, until serving time.

Bulgur, Couscous, Kasha

▼▼▼

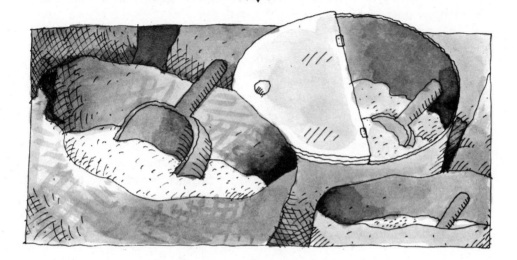

BULGUR (CRACKED WHEAT)

▲▲▲

For a moister consistency, good for pilafs and fillings, use one part bulgur to two parts water. For a drier consistency, for salads with dressings, use one part bulgur to one part water.

| 2 cups water
1 cup bulgur | **MOIST: YIELD**
2 ½ cups cooked
bulgur | 1 cup water
1 cup bulgur | **DRY: YIELD**
2 ¼ cups cooked
bulgur |

1. In a medium-size saucepan over medium heat, bring water to a boil. Stir in the bulgur and return to a boil for 1 minute.

2. Remove the pan from heat, cover, and let stand for 30 to 45 minutes.

3. Remove the cover and fluff the bulgur with a fork to separate the grains.

4. Divide for use. Refrigerate leftovers, covered.

COUSCOUS

▲▲▲

Couscous (semolina) is a tiny pearl-white grain. You may use it hot as a starch, or cold as a salad.

1 tablespoon unsalted butter
1¼ cups couscous grains (medium)
1¼ cups boiling water

YIELD
3 ½ cups cooked
couscous

1. In a medium-size saucepan over low heat, melt the butter. Add the couscous. To prevent burning, remove from the heat and stir until the butter is absorbed.
2. Stir in the boiling water. Cover. Let stand for 10 to 15 minutes.
3. Turn into a large bowl and separate with a fork.
4. Divide for use. Refrigerate leftovers, covered.

KASHA (BUCKWHEAT GROATS)

▲▲▲

Kasha has a rich, nutty flavor and crunchy texture. Usually served hot, it's also good cold in a salad (page 222).

2 cups water
¼ teaspoon salt
¼ teaspoon freshly ground pepper
1 teaspoon unsalted butter
1 cup medium kasha

YIELD
3 cups cooked
kasha

1. In a medium-size saucepan over high heat, combine the water, salt, pepper, and butter and bring to a boil.
2. Add the kasha and stir until thoroughly mixed. Reduce the heat until the mixture is at a simmer, cover, and cook the kasha for 10 minutes. If water has not been absorbed, cook an extra 5 minutes.
3. Remove the cover and fluff the kasha with a fork.
4. Divide for use. Refrigerate leftovers, covered.

FRUITED COUSCOUS SALAD

▲▲▲

Here is a salad that serves as a "starch" in a meal. It goes well with chicken, fish, or pork.

YIELD
3 servings

⅓ cup finely chopped dried apricots (about 4)
⅓ cup golden raisins
1 tablespoon freshly squeezed orange juice
1 cup cooked couscous (page 218), cooled
⅓ cup thinly sliced scallions
¼ teaspoon ground cinnamon
¼ teaspoon salt
¼ cup Citrus Vinaigrette (page 127)

1. In a medium-size bowl, mix the apricots and raisins. Pour the orange juice over them and let soak until all the juice is absorbed, about 20 minutes.
2. In a medium-size bowl, combine the apricots, raisins, couscous, scallions, cinnamon, and salt.
3. In a small bowl, whisk the Citrus Vinaigrette and pour over the salad. Toss to mix thoroughly.
4. Serve immediately.

BULGUR, CHICK-PEA, AND SCALLION SALAD

▲▲▲

Bulgur and chick-peas make a complementary protein/starch for an anytime-of-day snack or a quick starch for dinner.

YIELD
2 servings

1 cup cooked bulgur (page 217), cooled
1 can (10 ounces) chick-peas, drained and thoroughly rinsed
3 scallions, chopped
2 tablespoons Vinaigrette (page 125)

1. In a small bowl, combine the bulgur, chick-peas, and scallions.

2. In a small bowl, whisk the Vinaigrette and pour over the ingredients and blend thoroughly.

3. Serve immediately or refrigerate, covered, until serving time.

COUSCOUS WITH CARROTS, ALMONDS, AND CURRANTS

▲▲▲

It takes only minutes to "make" couscous. Prepare the couscous ahead in the morning, if you wish, then at serving time, add the remaining flavorful ingredients.

¼ cup currants
2 tablespoons water or sherry
1 tablespoon unsalted butter or corn oil
½ cup shredded carrots (hand grated)
½ cup roasted almonds, coarsely chopped
2 cups cooked couscous (page 218)

YIELD
4 servings

1. In a bowl, place the currants. Pour the water or sherry over them and let soak until the liquid is absorbed, about 20 minutes.

2. In a medium-size saucepan over medium heat, melt the butter or heat the corn oil. Add the carrots, almonds, and currants and sauté, about 3 to 4 minutes.

3. Add the cooked couscous and mix thoroughly. Heat about 5 minutes or until heated through.

4. Serve immediately or refrigerate, covered.

"KASHAED" MUSHROOMS

▲▲▲

Kasha and mushrooms have a great affinity. In this easy recipe, from Helen Nearing's book, *Simple Food for the Good Life*, vegetables are mixed with kasha for a hearty dish. Helen Nearing, in her 80's, continues her "homesteading" on her Maine farm. Her husband, Scott, died a few years ago—at age 100.

YIELD
4 servings

2 tablespoons corn oil
1 bunch scallions, trimmed and finely chopped
1 large sweet red pepper, rinsed, seeded, and finely
 chopped
1 large cucumber, peeled, seeded, and finely chopped
2 cups mushrooms, wiped clean with damp paper
 toweling and coarsely chopped
2 cups cooked kasha (page 218)

1. In a wok or heavy saucepan over medium heat, heat the oil. Add the scallions and red pepper and sauté until translucent.

2. Add the cucumber and sauté until it "wilts." Add the mushrooms. Raise the heat and cook until tender.

3. Mix the kasha with the vegetables and cook for about 5 minutes or until warmed through. Serve immediately.

BULGUR SALAD IN CUCUMBER BOATS

▲▲▲

A handsome way to serve this pretty yellow, green, and beige salad is to mound it in scooped-out cucumbers (see our Environmental Picnic Menu, page 90). It may also be served on greens as an everyday salad.

YIELD
4 servings

½ cup cooked bulgur (page 217), cooled
½ cup thinly sliced scallions
½ cup peeled, seeded, and finely diced cucumber
½ cup corn kernels, from the ear or frozen, thawed
¼ cup freshly squeezed lemon juice
2 tablespoons corn or olive oil
½ cup chopped fresh mint
Salt and freshly ground black pepper, to taste
2 medium-size cucumbers

1. In a medium-size bowl, combine the bulgur, scallions, diced cucumber, and corn.

2. In a small bowl, whisk together the lemon juice, oil, mint, and salt and pepper to taste. Pour over the salad ingredients and mix.

3. Cut off the ends of the whole cucumbers. With a vegetable peeler, rib the 2 cucumbers length-wise by removing alternate strips of peel. Then cut the cucumbers in half lengthwise. Scoop out the seeds with a small spoon. Fill each cucumber half with about 3 table-spoons of the bulgur filling.

4. Place the cucumber halves on a lemon leaf-lined platter.

5. Serve immediately or refrig-erate, covered, until serving time.

KASHA WITH CRISP GREEN AND YELLOW VEGETABLES

▲▲▲

Here kasha is served as a salad. Experiment with other combi-nations of vegetables, depending on the season.

———

2 cups cooked kasha (page 218), cooled
½ cup broccoli stems, peeled, sliced ½-inch thick, and then quartered
½ medium-size cucumber, rinsed, ribbed with the tines of a fork, quartered lengthwise, and sliced into ¼-inch slices
1 medium-size yellow squash, rinsed, trimmed, quartered lengthwise, and cut into ½-inch slices
¼ cup freshly squeezed lemon juice
4 tablespoons olive or corn oil
4 sprigs finely chopped Italian flat-leaf parsley
Salt and freshly ground pepper, to taste

YIELD
4 to 6 servings

———

1. In a serving bowl, combine the kasha and vegetables.

2. In a small bowl, whisk together the lemon juice, oil, parsley, and salt and pepper to taste. Pour the dressing over the kasha mixture and mix thoroughly.

3. Serve at room temperature immediately or refrigerate, covered, until serving time.

Beans

▼▼▼

Beans in our diet furnish protein and complex carbohydrates with a minimum of fat, and their versatility is almost unlimited. Here and elsewhere in this book you'll find them in a wide variety of dishes including soups, salads, and casseroles perfect for everyday feasting and entertaining friends. There are easy and delicious recipes for preparing beans from scratch as well as some quick-as-a-wink dishes that use canned beans. Enjoy them all.

BASIC BEAN RECIPE

▲▲▲

Beans need to be soaked overnight to give their full yield. One pound of dried beans equals two to two-and-a-half cups dried, or four-and-a-half to five cups cooked beans. Beans should be picked over to remove any small stones and broken beans before soaking.

The amount of water used in cooking the beans depends upon the texture desired. For soups, use four cups water to each cup of presoaked beans. For side dishes and salads, three cups water to one cup presoaked beans is the desired ratio. Exact cooking time and yield depend upon the size of the bean used.

1 cup dried beans, picked over and rinsed
3 to 4 cups water
1 bay leaf
1 teaspoon corn oil or olive oil

YIELD
2 to 2 ½ cups
cooked beans

PREP
Presoak beans
overnight

1. Soak the beans overnight in 4 cups of water. Drain and rinse.

2. In a large kettle or casserole combine the beans, water, bay leaf, and oil. Over medium heat, bring the water to a boil. Skim off any impurities that rise to the top.

2. Reduce heat, partially cover the pan, and simmer the beans for 45 minutes to 1 hour or until the beans are tender but still retain their shape.

3. Beans are now ready for use in other recipes.

KIDNEY BEAN SALAD OR ANTIPASTO SALAD

▲▲▲

I originally made this salad all from leftovers. In a pinch, canned kidney beans can be substituted. Serve as a quick bean salad on its own or as part of an antipasto.

2 cups cooked kidney beans (page 223), cooled
½ cup ¼-inch-thick scallion slices
8 ounces cherry tomatoes (about 10 to 12), halved
4 ounces pitted black olives, preferably marinated (page 152)
¼ cup Vinaigrette (page 125)

YIELD
4 servings

1. In a medium-size bowl, combine the kidney beans, scallions, tomatoes, and olives.

2. In a small bowl, whisk the Vinaigrette and pour over the salad ingredients. Mix thoroughly.

3. Serve or refrigerate, covered, until serving time.

BLACK BEAN AND VEGETABLE SALAD

▲▲▲

This cold salad is another way of enjoying the very popular black bean. Vary the vegetables according to what you have in your vegetable crisper. Another time you might have on hand carrots, summer squash, zucchini, and corn. It, too, will look lovely and give you loads of vitamins.

YIELD
4 servings

2 cups cooked black beans (page 223), cooled
1 cup diced sweet red pepper
½ cup diced scallions
½ cup diced, peeled Jerusalem artichokes or jícama
¼ cup Nene's Lemon-Garlic Dressing (page 128)
2 tablespoons chopped fresh cilantro or parsley

1. In a medium-size bowl, combine the black beans, red pepper, scallions, and Jerusalem artichokes.
2. In a small bowl, whisk the Lemon-Garlic Dressing with the chopped cilantro. Pour over the salad ingredients and mix.
3. Serve or refrigerate, covered, until serving time.

WHITE BEANS WITH LEMON

▲▲▲

Cold white beans are among the most versatile of vegetables. They're great in side dishes, as part of an antipasto, or combined with canned salmon and vegetables for an impromptu side salad.

YIELD
4 to 6 servings

4 cups cooked white beans (page 223), cooled
1 tablespoon olive oil
¼ cup freshly squeezed lemon juice
Freshly ground black pepper, to taste
Garnish: ½ lemon, thinly sliced

1. Place the beans in a 1-quart glass bowl.
2. In a small bowl, whisk together the olive oil, lemon juice, and pepper to taste. Pour the dressing over the beans and mix.
3. Garnish with the lemon slices and serve immediately.

TUSCANY BEANS

▲▲▲

This easy-to-make dish is both tasty and filling, and it freezes well too. It's especially nice with Three-Green Salad with Grapefruit and Olives (page 271).

1½ cups dried white beans, picked over and rinsed
1 teaspoon plus 2 tablespoons olive oil
1 bay leaf
1 teaspoon dried sage
Salt and freshly ground pepper, to taste
1 cup canned Italian plum tomatoes, drained and
    finely chopped

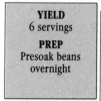

YIELD
6 servings

PREP
Presoak beans
overnight

1. Soak the beans overnight in 5 cups of water. Drain and rinse.

2. In a large casserole or kettle, combine the beans with water to cover. Add the 1 teaspoon olive oil and the bay leaf. Over medium heat bring the water to a boil. Reduce the heat to a simmer, and simmer, covered, for 45 minutes. The beans should be tender but not lose their shape.

3. In a large skillet over medium heat, heat the remaining 2 tablespoons of the oil. Add the beans, seasonings, and tomatoes and cook 3 or 4 minutes.

4. Remove the beans from the stove and serve immediately. Or cool and refrigerate, covered. You may freeze at this point. Thaw overnight in the refrigerator and reheat over low heat to serve.

Impromptu Bean Dishes

▼▼▼

FIVE-MINUTE SALMON AND WHITE BEAN SALAD

▲▲▲

Pink, white, green—and tasty. This salad supplies protein from two sources, and calcium from the bones in the fish.

1 can (10 ounces) small white beans, drained and thoroughly rinsed
1 can (3½ ounces) salmon, rinsed and thoroughly drained, skin removed, and salmon mashed with bones
3 scallions, trimmed and cut into ½-inch slices
2 tablespoons Basil Vinaigrette (page 128)

YIELD
2 servings

1. In a medium-size bowl, combine the beans, salmon, and scallions.

2. In a small bowl, whisk the Basil Vinaigrette. Pour over the salad mixture and mix.

3. Serve immediately or refrigerate, covered.

QUICK BLACK BEANS WITH RED PEPPER

▲▲▲

Black beans are good in any number of dishes, but this elegant dish is a special treat. It's prepared in a matter of minutes, and then baked for 20 minutes with vermouth and thyme. It tastes as though it baked for hours. And the colors are so dramatic! Whether as part of a grand buffet or as a simple meal, enjoy it often. This recipe can be prepared for four, forty, or a hundred.

1 teaspoon plus 1 tablespoon corn oil
1 can (10 ounces) black beans, drained and
      thoroughly rinsed
¼ to ⅓ cup dry vermouth
1 teaspoon dried leaf thyme
2 cloves garlic, peeled and finely chopped
2 medium-size sweet red peppers, seeded and cut lengthwise into ⅓-inch-
      wide strips

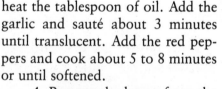

YIELD
4 servings
OVEN
350°F

1. In a baking dish rubbed with the 1 teaspoon oil, combine the beans, vermouth, and thyme.
2. Bake in the preheated 350°F oven about 20 minutes or until the beans are heated through but still retain their shape.
3. In a medium-size saucepan, heat the tablespoon of oil. Add the garlic and sauté about 3 minutes until translucent. Add the red peppers and cook about 5 to 8 minutes or until softened.
4. Remove the beans from the oven. Arrange the peppers over the beans. Serve immediately.

COLD BEAN AND PEA SALAD

▲▲▲

If you want to be the hit of your next "participation dinner," bring this salad. The dressing is also excellent on chicken salad and as a sauce for crudités and cold fish.

YIELD
8 servings

1 can (16 ounces) chick-peas, drained and thoroughly
   rinsed
1 can (16 ounces) kidney beans, drained and
   thoroughly rinsed
½ of 10-ounce package frozen green peas, thawed
2 medium-size red onions, peeled and cut into
   ¼-inch-thck slices
3 or 4 scallions, green parts only, cut into ⅛-inch slices
Garnish: chopped parsley or chopped cilantro

Dressing:

1 large ripe avocado, pitted, peeled, and cut into chunks
2 tablespoons corn oil
¼ cup Hellmann's Mayonnaise or Angie's Mayonnaise
   (page 121)
¼ cup sour cream or plain yogurt
Juice of 1 lime
Juice of ½ lemon
1 teaspoon salt
1 teaspoon freshly ground white pepper
1 teaspoon ground cumin
1 canned whole mild green chile, seeded (optional)

1. In a medium-size bowl, combine the first five ingredients. Cover and refrigerate.

2. In a food processor fitted with a metal blade or in a blender, combine the dressing ingredients. Whirl until smooth. Transfer the dressing to a bowl and chill, covered.

3. Shortly before serving, in a medium-size bowl, combine the dressing and salad ingredients. Garnish with the parsley or cilantro.

Lentils and Peas

▼▼▼

I like to serve lentils hot with white rice, and cold as a salad with red onions and Italian parsley. Those dishes are appetizing to look at, and delicious too.

Try using split peas in ways you may not have before—a yellow split-pea loaf with red, green, and yellow vegetables, and a yellow split-pea dahl with scallions, tomatoes, and tofu.

Experiment with recipes using these two inexpensive sources of good nutrients and good taste.

BASIC LENTIL/SPLIT-PEA RECIPE

▲▲▲

L entils and split peas, unlike beans, do not absolutely have to be soaked overnight. Because of their smaller size they cook in much less time. However, soaking them overnight produces a more generous yield. Two and a half cups dry give four and a half cooked. Both lentils and split peas should be picked over and thoroughly rinsed before soaking as they can be gritty. The amount of cooking water used depends on the specific lentil or split-pea recipe. The ratios generally used are as follows:

1 cup presoaked lentils or split peas to 4 cups water for soup
1 cup presoaked lentils or split peas to 3 cups water for loaf
1 cup presoaked lentils or split peas to 2 cups water for dahl
1 cup presoaked lentils or split peas to 1 ½ cups water for baked

---

1 cup dry lentils or split peas, picked over and rinsed
3 cups water
1 bay leaf
1 teaspoon corn oil or olive oil

YIELD
2 cups

PREP
Presoak lentils/
split peas
overnight

1. Soak the lentils or split peas overnight in 4 cups of water. Drain and rinse.

2. In a large kettle or casserole over medium heat, bring the lentils or split peas, the 3 cups water, bay leaf, and oil to a boil.

3. Skim off any impurities.

(Additional skimming may be necessary during the cooking process.)

4. Reduce heat, cover the pan, and simmer for 35 to 45 minutes or until the lentils or split peas are tender.

5. The lentils or split peas are now ready for use in other recipes.

YELLOW SPLIT-PEA LOAF WITH VEGETABLES, CHEESE, OR TOFU

▲▲▲

Yellow split-pea loaf is my own concoction that can be enjoyed hot or cold. This loaf is especially nutrient-rich, combining protein, calcium, and vitamins. Garden Tomato Sauce (page 241) is an attractive and tasty complement to this dish. Bake the loaf in a standard loaf-size pan, or two small ones. It freezes well.

———

YIELD
6 servings
OVEN
350°F

3 cups water

1 cup dried yellow split peas, picked over and rinsed

½ medium-size yellow onion, finely chopped

1 celery stalk, stringed and finely chopped

½ teaspoon dried summer savory

½ teaspoon dried thyme

1 bay leaf

¼ teaspoon coarse (kosher) salt

1 teaspoon freshly ground black pepper

1 egg plus 1 egg white

½ cup plain yogurt

4 ounces finely chopped tofu, or 4 ounces Swiss cheese, shredded with a hand grater

6 tablespoons fresh whole-wheat bread crumbs

½ medium-size zucchini, trimmed and cut into small dice

½ sweet green pepper, seeded and cut into small dice

½ sweet red pepper, seeded and cut into small dice

1. In a medium-size saucepan over medium heat, bring the water, split peas, onion, and celery to a boil. Reduce the heat and simmer about 5 minutes. Skim any impurities from the top.

2. Add the savory, thyme, bay leaf, salt, and pepper and simmer, partially covered, until the peas are tender, about 40 to 45 minutes. Remove from the heat and cool.

3. In a food processor fitted with a metal blade, add the split peas. Whirl until they are smooth and creamy, about 2 minutes. Remove and reserve. You should have about 2 cups.

4. In a large bowl, whisk together the eggs and egg white, yogurt, tofu or cheese, and bread crumbs. Add the vegetables and whisk again. Add the cooled split pea mixture and combine gently.

5. Into a 9x5x3-inch loaf pan or 2 5¾x3¼x2-inch pans sprayed with nonstick vegetable cooking spray and lined with parchment paper, pour the batter, shaking the pan to spread evenly. Bang the pan on the counter to remove any air bubbles.

6. Bake in the preheated 350°F oven about 45 minutes or until a knife inserted into the center of the loaf comes out clean. The loaf should be slightly brown around the edges.

7. Remove the loaf from the oven and cool about 20 minutes in the pan. Then remove from the pan and cool 10 minutes longer. Remove the parchment paper.

8. Cut the loaf into 1-inch-thick slices. Serve at room temperature. Or cool, wrap tightly in plastic freezer wrap and freeze.

SAM'S AUNT FANNY'S LENTILS AND RICE

▲▲▲

One Palm Sunday, just as I was beginning the recipe section of this book, I asked my neighbor, Sam Assaid, if we could have a Lebanese dish for dinner. Sam, a Lebanese from Virginia and a great cook, said, "Let's do my Aunt Fanny's lentils and rice. And a salad." I had two tomatoes, some romaine lettuce, some mushrooms, and green onions. Sam had lettuce, olive oil, lentils, and rice. In less than 45 minutes we were ready to eat what Sam described as a classic Lebanese Palm Sunday dinner. I went back for thirds.

1½ tablespoons olive oil
2 medium-size onions, diced
1 cup lentils, picked over and rinsed
1 cup raw long-grain rice
6 to 7 cups water
Salt and freshly ground pepper, to taste

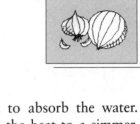

YIELD
6 servings

1. In a large saucepan over medium heat, heat the oil. Add the onions and sauté until translucent, about 5 minutes.

2. Add the lentils and the rice and stir until the lentils and rice are coated with oil.

3. Add the water and bring to a rolling boil.

4. Cook at a boil until the grains begin to absorb the water. Then reduce the heat to a simmer. Cook, partially covered, about 35 minutes or until the water is almost, but not quite all absorbed. Remove from the heat.

5. The mixture will dry out in 5 minutes. It should be mushy, like a stew. Season with salt and pepper to taste. Serve immediately.

Variation: Lentil-Rice Salad with Red Onion

This hearty and nutritious salad is made in mere minutes. The red onion and leafy parsley add verve and sparkle.

4 cups Sam's Aunt Fanny's Lentils and Rice, cooled
1 large red onion, peeled and thinly sliced
2 tablespoons finely chopped fresh parsley
5 tablespoons olive oil
3 tablespoons freshly squeezed lemon juice
½ teaspoon salt

YIELD
4 servings

1. In a large bowl, combine the 4 cups lentils and rice mixture, onion, and parsley.

2. In a small bowl, whisk together the oil, lemon juice, and salt. Pour the dressing over the salad and mix thoroughly.

3. Serve immediately.

DAHL WITH SCALLIONS, TOMATOES, AND LEMON

▲▲▲

Most of us are introduced to dahl as an accompaniment to curry. Madame Chitrabhanu, from whom I learned a great deal about Indian vegetarian cooking, says that Indian babies are given dahl at every meal as their main source of protein. Dahl can be served as a side starch or vegetable with any kind of meal, so no need to wait for a curry dinner. When tofu is added, it becomes a main dish.

2 cups dried yellow split peas, picked over and rinsed
4 cups water
1 tablespoon corn oil, margarine, or Clarified Butter (page 131)
1 tablespoon finely diced peeled fresh gingerroot
½ teaspoon mustard seeds or ⅛ teaspoon ground mustard
1 tomato, peeled and cubed
2 scallions, trimmed and finely chopped
½ lemon
4 ounces tofu, cut into ½-inch cubes (optional)

YIELD
4 servings
PREP
Presoak split peas overnight

1. Soak the split peas overnight in 6 cups of water. Drain and rinse.

2. In a medium-size saucepan over medium heat, bring the 4 cups water to a boil and add the split peas. Reduce the heat to a simmer. Skim off impurities as needed.

3. In a small skillet over medium heat, heat the oil. Add the spices and sauté 2 minutes.

4. Add the spices to the split peas and cook 20 to 25 minutes.

5. Add the tomato and scallions. Into the dahl, squeeze juice from the ½ lemon and continue to cook for 5 minutes.

6. The dahl is cooked when the split peas are partially puréed but still retain some shape.

7. For a smoother texture, remove 1 cup of the dahl mixture and place in a blender. Whirl until puréed and stir back into the saucepan. Add the tofu.

8. Serve immediately or refrigerate, covered. Reheat gently over low heat to serve.

PASTA

▼▼▼

For those of us who remember the humble macaroni and cheese of our childhood, the new trendiness of pasta—both gastronomic and nutritional—may still be a surprise. Until recently, pasta was usually banished from the diet of anyone who was the slightest bit weight-conscious. Now we know that pasta is actually a caloric bargain—a four-ounce serving is only 100 calories (no more than a small baked potato or an apple)—and it's also among our best sources of immediate energy, a far more healthful source than the simple sugars in sweets. In fact, it's pasta that distance runners stoke up on for fuel before starting a marathon.

We've learned from the Italians to serve pasta as a first course or as a light entrée. Here you'll find two versions of the ever-popular pesto sauce and a quick roasted red pepper sauce, for elegant first courses.

Then there are the small hot and cold pasta dishes that feature Oriental buckwheat noodles, the handsome Pasta Paella, and three different tomato sauces for light entrées.

Pasta is also featured in the entrée and side salad sections, in seven marvelous combinations using fish, chicken, and vegetables. Among the chicken recipes, I've also combined pasta with Chicken Moroccan and Chicken Gascony, two of my favorite entrées.

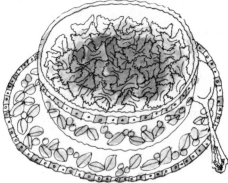

Hot Pasta Dishes

▼▼▼

Pasta... Cook It Right

• If the pot is too small and you don't use enough water, invariably the pasta will be gummy. Use at least a 6-quart pot. The ideal pot is both wide and deep, giving the roominess needed for the pasta to turn, toss, and roll over. Use enough water, even if you are cooking a small amount of pasta. You can never go wrong by having 3 to 4 quarts.

• Over high heat, bring the water to a rolling boil *before* you add the pasta. This means the water is boiling full out, not just starting to boil. Use a teaspoon of oil to prevent sticking. (It is not necessary to add salt—season when serving.)

• Ease the pasta into the boiling water so the water does not splash. For long noodles and linguine, lean them against the side of the pot and let them slide in. Add other shapes with a long-handled ladle that lets you put the pasta deep into the pot. Let the water return to a rolling boil. You may reduce the heat slightly, but the pasta must cook at a full boil at all times. Never cover the pot.

When Is Pasta Done?

Al dente. Pasta is best when it springs back to the bite, and bite you must to know whether your pasta is really still raw or just right. It is easy to overcook pasta. If cooking pasta from a package, always begin to check at least two or three minutes before the cooking time suggested on the package. "Homemade pasta," your own or the gourmet pastas, usually takes under five minutes, often as little as three to four.

Draining Pasta

For easier handling, turn off the heat and pour one cup cold water into the pot so the boiling stops immediately. Slowly pour the pasta into a large colander set in the sink. If the colander is large, there is room for the pasta so it won't stick. Pick up the colander and shake it so the water drains thoroughly. I put the colander back over the pot and cover it with a lid to keep it at room temperature.

Sauces

Pasta is ideal at room temperature. The heated sauce will make it as hot as you need it. I recommend for each serving a smaller amount of sauce: one-quarter cup is really quite sufficient for a thick intense sauce, one-third cup for a light sauce. And in some recipes, just two tablespoons is enough.

Portions

Pasta can be served as an appetizer, a salad, an entrée, or a party buffet dish. Portions for appetizers are 4 ounces, cooked, and for entrées eight ounces, cooked. Yields are based on dry measurement of pasta. Two ounces dry pasta yields one cup to one and one-half cups cooked, depending on the size and shape of the pasta.

ZUCCHINI LASAGNA

▲▲▲

Lasagna is the hands-down favorite pasta dish for parties. I've made it with meat, seafood, and chicken. This zucchini lasagna, inspired by a recipe in *The Northwest Cookbook* by Lila Gault, is delightfully rich yet light. The topping of sautéed mushrooms gives a distinct meatiness to the dish. Serve as an alternative to ham and turkey for a holiday buffet, or for a "friends-over" night and serve with salad and dessert.

———

6 tablespoons olive oil

2 medium-size yellow onions, finely chopped

6 cloves garlic, finely chopped

2 tablespoons fresh basil or 2 teaspoons dried

1 teaspoon dried oregano

2 cans (16 ounces each) tomatoes, drained and coarsely chopped

2 cans (6 ounces each) tomato paste

1 cup Italian flat-leaf parsley, finely chopped

Salt and freshly ground black pepper, to taste

2 cups ricotta cheese

1 cup low-fat cottage cheese

1 cup plain yogurt

6 quarts water

1 teaspoon corn oil

1½ pounds lasagna noodles

6 tablespoons unsalted butter

2 pounds mushrooms, wiped clean with damp paper toweling and cut lengthwise into ½-inch-thick slices

8 small zucchini, scrubbed, trimmed, and coarsely shredded on a hand grater or cut into ½-inch-thick slices (about 4 cups), pressed in a sieve to remove excess liquid if using shredded

2 pounds (about 4 cups) mozzarella, cut into ½-inch slices

Fresh parsley sprigs

YIELD
20 servings

OVEN
375°F

———

1. In a large casserole over medium heat, heat the olive oil. Add the onions and garlic and sauté until translucent, about 5 minutes.

2. Add the basil, oregano, tomatoes, tomato paste, and parsley. Reduce the heat and simmer, partially covered, for 20 minutes. Season with salt and pepper and remove the sauce from the heat.

3. In a large bowl, mix together the ricotta, cottage cheese, and yogurt. Beat with a whisk until smooth and set aside.

4. In a large 8-quart kettle, bring 6 quarts of water to a rolling boil and add the corn oil. Ease the lasagna noodles into the boiling water and cook until *al dente*. Drain in a colander.

5. In a medium-size saucepan, melt 2 tablespoons of the butter and sauté ⅓ of the mushrooms. Remove the sautéed mushrooms to a plate and in 2 batches repeat the process with the remaining butter and mushrooms.

6. Spray 2 8x15x2-inch baking dishes with nonstick vegetable cooking spray. In the bottom of each dish, arrange one-fourth of the noodles and layer with one-fourth each of the zucchini, the cottage cheese/ricotta/yogurt mixture, the sauce, and the mozzarella slices in that order. Repeat with the remaining ingredients.

7. Top each of the dishes with half the sautéed mushrooms and parsley sprigs.

8. Bake in the preheated 375°F oven for 35 to 45 minutes or until the lasagna is bubbling and brown on top. Remove from the oven and cool for 5 minutes.

9. Serve hot.

FARFALLE WITH CARIBBEAN ROUGE SAUCE

▲▲▲

These little bow-ties have always been popular in the classic Jewish favorite, kasha varnishkes. But they're charming enough to be served in many more ways. The Caribbean Rouge Sauce for baked fish makes a delightful and unusual sauce for pasta. The combination of tomatoes, cloves, and lemon perks up pasta, and the rich, rosy color is warmly inviting.

YIELD
2 servings

4 quarts water
1 teaspoon corn oil
8 ounces farfalle
½ cup Caribbean Rouge Sauce (page 311)

1. In a 6-quart kettle over medium heat, bring the water to a rolling boil and add the oil. With a ladle, add the farfalle and cook until *al dente*. Drain in a large colander. Place the colander over the cooking pot and cover.

2. In a small saucepan over low heat, heat ½ cup Caribbean Rouge Sauce, until heated through.

3. Place half the farfalle on each plate. Add half the sauce to each and lightly toss. Serve.

FUSILLI WITH HENRY GROSSI'S TOMATO SAUCE PICANTE WITH EGGPLANT

▲▲▲

This recipe and the recipe for Ratatouille (page 188) are among the two best meatless sauces for pasta I know. You can substitute a seventeen-ounce package of Pomi strained fresh tomatoes now available in supermarkets for one of the cans of plum tomatoes. They are smooth and have more flavor than regular canned plum tomatoes. This sauce freezes beautifully. I like to serve it with fusilli as a hearty entrée.

1 large or 2 medium-size eggplants (1½ pounds), unpeeled and cut into ½-inch cubes (4 cups, which reduces to 2 cups when cooked)

2 tablespoons salt

4 tablespoons olive oil

4 medium-size cloves garlic, finely chopped

1 medium-size yellow onion, finely chopped

2 teaspoons dried red pepper flakes or 1 whole dried red pepper

2 tablespoons chopped fresh basil or 1 tablespoon dried

3 cans (28 ounces each) Italian plum tomatoes (not packed in purée, low-sodium if possible), squeezed into pieces

4 quarts water

1 teaspoon olive oil

16 ounces fusilli

YIELD
2 quarts sauce
4 servings pasta

1. In a colander, sprinkle the eggplant with the salt and let drain for 30 minutes. Press the eggplant to remove moisture and pat dry with paper toweling.

2. In a medium-size saucepan over medium-high heat, combine 2 tablespoons of the oil, the garlic, onion, and red pepper flakes and sauté until the garlic browns, the onions are translucent, and the pepper flakes are a clear bright red, about 5 minutes.

3. Add the basil and tomatoes and heat over low to medium heat for 15 minutes. Remove the dried red pepper, if using.

4. In a medium-size skillet over medium-high heat, cook the eggplant in 2 tablespoons of oil until it has softened, about 6 to 8 minutes.

5. Combine the eggplant with the tomato sauce.

6. In a 6-quart kettle over high heat, bring the water to a rolling boil and add the teaspoon oil. With a ladle, add the fusilli and cook until *al dente*. Drain in a colander.

7. Use ½ cup of sauce for each serving and serve at room temperature. Or cool the sauce and freeze in boilable plastic freezer bags.

ANGEL HAIR WITH GARDEN TOMATO SAUCE

▲▲▲

This very thin spaghetti is delightful, and one of the best and simplest ways to serve it is with this tomato sauce with basil. You can put it together almost at a moment's notice, so it's perfect for when friends drop by unexpectedly. And if you make up a batch of the sauce in late summer and freeze it in boilable plastic freezer bags, you'll have it all through the winter.

5 pounds fresh tomatoes, rinsed
Boiling water as needed
3 tablespoons olive oil
2 cloves garlic, finely chopped
1 cup chopped fresh basil
4 quarts of water
1 teaspoon olive oil
8 ounces angel hair pasta

YIELD
1 quart sauce
2 servings pasta

1. Place the tomatoes in a very large kettle and cover them with boiling water. As soon as the skins begin to break, remove the tomatoes from the water with a slotted spoon. Peel the skins from the tomatoes and core. Working in batches, place the skinned tomatoes in a blender and whirl until they are small chunks.

2. In a large saucepan over medium-high heat, heat the 3 tablespoons oil. Add the garlic and sauté until translucent, 1 to 2 minutes. Add the tomatoes and basil and bring to a boil, stirring constantly.

Reduce the heat and simmer, stirring occasionally, for 10 minutes. Use at once or let the sauce cool and refrigerate, covered, until serving time. Or when cooled, freeze in boilable plastic freezer bags.

3. In a 6-quart kettle over medium heat, bring the 4 quarts of water to a rolling boil and add the 1 teaspoon oil. Ease in the pasta and cook until *al dente*. Drain in a large colander. Place the colander over the cooking pot and cover.

4. Place half of the angel hair on each plate. Add ¼ cup sauce to each plate. Toss lightly, and serve.

BUCKWHEAT NOODLES WITH ASPARAGUS, GINGER, AND SOY

▲▲▲

Buckwheat noodles, available in Oriental shops, are full of flavor, and cook in about the same time as ordinary pasta. This dish is quick to prepare. Use broccoli when asparagus is not in season. Serve as a delicious first course or light entrée.

4 quarts water
1 teaspoon corn oil
8 ounces thin buckwheat noodles
½ recipe Stir-Fry Asparagus with Ginger and Soy
    (page 194)
Additional soy or tamari (optional)

YIELD
2 servings

1. In a 6-quart kettle over medium heat, bring the water to a rolling boil and add the oil. Ease in the buckwheat noodles and cook until *al dente*. Drain in a large colander. Place the colander over the cooking pot and cover.

2. Prepare the Stir-Fry Aspara-

gus with Ginger and Soy according to the directions given in the recipe.

3. Place half the buckwheat noodles on each plate. Add half the asparagus to each serving, and additional soy, if needed. Serve.

INA FOX'S SPAGHETTI WITH TOMATO-SAUSAGE SAUCE

▲▲▲

My friend Ann Erwin's aunt has had this recipe since the 1930s—it came with her Merrit stove. It became their "take everywhere" casserole for trips to the mountains, outings with the kids, or covered-dish suppers. It is a simple yet wonderful combination of ingredients that is juicy and perfectly delicious. Omit the sausage for small meals at home, if you like, but I would include it if you are cooking for a crowd. The recipe doubles easily, and can be baked in two pans. If you freeze it, omit the cheese and add it only when you're warming it up to eat.

YIELD
6 servings

OVEN
350°F

6 to 8 sweet sausage links pricked all over with a fork

2 tablespoons unsalted butter

1 cup finely chopped yellow onion

1 cup finely chopped celery

1 cup finely chopped sweet green pepper

½ pound mushrooms, trimmed, wiped clean with damp paper toweling, and finely chopped

1 can (28 ounces) Italian plum tomatoes (not packed in purée), squeezed into pieces

1½ teaspoons Worcestershire sauce (optional)

½ pound thin spaghetti or linguine, broken into 1-inch pieces

⅔ cup shredded Monterey Jack or Cheddar cheese (shredded with a hand grater)

1. In a medium-size skillet over medium heat, cook the sausage until browned. Drain on paper toweling. When cool, slice thin.

2. Wash the skillet and return to the stove. Over medium heat,

melt 1 tablespoon of the butter. Add the onion, celery, and pepper and sauté until brown, about 7 minutes.

3. In a large saucepan over high heat, melt the remaining tablespoon of butter. Add the mushrooms and sauté for 2 to 3 minutes. Add the sausage, vegetable mixture, tomatoes, and Worcestershire, and bring to a boil.

4. Add the broken spaghetti to the hot sauce and mix carefully. Immediately transfer the mixture to a 2-quart baking dish and sprinkle the cheese over the top.

5. Bake in the preheated 350°F oven for 30 to 40 minutes or until bubbling and brown.

6. Serve hot or at room temperature.

PASTA PAELLA

▲▲▲

This makes a dramatic presentation for a Sunday supper. The bed of green and white noodles makes a lovely background for the colorful shrimp, mussels, chicken, and vegetables. Although there are a number of steps, the preparation is relatively brief, and well worth the effort. With salad, bread, and flan for dessert, it makes a grand meal.

1 pound fresh mussels
2 pounds boneless, skinned chicken breasts, rinsed
    and patted dry
2 tablespoons unbleached all-purpose flour, for dredging
2 strips bacon
2 tablespoons unsalted butter
½ teaspoon ground saffron or ¼ teaspoon turmeric
4 chorizo sausages or any other spicy sausage, pricked all over with a fork
1 teaspoon dried leaf thyme
Salt and freshly ground black pepper, to taste
1 sweet green pepper, seeded and cubed
1 sweet red pepper, seeded and cubed
1 small onion, cubed
4 quarts water
1 teaspoon oil
6 ounces white linguine

YIELD
6 servings

PREP
Soak mussels 2 hours

6 ounces spinach linguine
1 bottle (8 ounces) clam juice
1 jar (6½ ounces) quartered marinated artichoke hearts, thoroughly rinsed
   and drained
½ pound medium-size shrimp (about 15), peeled, deveined, and rinsed
½ of 10-ounce package frozen peas, thawed
Garnish: chopped fresh parsley or cilantro

1. Under cold running water, carefully wash the mussels, scrubbing them with a vegetable brush. Remove the beards. After scrubbing, let the mussels stand for 2 hours covered with cold water. Discard any that float.

2. Cut the chicken breasts lengthwise into 3 strips, then crosswise into 1-inch cubes. Dredge the cubes in the flour and set them aside.

3. In a large skillet over medium heat, cook the bacon until it is crisp. Remove and drain on paper toweling, reserving the fat in the skillet. Crumble the bacon when cool. Add 1 tablespoon of the butter, the saffron, and chorizo to the skillet and cook, stirring occasionally, until the chorizo is thoroughly browned. Cool about 20 minutes. Remove the chorizo with a slotted spoon and cut into ½-inch pieces. Set aside.

4. Combine the chicken cubes, thyme, and salt and pepper in the skillet and cook, turning once or twice, for 5 minutes or until the chicken is no longer pink in the center. Remove with a slotted spoon and set aside.

5. In a large casserole or kettle over medium heat, melt the remaining tablespoon butter. Add the peppers and onion and cook until translucent, about 5 minutes.

6. In a large saucepan with a lid, place the mussels and enough water to cover them halfway. Bring to a boil over high heat and cook until the shells open, about 3 minutes. Discard any mussels that do not open. Cool slightly and remove the mussels from their shells, reserving the shells for decoration.

7. In a 6-quart kettle, bring 4 quarts of water to a rolling boil and add the oil. Ease in the pasta and cook until *al dente*. Drain in a large colander. Place the colander over the cooking pot and cover.

8. Add the clam juice, mussels, chorizo, crumbled bacon, artichokes, shrimp, and chicken to the casserole and bring to a boil. Boil the shrimp until they just begin to turn pink, about 2 minutes. Add the thawed peas.

9. Transfer the linguine to a large platter. Arrange the chicken, sausage, vegetables, mussels, and shrimps attractively over the pasta. Use the mussel shells as a garnish around the outside of the platter. Sprinkle with parsley and serve.

PESTOS FOR ALL SEASONS

▲▲▲

Dorothy Rankin, in her lovely little book simply called *Pestos*, opens up a world of ideas for making pesto with all sorts of herbs from the garden or window box. Sometimes she combines the usual basil with mint, tarragon, cilantro, sorrel, or sage.

She also recommends using one and one-half cups chopped Italian flat-leaf parsley to one-third or one-half cup other fresh herbs when basil isn't in season, depending on how strongly flavored the herb used is. This offers a year-round choice of what she calls "herb pestos" that enhance pasta, as well as chicken, vegetables, and fish.

Remember that some herbs, such as oregano and thyme, are stronger and more overpowering than others, and should be used judiciously when combining with basil or parsley.

To cut back on the fat and calories, use cheese *or* nuts, rather than both together. (See Pesto Sauce Without Cheese, below.)

PENNE WITH PESTO SAUCE WITHOUT CHEESE

▲▲▲

Penne is a pretty shaped pasta. This is a quickly made first course or light entrée. If basil is unavailable, use spinach.

—

4 tablespoons corn oil

2½ cups basil or spinach (about 5 to 6 ounces), rinsed and roughly chopped

2 medium-size cloves garlic, coarsely chopped

2 tablespoons pignoli (pine nuts)

4 quarts water

1 teaspoon corn oil

4 ounces penne

YIELD
1 ⅓ cups sauce
2 servings pasta

1. In a blender, combine 2 tablespoons of the corn oil, all the basil or spinach, garlic, and nuts. Whirl until completely mixed. Continue blending while adding the other 2 tablespoons of oil.

2. In a 6-quart saucepan over high heat, bring the water to a rolling boil and add the 1 teaspoon oil.

With a ladle, add the penne and cook until *al dente*. Drain in a large colander. Place the colander over the cooking pot and cover.

3. Place 2 tablespoons of the pesto on each serving plate. Add half of the penne. Toss the sauce lightly yet thoroughly with the penne and serve.

RUOTE WITH THICK CHUNKY PESTO

▲▲▲

Because we are eating lighter, there is no need to drench our pastas in sauce. Two tablespoons of pesto are all you need per pasta serving. It keeps in the refrigerator, covered tightly, for two or three days and freezes well.

1 cup fresh basil leaves (2 ounces), rinsed and coarsely
   chopped
2 medium-size cloves garlic, finely chopped
2 tablespoons coarsely chopped walnuts
2 tablespoons freshly grated Romano cheese
2 tablespoons olive oil
2 tablespoons corn oil
4 quarts water
1 teaspoon olive oil
8 ounces medium-size ruote

YIELD
1 cup sauce
2 servings pasta

1. In a blender, combine the basil, garlic, nuts, cheese, and 1 tablespoon each of the oils. Whirl until chunky. Do not overpurée. Continue to blend while adding the remaining tablespoons of each oil.

2. In a 6-quart kettle over medium heat, bring the water to a rolling boil and add the 1 teaspoon

olive oil. With a ladle, add the ruote and cook until *al dente*. Drain in a large colander. Place the colander over the cooking pot and cover.

3. Place 2 tablespoons of the sauce on each of 2 serving plates. Add half of the ruote. Toss lightly and serve.

SMALL SHELLS WITH QUICK ROASTED RED PEPPER SAUCE

▲▲▲

I particularly like the small shells for a sauce like this. They are pretty and have a nice bounce to them against the teeth, yet they're not too much of a mouthful of pasta.

You can use either roasted red peppers from the supermarket or (better) Esther's Roasted Red Peppers for this quick sauce, which is also good on fish or chicken.

It is similar to pesto, and if you like, you can add nuts for extra richness. Use only two tablespoons of the sauce per serving. Covered tightly, it keeps at least two or three days in the refrigerator, and it freezes well, too.

---

1 jar (7 ounces) roasted red peppers, drained and thoroughly rinsed, or Esther's Roasted Red Peppers (page 196)

¼ cup cilantro or Italian flat-leaf parsley, rinsed, patted dry, and coarsely chopped

2 large cloves garlic, coarsely chopped

2 tablespoons freshly squeezed lime juice

2 tablespoons corn oil

4 quarts water

1 teaspoon corn oil

8 ounces small shells

> **YIELD**
> ¾ to 1 cup sauce
> 2 servings pasta

---

1. In a blender, combine the roasted red peppers, cilantro, garlic, lime juice, and 1 tablespoon of the oil. Whirl, and while blending, add the other tablespoon of oil.

2. Remove the sauce from the blender and refrigerate until ready to use.

3. In a 6-quart kettle over medium heat, bring the water to a rolling boil and add the 1 teaspoon oil. With a ladle, add the small shells and cook until *al dente*. Drain in a large colander. Place the colander over the cooking pot and cover.

4. Place 2 tablespoons of the sauce on each of 2 serving plates. Place half of the small shells over each. Toss lightly and serve.

Cold Pasta Dishes

▼▼▼

STRAW AND HAY

▲▲▲

Serve this as a first course, or as an entrée with one of the following: 5 ounces cooked fresh or frozen green peas, ½ cup broccoli flowerets, 3 ounces chopped prosciutto, or 6 ounces cooked scallops.

—

4 quarts water
1 teaspoon corn oil
4 ounces spinach linguine
4 ounces white linguine
½ cup freshly grated Parmesan cheese
¼ cup small capers, drained and thoroughly rinsed
3 tablespoons olive oil or corn oil
3 tablespoons freshly squeezed lemon or lime juice
¼ cup chopped parsley
Salt and freshly ground pepper, to taste

YIELD
2 servings

1. In a 6-quart kettle over high heat, bring the water to a rolling boil and add the 1 teaspoon corn oil. Ease in the linguine and cook until *al dente*. Drain in a large colander. Transfer to a serving bowl.

2. If using additional ingredients, add them now.

3. In a small bowl, thoroughly mix the cheese, capers, the 3 tablespoons oil, lemon juice, parsley, and salt and pepper. Pour over the pasta and mix thoroughly. Serve immediately. Or refrigerate, covered. Return to room temperature to serve.

PASTA SHELLS WITH SCALLOP SEVICHE

▲▲▲

Scallop Seviche is a very popular fish course from Spain and Mexico, and a mainstay of California cuisine. You'll find another version of it as an appetizer with kohlrabi and Bosc pears on page 150. I was delighted to find a new way of using seviche in a book called *Cold Pasta* by James McNair. He suggests using scallop seviche to fill medium-size shells. The pungent seviche combines well with the blander pasta for a first course or as a salad. Use the smaller bay scallops for this dish.

1 pound bay scallops, rinsed and patted dry
¼ cup dry vermouth or dry white wine (optional)
2 tablespoons freshly squeezed lime juice
2 canned green chiles, rinsed, drained, seeded, and finely chopped
3 ounces roasted red peppers, finely chopped, or 1 small fresh sweet red pepper, seeded and finely chopped
¼ teaspoon crushed red pepper flakes
2 tablespoons finely chopped fresh cilantro
4 quarts water
1 teaspoon corn oil
16 ounces medium-size pasta shells

YIELD
4 to 6 servings
PREP
Marinate 2 hours

1. In a medium-size saucepan, cover the scallops with water. Add the dry vermouth or white wine, if desired. Over medium heat, bring

the water to the gentlest of simmers. Poach about 5 minutes or until the scallops change from translucent to white. Do not overcook. Drain at once and cool.

2. In a medium-size stainless steel or glass bowl, combine the lime juice, chiles, red peppers, red pepper flakes, and cilantro. Toss with the scallops and marinate, covered, for 2 hours in the refrigerator.

3. In a 6-quart kettle over medium heat, bring the water to a rolling boil and add the oil. With a ladle, add the shells and cook until *al dente*. Drain in a large colander. Cool or refrigerate, covered.

4. When ready to serve, drain the seviche and spoon into the pasta shells as a stuffing. Or combine the pasta and seviche and serve on small plates.

ANGEL HAIR WITH BROCCOLI FLOWERETS AND PEAS

▲▲▲

This can be served both warm and cold, with equal success. If serving cold, add a drop or two of oil before refrigerating the pasta to keep it from sticking. Combine ingredients and dressing when ready to serve.

YIELD
4 servings

4 quarts water
1 teaspoon olive oil
16 ounces angel hair pasta
½ bunch broccoli, tips of flowerets cut into tiny ½-
    inch pieces, and stems reserved for soups or salad
1 package (10 ounces) frozen peas, thawed

Dressing:

½ cup olive oil
¼ cup red wine vinegar
2 tablespoons chopped fresh basil or snipped dill
¼ cup freshly grated Parmesan cheese
Salt and freshly ground pepper, to taste

1. In a 6-quart kettle over medium heat, bring the water to a rolling boil and add the 1 teaspoon oil. Ease in the pasta and cook until

al dente. Drain in a large colander.

2. In a medium-size bowl, combine the pasta, broccoli, and peas.

3. In a small bowl, whisk to-gether the dressing ingredients.

4. Pour the dressing over the pasta and mix thoroughly. Serve warm. Or refrigerate and serve chilled.

BUCKWHEAT NOODLES WITH SCALLIONS AND SMOKED OYSTERS

▲▲▲

Buckwheat noodles with sesame dressing is a very popular dish in Hunan Chinese restaurants. To enjoy it this way at home, use our Saté Dipping Sauce (page 121) thinned out with a little chicken broth. Or try the noodles with scallions and smoked oysters. Most supermarkets carry smoked oysters, and scallions should always be on hand in your vegetable crisper.

1 to 2 tablespoons good-quality cold-press sesame oil
4 scallions, trimmed and cut diagonally into 1-inch
    pieces
1 tin (3¾ ounces) smoked oysters, drained,
    thoroughly rinsed, and patted dry
1 tablespoon tamari or soy sauce
12 ounces cooked buckwheat noodles

YIELD
2 servings

1. In a small saucepan over medium heat, heat 1 tablespoon of the sesame oil. Add the scallions and sauté about 2 minutes. Add the oysters and heat through, about 2 minutes. Add the tamari and stir.

2. Place half of the buckwheat noodles on each plate, and half of the oyster and scallion mixture on top of the noodles. Add additional tamari and oil, if needed, and serve.

THE SALAD SCENE

▼▼▼

Entrée salads have always been a big feature in my cooking, probably because I come from California where there has always been an abundance of fresh produce year-round. It was a shock when I came to live in New York and found that my only choices on restaurant menus were a chefs salad and maybe a cold chicken or tuna salad. How dull!

Many of the recipes in my repertoire of salads, as it developed over the years, often originated with requests from our clients. For instance, I was asked to prepare a luncheon for a reunion of Smith College alumnae who had spent their junior year in France. The menu was to include a Niçoise salad made with chicken rather than tuna. That's just the kind of challenge I love. I created a chicken version that used a juxtaposition of fresh ingredients to make a salad both dramatic and different. It became our most popular buffet salad for corporate luncheons and buffet dinners. I also went on to develop a Steak Salad Niçoise and a Vegetable Salad Niçoise.

I did the same experimenting with a curried turkey salad from my friend Paula Schaengold—it became chicken, then shrimp, then ham, and even tofu.

Our entrée pasta salads, which include macadamia nuts and scallops—as well as our chicken pasta salads make wonderful hearty meals.

All of these healthy and beautiful salads are ideal for every day as well as for entertaining.

Entrée Salads

▼▼▼

CHICKEN SALAD NIÇOISE

▲▲▲

This salad is almost guaranteed to attract a fan club when you serve it.

½ pound green beans, trimmed and halved
1 pound poached chicken breasts (page 322), cut into
    1-inch cubes (about 32 pieces)
½ pound zucchini or yellow squash, trimmed, cut
    lengthwise into thirds, and then into ¼-inch-
    thick slices
½ pint cherry tomatoes (10 to 12), stemmed and halved
1 cup (4 ounces) pitted black olives, drained and thoroughly rinsed
¼ cup chopped parsley
½ cup Vinaigrette (page 125)

YIELD
6 servings

1. In a medium-size saucepan over medium heat, bring 2 quarts water to a boil. Add the green beans and cook until crisp-tender, about 6

to 8 minutes. Drain in a colander and refresh under cold water.

2. In a large bowl, combine the chicken, vegetables, olives, and parsley.

3. In a small bowl, whisk the Vinaigrette and pour over the salad. Mix thoroughly. Serve immediately, or refrigerate, covered, until ready to serve.

Variation: Steak Salad Niçoise

2 tablespoons corn oil
Replace the chicken with 1¼ pounds cubed filet or sirloin tips

1. In a medium-size saucepan over medium heat, heat the corn oil. Add the cubed steak and sauté until brown on the outside and pink on the inside, about 5 minutes.

2. Drain the liquid from the meat and cool the meat.

3. Continue the rest of the recipe precisely as written.

VEGETABLE SALAD NIÇOISE
▲▲▲

This is the perfect environmental salad. Serve it on individual savoy cabbage leaves to be eaten with your fingers.

YIELD
6 servings

PREP
Marinate 1 hour

½ pound green beans, trimmed and halved
½ pound zucchini, trimmed, halved lengthwise, and
    then cut into ¼-inch-thick slices
½ pound yellow squash, trimmed, cut into thirds
    lengthwise, and then into ¼-inch-thick slices
½ pint cherry tomatoes (10 to 12), stemmed and
    halved
1 cup (4 ounces) pitted black olives, drained and thoroughly rinsed
2 jars (6 ounces each) marinated artichoke hearts, drained and thoroughly
    rinsed
½ cup Fresh Herb Vinaigrette (page 128)
Savoy cabbage leaves (optional)

1. In a medium-size saucepan over medium heat, bring 2 quarts of water to a boil. Add the green beans and cook until crisp-tender, about 6 to 8 minutes. Drain in a colander and refresh under cold water.

2. In a large bowl, combine all of the vegetables.

3. In a small bowl, whisk the Vinaigrette and pour over the salad. Mix thoroughly.

4. Marinate, covered, 1 hour in the refrigerator.

5. Serve. Or refrigerate, covered, until ready to serve. If serving in cabbage leaves, drain salad in a colander to remove excess dressing.

CURRIED CHICKEN SALAD

▲▲▲

This quickly made entrée salad is welcome in any season.

1 pound poached chicken breasts (page 322), cut into
    1-inch cubes (about 32 pieces)
2 cups diagonally sliced ½-inch pieces celery
2 medium-size Golden Delicious apples with skins,
    cored, cut lengthwise into ½-inch-thick slices,
    and then into thirds (about 2 cups)
1 cup golden raisins
¼ cup walnuts or pecan pieces (optional)
½ cup Curry Dressing (page 130)

YIELD
6 servings

1. In a large glass bowl, combine the cubed chicken, celery, apples, raisins, and nuts if using. Mix thoroughly.

2. In a small bowl, whisk the dressing. Pour the dressing over the salad and mix so all the ingredients are well coated.

3. Serve immediately, or refrigerate, covered, until serving time.

For Curried Ham Salad
Substitute for the chicken 1 pound baked ham, cut into 1-inch cubes (about 16 pieces) and follow the rest of the recipe precisely.

For Curried Tofu Salad
Substitute for the chicken 1 pound firm tofu, cut into 1-inch cubes (about 20 pieces) and follow the rest of the recipe precisely.

Variation: Curried Shrimp Salad

1 pound large shrimp, peeled, deveined, and rinsed

1. In a medium-size saucepan over medium heat, bring the shrimp with water to cover to a boil. Reduce the heat and poach the shrimp until they turn pink and just begin to curl, 3 to 4 minutes. Drain.

2. Let the shrimp cool. Then cut in half lengthwise. Follow the rest of the recipe precisely.

GREEN-AND-WHITE TUNA SALAD

▲▲▲

Our old standby tuna fish makes a satisfying lunch or quick supper when combined with lots of the "greens" that are probably always in your vegetable crisper: celery, scallions, green pepper, and parsley. For the dressing I mix yogurt, mustard, and lime juice. Enjoy it in a sandwich, or if there's a home-grown tomato on hand, use it as an edible container for this salad.

YIELD
2 servings

**1 can (3½ ounces) tuna in oil or water, thoroughly
   drained**
¼ cup finely chopped scallions
¼ cup finely chopped celery
¼ cup finely chopped sweet green pepper
¼ cup finely chopped parsley

Dressing:

1 tablespoon plain yogurt
1 teaspoon Dijon-style mustard
1 teaspoon freshly squeezed lime juice

1. In a medium-size bowl, place the drained tuna and the chopped scallions, celery, pepper, and parsley.

2. In a small bowl, whisk together the yogurt, mustard, and lime juice. Pour over the tuna mixture, toss lightly, and serve.

GREEK ISLES PASTA-CHICKEN SALAD

▲▲▲

Salads as entrées have always been more popular with women than with men. Men perhaps think a salad is too light to eat as a main course. Not so. These two pasta-chicken-vegetable combinations will change that mistaken notion. They are very hearty and satisfying, and feature two favorites: pasta and chicken.

These salads are particularly attractive to serve for lunch or supper. If you are serving an all-cold meal, start with a cold soup, and finish with fresh fruit or an Italian or Greek sweet.

YIELD
4 servings

¼ pound green beans, trimmed and halved
1 medium-size carrot, peeled and cut into 2x¼-inch strips
3 cups cooked fusilli (6 ounces uncooked)
1 pound poached chicken breasts (page 322), cut into
        1-inch cubes (about 32 pieces)
1 jar (6 ounces) marinated artichoke hearts, drained,
        thoroughly rinsed, and halved

Dressing:

2 tablespoons corn oil
2 tablespoons olive oil
¼ cup freshly squeezed lemon juice
¼ teaspoon dried summer savory
¼ teaspoon dried oregano
2 medium-size garlic cloves, finely chopped
Salt and freshly ground pepper, to taste

1. In a medium-size saucepan over medium heat, bring 2 cups of water to a boil. Add the beans and cook until crisp-tender, about 5 minutes. Drain in a colander and refresh under cold water.

2. To blanch the carrots, place in a colander and pour boiling water over them. Cool briefly.

3. In a large bowl, combine the fusilli, chicken, green beans, carrots, and artichoke hearts.

4. In a small bowl, whisk together the dressing ingredients and pour over the salad. Mix thoroughly.

5. Serve at once, or refrigerate, covered, until serving time.

ROBUSTO PASTA AND CHICKEN SALAD WITH RED AND GREEN PEPPERS

▲▲▲

3 cups cooked fusilli (6 ounces uncooked)

1 pound poached chicken breasts (page 322), cut into
    1-inch cubes (about 32 pieces)

1 medium-size sweet red pepper, seeded, cut
    lengthwise into ½-inch-wide slices, and then into
    thirds

1 medium-size sweet green pepper, seeded, cut into ½-inch-wide slices, and
    then into thirds

3 scallions, trimmed and cut into medium dice

YIELD
4 servings

Dressing:

¼ cup olive oil
¼ cup freshly squeezed lemon juice
1 tablespoon snipped fresh dill

———

1. In a large bowl, combine the cooked pasta, chicken cubes, peppers, and scallions.

2. In a small bowl, whisk together the dressing ingredients. Pour over the salad and mix.

3. Serve at once, or refrigerate, covered, until serving time.

66The first time we saw radicchio was in an open air market in northern Italy. An Italian friend laughed when we asked why the sellers had taken all the stems of the "gorgeous red flowers." He explained the flowers were heads of winter lettuce. Cultivated in Treviso and Verona, Italy, radicchio is now available as an import nearly year round. The colors range from dark magenta to light pink and often the leaves are boldly streaked with white.... Just one or two well placed leaves of radicchio used as a garnish can dramatically enhance a simple plate presentation.99
Cucina Fresca, Vivian LaPlace and Evan Kleiman

ZITI WITH RED CABBAGE AND PIMIENTO-STUFFED OLIVES

▲▲▲

At The Party Box we were asked to devise a very simple salad for a large group. This one, with red cabbage and olives, is simple, inexpensive, and colorful.

YIELD
6 servings

16 ounces large ziti, cooked according to package
  directions and cooled
½ medium-size red or green cabbage (about 12
  ounces), halved and sliced lengthwise very thin
1 can (10 ounces) pitted large black olives or 1 jar (9
  ounces) pimiento-stuffed jumbo green olives,
  thoroughly rinsed and halved lengthwise
4 celery stalks, trimmed, halved lengthwise, and then cut diagonally into
  ¾-inch strips

Dressing:

⅓ cup rice vinegar
⅓ cup freshly squeezed lemon juice
⅓ cup safflower or corn oil

1. In a large salad bowl, toss together the ziti, cabbage, olives, and celery.

2. In a small bowl, whisk together the dressing ingredients and pour over the salad. Toss lightly to mix.

3. Serve immediately, or refrigerate, covered, until ready to serve.

GLORIOUS SEAFOOD SALAD

▲▲▲

A spectacular looking seafood salad is always a nice addition to anyone's salad repertoire. This one is a knockout. You can stretch the ingredients, which are expensive, by serving the salad as an appetizer in shells or on small plates.

1 pound (26 to 30) poached large shrimp (page 257)
1 pound poached sea scallops (page 148)
½ pound snow peas, strings removed and cut in half
2 sweet red peppers, seeded and cut lengthwise into
    ½-inch-wide strips
3 celery stalks, stringed and cut into ½-inch-thick slices
2 scallions, trimmed and thinly sliced
¾ cup Citrus Vinaigrette (page 127)

YIELD
6 to 8 servings

1. In a large salad bowl, combine all the ingredients but the vinaigrette.
2. In a small bowl, whisk the vinaigrette and pour over the salad ingredients. Mix thoroughly.
3. Serve immediately or refrigerate, covered, until serving time.

FUSILLI AND SCALLOP SALAD

▲▲▲

Scallops and pasta create an elegant salad. Slicing the scallops silver-dollar thin stretches this expensive ingredient.

YIELD
4 servings

1 pound sea scallops, rinsed
1 cup water
2 tablespoons freshly squeezed lemon juice
½ cup dry white wine or dry vermouth
2 cups cooked fusilli (4 ounces uncooked)
¼ cup freshly grated Parmesan cheese
¼ cup capers, coarsely chopped
¼ cup finely chopped Italian flat-leaf parsley
Salt and freshly ground white pepper, to taste

Dressing:

¼ cup olive oil
¼ cup freshly squeezed lemon juice

1. In a medium saucepan over low heat, poach the scallops in the water, lemon juice, and wine to cover until the scallops turn white,

about 3 to 5 minutes. Drain in a colander and rinse immediately under cold water. Cut each scallop into 3 silver-dollar-thin slices.

2. In a medium-size serving bowl, toss the fusilli gently with the scallops, Parmesan, capers, parsley, and salt and pepper.

3. In a small bowl, whisk together the dressing ingredients. Pour over the salad and mix thoroughly.

4. Serve at once, or refrigerate, covered, until serving time.

FUSILLI SALAD WITH ROASTED RED PEPPERS, ARTICHOKE HEARTS, AND BLACK OLIVES

▲▲▲

When you're in a hurry to make an entrée salad, here's where those "stores" in your pantry come in handy to create a colorful and hearty salad.

——

16 ounces white or green fusilli, cooked according to
    package directions and cooled
1 jar (7 ounces) roasted red peppers, drained,
    thoroughly rinsed, and cut into 1-inch strips
1 jar (6 ounces) marinated artichoke hearts, drained,
    thoroughly rinsed, and halved
1 can (6 ounces) pitted large black olives, drained and thoroughly rinsed

YIELD
6 servings

Dressing:

3 tablespoons corn oil
3 tablespoons rice vinegar
1 tablespoon freshly grated Parmesan cheese
1 teaspoon dried oregano
1 teaspoon chopped fresh basil or ¼ teaspoon dried

——

1. In a large serving bowl, gently combine the pasta with the vegetables and olives.

2. In a small bowl, whisk together the dressing ingredients. Pour the dressing over the salad and mix.

3. Serve immediately, or refrigerate, covered, until ready to serve.

FUSILLI AND MACADAMIA NUT SALAD

▲▲▲

This vegetable main course entrée comes from my friend Eleanor Tomic. It's an unusual blend of sharp-tasting radishes and mint, rich macadamia nuts, and a fresh ginger and lemon dressing. Serve it as a brunch or supper entrée (remember there is protein in both nuts and pasta) with hot or cold soup and finger fruit and finger pastries for dessert.

YIELD
4 servings

3 cups cooked fusilli (6 ounces uncooked)
1 medium-size zucchini or summer squash, trimmed, cut crosswise into thirds, and then into pieces to match the size of the fusilli
1 cup thinly sliced scallions
1 cup thinly sliced red radishes
¼ cup coarsely chopped fresh mint
12 macadamia nuts, coarsely chopped

Dressing:

⅓ cup corn oil
1½ teaspoons grated lemon rind
¼ cup freshly squeezed lemon juice
2 tablespoons rice vinegar
1 tablespoon chopped peeled fresh gingerroot
2 medium-size garlic cloves, finely chopped

1. In a large bowl, combine the pasta, vegetables, and nuts.
2. In a small bowl, whisk together the dressing ingredients. Pour over the salad ingredients and mix thoroughly.
3. Serve at once, or refrigerate, covered, until serving time.

> 66Salads need not be hampered by recipes. Use what is in season; use what is in the garden or meadow.99
> *Simple Food for the Good Life*
> by Helen Nearing

PAELLA SALAD

▲▲▲

Paella as an entrée salad is a splendid idea any time of year. However, the holidays offer us leftover turkey and ham as ingredients, along with shrimp, sausage, and many colorful vegetables to make a bountiful "Just Before Midnight, New Year's Eve" buffet dish. You can make it ahead, too.

YIELD
12 servings

1½ cups Chicken Stock (page 138) or canned chicken broth
1 cup tomato juice
½ cup finely chopped yellow onion
⅛ teaspoon saffron
2 cups raw converted long-grain rice
1½ pounds (42 to 48) poached large shrimp (page 257)
2 cups cooked and cubed chicken or turkey
½ pound cooked ham, cut into 1-inch cubes
½ pound chorizo or spicy Italian sausage, pricked all over with a fork,
    sautéed and drained
1 package (10 ounces) frozen peas, thawed
2 jars (6 ounces each) marinated artichoke hearts, thoroughly rinsed and
    drained
1 jar (7 ounces) roasted red peppers
1 medium-size sweet green pepper, cut lengthwise into ½-inch strips
Olive oil, as needed
Salt and freshly ground black pepper, to taste
Garnish: chopped fresh parsley or cilantro

1. In a large saucepan over medium heat, bring the stock and tomato juice to a boil. Add the onion and saffron.

2. Stir in the rice and return to a boil. Then reduce the heat, cover, and simmer for 20 to 25 minutes or until the rice has absorbed all the liquid.

3. Turn the rice out onto a shallow dish and cool completely.

4. In a large salad bowl or platter or copper paella pan, combine the shrimp, chicken, ham, chorizo, and vegetables, tossing lightly.

5. Add the cooled rice and toss again with enough oil to moisten to desired consistency.

6. Season with salt and pepper and chill, covered, until serving time. Toss again and garnish with chopped parsley or cilantro.

GADO GADO SALAD WITH SATÉ DIPPING SAUCE

▲▲▲

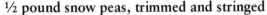

This salad, with Saté Dipping Sauce, has its origin in Asian-style food. The Oriental vegetables and the hard-cooked eggs and potatoes make this a salad that offers protein without meat.

Choose 5 or 6 of the following items:

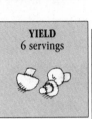

YIELD
6 servings

- 6 cooked unpeeled new or red potatoes, quartered
- 4 hard-cooked eggs, sliced
- 6 scallions, trimmed and cut into thirds
- ½ pound mushrooms, trimmed, wiped clean with damp paper toweling, and sliced lengthwise into thirds
- ½ pound snow peas, trimmed and stringed
- ½ pound daikon or white radishes, peeled and cut into ½-inch-thick slices
- ¼ pound spinach, thoroughly rinsed and stems removed
- ¼ pound fresh bean sprouts, rinsed

Saté Dipping Sauce (page 121)

On a large oval platter, arrange the ingredients in bunches, alternating the whites and greens. Serve with the sauce.

SALADS

66As an inexperienced gardener, I was nervous about planting delicate lettuces. I started a small garden with arugula and in three weeks, with just water and high hopes, I was serving my own first tender greens. Gradually I added some sucrine, leaf and romaine. While my methods may have been unorthodox and my furrows not perfectly tended, everything grew. I discovered that watching an edible plant progress through different stages was an education and there was almost always something to eat.99

Amy Nathan, author of the cookbook *Salad*

MÂCHE AND HADDOCK SALAD

▲▲▲

Use haddock or any leftover fish and whatever vegetables you have on hand to make this appetizing entrée salad. Mâche is a delicate salad green that is extremely hardy. It thrives partway through the winter, then dies, and comes back in the spring. (To order seeds by mail, see Thompson and Morgan, page 375.)

½ pound cooked haddock, cut into ½-inch cubes
1 cup (about 4 ounces) mâche or watercress, rinsed, patted dry, and stems removed
1 medium-size sweet red pepper, seeded, sliced lengthwise into ⅓-inch-wide strips, and then into thirds
4 scallions, trimmed and cut into ½-inch slices

YIELD
2 servings

Dressing:

2 tablespoons Hellmann's Mayonnaise or Angie's Mayonnaise (page 121)
2 tablespoons plain yogurt
2 tablespoons freshly squeezed lemon or lime juice
Salt and freshly ground pepper, to taste

1. In a medium-size bowl, combine the fish, mâche, pepper, and scallions.

2. In a small bowl, whisk together the dressing ingredients.

3. Pour the dressing over the salad and fold together lightly.

4. Serve immediately, or refrigerate, covered, until ready to serve.

Interchangeable Side Salads

▼▼▼

These salads may be small, but they're an important component of a meal. Here you'll find salads that look good, taste good, and are good for you.

Some of the combinations are novel and perhaps surprising, such as snow peas, raw mushrooms, and daikon. Some of these you may not think of as salads at all, such as stuffed artichokes with bulgur and golden raisins. But that's the fun and good taste of it.

There's no reason to confine these to their usual place as side salads. With their irrepressible and lively flavors, you can enjoy the lighter, more delicate ones as a first course or a palate refresher after a heavy entrée. Or you can combine three different kinds of salads as an entrée—for instance, artichokes, a fish, and a marinated vegetable choice.

You'll also find small salads a good energy booster as an off-hour meal or snack, along with grain and bean salads (pages 209–234). Try them for breakfast.

Take advantage of the versatility of these salads, whether improvised "salads of the moment" or marinated salads you do ahead. Their colors, textures, and flavors—not to mention the nutritional wallop they pack—can offer daily delight, and their makings are only as far away as your vegetable crisper or garden.

ARTICHOKES STUFFED WITH BULGUR AND GOLDEN RAISINS

▲▲▲

Artichokes with this stuffing make an excellent first course, side dish, or small meal.

2 medium-size to large artichokes, rinsed and stems removed
1 tablespoon red wine vinegar
2 tablespoons golden raisins
2 tablespoons dry sherry
1 cup cooked bulgur (page 217)

YIELD
2 servings

Dressing:

1 tablespoon safflower oil
2 tablespoons freshly squeezed orange juice
¼ teaspoon ground cinnamon

1. In a 4-quart saucepan, place the artichokes in enough water to cover and the vinegar. Over medium heat, bring to a boil. Reduce the heat and simmer 30 to 40 minutes or until tender. The leaves should pull out easily.

2. Drain the artichokes and cool slightly.

3. While the artichokes are cooking, plump the golden raisins in the sherry for about 15 minutes.

4. In a small bowl, whisk together the oil, orange juice, and cinnamon. Pour over the bulgur in a small bowl. Add the raisins. Toss lightly to mix.

5. Place each artichoke in a bowl small enough to keep it standing upright. Gently part the leaves,

being careful not to break them off at the base. Remove the choke with a spoon.

6. Spoon the bulgur-raisin mixture into each artichoke, dropping some into the opened leaves.

7. Serve at room temperature.

For Artichokes with Tamari-Lime Dressing

Cook the artichokes as directed above. Cool and refrigerate, covered. In a small bowl, whisk together 1 tablespoon distilled white vinegar, 2 tablespoons tamari, and the grated rind and juice of 1 lime. Serve the artichokes cold in glass bowls with the dressing on the side.

HANS' ENDIVE SALAD WITH PINK DRESSING

▲▲▲

Belgian endive is expensive by the pound, yet it adds up to less than a dollar per serving when prepared with this delicate pink dressing.

2 cups warm water
½ pound Belgian endive, trimmed, halved lengthwise, and then cut into ½-inch-wide pieces

Pink Dressing:

2 tablespoons Hellmann's Mayonnaise or Angie's Mayonnaise (page 121)
2 tablespoons plain yogurt
1 teaspoon paprika
Salt and freshly ground pepper, to taste

YIELD
2 servings

1. Place the warm water and endive in a bowl and let soak for 20 minutes to remove the bitter taste. Drain thoroughly.

2. In a medium-size bowl, whisk together the dressing ingredients.

3. Add the endive to the dressing and mix thoroughly.

4. Serve immediately, or refrigerate, covered, until ready to serve.

For Farfalle with Endive and Pink Dressing

Prepare ½ recipe Hans' Endive Salad with Pink Dressing according to the directions above. Cook 8 ounces of farfalle until *al dente*. Drain in a colander and cool. Place half of the farfalle on each of two plates. Add half the salad to each pasta serving. Toss lightly to mix and serve.

WATERCRESS RAITA

▲▲▲

Although we are most familiar with the cucumber raita served at Indian restaurants, many vegetables can be used in adapting raitas to everyday cuisine. I learned to do this with Pramoda Chitrabhanu in her Indian Vegetarian class. The following raitas are high in vitamins, minerals, and calcium and take minutes to prepare.

1 cup plain yogurt
1 tablespoon freshly squeezed lime juice
1 tablespoon chopped Italian flat-leaf parsley or 1
    tablespoon chopped fresh cilantro
1 teaspoon ground cumin
1 teaspoon ground cardamom
1 large bunch watercress, rinsed and stems removed

YIELD
2 servings

1. In a small bowl, whisk together the yogurt, lime juice, parsley, and seasonings.
2. In a medium-size bowl, combine the watercress and the yogurt mixture. Toss lightly to mix. Serve immediately, or refrigerate, covered, until ready to serve.

Variation: Carrot Raita

1 pound carrots, trimmed and peeled
2 cups plain yogurt
1 teaspoon ground cumin
1 teaspoon ground cardamom
1 teaspoon freshly squeezed orange juice

YIELD
4 servings

1. In a food processor fitted with a shredder disk or with a hand grater, shred the carrots.
2. In a medium-size bowl, combine the carrots with the remaining ingredients and mix thoroughly. Serve immediately, or refrigerate, covered, until ready to serve.

THREE-GREEN SALAD WITH GRAPEFRUIT AND OLIVES

▲▲▲

Here's a way to get your greens, three of them at a time: spinach, Chinese cabbage, and watercress. The grapefruit lends tartness, and the black olives, robustness.

YIELD
2 servings

1 cup fresh spinach leaves, thoroughly rinsed, patted dry, and stems removed
½ cup finely sliced Chinese, savoy, or green cabbage
¼ bunch watercress, rinsed, patted dry, and stems removed (about ½ cup)
½ grapefruit, seeded and sectioned
8 large pitted black olives, drained and thoroughly rinsed
¼ cup Nene's Lemon-Garlic Dressing (page 128)

1. In a large bowl, combine the spinach, cabbage, and watercress.
2. Add the grapefruit and black olives to the greens.

3. In a small bowl, whisk the dressing and pour over the salad. Toss lightly.
4. Serve immediately.

GARDEN GREENS AND VEGETABLES FOR SALADS

Celeriac and arugula, radicchio, Boston lettuce and cucumber, mâche and Jerusalem artichokes, dandelions and red lettuce—sound like the salads served at trendy expensive restaurants or seen in fancy cooking magazines?

You can grow most of these greens and vegetables in your own garden. Mâche and Jerusalem artichokes grow superbly in Hans Hartmann's backyard in Wilmington, Delaware. Upland cress grows wild on northern Long Island. I have some growing on the side of my house along with cucumbers. Dandelions grow wild everywhere.

Whether you grow leaf lettuce or Italian radicchio (To order seeds by mail, see Thompson and Morgan, page 375.), try to have as many lively greens as possible growing in your "edible landscape." Even a row of lettuce in a window box will do nicely.

FIRST-COURSE FINGER SALAD

▲▲▲

I love to use food itself as the centerpiece of many meals. In this instance, the lettuce surrounded by plates of finger vegetables becomes the centerpiece. The bright, graceful red and green leaf lettuces add special pleasure when they form part of an edible feast for you and your guests.

YIELD
4 to 6 servings

1 head red leaf lettuce, thoroughly rinsed but not
    separated into leaves
Carrots (allow 1 per person), trimmed and cut into
    matchsticks
Zucchini (allow 1 per person), scrubbed, peeled, and
    cut into matchsticks
Sweet peppers (allow ½ per person), seeded and cut into matchsticks
Celery (allow 1 stalk per person), cut into matchsticks
Lime wedges

1. Place the lettuce in the center of a shallow bowl or platter.
    2. Arrange the vegetable groups on small dishes in a circle around the lettuce and serve with the lemon wedges.

SNOW PEA, MUSHROOM, AND DAIKON SALAD

▲▲▲

This salad went to many Party Box parties, including the one for 1400 people at the Brooklyn Bridge centennial. It's always assembled at the last minute, and as I look back, slicing 75 pounds of mushrooms on the spot was rather foolhardy, but it was a glorious start to a very special meal. Daikon is a Japanese white radish; you may use white or red radishes.

10 snow peas, trimmed, stringed, and cut into thirds
4 mushrooms, wiped clean with damp paper toweling
    and cut lengthwise into ½-inch-thick slices
½ small daikon or 4 white radishes, trimmed, peeled,
    and cut into ¼-inch-thick slices

YIELD
2 servings

Dressing:

2 tablespoons corn oil
2 tablespoons rice vinegar
1 teaspoon Dijon-style mustard
1 tablespoon chopped parsley

1. In a medium-size salad bowl, combine the snow peas, mushrooms, and daikon.

2. In a small bowl, whisk together the oil, vinegar, mustard, and parsley. Pour the dressing over the salad. Toss well to mix.

3. Serve immediately, or refrigerate, covered, until ready to serve.

MANDARIN ORANGE, SCALLION, AND RED ONION SALAD

▲▲▲

This tart, dressy salad goes well on a buffet featuring a curry or couscous casserole. Also serve it for an elegant first course or after-entrée salad. But don't wait for company. Have it when you want to spoil yourself. The ingredients are often on hand.

½ head romaine lettuce, rinsed and broken into thirds
½ of 10-ounce package frozen peas, thawed
½ cup ⅛-inch-thick scallion slices (about 3 scallions)
½ cup ¼-inch-thick red onion slices
1 can (11 ounces) Mandarin oranges, drained and
    thoroughly rinsed
¼ cup Fresh Herb Vinaigrette (page 128)

YIELD
2 servings

1. In a large glass bowl or salad bowl, combine the lettuce, peas, scallions, red onion, and oranges.

2. In a small bowl, whisk the dressing and pour over the salad. Toss lightly.

3. Serve immediately, or refrigerate, covered, until ready to serve.

WATERCRESS, NEW POTATOES, AND WALNUT SALAD

▲▲▲

I first tasted this salad at an inn on Cape Cod as part of my small-meals-that-make-the-entrée way of eating (page 10). I had a small plate of shellfish from the seafood bar, this salad, some bread, and fresh raspberries for dessert. This "modular eating" is becoming popular at restaurants, which are outdoing themselves with sumptuous appetizers of fish, pasta, vegetables, and salads. The potatoes and walnuts in this particular salad are filling, yet the watercress makes it sharp and sprightly.

4 small new or red potatoes, scrubbed and not peeled
¼ teaspoon salt (optional)
1 bunch watercress, rinsed, patted dry, and stems
    removed
¼ cup chopped walnuts

YIELD
2 servings

Dressing:

2 tablespoons olive oil
2 tablespoons red wine vinegar
2 tablespoons freshly squeezed lime juice

1. In a small saucepan over medium heat, simmer the potatoes in enough water to cover until tender but very firm, about 15 minutes. You may salt the water with ¼ teaspoon salt if you wish.

2. Drain the potatoes. Cool slightly. Cut into small dice.

3. In a medium-size serving bowl, mix together the potatoes, watercress, and walnuts.

4. In a small bowl, whisk together the olive oil, vinegar, and lime juice. Pour the dressing over the salad ingredients and toss.

5. Serve immediately.

Satisfying Vegetable Salads

▼▼▼

HANS' CUCUMBER AND FRESH BEAN SALAD

▲▲▲

This yellow, green, and pale green pickled vegetable salad is particularly refreshing in spring and summer with cold foods and barbecues. If wax beans are unavailable, use all green beans.

½ pound wax beans, trimmed and cut into thirds

½ pound green beans, trimmed and cut into thirds

1 teaspoon dried summer savory

1 large cucumber or 2 medium-size cucumbers, peeled and cut into 1-inch cubes

3 scallions, trimmed and cut into 1-inch cubes

½ cup Italian flat-leaf parsley leaves, finely chopped

¼ cup white wine vinegar

2 tablespoons freshly squeezed lime juice

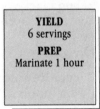

YIELD
6 servings
PREP
Marinate 1 hour

1. In a medium-size saucepan over medium heat, cook the beans with the savory in enough boiling water to cover for 6 to 8 minutes or until crisp-tender. Drain and refresh under cold water.

2. In a 2-quart serving bowl, mix the beans with the cucumbers, scallions, and parsley.

3. Pour the vinegar and lime juice over the vegetables and mix.

4. Marinate, covered, 1 hour in the refrigerator. Serve chilled or at room temperature.

YELLOW PEAR TOMATO SALAD WITH RED PEPPERS AND BLACK WALNUTS

▲▲▲

The end of summer bounty in northern Long Island produces not only gorgeous ripe tomatoes into the fall, but orange and yellow ones as well. Yellow pear tomatoes can be grown from seed or plant and are so sweet. This combination of ingredients was inspired by Marian Tracy's recipe in her book *Real Food*.

———

2 pints (about 36) yellow pear tomatoes, hulled
3 scallions, trimmed and sliced into 1/8-inch-thick circles
2 medium-size sweet red peppers, seeded and cut into small dice
1/4 cup black walnuts or regular English walnuts, coarsely chopped

Dressing:

1/4 cup rice vinegar
1 tablespoon walnut oil

YIELD
6 servings

———

1. In a medium-size bowl, combine all the salad ingredients.

2. In a small bowl, mix together the rice vinegar and walnut oil. Pour over the salad and toss.

3. Serve immediately.

YOGURT AND CUCUMBERS IN THE MIDDLE EASTERN STYLE

▲▲▲

Each month my women's entrepreneur group—there are eleven of us—meets at the house of a different member. When it was Cindy Annchild's turn, she prepared a Middle Eastern feast she learned to make while living there. She served chicken and a carrot-rice pilaf steamed together in a special Moroccan pot, but any large casserole will do. The condiments were stuffed grape leaves, fresh mint, sliced onions, and this refreshing yogurt. To make it even richer, Cindy suggests adding half a cup of light cream. In the summer she adds six ice cubes and serves it as a soup.

---

1 recipe Yogurt Cheese (page 122)
2 medium-size cucumbers, peeled, seeded, and finely
     chopped
¼ cup chopped scallions, white and light green parts only
2 tablespoons coarsely chopped fresh dill
2 tablespoons coarsely chopped fresh mint
2 tablespoons coarsely chopped parsley
½ teaspoon freshly ground black pepper
Salt, to taste
½ cup golden raisins, soaked 5 minutes in 1 tablespoon water or sherry to
     plump (optional)

YIELD
6 servings

---

1. Prepare Yogurt Cheese according to the recipe directions.
2. Transfer the yogurt cheese to a medium-size bowl and add the cucumbers, scallions, herbs, seasonings, and raisins if using.
3. Whisk to combine. Chill the mixture in the refrigerator until ready to serve.

HENRY'S CUCUMBER, RADISH, AND ORANGE SALAD

▲▲▲

Here is one of Chef Henry Grossi's favorite salads. It is surprisingly refreshing and very tart. This salad works well as a first-course salad or after-entrée salad.

YIELD
2 servings

½ bunch fresh radishes (white or red), sliced paper thin
1 medium-size cucumber, ribbed and cut into ¼-inch-
    thick slices
2 oranges, peeled, halved, thinly sliced crosswise, and
    seeded or 1 can (11 ounces) Mandarin oranges, drained

Dressing:

¼ cup rice vinegar
¼ cup freshly squeezed lime juice
2 tablespoons corn oil
1 tablespoon chopped fresh mint or 1 teaspoon dried

1. In a medium-size glass bowl, combine the radishes, cucumber, and oranges.

2. In a small bowl, whisk together the vinegar, lime juice, corn oil, and fresh mint and pour over the salad. Toss to mix thoroughly.

3. Serve at once, or refrigerate, covered, until ready to serve.

GREEN BEANS AND RED ONION IN LEMON DRESSING

▲▲▲

Lots of crunch here, and bright color too.

YIELD
2 servings

½ pound green beans, trimmed
1 red onion, sliced into ¼-inch-thick slices
1 tablespoon snipped fresh dill or 1 teaspoon dried dillweed

Lemon Dressing:

¼ cup freshly squeezed lemon juice
¼ cup olive oil
½ teaspoon Dijon-style mustard
Salt and freshly ground pepper, to taste

1. In a large saucepan of rapidly boiling water, cook the beans until they turn bright green but are still crisp, about 5 minutes. Drain and refresh under cold water.

2. Transfer the beans to a large salad bowl. Add the onion and dill and toss lightly.

3. In a small bowl, whisk together the dressing ingredients and pour over the salad.

4. Serve immediately.

MEDITERRANEAN POTATO SALAD

▲▲▲

This colorful potato salad has a dramatic Mediterranean look. The tiny, cured black olives are salty and oily, so you need no seasoning except a little oil. Serve as a side salad or as part of an antipasto.

2 medium-size new or red potatoes, scrubbed and unpeeled
½ cup diced sweet red pepper
¼ cup small cured black olives, rinsed to remove salt
⅓ cup finely chopped yellow onion
3 sprigs Italian flat-leaf parsley, finely chopped
2 tablespoons corn oil or olive oil
1 teaspoon freshly ground black pepper

YIELD
2 servings

1. In a medium-size saucepan over medium heat, cook the potatoes in enough boiling water to cover until tender, about 15 minutes. Drain, cool, and cut into 1-inch cubes.

2. In a medium-size bowl, combine the sweet red pepper, olives, onion, and parsley with the oil and black pepper. Add the potatoes and toss.

3. Serve immediately, or refrigerate, covered, until ready to serve.

RUTH AND HILARY BAUM'S YAM AND APPLE SALAD

▲▲▲

In their timely and wonderful *Lifespice Salt-Free Cookbook*, Ruth and Hilary Baum share a bounty of recipes, each one full of good taste and absolutely salt-free. This recipe invites us to try a colorful sweet potato or yam salad, especially nice for fall and winter eating. Yams are a darker orange color than sweet potatoes and are moister. They are an excellent source of Vitamin A.

4 medium-size yams or sweet potatoes
1 Granny Smith apple, unpeeled, cored, and thinly
    sliced
½ cup coarsely chopped red cabbage
½ cup roasted unsalted peanuts
2 small scallions, trimmed and sliced into 1-inch
    pieces

YIELD
4 servings

Dressing:

½ cup freshly squeezed orange juice
⅔ cup low-fat plain yogurt
1½ tablespoons freshly squeezed lemon juice

1. In a large saucepan over medium heat, cook the yams in boiling water to cover until they are just tender, about 25 minutes.

2. Drain the yams and rinse them under cold water. When the yams are cool enough to handle, peel and then slice into ¼-inch-thick rounds.

3. Combine the sliced yams, apple, cabbage, peanuts, and scallions in a serving bowl.

4. In a small bowl, whisk together the orange juice, yogurt, and lemon juice. Blend well and pour over the salad. Toss well.

5. Serve immediately, or refrigerate, covered, until ready to serve.

BLANCHE RIGAMONTI'S ANTIPASTO SALAD

▲▲▲

"This is a Mom recipe," my friend Robert Rigamonti said. "The amounts aren't precise. I grew up on it, eating it almost every day."

The vegetables will hold up well since they are "pickled" in oil and vinegar. Make a big batch to have on hand, and enjoy the salad often as a light luncheon entrée with a crusty bread and fresh fruit and cheese, or as a side salad for dinner or on a buffet.

YIELD
6 to 8 servings

½ cup olive oil
1 cup tarragon vinegar
¼ cup water
8 medium-size carrots, trimmed, peeled, and cut into
    small pieces
½ pound green beans, trimmed and halved
1 medium-size head cauliflower, broken into flowerets
1 can (3 ounces) pitted black olives, rinsed and drained
½ cup (about ½ of a 5¾-ounce jar) pimiento-stuffed green olives, rinsed
    and drained
⅓ cup tomato paste
1 teaspoon dried oregano
Salt and freshly ground black pepper, to taste
2 cans (7½ ounces each) tuna, drained and flaked
1 can (16 ounces) chick-peas, drained and thoroughly rinsed (optional)

—

1. In a large casserole over very low heat, bring the oil, vinegar, and water to a low simmer. Add the carrots, green beans, and cauliflower and cook, covered, with the lid slightly ajar, about 15 to 20 minutes or until crisp and bright in color. Do not overcook.

2. Add the olives, tomato paste, oregano, and salt and pepper

and heat through, about 2 minutes.

3. Transfer to a large serving plate. Add the tuna and the chick-peas, if using.

4. Serve immediately. Or cool and refrigerate, covered, and serve chilled.

Light and Lively Aspics

▼▼▼

A spics are a special category between cooked and raw foods. They can be one solution for those of us who find it hard to digest totally raw vegetables and fruit.

BEET ASPIC

▲▲▲

"What a nifty way to eat beets," my cousin-in-law Andy Russell said. Like many of us, Andy has difficulty digesting raw vegetables and fruits, but it had never occurred to him that he could enjoy cooked beets in an aspic. This is another of Nene Schardt's combinations that always brings color to the table.

1 can (16 ounces) small whole beets, drained and
   liquid reserved
1½ tablespoons (about 1½ envelopes) unflavored
   gelatin or 1 tablespoon agar-agar (page 283)
1 tablespoon freshly squeezed lime juice
3 scallions, trimmed and finely chopped

YIELD
4 servings

PREP
Chill 2 hours

1. In a glass measure, add enough water to the beet juice to make 3 cups of liquid. Pour into a medium-size saucepan. Sprinkle the gelatin over the top and let soften. Place over low heat and stir to dissolve, about 3 minutes. Remove the pan from the heat and cool.

2. In a blender or food processor fitted with a metal blade, combine the beets, lime juice, and scallions. Whirl until puréed but still lumpy.

3. Add the vegetables to the gelatin liquid, stirring to blend.

4. Spray a 1-quart mold with nonstick vegetable cooking spray. Pour the aspic mixture into the mold and refrigerate until firm, about 2 hours.

5. When ready to serve, unmold onto a glass or white platter.

ROSEMARY-SCENTED APRICOT ASPIC

▲▲▲

This aspic, from Marian Tracy's book *Real Food,* combines the sweetness of apricot, the fragrance of fresh rosemary, and the tartness of lemon. Serve with meat, fish, and chicken.

1 tablespoon finely chopped fresh rosemary or 1
    teaspoon dried
3 tablespoons freshly squeezed lemon juice
1½ tablespoons (about 1½ envelopes) unflavored
    gelatin or 1 tablespoon agar-agar (see below)
1 can (16 ounces) apricots, drained and juice reserved
Pinch salt
Garnish: fresh rosemary sprigs (optional)

YIELD
6 servings
PREP
Chill 2 hours

1. In a small bowl, soak the rosemary in the lemon juice, about 5 minutes.

2. In a small saucepan, sprinkle the gelatin or agar-agar over ½ cup of the reserved apricot juice and let soften. Place over low heat and stir until it dissolves, about 3 minutes. Remove from the heat.

3. In a blender, place ¾ cup of the drained apricots. Reserve the remaining apricots for other use. Whirl until a thick purée, about 1 minute.

4. In a large bowl, combine the puréed apricots with the gelatin mixture. Mix the rosemary-lemon juice mixture with enough water to make 2 cups. Stir in the puréed apricots and salt.

5. Spray a 1-quart mold with nonstick vegetable cooking spray. Pour the aspic mixture into the mold and refrigerate until it sets, about 2 hours.

6. When ready to serve, unmold onto a serving plate. Garnish with fresh rosemary, if desired.

GELATIN AND AGAR-AGAR

Gelatin has been used for years for preparing aspics, desserts, and glazes. People interested in not using any meat products may substitute agar-agar, a seaweed-based gelatin, for gelatin. It is available in health-food and Oriental stores.

One envelope (¼ ounce) of gelatin firms 2 cups of liquid, and 1 teaspoon of agar-agar firms 1 cup of liquid.

Light and Lively Slaws

▼▼▼

Slaws, like grain and bean salads, have become a part of my daily diet. They add fiber, now considered an important part of our diet.

One small to medium-size cabbage yields about 6 cups shredded. I usually work with half of a cabbage—3 cups—combined with 2½ to 3 cups of other vegetables and fruits. You may want to blanch the cabbage to remove the raw edge.

Because a slaw holds up well in the refrigerator, prepare enough so there's always some for small meals or snacks.

BOSC PEARS, GOLDEN RAISINS, AND GREEN CABBAGE SLAW

▲▲▲

When I decided to give myself a sixtieth birthday party, two of my favorite Party Box chefs, Anita Gorman and Henry Grossi, came early to help. Anita was baffled by this odd-seeming combination. But later she admitted laughingly, "To my surprise, it's a wonderful salad!" Like most of my salads, it was inspired by what I happened to have on hand. Bosc pears, golden raisins, and cabbage combine well for an interesting sweet, tart crispness. You can also make this with red cabbage.

3 cups finely sliced green cabbage (about ½ medium-size head)

2 medium-size Bosc pears, unpeeled, cored, and sliced lengthwise into ½-inch-thick slices

3 medium-size scallions, trimmed and cut into ½-inch pieces

1½ cups golden raisins

YIELD
6 servings

Dressing:

¼ cup rice vinegar
2 tablespoons freshly squeezed lime juice
2 tablespoons corn oil

1. In a large bowl, combine the cabbage, Bosc pears, scallions, and raisins.

2. In a small bowl, combine the rice vinegar, lime juice, and corn oil. Pour the dressing over the salad mixture. Toss to mix.

3. Let stand 30 minutes at room temperature before serving. Refrigerate, covered, to keep.

MAGENTA AND ORANGE SLAW (BEET AND CARROT)

▲▲▲

Who says slaws have to be made with cabbage? The combination of carrots and raw beets makes a breathtakingly vibrant combination of colors. Chopped almonds add crunch, extra calcium, and protein. This salad makes you feel healthy just looking at it.

YIELD
4 servings

1 cup shredded, peeled carrots (about 3 large or 5 medium-size)
1 large or 2 medium-size raw beets, peeled and shredded with a hand grater
3 tablespoons chopped roasted almonds

Dressing:

¼ cup rice vinegar
2 tablespoons plain yogurt
1 tablespoon freshly squeezed lime juice
Salt and freshly ground black pepper, to taste

1. In a medium-size bowl, combine the carrots, beets, and almonds.

2. In a small bowl, whisk together the vinegar, yogurt, lime juice, and salt and pepper. Add to

the slaw and mix well.

3. Serve immediately, or refrigerate, covered, until ready to serve.

MINNIE LEVY'S VEGETABLE RICH COLESLAW

▲▲▲

My friend Paula Schaengold's mother made this coleslaw for everyday as well as for parties. Paula used to eat it for breakfast, lunch, and dinner. This recipe makes a big bowlful, and it's perfect to take on a picnic with the grandchildren. Prepare it the night before.

3 cups shredded green cabbage (about ½ medium-size head)
1 cup shredded, peeled carrots (about 3 large or 5 medium-size)
4 celery stalks, stringed and finely diced
½ cup finely diced scallions (about 3 scallions)
1 bunch radishes, trimmed and finely diced
1 sweet green pepper, seeded and finely diced
½ pint (about 10 to 12) cherry tomatoes
½ cup finely chopped Italian flat-leaf parsley

YIELD
6 servings
PREP
Marinate 1 hour

Dressing:

6 tablespoons rice vinegar
2 to 3 tablespoons Hellmann's Mayonnaise or Angie's Mayonnaise (page 121)

1. In a large salad bowl, combine the vegetables.

2. In a small cup, whisk together the vinegar and mayonnaise until smooth. Pour the dressing over the slaw and mix thoroughly.

3. Marinate, covered, 1 hour in the refrigerator. Serve chilled or at room temperature.

CASSEROLES

▼▼▼

Most good cooks agree that making a casserole a day before improves the flavors. For entertaining, casseroles can be made even further ahead and then frozen. Defrost the casserole slowly the night before serving, and reheat just as the guests are coming in the door.

The less expensive "peasant" casseroles encourage us to reach out more often to friends and neighbors for easy, casual entertaining and for community projects when we need to feed a crowd. Other casseroles are great for special occasions or small parties. And remember to save a portion or two to freeze in plastic freezer bags, so you can have a favorite casserole any night for an impromptu feast.

Enjoy these casseroles often, whether as part of a theme party, or served simply with a first course, salad, bread, and a light dessert, or as part of a large buffet. And bring them to the table in your handsomest china, enamel, or pottery casserole.

Casseroles

▼▼▼

VEGETABLE COUSCOUS

▲▲▲

This is one of the dishes I did for a "Feast and Be Fit" series at B. Altman's Department Store in New York. Judy Janney, the director of special events, agreed to have me do four different vegetable entrées as an experiment to see how a general, non-vegetarian audience would react. The response was wonderful. People were agog at how quickly you could cook up huge, rainbow-hued potfuls of gorgeous vegetable concoctions, and in this case, all of them great ethnic dishes: chili, couscous, curry, feijoada.

I prepared them without meat, and I added vegetables not traditionally part of the dish in order to provide extra richness and variety so the meat was not missed. For meat eaters, serve with the Minted Lamb Balls with Pignoli or Persian Chicken Balls (pages 146–147).

2 tablespoons unsalted butter

2 tablespoons olive oil

1 tablespoon ground cumin

1 teaspoon fennel seeds, crushed

¼ teaspoon ground allspice

1 whole dried red pepper or ¼ teaspoon crushed red
    pepper flakes

3 cloves garlic, finely chopped

3 carrots, trimmed, peeled, halved lengthwise, and cut crosswise into
    ½-inch-thick slices

1 whole white turnip, peeled and sliced into ½-inch-thick rounds

½ pound green beans, trimmed and halved

3 new or red potatoes, unpeeled and cut into ½-inch-thick slices

1 sweet red pepper, seeded and cut lengthwise into ½-inch-wide slices

1 sweet green pepper, seeded and cut lengthwise into ½-inch-wide slices

1 large yellow onion, cut into ½-inch-thick slices

1 zucchini, cut lengthwise into thirds and then crosswise into ½-inch-thick
    slices

1 yellow squash, cut lengthwise into thirds and then crosswise into
    ½-inch-thick slices

2 cups All-Vegetable Soup Stock (page 139), heated

1 tomato, peeled and quartered

1 can (10 ounces) chick-peas, drained and thoroughly rinsed

Garnish: 1 navel orange, sliced into thin rounds

Couscous (page 218)

YIELD
6 to 8 servings

1. In a large casserole or kettle over medium heat, heat the butter and oil. Add the four spices and cook over low heat 1 minute. Add the garlic and sauté, about 2 minutes.

2. Add the carrots, turnip, green beans, and potatoes. Cover and cook over medium heat, stirring occasionally, about 10 minutes.

3. Add the sweet peppers and onion and cook, partially covered, 5 minutes.

4. Add the zucchini and yel-low squash and cook, partially covered, 5 minutes.

5. Add the stock, tomato, and chick-peas and cook 5 minutes.

6. Transfer the vegetables to a large serving bowl.

7. Remove the dried red pepper.

8. Garnish the vegetables with the orange slices. Serve hot with couscous.

CHICKEN AND LAMB COUSCOUS

▲▲▲

This casserole works perfectly for a Middle Eastern buffet. One of the prettiest ways I've seen to serve couscous was pictured in the volume *A Quartet of Cuisines* from the Time-Life series *Foods of the World*. A Moroccan woman stands in her court-yard, holds a huge serving tray, at least 30 inches in diameter, with the couscous, big meaty breasts of chicken, pumpkin, and large whole peppers. When you make these peasant dishes, garnish abundantly with whole Italian peppers, hard-cooked egg halves, circles of corn on the cob, and orange slices. It's a show stopper every time.

YIELD
6 servings

2 whole chicken breasts, rinsed, skinned (bone intact), and patted dry

1 pound lamb shoulder, rinsed, patted dry, fat trimmed, and cut into 1-inch cubes

2 teaspoons ground cumin

3 tablespoons Clarified Butter (page 131) or 2 tablespoons unsalted butter and 1 tablespoon bacon fat

2 cups Chicken Stock (page 138) or canned chicken broth

1 cup canned whole tomatoes, drained and squeezed by hand

3 carrots, trimmed, peeled, and cut diagonally into 1½-inch-thick pieces

2 medium-size white turnips, peeled and cut into small cubes

1 tablespoon arrowroot, softened in ½ cup warm water, or kuzu (page 293) (optional)

1 whole dried red pepper

2 medium-size yellow onions, peeled and sliced lengthwise into ½-inch-thick pieces

4 small zucchini, trimmed and cut diagonally into 1-inch-thick pieces

1 can (10 ounces) chick-peas, drained and thoroughly rinsed

Couscous (page 218)

Garnish: 4 hard-cooked eggs, halved; 2 whole green Italian peppers; 1 ear corn on the cob, cut into 1-inch-thick circles; and orange slices

1. Place the chicken and lamb in a bowl and rub with the cumin.

2. In a large casserole or kettle over medium heat, melt the butter.

Add the chicken and the lamb in batches and sauté until the chicken and lamb are a burnished brown, about 10 minutes. Remove batches as they brown to a platter.

3. Return the browned lamb to the casserole. Add the chicken stock, tomatoes, carrots, and turnips. Cook, partially covered, 15 minutes. At this point add the arrowroot if you wish a thicker sauce.

4. Remove the chicken from the bone in long strips and return it to the casserole. Reduce heat to a simmer and cook about 15 minutes.

5. Add the whole red pepper and onions and cook about 10 minutes.

6. Add the zucchini and cook about 5 minutes.

7. Add the chick-peas and cook 2 minutes.

8. Transfer to a large serving dish.

9. Serve with couscous. Garnish with eggs, green Italian peppers, corn, and orange slices.

BACALHAU À GOMES DE SÁ

▲▲▲

This classic Portuguese dish is one my brother-in-law served often. The combination of colors—black, red, white, and yellow—and the strong flavors of the olive oil, garlic, and smoked cod are irresistible. Portuguese cuisine is not as familiar to us as some of the other cuisines of Europe, and this dish is a good introduction to its many pleasures.

¾ pound dried salted cod, soaked in water to cover
    overnight (You should change the soaking water twice.)
¾ cup olive oil
3 small cloves garlic, finely chopped
4 medium-size potatoes, boiled or steamed
    and cut into ½-inch-thick slices
2 large yellow onions, peeled and cut into ½-inch-thick slices
½ cup dry vermouth or dry white wine
Freshly ground black pepper, to taste
Garnish: 4 hard-cooked eggs, quartered and dusted with paprika; 18 pitted
    Greek or Italian olives (see Marinated Olives, page 152); ½ cup
    chopped Italian flat-leaf parsley

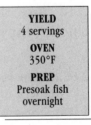

YIELD
4 servings

OVEN
350°F

PREP
Presoak fish
overnight

1. Place the drained, soaked cod in a bowl under cold tap water and keep it running over the cod for 15 minutes. Drain, pat dry with paper toweling, and cut into bite-size pieces.

2. In a medium-size skillet over medium heat, heat ¼ cup of the olive oil. Add the garlic and sauté until translucent, about 2 to 3 minutes.

3. In a 1½-quart baking dish or casserole, make a layer of half the ingredients as follows: potatoes, cod, and onions with half of the remaining oil and wine spooned over. Repeat the procedure with another layer.

4. Sprinkle the top with freshly ground black pepper.

5. Bake the casserole, uncovered, in the preheated 350°F oven for 20 minutes.

6. Raise the heat to 500°F and bake 5 minutes longer or until browned.

7. Remove from the oven and transfer to a platter.

8. Garnish the casserole with eggs, olives, and parsley and serve immediately. Or cool and refrigerate, covered.

MADELEINE BOULANGER'S CHICKEN WITH APPLES AND PEACHES

▲▲▲

This is a quick-cooking curry to have for every day or for as big a party as you like. It freezes well, either the sauce alone or with the shrimp or chicken, but add the apples at the last minute. Sautéing the chicken first in the butter and cumin adds flavor. And after the initial browning, it's not necessary to cook the chicken for a long time—otherwise it will toughen.

2 whole chicken breasts, split, rinsed, skinned (bones intact), and patted dry
1 teaspoon ground cumin
1 tablespoon Clarified Butter (page 131) or 1 tablespoon bacon fat
½ teaspoon mustard seeds
1 tablespoon curry powder
1½ cups Chicken Stock (page 138) or 1 can (13 ounces) chicken broth
¼ cup canned whole tomatoes, drained (not in purée)

YIELD
4 to 6 servings

1 tablespoon arrowroot, softened in ½ cup warm water, or kuzu (page 293) (optional)
1 cup coarsely chopped yellow onion
½ cup golden raisins
½ cup dried peaches or apricots
1 medium-size Golden Delicious apple, cored and cut into ¼-inch-thick slices (about 1 cup)

---

1. Rub the chicken with cumin.

2. In a large casserole or kettle over medium heat, melt the butter. Add the chicken, increase the heat to high, and sauté quickly on both sides until a burnished brown, about 5 minutes per side.

3. Remove the chicken from the pan to a plate.

4. Add the mustard seeds and sauté 1 minute. Add the curry powder and sauté about 3 minutes.

5. Add the chicken stock and tomatoes and cook until the liquid is reduced by one third, about 15 minutes. At this point add the arrowroot or kuzu if you wish a thicker sauce. Return the chicken to the casserole.

6. Reduce the heat to simmer and cook about 15 minutes. Add the onion and cook another 10 minutes.

7. Add the raisins and peaches and cook 5 minutes.

8. Remove the casserole from the stove.

9. Remove the chicken breasts with a slotted spoon to a cutting board. Remove the chicken from the bones in long strips. Return the meat to the casserole. Add the apple and heat through.

10. Transfer the curry to a serving dish and serve immediately.

For Shrimp Curry

Substitute for the chicken 1 pound shrimp, peeled, deveined, rinsed, and patted dry. Follow the directions exactly as for the chicken except sauté the shrimp only until it turns pink, about 2 to 3 minutes. Remove the shrimp and proceed with the recipe. Return the shrimp only 1 or 2 minutes before serving so they do not toughen.

KUZU

Kuzu, an extract from the root of the kuzu vine, often called the "Japanese cousin of arrowroot," is milder in flavor than cornstarch. Kuzu has no aftertaste, is low in sodium and high in iron. It is available in health-food and Japanese stores. Mix 1 tablespoon of kuzu powder with ½ cup to 1 cup liquid. Add the dissolved kuzu to the casserole, soup, or other liquid you want to thicken. Begin with a little and add more to reach the desired thickness.

Freeze-Aheads

▼▼▼

Cooking casseroles ahead is one way of streamlining time in the kitchen. The casseroles in this section can be cooked ahead, then frozen right in their covered casseroles or in portions in airtight freezer containers.

For freezing, undercook the vegetables, meat, fish, or chicken by about ten minutes so reheating won't overcook them.

Thaw casseroles overnight in the refrigerator before reheating in a slow oven or over low heat.

PICADILLO

▲▲▲

I learned how to make this popular Cuban and Mexican dish from Elizabeth DeUnda, my first catering teacher.

——

YIELD
6 servings

3 teaspoons corn oil
1½ pounds lean ground beef
2 tablespoons unsalted butter
1 tablespoon ground cumin
1 tablespoon dried oregano
1 medium-size sweet red pepper, seeded and cut
    lengthwise into 1-inch-wide strips
1 medium-size sweet green pepper, seeded and cut lengthwise into 1-inch-
    wide strips
1 medium-size yellow onion, coarsely chopped
2 medium-size cloves garlic, finely chopped
1 can (16 ounces) whole peeled tomatoes, coarsely chopped and liquid
    reserved
1 tablespoon rice vinegar
1 can (16 ounces) kidney beans, drained and thoroughly rinsed
1 cup medium-size pimiento-stuffed olives, drained and thoroughly rinsed
¾ cup golden raisins

2 tablespoons capers, drained and thoroughly rinsed
Salt and freshly ground black pepper, to taste

1. In a large casserole or kettle over medium heat, heat 1 teaspoon of the oil. Add the meat, broken into small pieces, and brown quickly, stirring constantly, about 5 minutes. Meat will release liquid and excess fat.

2. Remove the meat to a strainer and drain the liquid from the meat. Reserve the meat. Wash the casserole. Return the casserole to the stove over medium heat.

3. Add the remaining oil, butter, cumin, and oregano and sauté 1 minute. Stir in the peppers, onion, and garlic and cook until translucent, about 5 minutes.

4. Stir in the meat and the tomatoes with their liquid and mix thoroughly.

5. Add the vinegar, kidney beans, olives, raisins, capers, and salt and pepper. Reduce the heat and simmer 20 to 25 minutes.

6. Transfer to a serving platter. Serve immediately. Or cool in the casserole (you may freeze at this point) and refrigerate, covered.

Variation: Chickadillo

Substitute 1 pound boneless, skinned chicken breasts, cubed (about 30 to 32 pieces), for the beef and 1 can (16 ounces) chickpeas for the kidney beans.

1. In a large saucepan over medium heat, heat 1 tablespoon of the butter. Add the tablespoon cumin and sauté 1 minute. Add the garlic and cook until translucent, about 3 minutes.

2. Add the chicken and sauté 4 to 5 minutes, until it is pink inside. Remove the chicken and reserve. Wash the casserole. Return the casserole to the stove over medium heat.

3. Add the oil and oregano and sauté 1 minute. Stir in the peppers, onion, and garlic and cook until translucent, about 5 minutes.

4. Add the tomatoes with their liquid, the vinegar, olives, raisins, capers, and salt and pepper to taste. Reduce the heat and simmer about 20 to 25 minutes.

5. Return the chicken for the last 4 to 5 minutes of cooking time. Then add the drained chick-peas. Gently heat until heated through.

6. Serve at once. Or let cool in the casserole (you may freeze at this point) and refrigerate, covered.

MITZ PERLMAN'S CHICKEN DINNER IN A POT

▲▲▲

Mitz Perlman says, "I cook this ahead in the morning in my electric frying pan. Just before serving I transfer it to my Dansk casserole dish, reheat it, and serve it at the table. A green salad and bagel chips go with it, and for dessert, depending on the company, fresh fruit or a fruit pie."

1 tablespoon unsalted butter
2 tablespoons corn oil
2 large new or red potatoes, scrubbed, unpeeled, and cut into sixths
1 broiler chicken (2½ to 3 pounds), quartered, legs and thighs cut apart, rinsed, skinned, fat removed, and patted dry
1 cup dry sherry or dry vermouth
1 cup Chicken Stock (page 138) or canned chicken broth
1 large sweet green pepper, seeded, cut lengthwise into ½-inch-wide strips, and then in half
1 large sweet red pepper, seeded, cut lengthwise into ½-inch-wide strips, and then in half
2 medium-size yellow onions, peeled and sliced lengthwise in half
1 whole tomato, peeled and quartered
1 jar (6½ ounces) marinated artichoke hearts, drained and thoroughly rinsed
Salt and freshly ground black pepper, to taste

YIELD
4 servings

1. In a large casserole or kettle over medium heat, heat the butter and oil. Add the potatoes and sauté until golden brown, about 5 minutes. Remove and reserve them.

2. Add the chicken in batches and sauté about 10 minutes on each side or until browned. Return the chicken and potatoes to the casserole.

3. Add the sherry or vermouth, the stock, peppers, and onions. Cook over medium heat, partially covered, for about 30 minutes or until the chicken is no longer pink near the bone and the vegetables are crisp-tender. Stir frequently so the chicken and vegetables cook evenly.

4. Add the tomato and arti-

chokes. Cook another 10 minutes.

5. Season with salt and pepper. Transfer to a serving platter and serve immediately. Or cool in the casserole (you may freeze at this point) and refrigerate, covered.

JEFF'S CASSOULET

▲▲▲

This quickly made cassoulet freezes beautifully. The traditional version features duck, sausage, and pork. Here we've replaced these fatty meats with chicken, other beans, and vegetables.

YIELD
4 to 6 servings

¼ pound lean bacon slices

4 tablespoons (½ stick) unsalted butter

2 large onions, finely chopped

2 medium-size leeks, thoroughly rinsed and cut into 1-inch-thick pieces

2 cloves garlic, finely chopped

2 whole chicken breasts (about 1 pound each), bones intact, rinsed, skinned, and patted dry

2 medium-size carrots, peeled and cut into 1-inch-thick slices

1 can (16 ounces) kidney beans, drained and thoroughly rinsed

1 can (16 ounces) pinto beans, drained and thoroughly rinsed

1 can (16 ounces) small white beans, drained and thoroughly rinsed

1 can (16 ounces) black-eyed peas, drained and thoroughly rinsed

1 tablespoon chili sauce or 1 tablespoon tomato paste

1 tablespoon dried leaf thyme

2 cups canned beef stock

2 medium-size yellow squash, trimmed and cut into ½-inch-thick slices

1. In a large skillet over medium heat, cook the bacon until crisp. With a slotted spoon, remove the bacon to paper toweling to absorb excess fat. Cool and finely chop the bacon. Pour off the bacon fat, reserving 1 tablespoon in the skillet.

2. Melt 2 tablespoons of the butter in the skillet over medium heat. Add the onions, leeks, and garlic and sauté until translucent, about 5 to 7 minutes. With a slotted spoon, remove the cooked vegetables and set aside.

3. Heat the remaining 2 table-

spoons butter and the 1 tablespoon bacon fat in the skillet and sauté the chicken breasts, about 5 minutes on each side, until nicely browned.

4. In a large 6-quart casserole, combine the sautéed chicken with the butter and bacon fat along with the cooked vegetables, carrots, beans, chili sauce, and thyme.

5. Add the beef stock, and over medium-high heat bring to a boil. Reduce the heat to a simmer

and cook about 20 minutes. Add the yellow squash and cook 5 minutes longer. Remove the casserole from the heat.

6. With a slotted spoon, transfer the chicken breasts to a cutting board and bone the chicken in strips and return it to the casserole.

7. Garnish the casserole with the bacon. Serve hot. Or cool (you may freeze at this point) and refrigerate, covered.

LAMB NAVARIN

▲▲▲

Make this stew in the early spring with the first small tender vegetables (the *printanier*, the French call them).

1½ pounds boned lamb shoulder, fat trimmed and cut into 1½-inch cubes

1 tablespoon unbleached all-purpose flour for coating

¼ teaspoon each salt and freshly ground pepper or to taste

2 tablespoons corn oil

2 cans (13 ounces each) beef broth

6 small unpeeled new or red potatoes, halved

6 small peeled white onions or 1 package (10 ounces) frozen small onions, thawed

1 medium-size carrot, trimmed, peeled, and sliced diagonally into ½-inch-thick slices

1 teaspoon dried leaf thyme

2 tablespoons unsalted butter

1 pound mushrooms, wiped clean with damp paper toweling and thickly sliced

1 package (10 ounces) frozen peas, thawed

Garnish: chopped parsley

YIELD
6 servings

1. Lightly dust the lamb with the flour, salt, and pepper.

2. In a large casserole or kettle over medium heat, heat the oil. Add the lamb in batches and brown on all sides, about 5 minutes, removing the meat to a plate as it is done. Do not overcrowd the casserole.

3. Return the meat to the casserole.

4. In a medium-size saucepan over high heat, bring the broth to a boil. Pour it over the browned meat.

5. Bring the meat and liquid to a boil. Cover, reduce the heat, and simmer slowly for 1 to 1¼ hours or until almost tender.

6. Add the potatoes, onions, carrots, and thyme. Simmer, covered, 10 minutes more or until the vegetables are tender.

7. In a skillet over high heat, melt the butter. Add the mushrooms and quickly sauté until brown.

8. Add the mushrooms and the peas to the meat mixture. Gently heat through until just heated.

9. Serve in the casserole or transfer to a serving bowl. Garnish with chopped parsley. Or cool in the casserole (you may freeze at this point) and refrigerate, covered.

BELLE MEYERS' TSIMMES

▲▲▲

When Belle Meyers and her husband served this tsimmes at their annual party, it was the first dish that disappeared. This recipe makes enough for a friendly occasion and some portions for the freezer.

YIELD
6 to 8 servings

OVEN
375°F

3 teaspoons salt (or less, if desired)
½ teaspoon freshly ground black pepper
3 pounds lean short ribs (breast flanken), rinsed and
    patted dry
2 tablespoons corn oil
2 medium-size yellow onions, coarsely chopped
2 tablespoons unbleached all-purpose flour
3 cups boiling water
8 carrots, peeled and cut into eighths
3 medium-size sweet potatoes, peeled and cut into eighths
⅓ cup honey
1 cup pitted prunes

1. Combine 2 teaspoons of the salt and the pepper and rub into the meat.

2. In a large ovenproof casserole or kettle over medium heat, heat 1 tablespoon of the oil. Add the meat in batches and brown on all sides, removing the meat as it is done to a dish. Do not overcrowd the casserole.

3. Add the remaining tablespoon of oil to the casserole, and over medium heat sauté the onions, about 5 minutes. Remove the onions from the casserole and add to the meat.

4. Remove the casserole from the heat and stir in the flour until smooth. Gradually stir in the boiling water and continue to stir until the mixture is smooth. Add the remaining teaspoon of salt. Return the meat and onions to the casserole and bring the mixture to a boil over high heat. Reduce the heat to a simmer, cover, and cook 1 hour.

5. Add the carrots, sweet potatoes, honey, and prunes.

6. Bake, covered, in the preheated 375°F oven for 1½ to 1¾ hours or until the beef and vegetables are fork tender. Remove the lid during the last 15 minutes.

7. Transfer the meat and vegetables to a serving platter. Spoon the juices over the meat and serve immediately. Or cool in the casserole (you may freeze at this point) and refrigerate, covered.

VEGETABLE CHILI

▲▲▲

For many years The Party Box prepared soups and casserole entrées for the Guggenheim Museum Cafe. They asked us to come up with a vegetable chili for an increasing number of patrons interested in meat alternatives. All the vegetables in this chili remain crisp-tender, and served hot or cold, it's likely to become one of your standbys.

1 tablespoon unsalted butter
1 tablespoon oil
1 tablespoon chili powder
1 tablespoon ground cumin
1 teaspoon dried oregano
3 medium-size cloves garlic, finely chopped
5 carrots, peeled and cut diagonally into 1-inch-thick pieces

YIELD
6 servings

5 celery stalks, stringed and cut diagonally into 1-inch-thick pieces

4 ounces green beans, trimmed and halved

1 large sweet red pepper, seeded, cut lengthwise into ½-inch-wide slices, and then halved

1 large sweet green pepper, seeded, cut lengthwise into ½-inch-wide slices, and then halved

2 medium-size yellow onions, peeled and cut lengthwise into ½-inch-thick slices

1 can (16 ounces) whole tomatoes, coarsely chopped and liquid reserved

1 medium-size zucchini, trimmed and cut diagonally into ½-inch-thick slices

1 medium-size yellow squash, trimmed and cut diagonally into ½-inch-thick slices

1 can (16 ounces) kidney beans, drained and thoroughly rinsed, or 2 cups cooked kidney beans (page 223)

1 can (8 ounces) wax beans, drained and thoroughly rinsed

---

1. In a casserole or kettle over medium heat, heat the butter and oil. Add the seasonings and sauté 1 minute. Then add the garlic and sauté 2 to 3 minutes, stirring with a wooden spoon.

2. Add the carrots, celery, and green beans. Reduce the heat to a simmer and cook, covered, about 10 minutes.

3. Add the peppers, onions, and 1 cup of the tomatoes and cook, covered, about 10 minutes.

4. Add the zucchini, yellow squash, and the remaining tomatoes with their liquid and cook, covered, about 5 minutes.

5. Add the kidney beans and wax beans and cook, covered, about 5 minutes.

6. Transfer the chili to a serving platter and serve hot. Or cool in the casserole (you may freeze at this point) and refrigerate, covered.

CHICKEN CHILI

▲▲▲

Since many people are no longer eating red meat, try chicken chili. The trick is not to overcook the chicken when first browning it. The cumin-flavored chicken will quickly absorb flavor from the other seasonings when added to the pot for the final minutes of cooking.

---

1 pound boneless, skinned chicken breasts, rinsed, patted dry, cut into 1-inch cubes (about 30 to 32 pieces), or cut lengthwise into ½-inch-wide strips

YIELD
6 servings

1 tablespoon ground cumin
1 tablespoon unsalted butter
1 tablespoon corn oil
1 clove garlic, finely chopped
1 tablespoon chili powder
1 teaspoon dried oregano
1 large sweet green pepper, seeded, cut lengthwise into ½-inch-wide slices, and then halved
1 large sweet red pepper, seeded, cut lengthwise into ½-inch slices, and then halved
2 medium-size yellow onions, peeled and sliced lengthwise into ½-inch-thick slices
1 can (16 ounces) whole tomatoes, coarsely chopped and liquid reserved
½ cup Chicken Stock (page 138) or canned chicken broth
1 can (16 ounces) kidney beans, drained and thoroughly rinsed
1 can wax beans (8 ounces), drained and thoroughly rinsed
Salt and freshly ground pepper, to taste

---

1. Place the chicken in a large bowl and rub with the cumin.

2. In a large casserole or kettle over medium heat, melt the butter. Add the chicken in batches and sauté, stirring with a wooden spoon, for about 3 to 4 minutes. Remove the chicken and reserve.

3. Wash the casserole, dry, and return to the stove over medium heat. Add the oil, garlic, and seasonings and sauté about 1 minute, stirring frequently to prevent burning.

4. Add the peppers and cook until translucent, about 3 to 4 minutes.

5. Add the onions and cook

until translucent, about 3 to 4 minutes.

6. Add half of the tomatoes and half of the chicken stock and cook another 5 minutes.

7. Add the chicken and the remaining tomatoes and stock and cook, covered, 10 minutes. Stir occasionally.

8. Add the beans and heat 5 minutes or until heated through.

9. Season with salt and pepper to taste. Transfer the chili to a serving dish and serve hot. Or cool in the casserole (you may freeze at this point) and refrigerate, covered.

BLACK BEAN CHILI

▲▲▲

Black Bean Chili can star at a meal when served with an array of colorful accompaniments. Arrange the condiments in separate sections on a platter, with a small bowl of yogurt / sour cream in the center. To keep the fat and cholesterol low, omit the sour cream and the hard-cooked egg yolks.

2 cups black beans, picked over, rinsed, soaked
    overnight, and drained
10 cups water
2 tablespoons plus 1 teaspoon corn oil or safflower oil
1 bay leaf
2 tablespoons unsalted butter
2 teaspoons dried oregano
2 teaspoons ground cumin
2 teaspoons dried leaf thyme
1 whole dried red pepper
2 medium-size cloves garlic, thinly sliced
1 medium-size yellow onion, peeled and cut lengthwise into ½-inch-thick
    slices
Garnish: 2 hard-cooked eggs, halved; 1 avocado, peeled, pitted, and cut into
    ½-inch-thick slices; 3 scallions, trimmed and cut into ½-inch pieces; 1
    medium-size lime, cut into thin slices; 1 medium-size orange, cut into
    thin slices; ½ cup each plain yogurt and sour cream, mixed

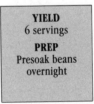

YIELD
6 servings

PREP
Presoak beans
overnight

1. In a very large, wide-bottomed casserole or kettle, place the

beans and cover with the water. Add the 1 teaspoon oil and the bay leaf.

Over medium heat, bring the beans to a boil. Skim off any impurities.

2. In a small saucepan over medium heat, heat 1 tablespoon of the oil and 1 tablespoon butter. Add half of the seasonings and the dried red pepper and sauté 2 minutes. Add the garlic and onion and sauté about 5 to 7 minutes until the onion becomes translucent.

3. Add the onion mixture to the beans. Adjust the heat to a brisk simmer. Cover the beans, leaving the top slightly ajar, and cook about 1 hour or until the beans are tender and soft, but are not broken and still retain their shape. Continue to skim off impurities and stir frequently. The mixture will have reduced by half.

4. In a small saucepan over medium heat, heat the remaining oil and butter. Add the rest of the seasonings and cook 3 to 4 minutes or until translucent. Add to the beans. Cook about 2 minutes. Remove the dried red pepper.

5. Transfer the chili to a serving dish. Serve with the garnishes arranged on a platter. Or cool in the casserole (you may freeze at this point) and refrigerate, covered.

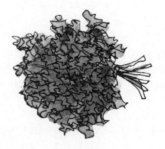

FISH AND SEAFOOD

▼▼▼

With today's rapid transport, we can have fish from around the world almost overnight. And the variety is incredible. Some of the newer fish now available, such as pollock, dogfish, and monkfish, offer bargains in terms of fat, calories, and protein without breaking the bank.

If you grew up like me in a household that decreed Friday night as fish night, you probably have memories of fish cooked to the consistency of tough rubber. We've learned since then to cook it gently, for only a few minutes so that it's moist, tender, and flaky.

Of all the "flesh foods," fish offers the most protein with the least amount of cholesterol and calories. And it's easy to prepare with a minimum amount of fat. There are fish recipes here that use all five of the low-fat cooking techniques—baking, poaching, steaming, low-fat sautéing, and broiling. Fish can also be stuffed or grilled, and served with an infinite variety of delicate or flavorful sauces. It's delicious, too, in salads.

Enjoy fish at almost any point in your meal—as an hors d'oeuvre, an entrée, or a salad. You'll find recipes featuring fish and seafood in other sections of this book.

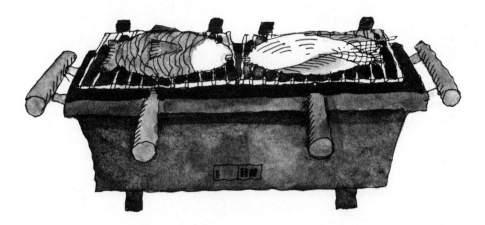

Baked Seafood

▼▼▼

FLAKY BAKED SALMON STEAK

▲▲▲

I use the same parchment-paper procedure for baking fish steaks as I do for baking chicken breasts (page 323). The fish comes out tender, yet firm, delicate, and flaky. And there is no risk of the fish breaking apart as there is when lifting poached fish out of water. The fish can be served hot or cold with a sauce, or used in recipes such as Salmon Quiche (page 309).

1 pound firm fish filet, such as salmon, halibut,
    weakfish, sea bass, or scrod, rinsed and patted
    dry
1 teaspoon corn oil
2 to 3 teaspoons freshly squeezed lemon juice
Freshly ground black pepper, to taste
Garnish: 2 tablespoons finely chopped parsley

YIELD
2 servings

OVEN
375°F

1. Line a baking tray with parchment paper or aluminum foil. Place the fish filet on the tray and brush the filet lightly with the corn oil. Sprinkle the lemon juice over the fish and season with the pepper to taste.

2. Cover the fish lightly with parchment paper or aluminum foil.

3. Bake in the preheated 375°F oven for about 15 minutes or until the fish flakes with a fork.

4. Remove the parchment or foil and transfer the fish to a serving platter.

5. Garnish with chopped parsley and serve. Or cool and reserve for use in other recipes.

MEAL IN A PACKAGE: FISH FILET WITH VEGETABLES

▲▲▲

Package dinners can be cooked in either parchment paper or aluminum foil; parchment is preferable, so do try to purchase it. In this recipe eight ounces of whole boned and skinned chicken breast can be substituted for the fish. It's another delicious, delicate, easy-to-prepare dinner.

½ pound fish filet such as tile, haddock, or scrod, rinsed and patted dry
½ teaspoon olive oil
½-inch-thick slice sweet potato
1-inch-thick slice yellow onion
1-inch-wide slice sweet red pepper
1-inch-thick slice zucchini or summer squash
1-inch-thick slice peeled tomato
1 tablespoon finely chopped fresh dill or thyme or 1 teaspoon dried
2 tablespoons freshly squeezed lime juice
Salt and freshly ground black pepper, to taste

YIELD
1 serving

OVEN
375°F

1. On an 11x15-inch sheet of parchment paper, place the fish. Spread the oil on the fish, then place the remaining ingredients on the fish in the order listed.

2. Fold the parchment in half over the fish and crimp and flatten and pleat the edges together until the package is closed.

3. Place on a baking tray

sprayed with nonstick vegetable cooking spray and bake in the preheated 375°F oven for 30 minutes.

4. Slit the parchment open and transfer the ingredients to a serving dish. Or place the package on a dinner plate and open at the table.

PACIFIC SALMON LOAF

▲▲▲

W hy should loaves always be made with meat? Pacific Salmon Loaf is a delicious and easy way to get more fish into your diet. If you use canned salmon, include the bones for extra calcium. The small diced vegetables add color and crisp texture. This loaf freezes well.

1 large egg plus 1 egg white
½ cup Hellmann's Mayonnaise or Angie's Mayonnaise
    (page 121)
¼ cup sour cream
1 can (15½ ounces) red salmon, drained, thoroughly
    rinsed, skin removed, and bones crushed, or 1
    pound baked fresh salmon steak (page 306), skin removed and boned
½ medium-size carrot, peeled and chopped into very small dice (about
    ½ cup)
1 celery stalk, stringed and finely diced (about ½ cup)
½ sweet red or green pepper, seeded and finely diced (about ½ cup)
1 small scallion, trimmed and finely diced (about ¼ cup)
¼ cup fresh whole-wheat bread crumbs
1 tablespoon freshly squeezed lemon juice
Salt and freshly ground pepper, to taste
Lemon slices

| YIELD |
| 6 to 8 servings |
| **OVEN** |
| 350°F |

1. In a medium-size bowl, beat the egg and egg white lightly. Blend in the mayonnaise and sour cream. Add the salmon, stirring to flake and incorporate.

2. Add the carrot, celery, sweet pepper, scallion, bread crumbs, lemon juice, and salt and pepper, and blend thoroughly.

3. To a 9x5x3-inch loaf pan sprayed with nonstick vegetable cooking spray or lined with parch-

ment paper, add the loaf mixture. Shake the pan so the mixture spreads evenly and bang the pan on the counter to remove air bubbles.

4. Bake in the preheated 350°F oven for 35 to 40 minutes. Remove the loaf and place the lemon slices on top. Return the loaf to the oven for 5 minutes to finish

cooking. The loaf should be firm to the touch.

5. Turn the loaf out onto a cooling rack. Let the loaf cool for about 20 minutes. Remove the parchment paper, slice, and serve at room temperature. Freeze extra slices in individual plastic freezer bags for quick and easy meals.

SALMON QUICHE

▲▲▲

The wonder of this recipe is that the custard mixes so thoroughly with the salmon that the pie becomes very solid. It is not only meaty, but it is the one quiche that travels well and is delicious cold. I always prefer to use fresh salmon.

1 pound fresh salmon steak, rinsed, or 1 can (15½ ounces) red salmon, drained, skin removed, and bones crushed
2 tablespoons unsalted butter
2 scallions, trimmed and cut into ¼-inch slices
4 large eggs plus 1 egg yolk
1 cup heavy cream
Salt and freshly ground black pepper, to taste
4 sprigs snipped fresh dill or 2 teaspoons dried dillweed
1 9-inch Cream Cheese Shell (page 369)

YIELD
6 to 8 servings
OVEN
400°F

1. In a shallow pan, bake the fresh salmon in the preheated 400°F oven for 25 minutes or until it flakes with a fork. (If using canned salmon, omit this and the next step.)

2. Transfer the salmon to a medium-size bowl and cool. Remove the skin and with a fork go

through the salmon to see if there are any bones. Remove them and flake the fish.

3. In a small saucepan over medium heat, melt the butter. Add the scallions and sauté for 3 minutes or until soft. Let cool.

4. In a medium-size mixing bowl, beat the eggs and egg yolk.

Add the cream and beat lightly. Add the cooked scallions, salmon and seasonings. If you are using canned salmon, omit adding any additional salt to the recipe.

5. Pour the mixture into the pie shell. Place the quiche on a baking tray and bake in the preheated 400°F oven for 15 minutes.

6. Reduce the oven temperature to 375°F and bake the quiche an additional 20 minutes or until brown and bubbly. The quiche is done when a knife inserted into the center comes out clean.

7. Cool on a rack for 10 minutes. Cut into wedges and serve at room temperature. Or refrigerate, covered, to serve chilled.

BAKED FISH WITH CAPERS AND ANCHOVY SAUCE

▲▲▲

Here's a way to prepare some of the newer fish such as monkfish, tilefish, weakfish, and dogfish now available to us. The sharp salty taste of the sauce enhances the flavor of the fish, for a delicious entrée low in cost and calories. Serve hot or cold.

1 pound fish filet, rinsed, skinned, and patted dry
2 tablespoons freshly squeezed lemon or lime juice
1 tablespoon drained capers
1 teaspoon anchovy paste
6 tablespoons dry vermouth or dry white wine, or
    balsamic or rice vinegar

> **YIELD**
> 2 servings
>
> **OVEN**
> 375°F

1. Spray a small baking pan with nonstick vegetable cooking spray.

2. Place the fish in the baking pan and sprinkle with the lemon or lime juice.

3. Bake in the preheated 375°F oven for 10 to 15 minutes or until the fish flakes when tested with a fork.

4. In a small bowl, whisk together the capers, anchovy paste, and the wine or vinegar. Transfer to a medium-size pan.

5. Over medium-high heat, bring the sauce to a boil, about 2 minutes. Remove pan from heat.

6. Transfer the fish to a serving plate and pour the sauce over the fish. Serve immediately. Or cool and refrigerate, covered, until ready to serve.

SUSAN DRESNER'S CARIBBEAN ROUGE FISH

▲▲▲

Everything Susan makes is a memorable balance of seasonings and flavors. Serve this dish for a lovely dinner.

1 tablespoon corn or olive oil
1 small yellow onion, finely diced
1 small sweet red pepper, seeded and finely diced
½ cup dry vermouth
½ teaspoon dried leaf thyme
4 whole cloves
2 strips lemon zest, each two inches long, cut into small chunks
1 whole dried red pepper
1 medium-size tomato, peeled and coarsely chopped
1 pound firm fish, such as red snapper, scrod, or tilefish,
    rinsed and patted dry

YIELD
2 servings

OVEN
375°F

1. In a medium-size skillet over medium heat, heat the oil. Add the onion and sweet red pepper and sauté until they become translucent, about 5 minutes.

2. Add the vermouth, seasonings, lemon chunks, dried red pepper, and tomato, and cook until the sauce is reduced by half, about 10 minutes.

3. In a shallow baking dish, place the fish and pour the sauce over the fish.

4. Bake in the preheated 375°F oven for 10 minutes or until the fish flakes when tested with a fork.

5. Transfer to a serving platter. Remove the cloves and dried red pepper. Run a fork through the fish to break it up slightly, and serve. Or serve the fish on individual plates.

Broiled, Sautéed, and Grilled Seafood

▼▼▼

BROILED SCROD WITH CHUNKY PESTO

▲▲▲

This fish entrée goes well with a salad of crisp Green Beans and Red Onion in Lemon Dressing (page 278).

½ pound scrod filet, rinsed and patted dry
1 medium-size lemon, halved
2 teaspoons unsalted butter, softened
2 tablespoons Pesto Sauce Without Cheese (page 247)
Garnish: 1 tablespoon finely chopped fresh basil

YIELD
2 servings
BROILER
Preheat
PREP
Marinate 2 hours

---

1. Place the fish in a shallow dish. Squeeze the juice from the

lemon halves over the fish.
2. In a small bowl, mix to-

gether the butter and the pesto. Pour over the fish.

3. Marinate, covered, 2 hours in the refrigerator.

4. In a shallow flameproof baking dish, place the fish and the marinade and broil 6 inches from the flame for 10 minutes or until the fish flakes when tested with a fork.

5. Transfer to a serving platter and garnish with basil. Serve hot.

BARBARA GROGAN'S "UNDER-THE-BROILER" GINGERED SHRIMP

▲▲▲

When you want to spoil yourself, fresh shrimp is hard to beat. This dish looks like springtime itself, with the pale green of the fresh limes and the pink of the shrimp. Double the recipe if you want to extend the treat to a friend or mate. Serve with Steamed Chayote (page 202), and rice pilaf or a cold rice salad.

8 large shrimp (about ¼ pound), shelled, leaving tails on, deveined, and rinsed
1 teaspoon olive oil
1 teaspoon dry vermouth
1 medium-size lime, halved
2 teaspoons shredded and finely chopped fresh gingerroot

YIELD
1 serving

BROILER
Preheat

PREP
Marinate 2 hours

1. Place the shrimp in a shallow dish and sprinkle with the olive oil and vermouth.

2. Squeeze half the lime over the shrimp. Cut the remaining half into thin slices and place on the shrimp.

3. Sprinkle the gingerroot over the top of the shrimp.

4. Marinate, covered, 2 hours in the refrigerator.

5. Place the shrimp and marinade in a shallow flameproof baking dish and broil the shrimp 6 inches from the flame 3 minutes on each side.

6. Transfer to a serving platter and serve hot.

GRILLED BLUEFISH WITH CILANTRO

▲▲▲

In late August and early September the "blues" are running in such large schools off Montauk Point that they almost jump into the fishing boats. The best way to enjoy bluefish, or any other fish, is to buy it at dockside, where it's cleaned and handed to you by the fishermen.

The sesame marinade is a strong complement for the fish. Cilantro or Chinese parsley has become the darling of the new wave of young chefs, but like most things it has been around for a long time and is found in a number of cuisines: Chinese, Mexican, Indian, Pan-Asian.

If you are catching or buying your fish where you are planning to hold your late summer picnic, bring the marinade in a container along with you, and marinate the fish while the coals are reaching just the right stage to grill the fish.

———

1 whole, cleaned bluefish (about 5 to 6 pounds) or 3 pounds filet of bluefish, rinsed and patted dry
1 cup freshly squeezed lime juice (about 12 medium-size limes)
½ cup tamari or good-quality soy sauce
4 teaspoons grated peeled fresh gingerroot
1 teaspoon salt
½ cup cold-press sesame oil
1 cup cilantro leaves, fresh snipped dill, or Italian flat-leaf parsley
2 large limes, thinly sliced

| **YIELD** |
| 6 servings |
| **GRILL** |
| Prepare coals |
| **PREP** |
| Marinate 1 to 2 hours |

———

1. In a shallow dish or a large plastic bag, arrange the fish.

2. In a medium-size bowl, combine the lime juice, tamari, gingerroot, salt, and sesame oil.

3. Pour the marinade over the fish and marinate, covered, 2 hours in the refrigerator. If marinating outdoors, place the fish in a plastic bag, pour the marinade over the fish, and close the bag. Scatter ice over the plastic-covered fish and marinate 1 hour.

4. Remove the fish from the marinade and sprinkle with herbs. Place the lime slices over the fish.

5. Enclose the fish securely in aluminum foil and seal and pleat the edges closed.

6. Grill the whole fish about 30 to 40 minutes or until the fish flakes when tested with a fork; the filets will take less time.

7. Serve immediately.

GRILLED RED SNAPPER WITH FENNEL AND SCALLIONS

▲▲▲

Firm yet delicate fish such as red snapper make wonderful barbecue fare. Marinate the fish ahead. A whole fish stuffed with lovely greens makes a striking presentation.

1 whole, cleaned red snapper (about 5 to 6 pounds) or
   3 pounds filets of any firm fish, rinsed and patted dry
½ cup freshly squeezed lime juice (about 6 medium-
   size limes)
¼ cup tamari or good-quality soy sauce
2 teaspoons grated peeled fresh gingerroot
½ teaspoon salt
1 teaspoon freshly ground black pepper
½ cup cold-press sesame oil
1 fennel bulb, trimmed and cut into 1-inch pieces
10 scallions, trimmed, green parts only, cut into 1-inch pieces

YIELD
6 servings
GRILL
Prepare coals
PREP
Marinate 2 hours

1. In a shallow dish, place the snapper or arrange filets in a single layer.

2. In a medium-size bowl, combine the lime juice, tamari, gingerroot, and salt and pepper with ¼ cup of the sesame oil.

3. Pour the marinade over the fish and marinate, covered, in the refrigerator, for 2 hours.

4. Remove the fish from the marinade. If you are using a whole snapper, stuff the fish with the fennel and scallions. If using filets, scatter the scallions and fennel on each filet. Drizzle the fish with the remaining ¼ cup sesame oil.

5. Enclose the fish securely in an aluminum foil envelope and seal and pleat the edges closed.

6. Grill the whole snapper 30 to 40 minutes or until the fish flakes; the filets will take less time.

7. Serve at once.

SKILLET FISH STEAK ON A BED OF PEPPERS AND ONIONS

▲▲▲

You can substitute chicken for the fish, and you can add other seasonal vegetables for color and variety.

½ pound firm fish filet, such as scrod, cod, salmon,
    halibut, weakfish, or sea bass, rinsed and patted dry
2 tablespoons freshly squeezed lime juice
¼ teaspoon dried leaf thyme
1 teaspoon unsalted butter
1 small yellow onion, finely chopped
½ small sweet green pepper, finely chopped
½ small sweet red pepper, finely chopped
½ tomato, coarsely chopped
2 slices lemon with rind, seeded and coarsely chopped
Garnish: 1 tablespoon coarsely chopped fresh basil or snipped dill

YIELD
2 servings
PREP
Marinate 1 hour

1. In a medium-size glass bowl, place the fish, lime juice, and thyme. Marinate, covered, 1 hour in the refrigerator.

2. In a medium-size skillet over low heat, melt the butter. Add the onion and peppers and sauté until translucent, about 3 minutes.

3. Add the fish. Cover and cook for about 7 minutes or until the fish just begins to flake when tested with a fork.

4. Add the tomato and lemon and cook 2 more minutes.

5. Transfer to a serving platter and garnish with basil. Serve hot.

THAI SHRIMP WITH CASHEWS

▲▲▲

This recipe combines just a half pound of shrimp with nuts, cabbage, carrots, and onions to serve six people. It's good as a light main course with rice and a salad. (The shrimp can be replaced with one large shredded cooked chicken breast.) Use as a filling for small biscuits and it will make at least 20 hors d'oeuvre servings.

½ pound poached shrimp (page 257), finely chopped
1 cup finely chopped yellow onion
1 cup peeled and shredded carrots
1 cup finely chopped Chinese or regular cabbage
¼ cup finely chopped cashews
2 teaspoons corn oil
1 teaspoon Oriental sesame oil
1 teaspoon curry powder
½ teaspoon ground cumin
Salt and freshly ground pepper, to taste

YIELD
6 servings

1. In a medium-size bowl, combine the shrimp, onion, carrots, cabbage, and cashews.

2. In a large saucepan over medium heat, heat the oils. Add seasonings and sauté 1 minute, stirring.

3. Add the shrimp mixture and sauté until heated through, about 5 minutes.

4. Transfer to a serving platter and serve hot. Or refrigerate, covered, and serve cool.

Poached and Steamed Seafood

▼▼▼

LEMON-SWEET STEAMED SCROD

▲▲▲

S teaming is an excellent cooking technique for keeping fish moist. Serve this with any of the pasta sauces.

½ pound scrod filet, rinsed and patted dry
2 tablespoons freshly squeezed lemon juice
2 teaspoons finely chopped cilantro or parsley
2 teaspoons finely chopped scallion, green part only
Salt and freshly ground black pepper, to taste
2 cups water

YIELD
2 servings

PREP
Marinate 1 hour

1. In a small stainless steel bowl, combine the scrod, lemon juice, cilantro, scallion, and salt and pepper. Marinate, covered, 1 hour in the refrigerator.

2. Place the scrod in a bam-

boo or stainless steel steamer.

3. Into a large wok or 6-quart saucepan, pour 2 cups of water and bring to a boil. Place the steamer, covered, over the boiling water and steam for about 10 minutes or until the fish flakes when tested with a fork. Remove the steamer.

4. Carefully lift the fish onto a platter and serve at once.

STEAMED SCALLOPS WITH SHADES OF JADE VEGETABLES

▲▲▲

Try preparing a one-dish meal in a Chinese bamboo steamer. Place all the ingredients on a plate inside the steamer.

½ pound bay scallops, rinsed and patted dry
2 tablespoons freshly squeezed lime juice
1 tablespoon rice vinegar or balsamic vinegar
4 dashes Tabasco sauce
3 scallions, trimmed and coarsely chopped
1 cup broccoli flowerets
½ cup ½-inch-thick slices yellow squash
½ cup ½-inch-thick slices zucchini
8 snow pea pods, stringed and cut into thirds
1 lemon, halved
2 cups water

YIELD
2 servings

PREP
Marinate 1 hour

1. In a small stainless steel bowl, place the scallops and sprinkle with the lime juice, vinegar, and Tabasco. Add the scallions and mix well. Marinate, covered, 1 hour in the refrigerator.

2. Place a glass or pottery plate in a bamboo steamer. Arrange the broccoli, squash, zucchini, and pea pods on the plate and top them with the scallops.

3. Squeeze half the lemon over the ingredients and then slice the remaining half into thin slices and place them on top of the ingredients.

4. Into a large wok or 6-quart saucepan, pour the 2 cups water and bring to a boil. Place the steamer, covered, over the boiling water and steam for about 10 minutes.

5. Remove the steamer from the stove and bring to the table, or remove the plate from the steamer and serve.

POACHED FILET OF SOLE WITH FRESH MUSHROOMS

▲▲▲

Sole (and flounder, which you can also use) is a light, lean, and delicately flavored fish that is an ideal form of animal protein—low in fat and calories. Cook at least a pound and a half at a time, about eight thick slices, so you can serve it twice (Mousse of Sole, page 155). You may add a teaspoon of arrowroot or kuzu for a slightly thickened sauce. Poach the fish lightly so that it is still firm, yet tender, and you have a most elegant entrée.

1½ pounds sole or flounder filet, rinsed and patted
    dry
Water to cover
½ cup dry white wine or dry vermouth
1 teaspoon arrowroot or kuzu (page 293) (optional)
½ cup water
8 mushrooms, sliced lengthwise into ½-inch-thick slices
2 tablespoons freshly squeezed lemon juice
Garnish: ½ lemon, thinly sliced, and 1 tablespoon chopped fresh parsley

YIELD
4 to 6 servings

1. In a large skillet, arrange the fish filets and cover them with water. Add the wine. Over medium heat, bring the liquid to a simmer and simmer for 5 minutes.

2. For a slightly thickened sauce, combine the arrowroot or kuzu in a 1-cup measuring cup with the ½ cup water. Mix thoroughly and add to the skillet and simmer for 3 more minutes.

3. Add the sliced mushrooms and lemon juice and simmer for another 3 minutes.

4. Remove from heat. With a slotted spatula, carefully lift the fish filets and mushrooms out of the pan and transfer to a serving platter.

5. Garnish with lemon slices and parsley. Or cool extra fish and refrigerate, covered, for later use.

POULTRY

▼▼▼

There's no meat quite as versatile as chicken, and here I've included all the best ways I know to prepare it. I almost always remove the skin first; that removes virtually all the fat. I don't ever use the ready-prepared chicken nuggets; they have cut-up fat mixed in. Nor will you find here any chicken dishes with heavy cream sauces. All the recipes in this book are low in fat and rich in flavor, and they include chicken for the barbecue, chicken in casseroles and pasta salads, and chicken steeped in marinades that totally transform the basic chicken and transport you around the world, from Mexico to Morocco to China.

I never buy a chicken or chicken breast and freeze it raw. I prefer to marinate or cook it first, then freeze it to have it on hand for heating up or to use as an ingredient in another dish.

Serve chicken as one component among several others from the vegetable kingdom, bearing in mind that we need only small amounts of animal protein daily.

The Versatile Chicken

▼▼▼

POACHED CHICKEN BREASTS

▲▲▲

I prefer to poach chicken breasts on the bone because it gives a better texture to the chicken. A one-pound whole breast yields eight ounces boned cooked chicken. If poaching boneless skinned chicken breasts, the yield will be almost exactly the same as the raw.

2½ cups water
1 tablespoon freshly squeezed lemon juice
4 whole white or green peppercorns, slightly crushed
1 bay leaf
2 whole chicken breasts (1 pound each), on the bone,
    skinned, rinsed, patted dry, and split, or 2
    boneless, skinned chicken breasts (1 pound), rinsed and patted dry

YIELD
1 pound boned
chicken

1. In a medium-size skillet over medium-high heat, bring the water to a boil with the lemon juice, peppercorns, and bay leaf.

2. Add the chicken breasts and reduce the heat so that the water is just below boiling and poach the chicken 8 to 10 minutes on the bone, 6 to 8 minutes if boneless. To test for doneness, lift the breast from the poaching liquid and prick with a fork. If the juices run clear, the chicken is done.

3. Remove the chicken from the skillet and cool. Discard the skin and bones if using whole breasts. The chicken breasts are ready to serve or use in recipes.

FORK-TENDER BAKED CHICKEN BREASTS

▲▲▲

Baking chicken breasts in parchment paper makes them absolutely tender, firm, succulent, and pure white, an important point when using them in dressy entrée chicken salads. Once you've tried baking chicken this way, you may prefer it to poaching, as I do.

—

2 whole chicken breasts (1 pound each), on the bone with skin, thoroughly rinsed, patted dry, and split, or 2 boneless, skinned chicken breasts (1 pound), rinsed and patted dry
1 teaspoon corn oil
2 teaspoons freshly squeezed lemon juice
Salt and freshly ground white pepper, to taste

YIELD
1 pound boned chicken

OVEN
325°F

—

1. Cover the bottom of an 8-inch-round or -square baking pan with a piece of parchment paper.

2. Arrange the chicken in one layer in the lined pan.

3. Rub the chicken with the oil and sprinkle with the lemon juice, and salt and pepper.

4. Cover the chicken with a second sheet of parchment paper.

5. Bake the chicken in the preheated 325°F oven about 20 to 25 minutes for breasts on the bone, 15 minutes for boneless breasts. The chicken is done if the juice runs clear when pricked with a fork.

6. Remove the chicken from the oven and serve. Or cool, and bone whole breasts for use in other recipes.

CHICKEN TACOS WITH SALSA

▲▲▲

When you're having vegetable chili as an entrée—which I hope you'll serve often at parties—try chicken with it, prepared this way. This recipe serves ten with just a few chicken breasts, and has that favorable carbohydrate-to-protein ratio of two-thirds to one-third. And the breasts are skinned, which eliminates most of the fat.

Letting guests assemble their own tacos with an assortment of vegetables and cheeses, and homemade salsa is great fun.

I remember one salsa that was so hot I could taste nothing for the rest of the meal. This salsa enhances the flavor of the dish, rather than overpowers it.

Serve the tacos in a napkin-lined basket and the salsa in a glass or earthenware bowl.

―――

Salsa:

YIELD
20 tacos

2 large tomatoes, peeled and coarsely chopped
½ cup finely chopped parsley
3 cloves garlic, finely chopped
2 medium-size sweet green peppers, seeded and
    finely chopped
3 tablespoons corn oil
1 small canned mild green chile, seeded and finely chopped
2 canned jalapeño peppers, seeded and finely chopped

Fillings:

2 zucchini, trimmed
2 summer squash, trimmed
1 pound Cheddar, Monterey Jack, or Colby cheese
1½ pounds poached chicken breasts (page 322), cut into ¼-inch strips
1 bunch scallions, trimmed and cut into 2-inch lengths
2 avocados, pitted, peeled, and sliced lengthwise into ½-inch-thick slices
1 medium-size head iceberg lettuce, finely shredded
2 medium-size sweet green peppers, seeded and cut lengthwise into ¼-inch-
    wide strips

20 taco shells
Garnish: ½ cup finely chopped parsley

1. Combine all the salsa ingredients in a small bowl. It is a thick, chunky salsa. Set aside.

2. In separate batches in a food processor fitted with the shredder disk, grate the zucchini, summer squash, and the cheese. Wash the processor between batches.

3. Place the chicken in a mound at the center of a platter. Arrange the other ingredients in sections around the chicken: zucchini, summer squash, cheese, scallions, avocados, lettuce, and sweet green peppers. Place the taco shells in a napkin-lined basket. Garnish the chicken with the parsley. Serve with the salsa and let each guest assemble his or her own taco.

CHICKEN PICCATA

▲▲▲

I first had this chicken dish at my friends Ann and John Erwin's house. Their original recipe called for much more butter. This adaptation can, in fact, be prepared with no butter at all, just lemon juice, wine, and herbs. The butter, of course, does give it a nice glaze and flavor. Veal Piccata can be made in exactly the same way.

1½ teaspoons unsalted butter
2 whole boneless, skinned chicken breasts (about 1 pound), thoroughly rinsed, patted dry, halved, and flattened between 2 pieces of wax paper
¼ cup freshly squeezed lemon juice (about 3 medium-size lemons)
¼ cup dry vermouth or dry white wine
Garnish: finely chopped parsley, cilantro, dill, or chives

YIELD
4 servings

1. In a medium-size skillet over medium-high heat, melt the butter. Add the chicken and sauté for about 3 minutes on each side.

2. Add half the lemon juice and all the vermouth and cover. Steam on high heat for 2 minutes.

3. Add the remaining lemon juice and return to a simmer, uncovered, for 1 minute. Transfer the chicken to a small heated platter.

4. Garnish and serve.

CHICKEN ACHIOTE

▲▲▲

The marinade for this grilled chicken is similar to that used in Chicken Madrid. Achiote, or annatto, a seed available in the Spanish food section of many markets, gives this dish its beautiful golden red color and delicate flavor.

---

2 frying chickens (about 2½ pounds each), quartered, thoroughly rinsed, and patted dry
¼ cup dry white wine
¼ cup olive oil
¼ cup chopped garlic
¼ cup freshly squeezed lime juice
¼ cup freshly squeezed orange juice
1 teaspoon ground cumin
1 teaspoon dried leaf thyme
1 teaspoon dried oregano
Salt and freshly ground black pepper, to taste
1 teaspoon achiote, if available
1 teaspoon dried red pepper flakes, or 1 whole dried red pepper
Garnish: 2 unpeeled navel oranges, cut crosswise into ⅛-inch-thick slices, or ½ bunch parsley, finely chopped

YIELD
6 to 8 servings
GRILL
Prepare coals
PREP
Marinate 4 hours

---

1. In a large shallow bowl, arrange the chicken in 1 layer.
2. In a small bowl, combine the remaining ingredients, except for the garnish. Pour over the chicken.
3. Marinate, covered, for 4 hours in the refrigerator, stirring 2 or 3 times.
4. Prepare the grill 1 hour ahead so the coals are covered with a fine white ash.
5. Remove the chicken from the marinade and pat dry.
6. Strain the marinade into a bowl and reserve it.
7. Place the chicken on the grill. Do not crowd the pieces.
8. Grill the chicken, brushing with the marinade, for 15 to 20 minutes on each side or until the juices run clear when the thigh joint is pricked with a fork.
9. Serve the chicken on a platter garnished decoratively with the orange slices or a sprinkling of parsley.

CHICKEN MADRID

▲▲▲

Olive oil, oranges, limes, cumin, oregano, thyme: these are the flavorings and seasonings of Spain.

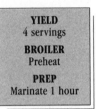

YIELD
4 servings

BROILER
Preheat

PREP
Marinate 1 hour

1 pound boneless, skinned chicken breasts, rinsed, patted dry, cut lengthwise into thirds, and then cut into 1-inch cubes (about 30 to 32 pieces)

3 medium-size garlic cloves, finely chopped

1 teaspoon dried oregano

1 teaspoon dried leaf thyme

1 teaspoon ground cumin

½ teaspoon freshly squeezed lime juice

1 teaspoon freshly squeezed orange juice

Slice of unpeeled orange (½ inch thick), seeded and finely chopped

1 tablespoon olive oil

1 tablespoon dry vermouth or dry white wine

1. In a medium-size glass or stainless steel bowl, place the cubed chicken.

2. In a small bowl, combine the garlic, seasonings, juices, chopped orange, oil, and vermouth or wine and whisk together. Pour the mixture over the cubed chicken and mix thoroughly.

3. Marinate, covered, for 1 hour in the refrigerator, stirring once or twice. (You may freeze the chicken at this point.)

4. Skewer 8 pieces of chicken on each of 4 9-inch metal skewers.

5. Broil the skewered chicken 6 inches from the flame for 3 minutes on each side. Baste with the marinade.

6. Remove from the broiler and gently push the chicken off the skewers with a fork onto a plate. Serve immediately.

CHICKEN GASCONY

▲▲▲

The French chef who created the marinade for this dish is from the Gascony region of France. I developed this version as a dry marinade for chicken, as well as for beef and lamb. Serve hot or cold.

---

1 pound boneless, skinned chicken breasts, rinsed, patted dry, and cut lengthwise into thirds, and then into 1-inch cubes (about 30 to 32 pieces)
3 medium-size cloves garlic, finely chopped
3 small shallots, finely chopped
½ teaspoon dried leaf thyme
½ teaspoon coarse (kosher) salt
¼ teaspoon freshly ground white pepper
¼ cup finely chopped Italian flat-leaf parsley
3 tablespoons corn oil

YIELD
4 servings
PREP
Marinate 4 hours

---

1. In a medium-size glass or stainless steel bowl, place the cubed chicken.

2. In a small bowl, stir together the garlic, shallots, thyme, salt, pepper, parsley, and 1 tablespoon of the oil. Add to the cubed chicken and mix thoroughly.

3. Marinate, covered, for 4 hours in the refrigerator, stirring 2 or 3 times.

4. Remove the chicken from the marinade and drain if any liquid has accumulated. (You may freeze the chicken at this point.)

5. In a large skillet over medium heat, heat the remaining 2 tablespoons of corn oil. Add the cubes of chicken and sauté 3 or 4 minutes, stirring frequently, until lightly browned. Do not overcook.

6. Remove the chicken from the skillet and transfer to a plate. Serve immediately. Or refrigerate, covered, and serve chilled.

For Ruote with Chicken Gascony

Prepare ½ recipe Chicken Gascony according to the directions above. Cook 8 ounces of ruote until *al dente* and drain in a colander. Place half of the ruote on each of two plates. Add half of the chicken to each serving of ruote and toss lightly to mix. Serve warm or chilled.

CHICKEN MOROCCAN

▲▲▲

The more marinades you use, the greater the range of authentic and unusual flavorings you can introduce into your meals. The seasonings in this recipe—cilantro, mint, and cumin—are Middle Eastern and Moroccan. This is another dish that works equally well served hot or cold.

1 pound boneless, skinned chicken breasts, rinsed, patted dry, cut lengthwise into thirds, then into 1-inch cubes (about 30 to 32 pieces)
3 medium-size cloves garlic, finely chopped
2 scallions, trimmed and finely chopped
2 tablespoons finely chopped cilantro or parsley
2 tablespoons finely chopped fresh mint
1 tablespoon ground cumin
3 tablespoons olive oil

> **YIELD**
> 4 servings
> **PREP**
> Marinate 4 hours

1. In a medium-size glass or stainless steel bowl, place the cubed chicken.

2. In a small bowl, stir together the garlic, scallions, cilantro or parsley, mint, and cumin with 1 tablespoon of the oil. Add to the cubed chicken and mix thoroughly.

3. Marinate, covered, for 4 hours in the refrigerator, stirring 2 or 3 times.

4. Remove the chicken from the marinade and drain if any liquid has accumulated. (You may freeze the chicken at this point.)

5. In a large skillet over medium heat, heat the remaining 2 tablespoons oil. Add the cubes of chicken and sauté, stirring frequently, for 3 to 4 minutes or until lightly browned. Do not overcook.

6. Remove the chicken from the skillet and transfer to a plate.

7. Serve immediately. Or refrigerate, covered, and serve cold.

For Lamb Moroccan
You may use the same marinade for 1 pound cubed lamb (from the shoulder or leg). Follow the directions as for chicken except sauté until the lamb is barely pink in the center, about 5 to 10 minutes.

For Ziti with Chicken Moroccan and Cilantro Sauce
Prepare ½ recipe Chicken Moroccan according to the directions above. Cook 8 ounces of ziti until *al dente* and drain in a colander. Place

half the ziti on each of two plates. Add half the chicken and 2 tablespoons Cilantro Sauce with Yogurt and Green Chiles (page 124) to each serving of ziti. Toss lightly to mix and serve.

LEMON-LIME CHICKEN

▲▲▲

The Party Box got its start with Lemon-Lime Chicken in boxes prepared for picnics and concerts in New York's Central Park. It remained our favorite chicken dish. I like it because it's baked, which keeps the calories down, yet it's crisp.

2 broiling chickens (about 2½ pounds each),
    quartered, thoroughly rinsed, and patted dry
½ cup freshly squeezed lemon juice (about 4 lemons)
½ cup freshly squeezed lime juice (about 4 limes)
2 teaspoons finely chopped peeled fresh gingerroot
2 teaspoons chopped garlic
½ teaspoon salt, or to taste
1¼ teaspoon freshly ground black pepper
3 tablespoons finely chopped parsley
3 tablespoons snipped fresh dill or 3 teaspoons dried dillweed
2 teaspoons finely chopped fresh tarragon or 1 teaspoon dried
6 tablespoons unsalted butter, melted

YIELD
6 to 8 servings

OVEN
450°F

PREP
Marinate 4 hours

1. In a large rectangular stainless steel or glass container, place the chicken pieces.

2. Combine the lemon and lime juices, the gingerroot, garlic, salt, and pepper. Pour over the chicken and marinate, covered, 4 hours in the refrigerator.

3. Line a large baking pan with parchment paper. Arrange the chicken in a layer, skin side up, and sprinkle with half the parsley, dill, and tarragon, and brush with the melted butter. Turn the chicken, skin side down, sprinkle with the remaining parsley, dill, and tarragon, and brush with the melted butter.

4. Bake the chicken in the preheated 450°F oven for 20 minutes, turning once.

5. Reduce the heat to 350°F and cook 30 to 35 minutes longer or until the juice runs clear when

the thigh joint is pricked with a fork. (If the skin has not crisped, run the chicken under the broiler until browned, about 8 minutes.)

6. Transfer the chicken to a platter and serve immediately. Or cool (you may freeze at this point) and serve chilled.

BUYING CHICKEN BREASTS

When you buy chicken breasts on the bone, you lose between a third and a half when the skin and bone are removed. Of course it's cheaper to begin with, but be aware that you will not end up with the full weight that's on the package. Chicken breasts, skinned and boned, are more expensive, but not that much more, ounce for ounce. And they do save a preparation step.

CHICKEN SESAME

▲▲▲

Sesame oil, soy sauce, and fresh gingerroot, the most popular Chinese flavorings, give this marinade its distinctive flavor— it's probably one you've used before. For a buffet dish, serve Chicken Sesame with snow peas and mushrooms. Or have it as a quick and delicious "feast every day" entrée. Either skewer and broil the chicken as described below, or simply sauté it.

———

1 pound boneless, skinned chicken breasts, rinsed, patted dry, cut lengthwise into thirds, and then into 1-inch cubes (about 30 to 32 pieces)
3 medium-size cloves garlic, finely chopped
1 tablespoon finely chopped peeled fresh gingerroot
1½ tablespoons tamari or good-quality soy sauce
1 tablespoon cold-press sesame oil or peanut oil
½ teaspoon freshly ground black pepper
2 tablespoons roasted sesame seeds (page 137) (optional)

YIELD
4 servings

BROILER
Preheat

PREP
Marinate 1 hour

1. In a medium-size glass or stainless steel bowl, place the cubed chicken.

2. In a small bowl, whisk together the remaining ingredients, except the sesame seeds. Pour over the cubed chicken and mix thoroughly.

3. Marinate, covered, in the refrigerator for 1 hour, stirring 1 or 2 times. (You may freeze the chicken at this point.)

4. Skewer 8 pieces of cubed chicken on each of 4 9-inch metal skewers. Sprinkle with the sesame seeds, if using.

5. Broil the skewered chicken 6 inches from the flame for 3 minutes on each side. Baste with the marinade.

6. Gently push the chicken cubes off the skewer with a fork onto a platter.

7. Serve immediately.

For Chicken Sesame with Snow Peas

For entertaining, double the amount of chicken. Add ¼ pound fresh snow peas, rinsed and stringed, and cut in half, or asparagus in season, and ½ pound fresh mushrooms, wiped clean with damp paper toweling, sliced lengthwise. In a skillet over medium heat, heat 2 tablespoons corn or peanut oil, add the snow peas and mushrooms, and sauté 2 to 3 minutes. Combine with the sautéed chicken and toss lightly. Serve in a chafing dish.

A TIP FOR BARBECUING CHICKEN

When grilling chicken for a group, split the chickens down the breast, flatten them, and cook them whole; this way you can turn the chickens in one motion. When done, cut the chickens into serving pieces with poultry shears or a cleaver.

MEAT

▼▼▼

In my travels about the country I have discovered one common fact almost everywhere—men will cut down on the meat in their daily meals, acknowledging the role that animal fats play in cardiovascular disease, but very few will eliminate it entirely. Meat at dinner is a custom too firmly entrenched to surrender completely. But when meat is presented in smaller amounts in interesting recipes, and in combination with other rich-tasting ingredients, it will not be missed as the main event.

I've found ways of reducing the quantity of meat without sacrificing its flavorful appeal. There are also techniques for preparing meat that enhance its flavor while reducing the quantity needed, as with paillards, flattened tender cuts of meat. Using marinades is another delicious way to keep flavor but with less meat.

Of course, we want to keep room in our lives for those special occasions when nothing but a roast will do. But rather than serving a big old-fashioned standing rib roast, try a small one, no more than three or four pounds—whether it's the "Spirited" Cold Roast Pork Tenderloin, a small roast leg of lamb with Greek flavorings, or the holiday and party favorite, Whole Standing Baked Ham.

And when you do serve roasts, whether for yourself, for company, or for large-scale entertaining, save the leftovers for sandwiches, a casserole with lots of vegetables, or perhaps for a salad. That way, even the special-occasion roast becomes part of our new style of eating.

Beef Dishes

▼▼▼

SHELL STEAK PAILLARD WITH THYME

▲▲▲

Paillard refers to a piece of meat that has been pounded very thin. Because the paillards are thin and marinated in oil, no further oil is needed for the skillet. The technique, also used for veal scallopini, makes expensive cuts of meat such as steak and veal go twice as far.

———

1 shell steak (about 8 or 9 ounces), rinsed and patted dry
1 large clove garlic, finely chopped
2 teaspoons finely chopped fresh thyme or 1 teaspoon dried leaf thyme
¼ teaspoon coarse (kosher) salt
1 tablespoon olive oil

YIELD
2 servings
PREP
Marinate 1 to 2 hours

———

1. Remove the bone, sinews, and fat from the steak. There should be about 4 ounces remaining. Cut the piece of meat horizon-

tally into 2 pieces. Between two sheets of wax paper, parchment paper or aluminum foil, flatten the 2 pieces of meat by either pounding with a mallet or the side of a cleaver. The meat should be about ¼ inch thick or less.

2. In a mortar combine the garlic, thyme, and salt and pound with the pestle until it forms a paste. Add the olive oil and blend thoroughly.

3. Rub the paste over both sides of the steaks. Reserve any remaining paste for sautéing the steak.

4. Marinate the steak, covered, for 1 hour at room temperature, or 2 hours in the refrigerator.

5. In the small skillet over medium-high heat, add the reserved paste and sauté the steak for 20 to 30 seconds on each side. Remove the meat from the skillet and place on a cutting board. Slice into 1½-inch wedges.

6. To serve, arrange the slices in a semicircle on 2 plates.

FILET MIGNON

▲▲▲

Usually we think of filet mignon as a very expensive and luxurious entrée dish, but it can also be served as part of a cocktail buffet, or "supper-by-the-bite," where it goes a very long way. The average filet, when defatted, yields between three and four and a half pounds, which might serve eight to ten people as an entrée. When served on a buffet, cubed or thinly sliced, with Sylvia Sherry's Horseradish Sauce (page 122) on whole-wheat baguettes, along with other buffet items, it will serve 20 to 30 people. This is a never-fail recipe that gives you perfect rare filet every time.

1 filet mignon (about 3 to 4½ pounds), rinsed, patted dry, and fat trimmed
1 tablespoon corn oil
2 tablespoons Dijon-style mustard
1 tablespoon freshly ground black pepper

YIELD
20 to 30 servings
on a buffet
8 to 10 servings
as an entrée

OVEN
500°F

1. Line a baking tray with parchment paper or aluminum foil and place the filet on it. Rub the filet with the oil.

2. In a small bowl, combine the mustard and pepper and, with a rubber spatula, spread it over the meat. Insert a meat thermometer into the thickest part.

3. Bake the filet in the preheated 500°F oven for 10½ to 12 minutes or until the thermometer reads 100°F.

4. Turn the oven off and let the filet remain in the oven another 10 minutes or until the thermometer reads 110°F to 115°F. Remove immediately from the oven. It will continue to cook. For medium filet, bake it 3 or 4 minutes longer.

5. Let the filet cool completely. Then refrigerate, covered, until thoroughly chilled.

6. For an entrée serving, cut the filet into ½- to ¾-inch-thick slices. For the buffet, halve or quarter the filet lengthwise before cutting into slices.

SKILLET SKIRT STEAK

▲▲▲

This quick skirt steak is a bargain in time, money, and calories. It's almost as tender as filet mignon, and some think more flavorful. Susan Dresner serves it often for herself or for a guest. When I made it for a friend one night, I served it with kale and pears and watercress salad.

Coarse (kosher) salt or regular salt
6 ounces skirt steak, washed, patted dry, and fat
    trimmed

YIELD
2 servings

1. In a heavy skillet over high heat, spread coarse salt to cover the bottom of the skillet. Heat until the salt flakes and forms a crust.

2. Place the skirt steak flat on the salt. Reduce the heat to medium-high. Cook the steak until rare, about 2 to 3 minutes on each side.

3. Transfer the steak to a cutting board. Scrape off the salt and cut the steak diagonally into 1-inch-thick slices.

For Skirt Steak with Lime Juice

Place the steak slices in a flat dish. Add ¼ cup freshly squeezed lime juice and 2 dashes of tamari or good-quality soy sauce. Marinate about 1 hour. Then proceed as above.

MAINLY MEAT MEAT LOAF WITH GREEN HERBS

▲▲▲

"This is really meaty, not like the usual bready-tasting meat loaf," said my neighbor Semlyn Saunders. Rich in herbs, this loaf is more flavorful when served cold. The loaf also freezes well. Sylvia Sherry's Horseradish Sauce (page 122) or Garden Tomato Sauce (page 241) are both good accompaniments.

1 egg plus 1 egg white
1½ pounds lean ground chuck or sirloin
6 tablespoons fresh whole-wheat bread crumbs
¼ teaspoon ground cumin
1 teaspoon dried tarragon or dried summer savory
1 teaspoon dried chervil
1 medium-size scallion, trimmed and finely chopped
2 tablespoons finely chopped Italian flat-leaf parsley
2 tablespoons finely chopped fresh basil
¼ cup milk
½ teaspoon coarse (kosher) salt
½ teaspoon freshly ground black pepper

YIELD
4 to 6 servings

OVEN
350°F

1. In a large bowl, beat the egg and egg white until well mixed. Add the meat and mix thoroughly.

2. Add the bread crumbs, cumin, tarragon or summer savory, and the chervil and work them into the meat.

3. Add the scallion, parsley, and basil and work into the meat.

4. Add the milk, salt, and pepper and work into the meat.

5. Spray a 9x5x3-inch loaf pan with nonstick vegetable cooking spray and line with parchment paper. Spread the meat mixture evenly in the pan.

6. Bake the meat loaf in the preheated 350°F oven for about 50 minutes. Increase the heat to 400°F and bake for 10 minutes to brown.

7. Remove the meat loaf from the oven and drain off the liquid. (There will be quite a lot.) Turn the drained meat loaf onto a rack and let cool at least 20 minutes.

8. Remove the parchment paper. Serve at room temperature. It slices best when chilled.

Other Meats

▼▼▼

ROAST LEG OF LAMB EL GRECO

▲▲▲

Spring is always the best time for lamb. A small roast of three to four pounds is the perfect size for this recipe.

1 teaspoon dried oregano
1 teaspoon dried rosemary
1 teaspoon ground cumin
1 tablespoon olive oil
1 leg of lamb (about 3 to 4 pounds), rinsed, patted dry, and fat trimmed
2 cloves garlic, thinly sliced
10 thin slivers of lemon rind, some flesh attached
Salt and freshly ground black pepper, to taste
½ cup dry vermouth or dry white wine

YIELD
4 to 6 servings

OVEN
450°F

PREP
Marinate overnight

1. In a small bowl, combine the herbs, spice, and oil and mix.

2. Rub the lamb with the oil and herb marinade.

3. Cut many slits, about ½ inch wide and 1 inch deep, all over the lamb. With a knife, insert the slices of garlic and lemon slivers into the slits. Add salt and pepper. Pour ¼ cup of the vermouth over the roast.

4. Marinate in the refrigerator, covered, overnight.

5. Place the roast on a rack in a small roasting pan. Insert the meat thermometer into the center of the meat away from the bone. Add the remaining ¼ cup vermouth to the bottom of the pan.

6. Roast the lamb in the preheated 450°F oven 15 minutes. It will release some of its juices and turn a burnished brown.

7. Reduce the heat to 350°F and cook an additional 30 to 40 minutes, uncovered, or until the temperature reaches 175°F to 180°F for meat well done.

8. Remove the roast from the oven and let the lamb stand for 15 minutes before carving.

9. Serve and carve the roast at the table, or carve slices for each plate in the kitchen before serving.

WHOLE STANDING BAKED HAM

▲▲▲

Ham on the bone is a festive, classic centerpiece on a buffet for holidays and parties. At The Party Box we served small slices of ham with raisin-pumpernickel bread and mustard sauce. Although you probably have your own favorite glaze, here is one that is especially flavorful.

1 precooked or smoked ham on the bone (about 6 to 8 pounds)
½ cup firmly packed light brown sugar
¼ cup Dijon-style mustard
¼ cup orange, lemon, or lime marmalade
¼ teaspoon ground cloves
¼ teaspoon ground ginger
¼ teaspoon ground allspice

YIELD
20 servings
OVEN
350°F

1. In a roasting pan, bake the ham, covered with aluminum foil, in the preheated 350°F oven for 1 hour.

2. In a small bowl, whisk together the sugar, mustard, marma-

lade, and seasonings until smooth.

3. Remove the foil from the ham. Brush the ham all over with the glaze.

4. Return the ham, uncovered, to the oven to bake for an additional 30 minutes. Remove from the oven and cool on a rack for 15 to 30 minutes before slicing.

5. Serve on the buffet.

MEAL IN A PACKAGE: KAY MESERVE'S LAMB CHOP DINNER WITH VEGETABLES

▲▲▲

Here is your entire dinner in one parchment-paper package. When it's done, take it out of the oven, open the package, and arrange the meat and vegetables on a plate. For more flavor, use one of our dry marinades for the lamb (see Chicken Moroccan, page 329, or Chicken Gascony, page 328).

—

1 shoulder lamb chop (about ½ pound), rinsed,
    patted dry, and fat trimmed
1 teaspoon chopped fresh rosemary or ¼ teaspoon dried
1 small baking potato, peeled and halved
1 medium-size carrot, peeled and halved
1 celery stalk, stringed and halved
1 large slice yellow onion, same thickness as lamb chop
1 large slice sweet red pepper, same thickness as lamb chop
Salt and freshly ground pepper, to taste

YIELD
1 serving
OVEN
350°F

—

1. Place the lamb chop on a sheet of parchment paper or aluminum foil and stack the remaining ingredients on top of the chop in exactly the order listed.

2. Fold the parchment in half over the lamb chop and crimp and flatten and pleat the edges together until the package is closed. Place the package in a shallow baking dish.

3. Bake in the preheated 350°F oven for 1 hour. Increase the temperature to 400°F and continue cooking for 15 additional minutes.

4. To serve, transfer the pack-

age to a serving plate and remove the parchment or foil. Or if serving guests, allow them to open the packets at the table.

"SPIRITED" COLD ROAST PORK TENDERLOIN

▲▲▲

This little roast is a beauty. The long marinating process and the slow baking keep the meat pristine white. Served with Rosemary-Scented Apricot Aspic (page 283), Fruited Couscous Salad (page 219), and Scandinavian Pickled Beets (page 195), the vibrant colors play off each other, especially when presented on glass plates.

1 center-cut boneless pork tenderloin roast (about 2 pounds), patted dry, and with an absolute minimum of fat
5 slightly crushed whole allspice
5 slightly crushed whole white peppercorns
¼ teaspoon coarse (kosher) salt
1 bay leaf
½ cup gin or dry vermouth for marinade
¼ cup dry vermouth for baking

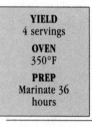

YIELD
4 servings

OVEN
350°F

PREP
Marinate 36 hours

1. On a platter or in a glass bowl, set the roast. Rub the roast with the allspice, white pepper, and salt. Break the bay leaf in half and place on top. Pour the ½ cup gin over the roast.

2. Weight the roast with a plate and a 1-pound can on top. Cover with foil and place in the refrigerator.

3. Marinate 36 hours, turning the roast every 12 hours and basting with the gin.

4. Remove the roast from the marinade.

5. Place the roast on a rack in a small roasting pan. Add the ¼ cup of vermouth to the bottom of the pan.

6. Roast, uncovered, in the preheated 350°F oven about 20 minutes per pound or until the juice runs clear when the roast is pricked with a fork.

7. Remove the roast from the pan and transfer to a plate to cool.

Then refrigerate until the roast is completely chilled (you may put it in the freezer for 10 minutes).

8. Cut into ½-inch-thick slices, allowing 3 slices per person. Present the roast on a platter.

THE OLD-FASHIONED MEAT GRINDER

We attached the hand meat grinder to our big kitchen table when it was time to grind meat for meatloaf or hamburgers. I can still hear that grumbly sound in my ear as I carefully turned the handle and watched the meat curl out into a bowl. When I was in New Hope, Pennsylvania, not long ago, I found three or four old-style grinders in an antique store. The proprietor said, "Young people grab these up." Going back to the old way is not such a bad idea. In fact, you may have one stored away. If you do, bring it out or buy one as I did. Then you can choose a good piece of meat with less fat and grind it yourself.

DESSERTS

▼▼▼

Feasting every day has to include dessert—what's a feast without it? Here you'll find many recipes neither high in calories nor in fat, beginning with perhaps the loveliest dessert of all, fruit in season—whether poached, baked, in aspic, frozen, pick-up-and-eat, sauced, or in crisps and cobblers. There's even an ice cream without cream, eggs, or sugar, yet it's creamy textured and rich in flavor.

There's a delicious flourless oat, nut, and coconut pastry shell, perfect for pies and tarts, and an oat, nut, and coconut topping for cobblers. I've also included three "there, there" desserts such as bread puddings and an Apricot Kugel—the kind of homey comfort we cherish from childhood. You'll also find several fruited quick breads and muffins.

Regardless of our resolve, there are always times when we can't resist the seduction of those double-deadly-rich desserts. I'm not going to be the one who says don't ever succumb. Why not—once in a while? But save them for special occasions.

Our Party Box solution to the irresistible allure of rich desserts was to shrink the portion size. We made our pastries in two-bite sizes, so that if you had four it felt like sinful indulgence. We served our mousses in large tulip glasses, which not only looked wonderfully elegant, but also made the dessert seem like more than just two and a half ounces.

A few of our other special desserts, such as Cranberry Jubilee, are meant to be served only during the holiday season, when we're licensed to indulge ourselves a little.

I could have included a hundred more desserts, but I've chosen for you only our top favorites. Alas, there's no substitute for eggs, butter, and cream, so when you splurge, splurge—just keep it for extra-special occasions. You'll appreciate them all the more!

Everyday Desserts

▼▼▼

ELANE'S AND BETSY'S FLOURLESS OAT, NUT, AND COCONUT PASTRY CRUST

▲▲▲

This pastry contains peanut butter but no flour or dairy, and is my all-purpose nut pastry. It goes well with fruit tarts, particularly smaller-size tarts, because it is so chewy.

⅔ cup rolled oats
⅓ cup large-flake unsweetened coconut
⅓ cup wheat germ
7 tablespoons smooth peanut butter
2 tablespoons ice water

---

1. In a food processor fitted with a metal blade, place the oats, coconut, and wheat germ. Pulse on

| YIELD |
| 1 9-inch pie shell or 6 2½-inch or 12 1½-inch tart shells |
| **OVEN** 400°F |
| **PREP** Refrigerate dough 1 hour |

and off until a fine texture, about 30 seconds.

   2. Add the peanut butter and pulse on and off until it is incorporated.

   3. Slowly add the water and pulse on and off until it is incorporated.

   4. Transfer the mixture to a sheet of wax paper and form into a ball. Refrigerate, covered, 1 hour to set.

   5. Remove the pastry from the refrigerator and let return to room temperature, about 20 minutes.

   6. To make a pie shell, spray a 9-inch pie pan with nonstick vegetable cooking spray. Gently spread the pastry with your hands to cover the bottom and sides of the pan. For tart shells, spray a standard 6-cup or 12-cup muffin pan with nonstick vegetable cooking spray. Divide the pastry into 6 or 12 equal parts and press the dough evenly to line the bottom and sides of the muffin-pan cups.

   7. Bake the pie or tart shells in the preheated 400°F oven for 8 to 10 minutes. Remove from the oven and cool on a rack. Fill according to the directions in individual recipes.

ELANE'S AND BETSY'S DATE AND APRICOT SQUARES

▲▲▲

These no-bake squares are soft and smooth and incredibly rich. The oat mixture forms the sandwich around the date and apricot filling. I make a large quantity of this healthful "topping" and store it in the refrigerator for my seasonal cobblers and for Apricot Kugel (page 360).

———

1 cup pitted dates
1 cup dried apricots
Boiling water
2 tablespoons freshly squeezed lemon or lime juice

YIELD
16 2-inch squares

PREP
Presoak dates
and apricots
overnight

Oat-Nut Topping:

½ cup rolled oats
½ cup roasted almonds, chopped
½ cup wheat germ
½ cup sesame seeds, toasted
½ cup plus 2 tablespoons large-flake unsweetened coconut

1. The night before baking, pack the dates and apricots in separate heatproof glass containers, pressing them into the containers with a spoon. Pour boiling water over the fruits to cover. Cool and refrigerate, covered, overnight. Most of the water will be absorbed.

2. In a food processor fitted with a metal blade, combine the fruits, lime juice, and 1 tablespoon of the soaking liquid from the fruit. Pulse on and off until the fruit is smooth and thick. Do not overpurée the fruit.

3. In a medium-size bowl, combine the topping ingredients.

4. Spray an 8x8x2-inch-pan with nonstick vegetable cooking spray. Line the bottom with half the topping mixture.

5. With a moistened spatula, spread the fruit mixture evenly over the oat topping so it touches all sides and press down lightly.

6. Sprinkle the remaining topping over the top of the fruit mixture.

7. Refrigerate or freeze until firm but not frozen. Cut into 2-inch squares, and transfer to a serving platter with a spatula.

SUSAN ZIGOURAS' APPLE CRISP

▲▲▲

Susan Zigouras, who worked for The Party Box over the years, developed this recipe for the Heart Association. Even though lighter in fat and cholesterol than the more traditional crisp, Susan's version is still delicious. Susan says "this dessert is simply wonderful warmed in the oven for breakfast or as a snack with just a smidge of low-fat milk."

10 Golden Delicious, Rome Beauty, Granny Smith, or
    other cooking apples (about 3¼ pounds)
3 tablespoons sugar
1 teaspoon ground cinnamon
1 teaspoon cornstarch or kuzu (page 293)
½ teaspoon ground nutmeg or allspice

Apple Crisp Topping:

1 cup rolled oats (not instant)
½ cup unbleached all-purpose flour
¼ cup sugar

YIELD
8 servings
OVEN
350°F

3 tablespoons chilled, unsalted margarine or butter, cut into small pieces
1 teaspoon ground cinnamon
½ teaspoon ground nutmeg or allspice

1. Peel and core the apples. Then cut them into quarters. Slice each quarter into 2 to 3 pieces and place in a large bowl.

2. In a small bowl, combine 3 tablespoons sugar, 1 teaspoon cinnamon, cornstarch, and ½ teaspoon nutmeg or allspice. Add to the apples and toss to mix.

3. Layer the apples in a baking dish, about 13x9x2 inches, sprayed with nonstick vegetable cooking spray.

4. In a medium-size bowl, by hand or in a food processor fitted with a metal blade, mix together the ingredients for the topping just until the topping reaches a crumbly consistency resembling rice grains. Sprinkle the mixture over the layered apples. Cover with aluminum foil.

5. Bake in the preheated 350°F oven for 45 to 50 minutes or until the apples are soft. Remove the foil during the last 10 to 15 minutes of baking time to "crispen" the topping.

6. Serve warm or at room temperature.

FRUIT DESSERTS

▲▲▲

All kinds of fruit should be enjoyed as part of our new style of eating. Some of us may have trouble digesting raw fruits, so included here is an interesting selection of baked and poached fruits. If you can, have fresh fruit on kabobs, or by themselves, enjoying each in turn in season: the citrus in winter, the pears, apples, persimmons, pomegranates in fall, the rhubarb and strawberries in spring, and apricots, cherries, plums, blueberries, and raspberries in full summer.

I have learned to enjoy fruits as a meal in themselves, and I find I digest them best when eaten separately, and preferably as the first meal of the day. Whether as a meal, a meal-starter, or as a dessert, enjoy them all.

PURE FRESH FRUIT "ICE CREAM"

▲▲▲

You can "splurge" on this healthy ice cream any day, any time you like. It's just pure fresh fruit.

1 banana, peeled and cut into thirds
¼ cup blueberries, rinsed and stems removed
½ cup fresh strawberries, rinsed and hulled

YIELD
1 ½ cups
PREP
Freeze fruits
overnight

1. Freeze each of the fruits separately in freezer bags overnight.

2. Remove the bags from the freezer about 20 minutes before serving.

3. In a food processor fitted with a metal blade, place the banana. Pulse on and off until smooth.

4. Add the blueberries and strawberries to the food processor. Whirl until a purée.

5. Serve at once. The mixture will have the consistency of frozen yogurt. For more of an ice cream texture, place in the freezer for 1 hour.

For Other Fruit "Ice Creams"
Substitute for the blueberries and strawberries, 1 mango, peeled and flesh coarsely chopped.

Or substitute for the blueberries, 1 kiwi, peeled and coarsely chopped.

Toppings:
1 teaspoon maple syrup and 2 tablespoons chopped walnuts; 2 teaspoons carob powder and 2 tablespoons chopped roasted almonds; 2 tablespoons carob chips and 2 tablespoons chopped roasted almonds.

SERVING FRUIT HANDSOMELY

Watermelon pieces on a black plate

Green grapes on a sienna-colored plate

Purple grapes on a terra-cotta saucer

Cherries on a white napkin on a silver tray

Strawberries in a basket or wooden-slotted box

Raspberries on demitasse-cup saucers

PICK-UP-AND-EAT FINGER FRUIT DESSERTS

▲▲▲

I like to serve fruit along with finger pastries as dessert. Have small plates for guests to make their own assortments.

1 pint (about 20) fresh strawberries, rinsed just before
    serving and hulled
2 kiwi fruits, unpeeled and cut into eighths
2 pears, unpeeled, cored, and cut into ½-inch-thick rounds

Arrange the fruit decoratively on a platter.

KUMQUATS, MANDARIN ORANGES, AND LITCHEE NUTS ON SKEWERS

▲▲▲

These go along on the Chinese-American Fourth of July Picnic.

1 can (10 ounces) preserved kumquats, drained
1 can (11 ounces) Mandarin oranges, drained
1 can (11 ounces) litchee nuts, drained

YIELD
6 to 8 servings

1. Divide and skewer the fruits, alternating them, among 8 bamboo skewers.

2. Arrange the skewers on a round platter.

3. Serve, or refrigerate in a covered container for a picnic.

For Fruit Kabobs
Substitute for the fruits above, 1 pint rinsed and hulled strawberries and 1 small pineapple peeled and cut into 1-inch cubes. Or use in-season melon instead of the pineapple. Cut the melon in half, seed it, and with a melon baller scoop out 1-inch balls. Drain on paper toweling. Alternately skewer two strawberries and pineapple cubes or melon balls on wooden picks.

SEASONAL FRUIT COBBLERS

▲▲▲

Fruit cobblers are always a delight, and each season offers its own variety of fresh fruits to enjoy. Spring and early summer strawberries and blueberries, summer peaches and nectarines, late summer blackberries and raspberries, fall pears and apples, and winter cranberries. I've used them all, and now I've got these cobblers down to a simple formula. I use six cups of prepared fruit per cobbler, either one or a combination of fruits, such as peaches and nectarines, strawberries and blueberries, pears and apples. For sweetness, I find ¼ cup of sugar, honey, or maple syrup is enough. To thicken the fruit, I use two tablespoons of tapioca, arrowroot, or kuzu (page 293). For tartness and to bring out the flavor, I usually add the juice of a lime or lemon, and with the cranberries, an orange as well as some slivers of the peel. For the crowning touch I use Elane's Oat-Nut Topping (page 345), which is both extremely healthful and delicious, or Susan Zigouras' Apple Crisp Topping.

Cobblers warm from the oven are a heavenly dessert to serve at the end of a "friendly occasions" dinner of casserole and salad. But don't wait until then—have them as an everyday treat. They hold up nicely in the refrigerator, covered, for two to three days.

Following is the recipe for Cranberry Cobbler. It calls for more sugar—cranberries are really tart. Most fruit cobblers cook 10 minutes at 400°F and then 30 minutes at 350°F, but the cranberries may take a bit longer.

———

2 bags (12 ounces each) cranberries, picked over, rinsed, and coarsely chopped (6 cups)
½ cup sugar
2 tablespoons quick-cooking tapioca
2 tablespoons freshly squeezed orange juice
1 teaspoon grated orange rind
1 recipe Susan Zigouras' Apple Crisp Topping (page 346)

YIELD
6 servings

OVEN
400°F

1. In a large bowl, mix together the cranberries, sugar, tapioca, orange juice and rind. Let stand 30 minutes. Pour the cranberries into a colander and drain.

2. In a 2-quart soufflé dish or ovenproof glass loaf pan sprayed with nonstick vegetable cooking spray, place the berries.

3. Prepare the Apple Crisp Topping according to the directions in the recipe. Sprinkle the topping mixture over the berries.

4. Bake in the preheated 400°F oven for 10 minutes or until the topping browns slightly. Reduce the oven temperature to 350°F and bake an additional 40 minutes.

5. Remove to a rack and cool 20 minutes.

6. Serve warm, or refrigerate, covered, and serve chilled.

FLORINE SNIDER'S SUMMER POACHED PEACHES

▲▲▲

Most supermarket peaches are usually under-ripe, and spoil before they reach perfect ripeness. Poaching makes them more tender, and easier to digest. Serve these peaches warm or cold; with or without the skins.

4 medium-size to large whole peaches or nectarines
3 cups water
1 tablespoon raspberry conserve or Hans' Strawberry Fruit Jam (page 133)
½ cup white grape juice
1 large wedge unpeeled lemon
1 cinnamon stick (about 1 inch long)

YIELD
4 servings

1. In a medium-size saucepan over medium heat, combine all the ingredients and bring to a boil. Reduce the heat and simmer the mixture for 10 to 12 minutes or until the peaches are tender when pricked with a fork.

2. Turn off the heat and cover the saucepan. Let the mixture stand on the stove for 5 to 10 minutes.

3. Serve hot in a glass bowl or dessert dishes. Or remove the peaches to a bowl, cool, and refrigerate, covered, and serve chilled. Reserve a small amount of the liquid to pour over the peaches.

RASPBERRY ASPIC WITH CHOPPED FRESH LIMES

▲▲▲

What a lovely dessert this is—so easy to fix and so shimmering. The idea came from *The Festive Vegetarian* by Rose Elliot. She combined raspberries, cranberry juice, and agar-agar.

I chose frozen raspberries and added, for tartness, a slice or two of lime with rind on and a squeeze or two of lime juice. I often serve this aspic on dessert plates with fresh raspberries, Mandarin oranges, and kiwi fruit.

1½ cups cranberry juice

2 tablespoons freshly squeezed lime juice

2 lime slices with rind, ¼ inch thick, seeded and cut into tiny cubes

1½ teaspoons agar-agar (page 283) or 1½ teaspoons gelatin (if using gelatin, soften 3 minutes in cranberry juice before heating)

10 ounces (1 pint) fresh or frozen raspberries (juice drained if frozen)

YIELD
4 servings

PREP
Refrigerate 2 hours

1. In a medium-size saucepan over medium heat, heat the cranberry juice, lime juice, and lime cubes. Add the agar-agar, bring to a boil, and boil for 2 minutes, stirring constantly. Remove the pan from the heat.

2. In a large bowl, place the raspberries. Add the lime mixture and gently stir. Cool slightly.

3. Refrigerate until set, about 2 hours.

Muffins and Quick Breads

▼▼▼

ELANE'S HEARTY APPLE AND OAT MUFFINS

▲▲▲

Muffins for breakfast, for dessert, and for a snack any time of day are always a welcome treat. These muffins are made without milk, eggs, flour, or baking soda. They've got a chewy texture and are delicious with Hans' Strawberry Fruit Jam or Quince Fruit Jam (page 133).

½ cup pitted dates

Boiling water

7 apples (any firm cooking apple), peeled, cored, and coarsely chopped

3 cups rolled oats

½ cup golden raisins

½ cup safflower oil

½ cup large-flake unsweetened coconut

1 teaspoon ground cinnamon

YIELD
12 to 18 2½-inch muffins

OVEN
375°F

PREP
Presoak dates overnight

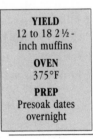

1. The night before baking, pack the dates in a heatproof glass container. Press down firmly with a spoon. Pour in boiling water to cover. Cool slightly and refrigerate, covered, overnight.

2. Drain the dates and reserve the liquid. Squeeze the remaining liquid from the dates. Place all the ingredients, plus 1 tablespoon of the reserved liquid, in a food processor fitted with a metal blade. Let stand 5 minutes.

3. Pulse on and off, about 1 minute. Leave the apples chunky.

4. Spray 3 6-cup muffin pans with nonstick vegetable cooking spray. Spoon the muffin batter into the muffin cups, filling almost to the top and pressing down slightly.

5. Bake in the preheated 375°F oven for about 25 minutes or until firm to the touch.

6. Transfer the muffins to a rack.

7. Serve hot. Or let cool (you may freeze at this point) and refrigerate, covered, and serve cold.

PINEAPPLE MUFFINS

▲▲▲

This recipe comes from Bonnie Liebman of *Nutrition Action,* the Washington-based consumer watchdog newsletter, and it has no milk and very little oil.

1 cup whole-wheat flour or whole-wheat pastry flour
1½ teaspoons baking powder, low sodium
¼ to ½ teaspoon ground cinnamon
¼ to ½ teaspoon ground nutmeg or allspice or coriander
1 can (8 ounces) crushed pineapple in its own juice
1 large egg, slightly beaten
1 tablespoon corn oil
2 tablespoons honey
1 tablespoon unsulphured molasses
2 tablespoons slivered almonds or whole sunflower seeds

YIELD
6 2½-inch muffins

OVEN
375°F

1. In a medium-size bowl, sift together the flour, baking powder, and spices.

2. In a medium-size bowl, combine the pineapple, egg, oil, honey, and molasses and blend with a whisk.

3. Pour the pineapple mixture

into the dry mixture and mix together quickly with a rubber spatula just until the ingredients are evenly moistened. Fold in the nuts.

4. Spray a 6-cup muffin pan with nonstick vegetable cooking spray. Fill each cup three quarters full, and press down slightly.

5. Bake in the preheated 375°F oven for 10 minutes. Reduce heat to 350°F and bake 15 minutes more or until a skewer inserted into a muffin comes out clean.

6. Run a knife around the edge of each muffin so muffins do not stick, and turn the muffins out onto a plate.

7. Serve warm. Or let cool and refrigerate, covered. You may freeze the muffins at this point, wrapped tightly in plastic freezer wrap. Thaw overnight in the refrigerator.

ELEANOR TOMIC'S PRUNE AND WALNUT BREAD WITH CARROTS

▲▲▲

There are countless recipes for carrot bread and cake. This one is an unexpected combination, and a delicious one. The prunes provide a rich, mellow flavor. It's an especially delightful fall and winter bread, and lasts for days in the refrigerator when well wrapped. It also freezes well.

½ cup freshly squeezed orange juice
1 cup coarsely chopped pitted prunes
½ to ¾ cup firmly packed light brown sugar
½ cup corn oil
1 teaspoon vanilla extract
2 large eggs plus 1 egg white
2 cups shredded carrots (3 medium-size carrots)
2 cups unbleached all-purpose flour
2 teaspoons baking powder
1½ teaspoons ground cinnamon
¼ teaspoon coarse (kosher) salt
1 cup coarsely chopped walnuts

| YIELD |
| 1 large loaf |
| **OVEN** |
| 350°F; 325°F if using glass or Pyrex |

1. In a small saucepan over medium heat, bring the orange juice to a boil. Add the prunes and remove the pan from heat.

2. In a medium-size mixing bowl, beat the sugar, oil, and vanilla with an electric mixer on medium speed until smooth, about 5 minutes. Clean the beaters.

3. In a large mixing bowl, beat the eggs and egg white with the electric mixer on high speed until their volume increases about 4 times, about 5 minutes. Gradually beat the sugar/oil mixture into the eggs and beat until smooth.

4. With a spatula, fold in the carrots. Add the chopped prunes and orange juice and mix.

5. In a medium-size bowl, sift together the dry ingredients. Stir into the carrot mixture, mixing just until the flour is absorbed. Fold in the nuts.

6. Spray a 9x5x3-inch loaf pan with nonstick vegetable cooking spray and line with parchment paper. Pour in the batter.

7. Bake in the preheated 350°F oven for 1 hour or until small cracks appear on top of the loaf and a skewer inserted into the center comes out clean.

8. Let the bread cool in the pan on a rack for 25 minutes. Then turn the loaf out onto the rack, remove the parchment paper, and let cool completely. This loaf slices better the next day. You may freeze the bread at this point, wrapped tightly in plastic freezer wrap. Thaw overnight in the refrigerator.

APRICOT LOAF

▲▲▲

This is a moist, dense, rich loaf, with a texture similar to a fruit cake rather than a bread. I think it's really special. There is no oil in it, and most of the sugar comes from the fruit. The loaf will last for days in the refrigerator, and it freezes beautifully. It also makes a handsome gift.

1½ cups water or 1 cup apricot nectar and ½ cup water
2 tablespoons unsalted butter
⅓ cup firmly packed light brown sugar
2 cups finely chopped dried apricots
1¼ cups unbleached all-purpose flour
1 cup whole-wheat pastry flour
2 teaspoons baking powder

YIELD
1 loaf

OVEN
350°F; 325°F, if using glass or Pyrex

½ teaspoon coarse (kosher) salt
2 large eggs, well beaten
1 teaspoon lemon extract

1. In a medium-size saucepan, combine the water or nectar, butter, and sugar and bring to a boil. Continue to boil, stirring occasionally, for 1 minute. Remove the pan from heat.

2. Add the apricots to the hot liquid and let cool, 30 to 45 minutes.

3. In a medium-size bowl, sift together the flours, baking powder, and salt. Add the cooled apricots and their liquid to the dry ingredients.

4. In a medium-size bowl, beat the eggs with an electric or hand mixer on high speed until they increase about 4 times in volume, about 5 minutes. Add to the apricot mixture along with the lemon extract and mix well.

5. Spray a 9x5x3-inch loaf pan with nonstick vegetable cooking spray and line with parchment paper. Add the batter and let stand for 30 minutes to set up.

6. Bake the loaf in the preheated 350°F oven for 50 to 60 minutes or until a skewer inserted into the center comes out clean.

7. Immediately turn the loaf out onto a rack to cool. Cool 15 minutes, then remove the parchment paper, cover, and let stand overnight before slicing. You may freeze the bread at this point, wrapped tightly in plastic freezer wrap. Thaw overnight in the refrigerator.

For Pineapple and Date Bread

Substitute 1 cup each of coarsely chopped dried pineapple (available from most health-food stores) and dates for the apricots and use 1 cup pineapple juice instead of apricot juice.

For Peach and Pear Bread

Substitute 1 cup each of coarsely chopped dried peaches and pears for the apricots and use 1 cup pear nectar instead of apricot juice.

RONA PIMENTEL'S DO-AHEAD BAKING TIPS

Rona baked into her eighty-seventh year. Although the Portuguese sweet bread and some of the other elaborate baking went by the board, she continued to make her special fruit cakes, cup cakes, and oat cakes. "I like to do some of the steps ahead," she said.

Squeeze a number of lemons and freeze the juice in ice-cube trays, ready for use.

Pre-sift baking ingredients when called for.

Marinate dried fruits in brandy, so they are always ready and fragrant.

Pre-cut wax or parchment paper for lining pans.

"There, There" Desserts

▼▼▼

W hen I was a little girl and I skinned my knee or had to be in a croup tent for a bad cold, grown-ups used to say to me, "There, there, don't cry, everything's going to be all right." And then I was allowed junket, rice pudding, bread pudding, all those special childhood treats that have lost none of their power to comfort. They contain what for most of us is too many eggs and too much cream—but once in a while we still need a little "there, there" consoling.

MEXICAN BREAD PUDDING (CAPRIOTADO)

▲▲▲

T his bread pudding is best in the fall when pears and apples are at their peak.

1½ cups firmly packed brown sugar
2 cups apple juice
1 cinnamon stick, broken up
6 cups ½-inch cubes day-old bread (French or Italian)
2 ounces pignoli (pine nuts)
½ cup walnuts, chopped
2 tablespoons grated orange rind
3 firm cooking apples, unpeeled, cored, and cut lengthwise in ¼-inch-thick strips
3 firm Bosc or Bartlett pears, peeled, cored, and cut lengthwise in ¼-inch-thick strips

YIELD
6 servings

OVEN
350°F

1. In a small saucepan over medium heat, combine the sugar, apple juice, and cinnamon stick and cook until the mixture thick-

ens, about 10 minutes. It will be a light syrup. Remove any pieces of cinnamon stick.

2. Spray a 13x9x2-inch baking pan or oven-to-table dish with nonstick vegetable cooking spray.

3. In a large bowl, combine the bread cubes and two thirds of the syrup and mix thoroughly.

4. In a small bowl, combine the nuts and orange rind.

5. In the baking pan, layer half the bread, then half the fruit, and half the nut mixture. Repeat the layers.

6. Pour the remaining third of the hot syrup over the mixture.

7. Bake in the preheated 350°F oven until firm, about 20 minutes.

8. Remove from the oven and cool on a rack.

9. Serve with fresh fruit, ice cream, or whipped cream.

FRANK PIMENTEL'S RAISIN BREAD PUDDING

▲▲▲

This bread pudding recipe from my brother-in-law isn't particularly fancy—just one of the best.

1 teaspoon butter
3 slices raisin bread, crusts removed and cut into cubes
3 cups half-and-half
3 large eggs
1 tablespoon sugar
1 teaspoon vanilla extract

YIELD
4 servings
OVEN
350°F

1. Grease a 1-quart soufflé dish with the butter.

2. Layer the bread in the bottom of the soufflé dish. Add 1½ cups of the half-and-half.

3. In a bowl, beat the eggs lightly. Then add the remaining half-and-half, sugar, and vanilla and blend.

4. Strain the egg mixture through a fine sieve over the bread. Place the soufflé dish in a larger baking pan. Fill the pan with hot water to come halfway up the soufflé dish.

5. Bake in the preheated 350°F oven for 35 minutes or until the pudding is firm.

6. Serve hot or cool and refrigerate, covered, and serve chilled.

APRICOT KUGEL

▲▲▲

Macaroni and noodles are definitely "there, there" food. Whenever I feel bad, I always cook one of them and immediately feel better. Whether you serve this dish as a main course, a dessert, or just something to pull out of the refrigerator and warm in the oven, you'll find that the apricots make it a special treat. I have cut back on the dairy fat, and Elane's Oat-Nut Topping is delicious on this.

1 cup dried apricots, soaked overnight and finely chopped (see Elane's and Betsy's Date and Apricot Squares, page 345) or 1 can (16 ounces) apricots in syrup, drained, pitted, and finely chopped, reserving 1 cup of the syrup for other use
¼ cup (½ stick) unsalted butter, melted, plus 1 tablespoon, unmelted
½ cup low-fat, large-curd cottage cheese
1½ tablespoons finely chopped lemon rind
3 large eggs, well beaten
½ cup half-and-half or heavy cream
4 ounces spinach noodles, broken in half and cooked according to package directions

| YIELD |
| 8 servings |
| OVEN |
| 350°F |
| PREP |
| Presoak apricots overnight |

Topping:

1 cup whole-wheat bread crumbs
¼ cup maple syrup
1 teaspoon ground cinnamon
½ teaspoon ground nutmeg

1. In a large bowl, combine the apricots, the melted butter, cottage cheese, lemon rind, eggs, and half-and-half. Mix well.

2. Add the noodles and blend well.

3. In a small bowl, mix together the topping ingredients.

4. Spray an 8-inch-square baking pan with nonstick vegetable cooking spray. Pour in the mixture and spread evenly with a spatula.

5. Sprinkle the topping mixture over the top. Dot with the 1 tablespoon butter.

6. Bake in the preheated

350°F oven for 45 to 60 minutes or until a skewer inserted into the center comes out clean.

7. Remove from the oven and cool slightly on a rack.

8. Cut the kugel into 2-inch squares and serve warm. Or cool and refrigerate, covered. Reheat in a low oven to serve.

Cookies

▼▼▼

C ookies and small finger pastries along with finger fruits offer a light approach to dessert without giving it up all together. The best way to spoil your guests, I'm convinced, is *not* to gorge them with sugars and fats, but to offer them intensity of flavor and variety in smaller quantities.

The selection of cookies are some of the all-time favorites served at our parties. All of them can be made ahead of time and many of them freeze well. Serve them on flat baskets with handles or with baskets of fruit on a buffet. For sit-down dinners, serve on dessert plates surrounding clusters of grapes and strawberries.

SWEDISH SWEET BUTTER COOKIES

▲▲▲

T his was my first commercial cookie, shared with me by my friend Rene Taubenblatt. I always hid them in a bag in my freezer in the bedroom, and it was so hard not to devour them.

¾ cup (1½ sticks) unsalted butter, softened

½ cup superfine sugar

1 egg yolk

½ teaspoon vanilla extract

1¼ cups sifted unbleached all-purpose flour

YIELD
2 dozen

OVEN
325°F

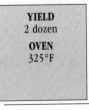

1. In a medium-size bowl, beat together the butter and sugar until fluffy, about 3 minutes.

2. Beat in the egg yolk and vanilla.

3. Stir in the flour in 3 batches and blend well after each addition.

4. Remove the dough to wax paper and refrigerate for 5 to 10 minutes until it becomes firm enough to handle.

5. Spray a cookie sheet with nonstick vegetable cooking spray or line it with parchment paper.

6. Remove the dough from the refrigerator and pinch off pieces about the size of a walnut. With lightly floured hands, roll the dough into 1-inch balls and place them on the cookie sheet 2 inches apart (you will have 2 dozen). With your forefinger, make a slight indentation in the middle of the ball, pressing it down slightly. This will help the cookie bake into a high round cookie.

7. Bake in the preheated 325°F oven for 8 to 10 minutes or until the cookies turn a delicate light brown. They should retain a slightly soft center.

8. With a spatula, remove the cookies immediately to a rack and let cool completely. Store in an airtight container, or freeze them.

MARLU'S CHOCOLATE BURSTS

▲▲▲

Unashamedly rich, unbelievably delicious—that's what these chocolate confections are. A teaspoon of batter puffs up into a little pillow of delight. If you want a chewy, fudge-like texture, bake for only seven to eight minutes. Bake them a minute or two longer and you'll get a crisp cookie.

1 cup sifted unbleached all-purpose flour
1 teaspoon baking powder
¼ teaspoon salt
1 cup superfine or granulated sugar
¼ cup (½ stick) unsalted butter, softened
2 ounces unsweetened chocolate, melted and cooled
1 teaspoon vanilla extract
2 large eggs
½ cup superfine or confectioners' sugar

YIELD
3 dozen

OVEN
350°F

PREP
Refrigerate dough
12 hours or
overnight

1. Into a medium-size bowl, sift together the flour, baking powder, and salt.

2. In a medium-size bowl, combine the granulated sugar, butter, melted chocolate, and vanilla extract. With an electric beater or hand mixer, beat until the ingredients are thoroughly incorporated.

3. Blend in 1 egg at a time, beating the first for about 3 minutes before adding the second. Beat another 3 minutes.

4. Beat in the dry ingredients, about one third at a time, until thoroughly incorporated. The batter will be quite soft. Refrigerate in the bowl until it firms slightly. Remove the dough from the bowl to a sheet of wax paper and shape into a ball. Wrap loosely and refrigerate 12 hours or overnight.

5. Spray a standard cookie sheet with nonstick vegetable cooking spray or line it with parchment paper. With a teaspoon, take small pieces of batter, which will now be quite firm. With lightly floured hands, roll the pieces into small balls. Drop into a small bowl of superfine or confectioners' sugar and roll around to coat. Then set on the cookie sheet, 2 inches apart, making a small indentation in each cookie with your forefinger.

6. Bake in the preheated 350°F oven for 7 to 8 minutes or until just firm.

7. Remove the cookie sheet from the oven. With a spatula, immediately move cookies around on the cookie sheet. Then place them on a rack to cool completely, about 30 minutes.

8. Serve, or store in an airtight container.

MEXICAN WEDDING COOKIES

▲▲▲

I always serve these with the Vegetable Chili (page 300) and the Mexican Fiesta (page 87). These cookies feel light as air in the mouth but, alas, they are very, very rich. "Moderation" is the watchword with these.

½ cup (1 stick) unsalted butter, softened
¼ cup plus ½ cup confectioners' sugar
Pinch salt
½ cup sifted unbleached all-purpose flour
½ cup sifted whole-wheat flour
½ cup walnuts, finely chopped
½ teaspoon vanilla extract

YIELD
20 to 24 cookies

OVEN
350°F

1. In a medium-size bowl with an electric beater or hand mixer, beat the butter with the ¼ cup confectioners' sugar and the salt until fluffy, about 3 to 4 minutes.

2. Add the flours, walnuts, and vanilla and mix until smooth.

3. Spray a baking sheet with nonstick vegetable cooking spray or line with parchment paper.

4. With lightly floured hands, roll the dough into 1-inch balls and place about 2 inches apart on the baking sheet.

5. Bake in the preheated 350°F oven for 20 minutes or until firm.

6. Transfer the cookies to a rack to cool completely.

7. Dust with the remaining ½ cup confectioners' sugar. Store in an airtight container or freeze.

Note: If preparing in a food processor with a metal blade, all the ingredients can be combined at once. Pulse on and off until the mixture forms a ball.

GINGER ICEBOX COOKIES

▲▲▲

If, like me, you love crystallized ginger, you'll love these cookies. These cookies are made the same way our housekeeper Esther made plain old-fashioned ice-box cookies: a stiff dough is rolled into logs, chilled, and sliced. This recipe will make about three small logs that you can freeze, so you need bake only ten or twelve at a time when friends drop by or when you want a special dessert treat.

½ cup (1 stick) unsalted butter, softened
½ cup firmly packed dark brown sugar
¼ cup molasses
1½ cups sifted unbleached all-purpose flour
1 teaspoon baking soda
½ cup pecan halves, finely chopped
⅓ cup crystallized ginger, finely chopped

YIELD
3 3x1-inch logs;
number of
cookies depends
on size, about 36

OVEN
350°F

1. In a large mixing bowl with an electric beater or hand mixer, beat together the butter and sugar

until fluffy, about 3 minutes. Beat in the molasses.

2. In a medium-size bowl, stir

together the flour and baking soda. Add to the butter mixture, beating at low speed just until blended.

3. With a wooden spoon or rubber spatula, stir in the nuts and the crystallized ginger until they are evenly distributed.

4. Form the dough into 2 or 3 logs, 1 to 3 inches in diameter. Wrap each log in wax paper and chill thoroughly, or partially freeze to make slicing easier.

5. Slice the logs into ⅛- to ¼-inch-thick slices and arrange ½ inch apart on a standard baking sheet sprayed with nonstick vegetable cooking spray or lined with parchment paper cut to fit.

6. Bake in the preheated 350°F oven for 7 to 10 minutes, depending on the thickness of the slices. When done, the cookies should be golden brown and the centers should be set.

7. Remove the baking sheet from the oven. With a spatula, immediately move the cookies around on the sheet. Then transfer to racks to cool until crisp.

8. Store the cookies in an airtight tin, or freeze them.

ELEANOR TOMIC'S "COOKIE BAKING WITH PARCHMENT" SECRET

"Investing in parchment paper is a good idea for the person who likes to bake. Drop cookies tend to brown too much around the edges when baked on an unlined cookie sheet. Not so with parchment. And bar cookies, such as brownies, can be cut more easily when the pan is lined with parchment. When cool enough to handle, the baked good can be lifted out onto a rack and the parchment peeled off."

CHOCOLATE-PISTACHIO SQUARES

▲▲▲

This rich finger pastry combines a baked shortbread base with a chocolate-pistachio topping.

2 cups sifted unbleached all-purpose flour
½ cup sifted confectioners' sugar
1 cup (8-ounce tub) soft margarine
1 bag (12 ounces) semisweet chocolate chips
½ cup water
¼ cup pistachio nuts, finely chopped

YIELD
About 60 1½-inch squares

OVEN
350°F

1. In a small bowl, combine the flour and sugar with a fork or whisk.

2. Add the soft margarine and form into a dough, mixing with the fork or whisk. The dough will be soft.

3. Spray a 15x10-inch jelly-roll pan with nonstick vegetable cooking spray. Press the dough into the pan.

4. Bake the shortbread base in the preheated 350°F oven for 21 to 22 minutes or until brown. Cool on a wire rack.

5. In the top of a double boiler, melt the chocolate chips with the water. Whisk until smooth. Remove from over the water and let cool.

6. When cool, pour the chocolate mixture evenly over the baked and cooled shortbread crust and spread to the ends of the pan.

7. Sprinkle the pistachios over the chocolate. Refrigerate until the chocolate is set.

8. Cut into 1½-inch squares.

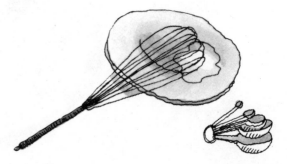

Special Splurge Desserts

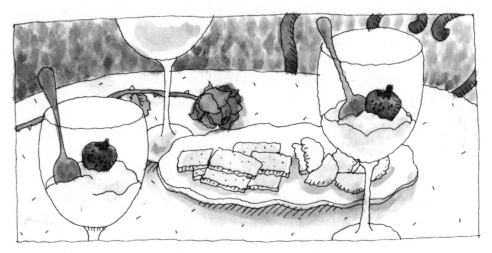

Here are just a few of those "Oh, My God" desserts—the ones we consider sinful and have to repent for later. While it's tempting to serve large portions, the art of indulging in moderation can make us dessert connoisseurs.

FLAN WITH ORANGE CURAÇAO OR AMARETTO

▲▲▲

Everybody adores this. And it's so easy—slip it into the oven just as you and your guests sit down to dinner, and you can serve it hot right from the oven at dessert time.

2 cups (1 pint) half-and-half
¼ cup superfine sugar
⅛ teaspoon salt
4 large egg yolks
¼ cup orange Curaçao or Amaretto or Triple Sec

YIELD
6 servings

OVEN
325°F

1. In a small saucepan over low heat, combine the half-and-half, sugar, and salt and cook until the sugar and salt have dissolved.

2. In a bowl with an electric beater or hand mixer, beat the egg yolks for 1 minute. Slowly, in a thin, steady stream, add 1 cup of the heated half-and-half mixture to the yolks, beating constantly. Pour the mixture back into the remaining half-and-half and stir in the liqueur.

3. Divide the mixture among 6 custard cups. Set the cups in an 8x8x2-inch baking pan. Fill the pan with enough hot water to come halfway up the sides of the custard cups.

4. Bake in the preheated 325°F oven for 25 to 30 minutes or until a knife inserted near the edge comes out clean.

5. Remove the custard cups from the water bath at once. Serve hot, at room temperature, or chilled.

Note: This flan may also be baked in a 1-quart soufflé dish set in a water bath. Increase the baking time to 35 to 40 minutes.

CRANBERRY JUBILEE

▲▲▲

This is a variation of Cherries Jubilee that is perfect for the holiday season when you want a spectacular dessert. You can cook it ahead, and then ignite it just before pouring over vanilla ice cream.

1 bag (12 ounces) fresh or thawed frozen cranberries
1 jar (12 ounces) red currant jelly
¼ cup sugar
½ cup light rum
½ cup plus 2 tablespoons brandy
Rind of 1 orange, finely chopped
½ gallon vanilla ice cream

YIELD
8 servings

1. In a large saucepan over medium heat, combine the cranberries, jelly, sugar, rum, the ½ cup brandy, and the orange rind. Bring to a boil and cook for about 5 minutes, stirring constantly, until the berries pop and the sauce thickens. You want some of the berries whole, so don't overcook.

2. Cool slightly and transfer the sauce to a bowl. Pour the remaining brandy over it and ignite.

3. Serve 2 to 3 tablespoons over each serving of ice cream.

CREAM CHEESE SHELL

▲▲▲

This is a slightly sweet, really rich pie shell. I use it for small and regular-size tarts as well as for a full crust. It refrigerates and freezes well, so you can make it ahead. This no-fail shell is my all-purpose pie shell. It requires no liquid and no special baking know-how.

½ cup (1 stick) butter, softened to room temperature
4 ounces cream cheese, softened to room temperature
1 cup unsifted unbleached all-purpose flour

YIELD
1 9-inch pie shell
or 6 2½-inch or
12 1½-inch tart
shells

OVEN
350°F

PREP
Refrigerate dough
1 hour

1. In a food processor fitted with a metal blade or medium-size bowl with an electric beater, cream together the butter and cream cheese. Add the flour and incorporate by pulsing on and off for about 30 seconds or blending with the electric beater until the flour is just incorporated and the dough comes away from the sides of the bowl. Do not overmix. The dough should just come together; it will be soft.

2. Place the dough on a sheet of wax paper and gently shape it into a ball. Wrap it in wax paper and refrigerate for at least 1 hour.

3. Remove the dough from the refrigerator and let it come to room temperature, about 20 minutes. Do not let it get overly soft.

4. *If using the dough for tarts:* Divide into 6 or 12 equal parts depending on the size of the muffin-pan cups and shape into balls. Spray 6 2½-inch or 12 1½-inch muffin-pan cups with nonstick vegetable cooking spray. Press the dough evenly to line the bottom and sides of the muffin-pan cups. Prick the dough all over with a fork. *If making a pie shell:* Roll out the dough on wax paper lightly sprinkled with flour to fit a 9-inch pan. Spray the pie pan with nonstick vegetable cooking spray. Gently lift the pastry into the pan. Cut off extra dough with a knife or scissors and crimp the edge.

5. Bake the pie or tart shells in the preheated 350°F oven for 8 to 10 minutes or until lightly brown. Remove and cool on a rack. You may also freeze the shells at this time wrapped tightly in plastic freezer wrap. Thaw to room temperature before using.

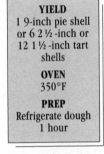

CHOCOLATE-PECAN CHESS TARTS

▲▲▲

The Party Box catered the launching party for *Chocolatier Magazine,* for which we prepared a huge chocolate table. I hate to think of how many kinds and quantities of chocolate there were on that table, and how quickly they were all devoured. These chocolate-pecan chess tarts made such a hit, they were chosen as a dessert recipe by the magazine for a Top Caterers of New York picnic. Save these for an extra-special fling.

1 recipe Cream Cheese Shell (page 369)
½ cup firmly packed light brown sugar
¼ cup granulated sugar
1 egg
2 tablespoons half-and-half
2 tablespoons light corn syrup
½ teaspoon vanilla extract
1 tablespoon melted unsalted butter
1 ounce unsweetened chocolate, melted and cooled
⅔ cup coarsely broken pecans

YIELD
6 2 ½ -inch tarts

OVEN
350°F

1. Prepare the Cream Cheese Shell for 6 tarts according to the directions given in the recipe.

2. In a medium-size bowl with an electric beater or hand mixer, cream together the sugars, egg, half-and-half, corn syrup, vanilla, melted butter and melted chocolate until smooth.

3. Divide the broken pecans among the tart shells. Add the filling almost to the top of each.

4. Bake in the preheated 350.°F oven until the filling is just set, about 10 minutes. The tarts will puff up, then fall slightly. The filling will still be slightly soft; it will harden later.

5. Transfer to a rack and let cool. Serve immediately, or refrigerate, covered, until ready to serve.

For Pecan Chess Tarts
Omit the 1 ounce cooled, melted unsweetened chocolate and proceed precisely according to the remaining recipe instructions.

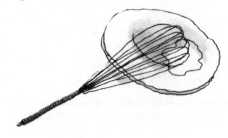

LATE SUMMER PLUM-PEAR TARTS

▲▲▲

In late August and early September, all varieties of plums are in season—the tiny prune plums, the golden-green greengages, and every kind of purple and red plum. And at the same time, the first Seckel and Bartlett pears arrive. With the addition of crisp apples, the combination makes a rich and fruity tart. I found this recipe in *Cooking by the Calendar*, edited by Marilyn Hansen. The tarts will freeze. They can also be made into a 9-inch open-face pie.

1 pound plums, unpeeled, rinsed, stoned, and
    coarsely chopped
2 pears, cored, peeled, and coarsely chopped
2 firm cooking apples or 1 apple and 1 peach, rinsed,
    cored, unpeeled, and coarsely chopped (optional)
1 tablespoon grated lemon rind
1 tablespoon grated orange rind
⅓ cup firmly packed light brown or granulated sugar
1 teaspoon ground cinnamon
1 teaspoon ground cloves
1 teaspoon ground allspice
2 tablespoons unbleached all-purpose flour
2 batches Cream Cheese Shell dough, unbaked (page 369)

YIELD
12 2½-inch
muffin-sized tarts

OVEN
375°F

1. In a 2-quart bowl, combine the fruits, rinds, sugar, spices, and flour and mix well. Let stand for 30 minutes.

2. Using the Cream Cheese Shell dough, pinch off 1-inch balls of dough and press into 12 2½-inch-size muffin-pan cups. Prick the dough all over with a fork.

3. Bake the shells in the preheated 375°F oven for 8 to 10 minutes or until a light brown.

4. Spoon the fruit filling into the pastry-lined cups.

5. Bake in the preheated 375°F oven for 20 minutes or until the crust is brown and the fruit is firm. Cool the tarts on a rack.

6. Serve on a dessert platter or refrigerate, covered, until ready to serve.

LIME MOUSSE

▲▲▲

L ime mousse is so refreshing and delicate. And it's not green as you might expect, but a pale yellow.

1 cup heavy cream
1¼ cups water
1 envelope unflavored gelatin
5 egg yolks
1 cup sugar
⅔ cup freshly squeezed lime juice (about 5 or 6 limes)
1 tablespoon grated lime rind

YIELD
6 to 8 servings
PREP
Refrigerate 1 hour

1. Pour the cream into a stainless steel bowl and refrigerate.

2. In a small saucepan over medium heat, bring 1 cup water to a boil. Reduce heat to a simmer. To a 1-cup heatproof glass measure, add ¼ cup water. Sprinkle the gelatin over the water and stir to soften. Place the measuring cup in the simmering water and stir until the gelatin dissolves. Remove and let cool 5 minutes.

3. In a medium-size bowl, with an electric beater or hand mixer, beat the egg yolks for 5 minutes or until the mixture forms a ribbon when beaters are lifted. Gradually add the sugar, beating until thick and lemon colored.

4. On low speed, beat in the lime juice, rind, and then the dissolved gelatin.

5. Beat the cream in the refrigerated bowl until soft peaks form, then fold into the gelatin mixture. Transfer the mousse to a serving bowl or individual tulip glasses and refrigerate, covered, 1 hour. You may freeze the mousse at this point in a covered container. Thaw overnight in the refrigerator.

For Mousse with Liquor or Liqueur

Substitute for the lime juice and rind, ⅓ to ½ cup of liquor or liqueur such as rum or cassis. Place the liquid in a small saucepan over high heat until it ignites (remove the pan from the heat at once) and the alcohol burns off. Let cool, then add to the egg-sugar mixture and continue to follow the recipe directions above.

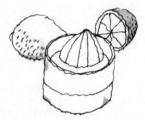

APPENDIX

MAIL-ORDER SHOPPING

▲▲▲

The following mail-order sources offer fresh and canned foods, pickles, spices, nuts, teas and coffees, and cookware, as well as information on special and unusual ingredients. Most have free catalogs.

The sources in New York I have known for years. Also, books, guides, and friends directed me to sources from around the country. This is a burgeoning field, with new specialty firms appearing all the time.

CASA MONEO, *210 W. 14 St., New York, NY 10011—(212) 929-1644.* At this heaven-sent supermarket for Mexican and Latin American foods and gifts, you can buy green chiles in large cans, Mexican chocolate, chiles and peppers, fruits such as jícama, cactus, and plantains, and many Mexican serving pieces. Catalog available.

COOKWORKS, INC., *316 Guadalupe St., Santa Fe, NM 85701—(505) 988-7676.* Housed in an 1855 warehouse and an 85-year-old adobe house, Cookworks offers one of the country's finest and most extensive selections of food, cookware, and gifts. They ship gourmet coffees, vacuum-sealed, from all over the world, feature blocks of Caillebaut white and bittersweet chocolate as well as a great variety of Southwest specialty food items.

FULL MOON MUSHROOM CO., *P.O. Box 6138, Olympia, WA 98502—(206) 866-9362.* This unusual business offers two kits for growing your own mushrooms: for the ambitious, there is an outdoor mix called Garden Giant Spawn, which you mix into a sawdust bed and dirt and water; the indoor kit is called the Oyster Mushroom Garden Kit. Soon to be offered is a Mushroom-of-the-Month subscription service—a different variety of mushroom will be shipped every month. Brochure available.

GOODBEE PECANS, *Goodbee Pecan Plantations, P.O. Box 3650, Albany, GA 31708—(800) 841-4352.* This firm guarantees the best pecans you've ever tasted or your money back. Prices are reasonable, and you can order nuts salted, unsalted, or with various flavorings. Catalog available.

HARRY AND DAVID, *Bear Creek Or-* *chards, Medford, OR 97501—(800) 547-3033.* This fruit-of-the-month club is the granddaddy of them all. Harry and David ship fruit and other gourmet goodies year round. Catalog available.

KATAGIRI COMPANY, *224 E. 59 St., New York, NY 10022—(212) 755-3566.* This store combines Japanese gourmet foods with a large selection of porcelain serving pieces. Ask for the Japanese pepper imported under the brand name "House Sansho"; it is mild and fragrant with an almost floral bouquet. Catalog available.

THE KOBOS COMPANY, *The Water Tower at Johns Landing, 5331 S.W. Macadam, Portland, OR 97201—(503) 222-5226.* Kobos ships its specialty coffees and teas from all over the world. Also available are excellent cookware, tools, and serving items for the buffet. If you are in the Portland area, visit their three retail stores. Brochure available.

McNULTY'S TEA AND COFFEE, *109 Christopher St., New York, NY 10014—(212) 242-5351.* To step into this Greenwich Village store is like stepping into another century. Exotic teas and coffees from all over the world fill barrels and jars from floor to ceiling. There is a selection of over 150 teas, including McNulty's own blends, and over 75 coffees to choose from. Here are beautiful tea and coffee services, coffee mills, and other kitchen items. Brochure available.

THE NEW ORLEANS COOKING SCHOOL AND GENERAL STORE, *620 Decatur St., New Orleans, LA 70130—(504) 525-2665.* This combination general store/cooking school run by Joe and Karen Cahn has the largest collection of Louisiana and Cajun products in the state, including foods, crafts, and even music. You can order Creole mustard, jambalaya and okra mix, pickled okra, remoulade sauce, coffee and chickory, beignet mix, and many hot sauces and spices. Catalog available.

PAPRIKA WEISS, *1546 Second Ave., New York, NY 10028—(212) 288-6117.* Formerly rare and unusual spices from the Far East, India, and Indonesia; baking utensils; unusual molds; and over a hundred cookie cutters. Owner Ed Weiss says he has sold literally tons of Hungarian paprika. Catalog available.

PIONEER SEMINOLE GROVES, *P.O. Box 2209, Cocoa, FL 32992—(305) 452-3833.* There is nothing better than great citrus. This establishment offers a variety of premium citrus fruit and also ships numerous jams, jellies, and preserves made from citrus and other tropical fruits. Catalog available.

PRAGTREE FARMS, *13217 Mattson Rd. Arlington, WA 98223—(206) 435-4648.* For only $25, you can have organically grown seasonal greens and four dozen flowers from the farm shipped by second-day airmail. (Overnight air is extra.) Pragtree Farms ships from March through Thanksgiving. Call for current availability of specific greens. Brochure available.

G. B. RATTO INTERNATIONAL GROCERS, *821 Washington St., Oakland, CA 94607—(800) 325-3483.* A truly wonderful mail-order "treasure house of ethnic foods since 1897." Ratto's catalog offers kitchenware, smoked and dried fish, exotic and unusual oils, vinegars, preserves and condiments, confections, and a large selection of Italian gourmet items, as well as French and Italian sweets. Catalog available.

ROSSI PASTA, *114 Green St., Marietta, OH 45750—(614) 373-5155.* From the Midwest comes an unusual and extensive selection of pastas that include jalapeño, saffron, pimiento, artichoke, and black olive in many sizes and shapes. Catalog available.

S. E. RYKOFF & CO., *P.O. Box 21467, Los Angeles, CA 90021—(800) 421-9873.* This West Coast mail-order house offers an outstanding array of fine foods and cookware, including wicker gift baskets filled with dozens of specialty gourmet items from around the world. Rykoff's Gourmet-Food-of-the-Month Club ships subscribers everything from soup to nuts.

SELECT ORIGINS, *Box "N", Southampton, NY 11968—(516) 288-1382.* This is the store for pepper. Its classic Pepper Melange features green, white, and black peppercorns. Szechuan peppers are also offered here, as are Muntok white and freeze-dried green peppercorns. Pepper Melange Rosé includes lovely pink peppercorns. You can also choose from a fine selection of herbs, spices, oils, vinegars, rices, and wild mushrooms. Catalog available.

THOMPSON AND MORGAN, *P.O. Box 1308, Jackson, NJ 08527—(201) 363-2225.* This seed company features a large selection of vegetable and flower seeds including those for radicchio, mâche, and a variety of Chinese vegetables such as Chinese cabbage (also called celery or Napa) and Meiquing Choy, a hybrid version of Bok Choy. There is also a Flower Salad Mix, a packet of mixed flower seeds specially selected for use in salads. Catalog available.

WALNUT ACRES, *Penns Creek, PA 17862—(717) 837-0601.* Established in 1946 as one of the first organic health farms, Walnut Acres now sells nationwide and has consistently maintained the quality of its flours, grains, dried beans, soups, vegetables, chiles, nuts, and fresh and dried fruits. Catalog available.

THE WHOLE CHILI PEPPER CATALOGUE, *published by Outwest Pub. Co., P.O. Box 4278, Albuquerque, NM 87196—(505) 268-0288.* The catalog contains everything from seed to salsa, where to get chili, the history of chili, and a world of recipes. The catalog lists sources for hundreds of ingredients from reputable producers, featuring products from the Southwest—chiles, fruit baskets, garden supplies, and ornaments.

BIBLIOGRAPHY

▲▲▲

Ackart, Robert. *A Celebration of Soups.* Garden City, N.Y.: Doubleday, 1982.
——. *A Celebration of Vegetables.* New York: Atheneum, 1979.
Adams, Catherine F. *Nutritive Value of American Foods in Common Units.* Washington, D.C.: United States Agricultural Research Service, Nov. 1975.
Annechild, Annette. *Annette Annechild's Wok Your Way Skinny 30-Day Menu Plan.* New York: Wallaby/Simon & Schuster, 1984.
Bailey, Covert. *Fit or Fat.* Boston: Houghton-Mifflin, 1978.
Ballentine, R. M., M.D. *Diet and Nutrition.* Honesdale, Pa.: Himalayan International Institute, 1978.
Barry, Beryl, and Sachs, Barbara Turner, eds. *The Artists' and Writers' Cookbook.* Sausalito, Calif.: Contact Editions, 1961.
Bartholomew, Mel. *Square Foot Gardening: A New Way to Garden in Less Space with Less Work.* Emmaus, Pa.: Rodale Press, 1981.
Bateman, Ruth C. *The Zucchini & Carrot Cookbook.* New York: Crown, 1980.
Baum, Ruth, and Baum, Hilary. *Lifespice Salt-Free Cookbook.* New York: Perigee/Putnam Publishing Group, 1985.
Blanchard, Marjorie Page. *The Home Gardener's Cookbook.* Pownal, Vt.: Garden Way Publishing, 1974.
Bracken, Peg. *A Window over the Sink.* New York: Avon, 1982.
Brody, Jane. *Jane Brody's Good Food Book: Living the High Carbohydrate Way.* New York: W. W. Norton, 1985.
Brown, Barbara B. *Between Health and Illness: New Notions on Stress & The Nature of Well Being.* New York: Bantam, 1985.
Brown, Edward E. *Tassajara Cooking.* Boston: Shambhala Publications, 1985.
——. *The Tassajara Recipe Book: Favorites of the Guest Season.* Boston: Shambhala Publications, 1985.
Burros, Marian. *Pure and Simple: A Cookbook.* New York: Morrow, 1978.

Butler, Robert N., and Lewis, Myrna I. *Love and Sex After Sixty: A Guide for Men and Women in Their Later Years.* New York: Harper & Row, 1976.
Capon, Robert Farrar. *The Supper of the Lamb: A Culinary Reflection.* Garden City, N.Y.: Doubleday, 1969.
Cavanna, E., and Welton, J. B. *Gourmet Cookery for a Low-Fat Diet.* Englewood Cliffs, N.J.: Prentice-Hall, 1961.
Claiborne, Craig. *Craig Claiborne's Gourmet Diet.* New York: Ballantine, 1981.
——. *The New York Times Food Encyclopedia.* New York: Times Books, 1985.
Colbin, Annemarie. *Food and Healing.* New York: Ballantine, 1986.
Constable, George, ed. *Fresh Ways with Soups and Stews.* Alexandria, Va.: Time-Life Books, 1986.
Cost, Bruce. *Ginger East to West: A Cook's Tour with Recipes, Techniques & Lore.* Berkeley, Calif.: Aris Books, 1984.
David, Elizabeth. *French Provincial Cooking.* Toronto: Collins, 1960.
De Gouy, Louis P. *The Gold Cook Book.* New York: Chilton, 1960.
De Groot, Roy. *Feasts for All Seasons.* New York: McGraw-Hill, 1976.
Doyle, Roger. *The Vegetarian Handbook.* New York: Crown, 1979.
Doyle, Rodger P., and Redding, James L. *The Complete Food Handbook.* New York: Grove, 1977.
Dunn, William J. *Out of the Stock Pot.* New York: Scribner, 1971.
Durand, Pauline, and Languirand, Yolande. *Brunch: Great Ideas for Planning, Cooking, and Serving.* Woodbury, N.Y.: Barron, 1978.
Eckhardt, Linda W. *The New West Coast Cuisine.* Los Angeles: J. P. Tarcher, 1985.
Elliot, Rose. *The Festive Vegetarian.* New York: Pantheon, 1983.
Famularo, Joe, and Imperiale, Louise. *Vegetables: The New Main Course Cookbook.* Woodbury, N.Y.: Barron, 1985.
Farb, Peter, and Armelagos, George. *Consuming Passions: The Anthropology of Eating.* Boston: Houghton-Mifflin,

1980.

Farwagi, Peta L. *Full of Beans: An International Bean Cookbook.* London: Harper & Row Ltd., 1978.

Fischer, Teri A. *Seattle's Seasonal Bounty.* Seattle: Teri A. Fischer, 1983.

Friedman, Jo-Ann. *Home Health Care: A Complete Guide for Patients and Their Families.* New York: Norton, 1986.

Fuchs, Estelle, Ph.D. *The Second Season: Life, Love and Sex for Women in the Middle Years.* Garden City, N.Y.: Doubleday, 1977.

Fukuoka, Masanobu. *The One Straw Revolution.* New York: Bantam, 1985.

Galton, Lawrence. *Save Your Stomach.* New York: Crown, 1977.

Gault, Lila. *The Northwest Cookbook.* New York: Quick Fox/Putnam Publishing Group, 1978.

Gewanter, Vera. *A Passion for Vegetables: Recipes from European Kitchens.* New York: Viking, 1980.

Gorman, Judy. *The Culinary Craft.* Dublin, N.H.: Yankee Books, 1984.

Grigson, Jane. *Jane Grigson's Vegetable Book.* New York: Atheneum, 1979.

Hagler, Louise. *Tofu Cookery.* Summertown, Tenn.: Book Publishing, 1982.

Hansen, Marilyn, ed. *Cooking by the Calendar: A Family Weekly Cookbook.* New York: Times Books, 1978.

Hardigree, Peggy. *Mail Order Gourmet.* New York: St. Martin's, 1983.

Hartbarger, Janine Coulter, and Hartbarger, Neil J. *Eating for the Eighties.* Philadelphia: Saunders, 1981.

Hawken, Paul. *The Next Economy.* New York: Holt, Rinehart & Winston, 1983.

Hazelton, Nika. *The Unabridged Vegetable Cookbook.* New York: M. Evans, 1976.

Hendrickson, Audra, and Hendrickson, Jack. *The Carrot Cookbook.* Pownal, Vt.: Storey Communications, 1987.

Hewitt, Jean. *The New York Times Natural Foods Cookbook.* New York: Avon, 1972.

Johnston, Mireille. *The Cuisine of the Sun: Classical French Cooking from Nice & Provence.* New York: Vintage/Random House, 1979.

Kimball, Jeffe, and Anderson, Jean. *Art of American Indian Cooking.* Garden City, N.Y.: Doubleday, 1965.

Langham, Derald G. *Circle Gardening.* Old Greenwich, Conn.: Devin-Adair Publishing, 1977.

LaPlace, Vivian, and Kleiman, Evan. *Cucina Fresca.* New York: Harper & Row, 1985.

Lappe, Frances M. *Diet for a Small Planet.* New York: Ballantine, 1982.

—— and Collins, Joseph. *Food First: Beyond the Myth of Scarcity.* Boston: Houghton-Mifflin, 1977.

Lederman, Martin. *The Slim Gourmet.* New York: Simon & Schuster, 1954.

LeShan, Eda. *Oh, To Be Fifty Again: On Being Too Old for a Midlife Crisis.* New York: Times Books, 1986.

Lewis, Edna. *The Taste of Country Cooking.* New York: Knopf, 1976.

Lo, Kenneth H. *Chinese Vegetarian Cooking.* New York: Pantheon, 1974.

London, Mel. *Second Spring.* Emmaus, Pa.: Rodale Press, 1982.

London, Sheryl, and London, Mel. *The Herb and Spice Cookbook.* Emmaus, Pa.: Rodale Press, 1986.

Lynch, James J. *The Broken Heart: The Medical Consequences of Loneliness.* New York: Basic, 1979.

McGill, Michael E. *The Forty- to Sixty-Year-Old Male.* New York: Simon & Schuster, 1980.

McNair, James. *Cold Pasta: Elegant Pasta Recipes for Cold Presentation.* San Francisco: Chronicle, 1985.

Madison, Deborah, with Brown, Edward Espe. *The Greens Cook Book.* New York: Bantam, 1987.

Manners, Ruth Ann, and Manners, William. *The Quick & Easy Vegetarian Cookbook.* New York: M. Evans, 1979.

Montagu, Ashley. *Growing Young.* New York: McGraw-Hill, 1981.

Nathan, Amy. *Salad.* San Francisco: Chronicle, 1985.

Nearing, Helen. *Simple Food for the Good Life.* New York: Delta/Eleanor Friede, 1982.

Norman, Barbara. *Spanish Cookbook.* New York: Bantam, 1966.

Ortiz, Elisabeth Lambert. *The Book of Latin American Cooking.* New York: Knopf, 1979.

Pappas, Lou S. *Entertaining in the Light Style.* San Francisco: One Hundred One Productions, 1982.

Pepper, Claude. *Ask Claude Pepper.* Garden City, N.Y.: Doubleday, 1984.

Peter, Madeleine; Simmons, Nancy, ed. *Favorite Recipes of the Great Women Chefs of France.* New York: Holt, Rinehart & Winston, 1979.

Plaut, Martin E., M.D. *The Doctor's Guide to You and Your Colon: A Candid, Helpful Guide to Our Number One Hidden Health Complaint.* New York: Harper & Row, 1982.

Powledge, Fred. *Fat of the Land: What's Behind Your Shrinking Food Dollar & What You Can Do About It.* New York: Simon & Schuster, 1984.

Prudden, Bonnie. *Bonnie Prudden's After Fifty Fitness Guide.* New York: Villard, 1986.

Puner, Morton. *Getting the Most Out of Your Fifties.* New York: Crown, 1977.

Rankin, Dorothy. *Pestos! Cooking with Herb Pastes.* Trumansburg, N.Y.: Crossing Press, 1985.

Rawlings, Marjorie Kinnan. *Cross Creek Cookery.* New York: Scribner, 1942.

Romagnoli, Margaret, and Romagnoli, G. Franco. *The Romagnolis' Table.* New York: Bantam, 1977.

Root, Waverly. *Food: An Informal Dictionary.* New York: Simon & Schuster, 1980.

Rosenberg, Magda. *Sixty Plus and Fit Again.* New York: M. Evans, 1977.

Rosenfeld, Isadore. *Second Opinion.* New York: Simon & Schuster, 1980.

Rozin, Elizabeth. *The Flavor-Principle Cookbook.* New York: Hawthorn Books, 1973.

Sanders, Sharon. *Slim Snacks.* Chicago: Contemporary Books, 1982.

Sax, Richard. *From the Farmer's Market.* New York: Harper & Row, 1986.

Schoen, Elin, and Golbitz, Pat. *Widower.* New York: Morrow, 1984.

Seskin, Jane. *Alone Not Lonely: Independent Living for Women over Fifty.* Glenview, Ill.: Scott, Foresman, 1985.

Sherman, Kay L. *The Findhorn Family Cookbook.* Boulder, Colo.: Shambhala Publications, 1982.

Shulman, Martha R. *The Vegetarian Feast.* New York: Harper & Row, 1979.

Shurtleff, William, and Aoyagi, Akiko. *The Book of Tofu.* New York: Ballantine, 1979.

Spencer, Colin. *The New Vegetarian.* New

York: Viking, 1986.

Steinberg, Rafael. *Cooking of Japan.* Alexandria, Va.: Time-Life Books, 1969.

Stidham, Martin. *The Fragrant Vegetable: Simple Vegetarian Delicacies from the Chinese.* Los Angeles: J. P. Tarcher, 1986.

Tannahill, Reay. *Food in History.* New York: Stein & Day, 1974.

Thompson, Sylvia V. *Economy Gastronomy: A Gourmet Cookbook for the Budget-Minded.* New York: Atheneum, 1963.

Tracy, Marian. *Real Food: Simple, Sensuous, and Splendid—A Treasure of Over 230 Favorite Recipes.* New York: Penguin Books, 1978.

Tudge, Colin. *Future Food: Politics, Philosophy & Recipes for the Twenty-First Century.* New York: Harmony/Crown, 1980.

Turner, James S. *The Chemical Feast: Report on the Food and Drug Administration.* New York: Grossman/Viking, 1970.

Turvey, Valerie. *Bean Feast: An International Legumes Cookbook.* San Francisco: One Hundred One Productions, 1979.

Van Hoose, William H. *Midlife Myths & Realities.* Atlanta, Ga.: Humanics Ltd, 1985.

Williams, Jacqueline B., and Silverman, Goldie. *Hold the Fat, Sugar & Salt.* New York: Putnam Publishing Group, 1984.

Williams, Milton, and Windeler, Robert. *The Party Book.* Garden City, N.Y.: Doubleday, 1981.

Willing, Jules Z. *The Reality of Retirement: The Inner Experience of Becoming a Retired Person.* New York: Quill/Morrow, 1981.

——. *The Lively Mind: How to Enjoy Life by Becoming More Mentally Alert.* Chapel Hill, N.C.: Lively Mind Books, 1982.

Wilson, Lynne C. *The Wilson Farm Country Cookbook: Recipes from New England's Favorite Farm Stand.* Reading, Mass.: Addison-Wesley, 1985.

Worthington, Diane R. *Cuisine of California.* Los Angeles: J. P. Tarcher, 1982.

Yanker, Gary. *Gary Yanker's Walking Workouts.* New York: Warner Books, 1985.

INDEX

▲▲▲

A

Achiote, chicken, 93, 326–27
Acorn squash with fruit, 37,
  190
Agar-agar, 283
Almonds, couscous with
  carrots, currants and, 69,
  101, 220
Amaretto, flan with, 86,
  367–68
Anchovy and capers sauce,
  310–11
Angel hair:
  with broccoli flowerets and
    peas, 13, 68, 251–52
  with garden tomato sauce,
    68, 241–42
Antipasto:
  Italian, 98, 158
  Middle Eastern, 159
  salad, Blanche Rigamonti's,
    281
  salad, kidney bean, 224
Apple(s):
  chicken curry with peaches
    and, Madeleine
    Boulanger's, 102, 292–93
  crisp, Susan Zigouras',
    346–47
  Mexican bread pudding
    (capriotado), 87, 102,
    358–59
  and oat hearty muffins,
    Elane's, 353–54
  shrimp curry with peaches
    and, Madeleine
    Boulanger's, 102, 293
  stir-fry vegetables with, 187
  and yam salad, Ruth and
    Hilary Baum's, 67, 280
  zucchini soup, Nene's, 41,
    166, 167–68
Apricot:
  aspic, rosemary-scented, 95,
    283
  kugel, 68, 360–61
  loaf, 72, 356–57
  squares, 345–46
Artichoke(s):
  hearts, fusilli salad with
    roasted red peppers, black
    olives and, 68, 262
  soufflé squares, 144–45
  stuffed with bulgur and
    golden raisins, 41, 268

  with tamari-lime dressing,
    41, 268
Asparagus:
  buckwheat noodles with
    ginger, soy and 68, 242–43
  stir-fry with ginger and soy,
    37, 67, 91, 194–95
Aspics, 282–83
  beet, 282
  fruit dessert, 135
  gazpacho, 106, 166
  raspberry with chopped fresh
    limes, 352
  rosemary-scented apricot,
    95, 283

B

Baba ganouch, 65, 67, 153
Bacalhau à gomes de sá, 80,
  291–92
Baked:
  eggplant with nutmeg and
    ginger, 67, 205
  fish with capers and anchovy
    sauce, 310–11
  fork-tender chicken breasts,
    114, 323
  onions with balsamic
    vinegar, 35, 41, 114, 207
  salmon steak, flaky, 114,
    306–7
  whole standing ham, 99,
    105, 339–40
Baking with parchment paper,
  114, 116–18
Barbecues, 91–93, 332
  luau on the grill menu, 93
  Spanish supper on the grill
    menu, 92–93
Basil vinaigrette, 82, 128–29
Bean(s), 49, 209, 223–29
  basic recipe, 223–24
  cassoulet, Jeff's, 81, 297–98
  cook once, eat twice, 69
  impromptu dishes, 227–29
  kidney, salad or antipasto
    salad, 224
  and pea salad, cold, 93, 105,
    229
  See also Black bean(s); Green
    bean(s); White bean(s)
Beef, 334–37
  filet mignon, 13, 98, 106,
    335–36
  mainly meat meat loaf with
    green herbs, 9, 15, 62, 337

  mini Dijon burgers, 62,
    142–43
  picadillo, 15, 62, 63, 102,
    294–95
  shell steak paillard with
    thyme, 114, 334–35
  skillet skirt steak, 35, 114,
    336
  skirt steak with lime juice,
    336
  steak salad Niçoise, 34, 91,
    255
  tsimmes, Belle Meyers',
    299–300
  and vegetable stew, 84,
    178–79
Beet(s):
  aspic, 282
  and carrot slaw (magenta and
    orange), 9, 37, 285–86
  and carrot soup, 163
  and cucumber soup, 15, 37,
    41, 95, 162–63, 171
  ruby-red cranberry borscht,
    181–82
  Scandinavian pickled, 67,
    95, 195–96
Black, yellow, and green rice
  salad, 69, 91, 214
Black bean(s):
  chili, 69, 102, 303–4
  with red peppers, quick, 41,
    107, 228
  and vegetable salad, 69,
    224–25
Bluefish with cilantro, grilled,
  314–15
Borscht, ruby-red cranberry,
  181–82
Brazilian vegetable feijoada, 86,
  186–87
Bread(s), 37, 51
  apricot loaf, 72, 356–57
  do-ahead baking tips for, 357
  hearty apple and oat muffins,
    Elane's, 353–54
  peach and pear, 357
  pineapple and date, 357
  pineapple muffins, 354–55
  prune and walnut with
    carrots, Eleanor Tomic's,
    355–56
  pudding, Mexican
    (capriotado), 87, 102,
    358–59
  raisin, pudding, Frank
    Pimentel's, 95, 359

Breakfast, 7–8
Broccoli:
  flowerets, angel hair with
    peas and, 13, 68, 251–52
  soup, emerald, 37, 41, 166,
    169–70
  stir-fry with garlic, ginger,
    and soy, 37, 41, 195
Broiled:
  scrod with chunky pesto,
    114, 312–13
Brunch, 13, 78–80
Brussels sprouts:
  with Vermont Cheddar
    cheese, 37, 67, 198–99
  with vinaigrette, 37, 67, 199
Buckwheat groats. See Kasha
Buckwheat noodles:
  with asparagus, ginger and
    soy, 68, 242–43
  with scallions and smoked
    oysters, 68, 252
Buffet menus:
  birthday, 64–65
  elegant cocktail, 98
  just before midnight New
    Year's Eve, 106–7
  standard cocktail, 99
  summer solstice
    environmental, 89–90
  traditional holiday, 104–5
Bulgur (cracked wheat), 102,
    217
  artichokes stuffed with
    golden raisins and, 41, 268
  chick-pea, and scallion salad,
    219–20
  rice pilaf with walnuts,
    Eleanor Tomic's, 69,
    212–13
  salad in cucumber boats, 69,
    90, 221–22
Burgers, mini Dijon, 142–43
Butter(s):
  chive, Party Box, 105, 134
  clarified, 63, 131–32
  compound, 132
  cookies, Swedish sweet, 9,
    81, 361–62
  herb, 132
  lemon and lime, 132

C
Cabbage:
  Chinese, in three-green salad
    with grapefruit and olives,
    37, 85, 271
  red, ziti with pimiento-
    stuffed olives and, 68, 260
  ruby-red cranberry borscht,
    181–82
  See also Slaws

Canning, 135
Capers and anchovy sauce,
    310–11
Capriotado (Mexican bread
    pudding), 87, 102,
    358–59
Caribbean rouge sauce, 311
  farfalle with, 239–40
  fish in, Susan Dresner's, 311
Carrot(s):
  and beet slaw (magenta and
    orange), 9, 37, 285–86
  and beet soup, 163
  couscous with almonds,
    currants and, 69, 101, 220
  marinated red peppers with,
    35, 37, 41, 204
  and pignoli loaf, 9, 15, 37,
    184–85
  prune and walnut bread
    with, Eleanor Tomic's,
    355–56
  purée of parsnips and, 37,
    41, 202
  raita, 37, 95, 102, 270
  vichyssoise, 41, 90, 166, 172
Cashews, Thai shrimp with,
    317
Casserole dinners, 80–82
Casseroles, 287–304
  bacalhau à gomes de sá, 80,
    291–92
  black bean chili, 69, 102,
    303–4
  cassoulet, Jeff's, 81, 297–98
  chickadillo, 15, 63, 64, 72,
    102, 295
  chicken and lamb couscous,
    63, 101, 290–91
  chicken chili, 64, 102, 302–3
  chicken curry with apples
    and peaches, Madeleine
    Boulanger's, 102, 292–93
  chicken dinner in a pot, Mitz
    Perlman's, 62, 82, 296–97
  freeze-ahead, 63, 294–304
  lamb Navarin, 298–99
  picadillo, 15, 62, 63, 102,
    294–95
  shrimp curry with apples and
    peaches, Madeleine
    Boulanger's, 102, 293
  tsimmes, Belle Meyers',
    299–300
  vegetable chili, 15, 67, 102,
    300–301
  vegetable couscous, 37, 65,
    101, 288–89
Cassoulet, Jeff's, 81, 297–98
Cauliflower:
  lemon-zest soup, 41, 166,
    168–69
  steamed with fennel and

cumin, 41, 114, 206–7
Chayote, steamed, 114, 202–3
Cheddar:
  pennies, 142–43
  potted, with port and
    walnuts, 99, 156
  Vermont, Brussels sprouts
    with, 37, 67, 198–99
Cheese:
  cream, shell, 369
  feta and spinach stuffed
    mushrooms, 41, 145–46
  horseradish-yogurt, spread
    with strawberries, 123
  yellow split-pea loaf with,
    15, 69, 231–32
  yogurt, 122–23
  See also Cheddar
Chess tarts:
  chocolate-pecan, 370
  pecan, 101, 370
Chickadillo, 15, 63, 64, 72,
    102, 295
Chicken, 50, 115–18, 321–32
  achiote, 93, 326–27
  balls, Persian, 65, 147
  breasts, fork-tender baked,
    114, 323
  breasts, poached, 114,
    322–23
  cassoulet, Jeff's, 81, 297–98
  chickadillo, 15, 63, 64, 72,
    102, 295
  chili, 64, 102, 302–3
  curry with apples and
    peaches, Madeleine
    Boulanger's, 102, 292–93
  dinner in a pot, Mitz
    Perlman's, 62, 82, 296–97
  freeze-aheads, 62
  Gascony, 79, 328
  Gascony, ruote with, 68, 328
  and lamb couscous, 63, 101,
    290–91
  lemon-lime, 62, 91, 330–31
  Madrid, 327
  Moroccan, 98, 329
  Moroccan, ziti with cilantro
    sauce and, 68, 329
  pasta paella, 68, 244–45
  piccata, 35, 114, 325–26
  sesame, 64, 93, 331–32
  sesame with snow peas, 332
  shrimp gumbo, Dick Dorn's
    Texas-style, 180–81
  stock, 63, 138
  tacos with salsa, 324–25
Chicken salads:
  curried, 64, 67, 256
  Niçoise, 64, 254–55
  paella, 107, 264
  pasta and, Greek Isles, 258
  robusto pasta and, with red

and green peppers, 41, **259**

Chick-pea(s):
  bulgur, and scallion salad,
    219–20
  hummus, **158–59**
  kale with linguiça and, 80,
    107, **185–86**

Chiles, green, cilantro sauce
  with yogurt and, **124**

Chili:
  black bean, 69, 102, **303–4**
  chicken, 64, 102, **302–3**
  vegetable, 15, 67, 102, **300–1**

Chinese:
  -American Fourth of July
    picnic menu, 90–91
  cabbage, in three-green salad
    with grapefruit and olives,
    37, 85, **271**
  emerald brown rice, 37, 69,
    211

Chive butter, Party Box, 105,
  134

Chocolate:
  bursts, Marlu's, 13, 90,
    362–63
  pecan chess tarts, **370**
  pistachio squares, **366**

Chowders:
  classic New England fish, 85,
    166, **177–78**
  corn-potato-mushroom, 166,
    173–74

Christmas Eve supper menu,
  105–6

Chutney, summer/winter, **140**

Cilantro:
  butter, 85, **132**
  grilled bluefish with, **314–15**
  sauce, ziti with chicken
    Moroccan and, 68, **329**
  sauce with yogurt and green
    chiles, **124**

Citrus vinaigrette, 63, **127**

Clarified butter, 63, **131–32**

Cobblers:
  cranberry, **350–51**
  seasonal fruit, **350**

Cocktail buffets, 96–97,
  98–100

Coconut, oat, and nut flourless
  pastry crust, Elane's and
  Betsy's, **344–45**

Cod, salted, in bacalhau à
  gomes de sá, 80, **291–92**

Cold suppers, 94–95

Coleslaws. *See* Slaws

Component cooking, 63–72
  cook once, eat all week,
    70–72
  cook once, eat twice, 66–69

Compote, winter/summer fruit,
  105, **134–35**

Compound butters, **132**

Condiments:
  holiday spiced fruit, **136**
  quince fruit jam, **133**
  strawberry fruit jam, Hans',
    133
  summer/winter chutney, **140**
  winter/summer fruit
    compote, 105, **134–35**
  See also Butter(s)

Cookies, 361–65
  chocolate bursts, Marlu's,
    13, 90, **362–63**
  ginger icebox, 9, 91, 95,
    364–65
  Mexican wedding, 93, 102,
    363–64
  Swedish sweet butter, 9, 81,
    361–62

Cooking techniques. *See*
  Low-fat cooking
  techniques; Streamlined
  preparation techniques

Cook once, eat all week
  technique, 70–72

Cook once, eat twice
  components, 66–69
  beans, lentils, and peas, 69
  grains, 69
  pasta, 68
  vegetables, 67–68

Corn:
  black, yellow, and green rice
    salad, 67, 69, 91, **214**
  grilled peppers, pineapple
    and, 93, **203**
  potato-mushroom chowder,
    166, **173–74**

Couscous (semolina), 49, **218**
  with carrots, almonds, and
    currants, 69, 101, **220**
  chicken and lamb, 63, 101,
    290–91
  fruited, 69, 95, **219**
  vegetable, 37, 65, 101,
    288–89

Cracked wheat. *See* Bulgur

Cranberry(ies):
  borscht, ruby-red, **181–82**
  cobbler, **350–51**
  jubilee, 106, **368**
  vinaigrette, Mangetout, **126**

Cream cheese shell, **369**

Crudités with sauce Niçoise,
  99, **155**

Crusts:
  cream cheese shell, **369**
  flourless oat, nut, and
    coconut pastry, Elane's
    and Betsy's, **344–45**

Cucumber(s):
  and beet soup, 15, 37, 41,
    95, **162–63**, 171

boats, bulgur salad in, 69,
  90, **221–22**
  curried, 41, 102, **199–200**
  and fresh bean salad, Hans',
    41, **275–76**
  potatoes with fresh dill, Elise
    Cavanna's, 67, **201**
  radish, and orange salad,
    Henry's, 101, 107, **278**
  and yogurt in the Middle
    Eastern style, 65, 101, **277**

Curaçao, flan with, 86, **367–68**

Currants, couscous with
  carrots, almonds and, 69,
  101, **220**

Curry(ied):
  chicken salad, 64, 67, **256**
  chicken with apples and
    peaches, Madeleine
    Boulanger's, 102, **292–93**
  cucumber, 41, 102, **199–200**
  dressing, 41, 63, **130**
  ham salad, **256**
  shrimp salad, 95, **257**
  shrimp with apples and
    peaches, Madeleine
    Boulanger's, 102, **293**
  tofu salad, **256**

D

Dahl with scallions, tomatoes,
  and lemon, 69, **234**

Daikon, snow pea, and
  mushroom salad, 41,
  272–73

Date:
  and apricot squares, Elane's
    and Betsy's, **345–46**
  and pineapple bread, **357**

Desserts, 343–72
  apple crisp, Susan Zigouras',
    346–47
  apricot kugel, 68, **360–61**
  chocolate-pistachio squares,
    366
  cranberry jubilee, 106, **368**
  cream cheese shell, **369**
  date and apricot squares,
    Elane's and Betsy's,
    345–46
  flan with orange Curaçao or
    amaretto, 86, **367–68**
  flourless oat, nut, and
    coconut pastry crust,
    Elane's and Betsy's,
    344–45
  lime mousse, **372**
  mousse with liquor or
    liqueur, 102, **372**
  See also Bread(s); Cookies;
    Tarts

Desserts, fruit, 347–52

aspic, 135
cranberry cobbler, 350–51
kabobs, **349**
kumquats, Mandarin
  oranges, and litchee nuts
  on skewers, 91, **349**
pick-up-and-eat finger, **349**
pure fresh fruit "ice cream,"
  95, **348**
raspberry aspic with chopped
  fresh limes, 352
seasonal cobblers, 350
summer poached peaches,
  Florine Snider's, 9, 114,
  351
winter/summer compote,
  105, **134–35**
Dijon mini burgers, 62, **142–43**
Dinner, 7, 10
  menus for. *See* Menus
Dipping sauce, saté, 62, 63, **121**
Dips:
  baba ganouch, 65, 67, **153**
  guacamole with tofu, **151**
  hummus, **158–59**
  sauce Niçoise, Party Box, 63,
    120
Dressings. *See* Salad dressings;
  Sauces, cold;
  Vinaigrette(s)
  pink, **269**

E

Eggplant:
  baba ganouch, 65, 67, **153**
  baked with nutmeg and
    ginger, 67, **205**
  ratatouille, 68, 79, **188–89**
  tomato sauce picante with,
    Henry Grossi's, **240–41**
Eggs, 51
  gado gado salad with saté
    dipping sauce, 67, 93, **265**
Emerald broccoli soup, 37, 41,
  166, **169–70**
Endive:
  and farfalle with pink
    dressing, 68, **269**
  salad with pink dressing,
    Hans', **269**
Entertaining, 73–107
  at barbecues, 91–93
  for a crowd, 96–103
  at friendly occasions, 77–87
  at group events, 74
  holiday, 97, 103–7
  at lunchtime, 9–10
  at momentous occasions,
    73–74
  at picnics, 89–91
  in summer, 88–95
  See also Menus

Equipment, 59–61
  nonstick pans, 51, 114
  steaming utensils, 116

F

Farfalle:
  with Caribbean rouge sauce,
    68, **239–40**
  and endive with pink
    dressing, 68, **269**
Feijoada, Brazilian vegetable,
  86, **186–87**
Fennel:
  grilled red snapper with
    scallions and, 93, **315**
  sautéed in tarragon butter,
    41, **197**
  steamed cauliflower with
    cumin and, 41, 114,
    206–7
Feta and spinach stuffed
  mushrooms, 41, **145–46**
Fettuccine, green, with skillet
  slaw, **193**
Fiery pumpkin soup, 37, **170–71**
Filet mignon, 13, 98, 106,
  335–36
First courses:
  finger salad, **272**
  shrimp seviche with kohlrabi
    and Bosc pears 35, 87,
    150–51
  See also Hors d'oeuvres,
    cold; Hors d'oeuvres, hot;
    Salads, side; Soups
Fish, 50–51, 114–18, 305–20
  bacalhau à gomes de sá, 80,
    291–92
  baked, with capers and
    anchovy sauce, **310–11**
  broiled scrod with chunky
    pesto, 114, **312–13**
  Caribbean rouge, Susan
    Dresner's, **311**
  chowder, classic New
    England, 85, 166, **177–78**
  filet with vegetables (meal in
    a package), 114, **307–8**
  green-and-white tuna salad,
    257
  grilled bluefish with cilantro,
    314–15
  grilled red snapper with
    fennel and scallions, 93,
    315
  lemon-sweet steamed scrod,
    114, **318–19**
  mâche and haddock salad, **266**
  poached filet of sole with
    fresh mushrooms, 114, **320**
  sole mousse, **155**
  steak on a bed of peppers

and onions, skillet, 114,
    316
  See also Salmon; Scallop(s);
    Seafood; Shrimp
Flan with orange Curaçao or
  amaretto, 86, **367–68**
Fourth of July Chinese-
  American picnic menu,
  90–91
Freeze-aheads, 15, 62–63,
  294–304
French:
  cassoulet dinner, Jeff's, 81,
    297–98
  chicken Gascony, 79, **328**
  country brunch or supper
    menu, 78–79
  ratatouille, 68, 79, **188–89**
  See also Niçoise
Fruit(s), 8, 36, 48, 115
  acorn squash with, 37, **190**
  aspic dessert, **135**
  for buffets, 160
  couscous with, 69, 95, **219**
  desserts, *See* Desserts, fruit
  holiday spiced, 136
  winter/summer compote,
    105, **134–35**
  See also specific fruits
Fusilli:
  and macadamia nut salad,
    263
  salad with roasted red
    peppers, artichoke hearts,
    and black olives, 68, **262**
  and scallop salad, 34,
    261–62
  and tomato sauce picante
    with eggplant, Henry
    Grossi's, 68, **240–41**

G

Gado gado salad with saté
  dipping sauce, 67, 93, **265**
Gala vegetables, 13, 37, **191**
  chilled, **191**
Garden tomato sauce, 62,
  241–42
Garlic-lemon dressing, Nene's,
  37, 41, 63, 64, **253**
Gascony chicken, 79, **328**
  ruote with, 68, **328**
Gazpacho, 93, 107, **165–66**,
  171
  aspic, 106, **166**
Gelatin, 283
Ginger(ed):
  baked eggplant with nutmeg
    and, 67, **205**
  buckwheat noodles with
    asparagus, soy and, 68,
    242–43

Chinese emerald brown rice, 37, 69, **211**
icebox cookies, 9, 91, 95, **364–65**
nut mix, Party Box, **137**
stir-fry asparagus with soy and, 37, 67, 68, **194–95**
stir-fry broccoli with garlic, soy and, 37, 41, 91, **195**
"under-the-broiler" shrimp, Barbara Grogan's, 114, **313**
Grains, 49, **209–22**
  cook once, eat twice, 69
  See also Bulgur; Couscous; Kasha; Rice; Rice salads; Wild rice
Grapefruit, three-green salad with olives and, 37, 85, **271**
Gravlax, 98, **157**
Greek:
  lemon potatoes, **200–1**
  pasta-chicken salad, **258**
Green(s), 35–36, 37, **265**
  garden, for salads, **271**
  interchangeable, 37, 114, **208**
  three-, salad with grapefruit and olives, 37, 85, **271**
Green-and-white tuna salad, 15, **257**
Green bean(s):
  antipasto salad, Blanche Rigamonti's, **281**
  fresh, and cucumber salad, Hans', 41, **275–76**
  and red onion in lemon dressing, 41, 106, **278–79**
  vegetable salad Niçoise, 90, **255–56**
Green noodles with skillet slaw, 68, **193**
Grilled:
  bluefish with cilantro, **314–15**
  corn, peppers, and pineapple, 93, **203**
  red snapper with fennel and scallions, 93, **315**
Guacamole with tofu, **151**
Gumbo, shrimp-chicken, Dick Dorn's Texas-style, **180–81**

H

Haddock and mâche salad, **266**
Ham:
  paella salad, 107, **264**
  salad, curried, **256**
  whole standing baked, 99, 105, **339–40**

Herb(s):
  butters, **132**
  fresh, vinaigrette, 105, **128–29**
  oil flavored with, 127
  vinegars, 52, 129
Holiday entertaining, **103–7**
Holiday spiced fruit, **136**
Hors d'oeuvres, cold, 141, **148–51**
  baba ganouch, 65, 67, **153**
  cherry tomatoes with salmon cream, **149–50**
  crudités with sauce Niçoise, 99, **155–56**
  fruit, **160**
  gravlax, 98, **157**
  guacamole with tofu, **151**
  hummus, **158–59**
  Italian antipasto, 98, **158**
  marinated olives, 65, **152–53**
  marinated shrimp and snow pea kebabs, **149**
  Middle Eastern antipasto, **159**
  mousse of salmon, 99, **154–55**
  mousse of sole, **155**
  Oriental vegetables with saté dipping sauce, 98, **160**
  potted Cheddar with port and walnuts, 99, **156**
  shrimp seviche with kohlrabi and Bosc pears, 35, 87, **150–51**
  skewered scallops with zucchini and summer squash, **148–49**
Hors d'oeuvres, hot, 141–47
  artichoke soufflé squares, **144–45**
  Cheddar pennies, **142–43**
  fennel sautéed in tarragon butter, **197**
  mini Dijon burgers, 62, **142–43**
  minted lamb balls with pignoli, 65, **146**
  Persian chicken balls, 65, **147**
  spinach and feta stuffed mushrooms, 41, **145–46**
Horseradish:
  sauce, Sylvia Sherry's, 13, 98, 106, **122**
  yogurt cheese spread with strawberries, **123**
Hummus, **158–59**
Hungarian plum soup, Arthur Cafiero's, **164–65**

I

Icebox cookies, ginger, 9, 91, 95, **364–65**

"Ice cream," pure fresh fruit, 95, **348**
Impromptu meals, 15
Interchangeable greens, 37, 114, **208**
Italian:
  antipasto, 98, **158**
  red or green Swiss chard, 37, 84, 114, **208**
  zucchini, 35, 37, 41, **200**

J

Jams, 63
  quince fruit, **133**
  strawberry fruit, Hans', **133**

K

Kabobs and skewers:
  fruit, **349**
  kumquats, Mandarin oranges, and litchee nuts on, 91, **349**
  marinated shrimp and snow pea, **149**
  scallops with zucchini and summer squash, **148–49**
Kale with linguiça and chick-peas, 80, 107, **185–86**
Kasha (buckwheat groats), **218**
  with crisp green and yellow vegetables, 69, **222**
  "kashaed" mushrooms, 69, **220–21**
Kidney bean:
  and pea salad, cold, 93, 105, **229**
  salad or antipasto salad, **224**
Kohlrabi, shrimp seviche with Bosc pears and, 35, 87, **150–51**
Kugel, apricot, 68, **360–61**
Kumquats, Mandarin oranges, and litchee nuts on skewers, 91, **349**
Kuzu, **293**

L

Lamb:
  balls with pignoli, minted, 65, **146**
  and chicken couscous, 63, 101, **290–91**
  chop dinner with vegetables (meal in a package), 114, **340–41**
  Moroccan, 98, **329**
  Navarin, **298–99**
  roast leg of, El Greco, 72, **338–39**

Lasagna, zucchini, 105, 238–39

Lemon:
butter, 132
dahl with scallions, tomatoes and, 69, 234
dressing, 41, 106, 278–79
garlic dressing, Nene's, 37, 41, 63, 64, 128
lime chicken, 62, 91, 330–31
mushrooms in oil and, 41, 204–5
potatoes, Greek, 200–1
sweet steamed scrod, 114, 318–19
white beans with, 9, 69, 72, 225
zest cauliflower soup, 41, 166, 168–69

Lentils, 230–31
cook once, eat twice, 69
and rice, Sam's Aunt Fanny's, 69, 232–33
rice salad with red onion, 69, 233

Lime:
butter, 132
juice, skirt steak with, 336
lemon chicken, 62, 91, 330–31
mousse, 372
tamari dressing, 41, 268

Linguiça, kale with chick-peas and, 80, 107, 185–86

Liquor, mousse with liqueur or, 372

Litchee nuts, kumquats, and Mandarin oranges on skewers, 91, 349

Loaves:
carrot and pignoli, 9, 15, 37, 184–85
freeze-ahead, 62–63
for impromptu meals, 15
mainly meat meat, with green herbs, 9, 15, 62, 337
Pacific salmon, 15, 72, 308–9
yellow split-pea, with vegetables, cheese, or tofu, 15, 69, 231–32
See also Bread(s)

Low-fat cooking techniques, 31, 113–18

Luau on the grill menu, 93

Lunch, 7, 9–10, 14

M

Macadamia nut and fusilli salad, 263

Mâche and haddock salad, 266

Magenta and orange slaw (beet and carrot), 9, 37, 285–86

Mandarin orange(s):
kumquats, and litchee nuts on skewers, 91, 349
scallion, and red onion salad, 41, 273–74

Mango summer/winter chutney, 140

Marinated:
carrots with red peppers, 35, 37, 41, 204
olives, 65, 152–53
shrimp and snow pea kabobs, 149

Mayonnaise:
Angie's, 121–22

Meat, 333–42
loaf with green herbs, 9, 15, 62, 337
"spirited" cold roast pork tenderloin, 95, 341–42
See also Beef; Ham; Lamb; Sausage

Mediterranean potato salad, 67, 279

Menus:
for barbecues, 91–93
beef-and-vegetable stew, 83–84
birthday, 64–65
Brazilian vegetable feijoada, 86
cassoulet dinner, Jeff's, 81
chicken dinner in a pot, Mitz Perlman's, 82
Chinese-American Fourth of July picnic, 90–91
classic New England dinner, 84–85
for cold suppers, 94–95
deluxe dining at home, 13
elegant cocktail buffet, 98
elegant cold roast pork supper, 95
French country brunch or supper, 78–79
glamorous cold salad supper, 94–95
hearty Portuguese brunch or supper, 80
for interchangeable brunches and suppers, 78–80
just before midnight New Year's Eve buffet, 106–7
late Christmas Eve supper, 105–6
luau on the grill, 93
lunches to go, 9
Mexican fiesta, 87
for picnics, 89–91
for soup dinners, 83–85
Spanish supper on the grill, 92–93
standard cocktail buffet, 99
for stove-top to table-top casserole dinners, 80–82
summer solstice environmental buffet, 89–90
traditional holiday buffet, 104–5
for variations on a theme, 100–103
for vegetable dinners, 85–87

Mexican:
bread pudding (capriotado), 87, 102, 358–59
chickadillo, 15, 63, 64, 72, 102, 295
chicken piccata, 35, 114, 325–26
chicken tacos with salsa, 324–25
fiesta menu, 87
fiesta vegetables, 37, 67, 87, 192–93
picadillo, 15, 62, 63, 102, 294–95
wedding cookies, 93, 102, 363–64

Middle Eastern:
antipasto, 159
baba ganouch, 65, 67, 153
birthday menu, 64–65
chicken and lamb couscous, 63, 101, 290–91
hummus, 158–59
Persian chicken balls, 65, 147
yogurt and cucumbers, 65, 101, 277
See also Moroccan

Mini Dijon burgers, 62, 142–43

Minted lamb balls with pignoli, 65, 146

Miso soup with vegetables, 171, 176

Moroccan:
chicken, 329
chicken, ziti with cilantro sauce and, 68, 329
lamb, 98, 329

Mousse:
lime, 372
with liquor or liqueur, 102, 372
of salmon, 99, 154–55
of sole, 155

Muffins:
hearty apple and oat, Elane's, 353–54
pineapple, 354–55

Mushroom(s):
corn-potato chowder, 166, 173–74

fresh, poached filet of sole
with, 114, **320**
"kashaed," 69, **220–21**
in lemon and oil, 41, **204–5**
shiitake, wild rice with, 69,
215–16
snow pea, and daikon salad,
41, **272–73**
spinach and feta stuffed, 41,
145–46
Mussels, in pasta paella, 68,
244–45

N

New England:
classic dinner menu, 84–85
classic fish chowder, 85, 166,
177–78
New Year's Eve buffet menu,
106–7
Niçoise:
chicken salad, 64, **254–55**
sauce, crudités with, 99, **155**
sauce, Party Box, 63, **120**
steak salad, 34, 91, **255**
vegetable salad, 90, **255–56**
Noodles:
buckwheat, with asparagus,
ginger, and soy, 68,
242–43
buckwheat, with scallions
and smoked oysters, 68,
252
green, with skillet slaw, 68,
193
Nut(s), 37
mix, Party Box, **137**
oat, and coconut flourless
pastry crust, Elane's and
Betsy's, **344–45**
oat topping, **345–46**
oven-roasted, **137**
See also specific nuts
Nutmeg, baked eggplant with
ginger and, 67, **205**

O

Oat:
and apple hearty muffins,
Elane's, **353–54**
nut, and coconut flourless
pastry crust, Elane's and
Betsy's, **344–45**
nut topping, **345–46**
topping, **346–47**
Oils, 31, 51, 52, 127
saturated, 46
Olives:
antipasto salad, Blanche
Rigamonti's, **281**
black, fusilli salad with

roasted red peppers,
artichoke hearts and, 68,
262
black, yellow, and green rice
salad, 67, 69, 91, **214**
marinated, 65, **152–53**
pimiento-stuffed, ziti with
red cabbage and, 68, **260**
three-green salad with
grapefruit and, 37, 85,
271
vegetable salad Niçoise, 90,
255–56
Onion(s):
baked, with balsamic
vinegar, 35, 41, 114, **207**
red, green beans and, in
lemon dressing, 41, 106,
278–79
red, lentil-rice salad with, 69,
233
red, Mandarin orange, and
scallion salad, 41, **273–74**
skillet fish steak on a bed of
peppers and, 114, **316**
Orange(s):
cucumber, and radish salad,
Henry's, 101, 107, **278**
Curaçao, flan with, 86,
367–68
Mandarin, kumquats, and
litchee nuts on skewers,
91, **349**
Mandarin, scallion, and red
onion salad, 41, **273–74**
Oriental vegetables with saté
dipping sauce, 98, **160**
Oven-baked brown rice or
converted white rice, **210**
Oysters, smoked, buckwheat
noodles with scallions
and, 68, **252**

P

Pacific salmon loaf, 15, 72,
308–9
Package dinners, 117
fish filet with vegetables,
114, **307–8**
lamb chop dinner with
vegetables, Kay Meserve's,
114, **340–41**
Paella:
pasta, 68, **243–44**
salad, 107, **264**
Parchment paper, baking with,
114, 116–18
cookies, **365**
flaky salmon steak, 114,
306–7
fork-tender chicken breasts,
114, **323**

onions with balsamic
vinegar, 35, 41, 113, **207**
See also Package dinners
Parsley, Italian:
brown rice with pepita nuts
and, 102, **212**
rice pilaf with pignoli and,
35, 69, 72, **212**
Parsnips, purée of carrots
and, 37, 41, **202**
Pasta, 235–52
angel hair with garden
tomato sauce, 68, **241–42**
cook once, eat twice, 68
farfalle with Caribbean rouge
sauce, 68, **239–40**
fusilli and tomato sauce
picante with eggplant,
Henry Grossi's, 68,
240–41
green noodles with skillet
slaw, 68, **193**
paella, 68, **244–45**
penne with pesto sauce
without cheese, 68,
246–47
ruote with chicken Gascony,
328
ruote with thick chunky
pesto, **247**
small shells with quick
roasted red pepper sauce,
68, **248**
spaghetti with tomato-
sausage sauce, Ina Fox's,
243–44
ziti with chicken Moroccan
and cilantro sauce, 68,
329
zucchini lasagna, 105,
238–39
See also Buckwheat noodles
Pasta salads, 249–52
angel hair with broccoli
flowerets and peas, 10, 68,
251–52
chicken, Greek Isles, **258**
with chicken and red and
green peppers, robusto,
41, **259**
farfalle and endive with pink
dressing, 68, **269**
fusilli and macadamia nut,
263
fusilli and scallop, 34,
261–62
fusilli with roasted red
peppers, artichoke hearts,
and black olives, 68, **262**
shells with scallop seviche,
68, **250–51**
straw and hay, 68, **249–50**
ziti with red cabbage and

pimiento-stuffed olives, 68, 260
Pasta sauces, 237
    freeze-ahead, 62
    garden tomato, 241–42
    pesto without cheese, 246–47
    quick roasted red pepper, 62, 248
    spaghetti squash with, 188
    thick and chunky pesto, 62, 247
    tomato picante with eggplant, Henry Grossi's, 240–41
    tomato-sausage, 243–44
Pastry crust, flourless oat, nut, and coconut, Elane's and Betsy's, 344–45
Pea(s), 230
    angel hair with broccoli flowerets and, 13, 68, 251–52
    basic recipe, 230–31
    and bean salad, cold, 93, 105, 229
    cook once, eat twice, 69
    skillet slaw with peppers, golden raisins and, 67, 193
    soup, five-minute, 15, 163, 166, 171
    soup with watercress, 163
    See also Yellow split pea(s)
Peach(es):
    chicken curry with apples and, Madeleine Boulanger's, 102, 292–93
    and pear bread, 357
    poached summer, Florine Snider's, 9, 114, 351
    shrimp curry with apples and, Madeleine Boulanger's, 102, 293
Pear(s):
    Bosc, golden raisins, and green cabbage slaw, 67, 284–85
    Bosc, shrimp seviche with kohlrabi and, 35, 87, 150–51
    Mexican bread pudding (capriotado), 87, 102, 358–59
    and peach bread, 357
    plum tart, late summer, 371
Pecan:
    chess tarts, 101, 370
    chocolate chess tarts, 370
Penne with pesto sauce without cheese, 68, 246–47
Pepita nuts, brown rice with Italian parsley and, 102, 212

Pepper(s):
    grilled corn, pineapple and, 93, 203
    skillet fish on a bed of onions and, 114, 316
    skillet slaw with peas, golden raisins and, 67, 193
    tri-color, wild rice with, 69, 95, 106, 216
Pepper(s), red:
    marinated carrots with, 35, 37, 41, 204
    quick black beans with, 41, 107, 228
    roasted, Esther's, 41, 196–97
    roasted, fusilli salad with artichoke hearts, black olives and, 68, 262
    roasted, quick sauce, 62, 248
    yellow pear tomato salad with black walnuts and, 276
Persian chicken balls, 65, 147
Pesto, 246–67
    without cheese, 246–47
    chunky, broiled scrod with, 114, 312–13
    thick chunky, 62, 247
Picadillo, 15, 62, 63, 102, 294–95
Piccata, chicken, 35, 114, 325–26
Pickled beets, Scandinavian, 67, 95, 195–96
Picnics, 89–91
Pignoli:
    and carrot loaf, 9, 15, 37, 184–85
    minted lamb balls with, 65, 146
    rice pilaf with Italian parsley and, 35, 69, 72, 212
Pilafs:
    rice, with pignoli and Italian parsley, 35, 69, 72, 212
    rice-bulgur, with walnuts, Eleanor Tomic's, 69, 212–13
Pineapple:
    and date bread, 357
    grilled corn, peppers and, 93, 203
    muffins, 354–55
Pink dressing, 269
Pistachio-chocolate squares, 366
Plum(s):
    pear tart, late summer, 371
    soup, Arthur Cafiero's Hungarian, 164–65
Poached:
    chicken breasts, 114, 322–23
    filet of sole with fresh

mushrooms, 114, 320
    scallops, 148
    shrimp, 257
    summer peaches, Florine Snider's, 9, 114, 351
Poaching, 114, 115–16
Pork:
    tenderloin, "spirited" cold roast, 95, 341–42
    See also Ham; Sausage
Port, potted Cheddar with walnuts and, 99, 156
Portuguese:
    bacalhau à gomes de sá, 80, 291–92
    hearty brunch or supper menu, 80
    kale with linguiça and chick-peas, 80, 107, 185–86
Potato(es):
    corn-mushroom chowder, 166, 173–74
    cucumber, with fresh dill, Elise Cavanna's, 67, 201
    Greek lemon, 200–201
    new, watercress, and walnut salad, 274
    salad, Mediterranean, 67, 279
    sweet, in Brazilian vegetable feijoada, 86, 186–87
    as thickener, 166
Potted Cheddar with port and walnuts, 99, 156
Poultry. See Chicken
Prune and walnut bread with carrots, Eleanor Tomic's, 355–56
Puddings:
    flan with orange Curaçao or amaretto, 86, 367–68
    Mexican bread (capriotado), 87, 102, 358–59
    raisin bread, Frank Pimentel's, 95, 359
Pumpkin soup, fiery, 37, 170–71
Purée of parsnips and carrots, 37, 41, 202

Q

Quiche, salmon, 79, 309–10
Quick-broiling, 114, 118
Quince fruit jam, 133

R

Radicchio, 259
Radish, cucumber, and orange salad, Henry's, 101, 107, 278
Raisin bread pudding, Frank

Pimentel's, 95, 359
Raisins, golden:
  artichokes stuffed with
    bulgur and, 41, 268
  Bosc pear, and green cabbage
    slaw, 67, 284–85
  skillet slaw with peas,
    peppers and, 67, 193
Raitas:
  carrot, 37, 95, 102, 270
  watercress, 37, 102, 270
Raspberry aspic with chopped
  fresh lime, 352
Ratatouille, 68, 79, 188–89
Red cabbage, ziti with pimiento-
  stuffed olives and, 68, 260
Red snapper with fennel and
  scallions, grilled, 93, 315
Rice, 102, 209
  brown, with pepita nuts and
    Italian parsley, 102, 212
  bulgur pilaf with walnuts,
    Eleanor Tomic's, 69,
    212–13
  Chinese emerald brown, 37,
    69, 211
  and lentils, Sam's Aunt
    Fanny's, 69, 232–33
  lentil salad with red onion,
    69, 233
  oven-baked brown or
    converted white, 210
  pilaf with pignoli and Italian
    parsley, 35, 69, 72, 212
  as thickener, 166
  top-of-the-stove cooked
    brown or converted white,
    211
  See also Wild rice
Rice salads:
  black, yellow, and green, 67,
    69, 91, 214
  cold brown, with seasonal
    vegetables, 69, 213–14
  paella, 107, 264
  spring green-and-white, 41,
    69, 214
Rice wine vinegar, 52
Roast(ed):
  leg of lamb El Greco, 72,
    338–39
  nuts and seeds, 137
  red peppers, Esther's, 41,
    196–97
  red peppers, fusilli salad with
    artichoke hearts, black
    olives and, 68, 262
  red pepper sauce, quick, 62,
    248
  "spirited" cold pork
    tenderloin, 95, 341–42
Robusto pasta and chicken
  salad with red and green

peppers, 41, 259
Rosemary-scented apricot aspic,
  95, 283
Ruby-red cranberry borscht,
  181–82
Ruote:
  with chicken Gascony, 328
  with thick chunky pesto, 247
Russian dressing, 123–24

S

Salad dressings, 125–30
  curry, 41, 63, 130
  lemon, 41, 106, 278–79
  lemon-garlic, Nene's, 37, 41,
    63, 64, 128
  pink, 269
  Russian, 123–24
  tamari-lime, 41, 268
  See also Vinaigrette(s)
Salads, entrée, 253, 254–66
  curried ham, 256
  curried shrimp, 95, 257
  curried tofu, 256
  gado gado, with saté dipping
    sauce, 67, 93, 265
  glamorous cold supper menu,
    94–95
  glorious seafood, 260–61
  green-and-white tuna, 15,
    257
  impromptu meals, 15
  mâche and haddock, 266
  salmon and white bean,
    five-minute, 9, 15, 227
  steak, Niçoise, 34, 91, 255
  vegetable, Niçoise, 90,
    255–56
  See also Chicken salads;
    Pasta salads
Salads, side, 267–86
  antipasto, Blanche
    Rigamonti's, 281
  artichokes stuffed with
    bulgur and golden raisins,
    41, 268
  artichokes with tamari-lime
    dressing, 41, 268
  beet aspic, 282
  black bean and vegetable, 69,
    224–25
  bulgur, chick-pea, and
    scallion, 219–20
  bulgur, in cucumber boats,
    69, 90, 221–22
  carrot raita, 37, 95, 102, 270
  cold bean and pea, 93, 105,
    229
  cucumber, radish, and
    orange, Henry's, 101,
    107, 278
  cucumber and fresh bean,

Hans', 41, 275–76
  endive with pink dressing,
    Hans', 269
  farfalle and endive with pink
    dressing, 68, 269
  first-course finger, 272
  fruited couscous, 69, 95, 219
  garden greens and vegetables
    for, 271
  gazpacho aspic, 106, 166
  green beans and red onion in
    lemon dressing, 41,
    278–79
  kasha with crisp green and
    yellow vegetables, 69, 222
  kidney bean or antipasto,
    224
  lentil-rice, with red onion,
    69, 233
  Mandarin orange, scallion,
    and red onion, 41, 273–74
  Mediterranean potato, 67,
    279
  with orange and green
    vegetables, 37
  rosemary-scented apricot
    aspic, 95, 283
  snow pea, mushroom, and
    daikon, 41, 272–73
  three-green, with grapefruit
    and olives, 37, 85, 271
  watercress, new potatoes,
    and walnut, 274
  watercress raita, 37, 102,
    270
  wild rice with tri-color
    peppers, 95, 106, 216
  yam and apple, Ruth and
    Hilary Baum's, 67, 69,
    280
  yellow pear tomato, with red
    peppers and black
    walnuts, 276
  yogurt and cucumbers in the
    Middle Eastern style, 65,
    101, 277
  See also Pasta salads; Rice
    salads; Slaws
Salmon:
  cream, cherry tomatoes with,
    149–50
  gravlax, 98, 157
  mousse of, 99, 154–55
  Pacific, loaf, 15, 72, 308–9
  quiche, 79, 309–10
  steak, flaky baked, 114,
    306–7
  and white bean salad,
    five-minute, 9, 15, 227
Salsa, 102, 324–25
Saté dipping sauce, 62, 63, 121
  gado gado salad with, 67,
    93, 265

Oriental vegetables with, 98, 160

Sauces, cold:
cilantro, with yogurt and green chiles, 124
horseradish, Sylvia Sherry's, 13, 98, 106, 122
mayonnaise, Angie's, 121–22
Party Box, Niçoise, 63, 120
salsa, 102, 324–25
saté dipping, 62, 63, 121
See also Salad dressings; Vinaigrette(s)

Sauces, hot:
capers and anchovy, 310–11
Caribbean rouge, 311
See also Pasta sauces

Sausage:
linguiça, kale with chick-peas and, 80, 107, 185–86
paella salad, 107, 264
pasta paella, 68, 244–45
tomato sauce, 243–44

Sautéed fennel in tarragon butter, 197

Sautéing, low-fat, 113–15

Scallion(s):
buckwheat noodles with smoked oysters and, 68, 252
bulgur, and chick-pea salad, 219–20
dahl with tomatoes, lemon and, 69, 234
grilled red snapper with fennel and, 93, 315
Mandarin orange, and red onion salad, 41, 273–74

Scallop(s):
and fusilli salad, 34, 261–62
glorious seafood salad, 260–61
poaching, 148
seviche, pasta shells with, 68, 250–51
skewered with zucchini and summer squash, 148–49
steamed, with shades of jade vegetables, 114, 319

Scandinavian pickled beets, 67, 95, 195–96

Scrod:
broiled, with chunky pesto, 114, 312–13
lemon-sweet steamed, 114, 318–19

Seafood:
salad, glorious, 260–61
smoked oysters with buckwheat noodles and scallions, 68, 252
See also Fish; Salmon; Scallop(s); Shrimp

Seeds, oven-roasted, 137

Semolina. See Couscous

Sesame:
chicken, 64, 93, 331–32
chicken with snow peas, 332
marinade, 314

Seviche:
scallop, pasta shells with, 68, 250–51
shrimp, with kohlrabi and Bosc pears, 35, 87, 150–51

Shell steak paillard with thyme, 114, 334–35

Shiitake mushrooms, wild rice with, 69, 215–16

Shopping, 37, 45–57, 71
weekly supermarket guide for, 47–54

Shrimp:
with cashews, Thai, 317
chicken gumbo, Dick Dorn's Texas-style, 180–81
curry with apples and peaches, Madeleine Boulanger's, 102, 293
glorious seafood salad, 260–61
marinated, and snow pea kabobs, 149
paella salad, 107, 264
pasta paella, 68, 244–45
poached, 148
salad, curried, 95, 257
seviche with kohlrabi and Bosc pears, 35, 87, 150–51
"under-the-broiler" gingered, Barbara Grogan's, 114, 313

Skillet:
fish steak on a bed of peppers and onions, 114, 316
skirt steak, 35, 114, 336
slaw, green noodles with, 68, 193
slaw with peas, peppers, and golden raisins, 67, 193

Skirt steak:
with lime juice, 336
skillet, 35, 336

Slaws, 284–86
Bosc pears, golden raisins, and green cabbage, 67, 284–85
magenta and orange (beet and carrot), 9, 37, 285–86
skillet, green noodles with, 68, 193
skillet, with peas, peppers, and golden raisins, 67, 193
vegetable rich, Minnie Levy's, 37, 286

Smoked oysters, buckwheat noodles with scallions and, 68, 252

Snow pea(s):
chicken sesame with, 332
and marinated shrimp kabobs, 149
mushroom, and daikon salad, 41, 272–73

Sole:
mousse of, 155
poached filet of, with fresh mushrooms, 114, 320

Soufflé(s):
artichoke, squares, 144–45
turnip, Ceil's, 67, 198

Soup dinners, 83–85
beef-and-vegetable stew menu, 83–84
classic New England dinner menu, 84–85

Soups, 161–76
beet and carrot, 163
beet and cucumber, 15, 37, 41, 95, 162–63, 171
broccoli, emerald, 37, 41, 166, 169–70
carrot vichyssoise, 37, 41, 90, 166, 172
cold, 162–72
cooling, 176
corn-potato mushroom chowder, 166, 173–74
creamy, with no cream, 166
gazpacho, 93, 102, 107, 165, 171
hot, 173–76
hot or cold, 167–72
impromptu, 15, 171
lemon zest cauliflower, 41, 166, 168–69
miso, with vegetables, 171, 176
with orange and green vegetables, 37
pea, five-minute purely, 15, 163, 166, 171
pea, with watercress, 163
plum, Arthur Cafiero's Hungarian, 164–65
pumpkin, fiery, 37, 170–71
vegetable, 34
white-satin bean, 72, 166, 175
yellow split-pea with vegetables, mellow, 166, 174–75
zucchini-apple, Nene's, 41, 166, 167–68

Soup-stews, entrée, 177–82
beef-and-vegetable, 84, 178–79
New England fish chowder,

classic, 166, **177–78**
ruby-red cranberry borscht, **181–82**
Texas-style shrimp-chicken gumbo, Dick Dorn's, **180–81**
Spaghetti squash with pasta sauce, 37, **188**
Spaghetti with tomato-sausage sauce, Ina Fox's, **243–44**
Spanish:
chicken achiote, 93, **326–27**
chicken Madrid, **327**
paella salad, 107, **264**
supper on the grill menu, 92–93
Spiced fruit, holiday, **136**
Spinach:
and feta stuffed mushrooms, 41, **145–46**
interchangeable greens, 37, 114, **208**
three-green salad with grapefruit and olives, 37, 85, **271**
"Spirited" cold roast pork tenderloin, 95, **341–42**
Spreads:
horseradish-yogurt cheese spread with strawberries, **123**
potted Cheddar with port and walnuts, 99, **156**
strawberry fruit jam, Hans', **133**
yogurt cheese, **122–23**
Spring green-and-white rice salad, 41, 69, **214**
Squash:
acorn, with fruit, 37, **190**
crookneck, in summer/ winter chutney, **140**
fiery pumpkin soup, 37, **170–71**
spaghetti, with pasta sauce, 37, **188**
See also Yellow squash; Zucchini
Steak:
salad Niçoise, 34, 91, **255**
shell, paillard, with thyme, 114, **334–35**
skillet skirt, 35, 114, **336**
skirt, with lime juice, **336**
Steaming, 114, 116, **206**
Stews:
lamb Navarin, **298–99**
See also Soup-stews, entrée
Stir-fries:
asparagus with ginger and soy, 37, 67, 91, **194–95**
broccoli with garlic, ginger, and soy, 37, 41, **195**

vegetables with apples, **187**
Stocks:
all-vegetable soup, 63, **139**
chicken, 63, **138**
Straw and hay, 68, **249–50**
Strawberry(ies):
fruit jam, Hans', **133**
horseradish-yogurt cheese spread with, **123**
Streamlined preparation techniques, 58–71
component cooking, 63–65
cook once, eat all week, 70–72
cook once, eat twice, 66–69
equipment for, 59–60
freeze-aheads, 62–63
Summer entertaining, 88–95
barbecues, 91–93
cold suppers, 94–95
picnics, 89–91
Summer solstice environmental buffet menu, 89–90
Summer/winter chutney, **140**
Supper-by-the-bite, 96–97, 98–100
elegant cocktail buffet menu, 98
standard cocktail buffet menu, 99
Supper menus. *See* Menus
Swedish sweet butter cookies, 81, **361–62**
Sweet potato, in Brazilian vegetable feijoada, 86, **186–87**
Swiss chard, red or green, Italian style, 37, 84, 114, **208**

T

Tacos, chicken, with salsa, **324–25**
Tamari-lime dressing, 41, **268**
Tapioca, as thickener, 166
Tarragon butter, fennel sautéed in, **197**
Tarts:
chocolate-pecan chess, **370**
late summer plum-pear, **371**
pecan chess, 101, **370**
Texas-style shrimp-chicken gumbo, Dick Dorn's, **180–81**
Thai shrimp with cashews, **317**
Three-green salad with grapefruit and olives, 37, 85, **271**
Tofu:
guacamole with, **151**
salad, curried, **256**
yellow split-pea loaf with, 15, 69, **231–32**

Tomato(es):
cherry, in vegetable salad Niçoise, 90, **255–56**
cherry, with salmon cream, **149–50**
dahl with scallions, lemon and, 69, **234**
yellow pear, salad with red peppers and black walnuts, **276**
See also Pasta sauces
Top-of-the stove cooked brown rice or converted white rice, **211**
Toppings:
apple crisp, **346–47**
apricot kugel, **360–61**
oat-nut, **345–46**
for pure fresh fruit "ice cream," 348
Tsimmes, Belle Meyers', **299–300**
Tuna:
antipasto salad, Blanche Rigamonti's, **281**
salad, green-and-white, 15, **257**
Turnip soufflé, Ceil's, 67, **198**
Tuscany beans, 69, **226**

V

Variations on a theme, 100–103
chili menu, 102
Middle Eastern menu, 101
picadillo or chickadillo menu, 102
shrimp or chicken curry menu, 102
Vegetable(s), 25, 26, 32, 36, 39–41, 47, 48, 183–208
cook once, eat twice, 67–68
green and orange, 35–36, 37
for salads, 271
soups, 34
soup stock, 63, **139**
steaming, 116, 206
See also specific vegetables
Vegetable dinners, 85–87
Brazilian feijoada menu, 86
Mexican fiesta menu, 87
Vegetable entrées, 184–93
acorn squash with fruit, 37, **190**
Brazilian feijoada, 86, **186–87**
carrot and pignoli loaf, 9, 15, 37, **184–85**
chili, 15, 67, 102, **300–1**
chilled gala, **191**
couscous, 37, 65, 101, **288–89**
gala, 13, 37, **191**

green noodles with skillet slaw, 68, **193**
kale with linguiça and chick-peas, 80, 107, **185–86**
Mexican fiesta, 37, 67, 87, **192–93**
ratatouille, 68, 79, **188–89**
skillet slaw with peas, peppers, and golden raisins, 67, **193**
spaghetti squash with pasta sauce, 37, **188**
stir-fry with apples, **187**
Vegetable side-dishes, **194–208**
baked eggplant with nutmeg and ginger, 67, **205**
baked onions with balsamic vinegar, 35, 41, 114, **207**
Brussels sprouts with Vermont Cheddar cheese, 37, 67, **198–99**
Brussels sprouts with vinaigrette, 37, 67, **199**
cucumber potatoes with fresh dill, Elise Cavanna's, 67, **201**
curried cucumber, 41, 102, **199–200**
fennel sautéed in tarragon butter, 41, **197**
Greek lemon potatoes, **200–201**
grilled corn, peppers, and pineapple, 93, **203**
interchangeable greens, 37, 114, **208**
marinated carrots with red peppers, 35, 37, 41, **204**
mushrooms in lemon and oil, 41, **204–5**
purée of parsnips and carrots, 37, 41, **202**
red or green Swiss chard, Italian style, 37, 84, 114, **208**
roasted red peppers, Esther's, 41, **196–97**
Scandinavian pickled beets, 67, 95, **195–96**
steamed cauliflower with fennel and cumin, 41, 114, **206–7**
steamed chayote, 114, **202–3**

stir-fry asparagus with ginger and soy, 37, 67, 91, **194–95**
stir-fry broccoli with garlic, ginger, and soy, 37, 41, **195**
turnip soufflé, Ceil's, 67, **198**
zucchini Italienne, 35, 37, 41, **200**
See also Salads, side
Vichyssoise, carrot, 37, 41, 90, 166, **172**
Vinaigrette(s):
basil or fresh herb, 82, 105, **128–29**
Brussels sprouts with, 37, **199**
citrus, 63, **127**
classic, **125–26**
cranberry, Mangetout, **126**
Vinegars:
balsamic, baked onions with, 35, 41, 114, **207**
herb, 52, **129**

W

Walnut(s):
black, yellow pear tomato salad with red peppers and, **276**
potted Cheddar with port and, 99, **156**
and prune bread with carrots, Eleanor Tomic's, **355–56**
rice-bulgur pilaf with, Eleanor Tomic's, 69, **212–13**
watercress, and new potatoes salad, **274**
Watercress:
new potatoes, and walnut salad, **274**
pea soup with, **163**
raita, 37, 102, **270**
three-green salad with grapefruit and olives, 37, 85, **271**
White bean(s):
with lemon, 9, 69, 72, **225**
and salmon salad, five-minute, 9, 15, **227**
satin soup, 72, 166, **175**
Tuscany, 69, **226**

Wild rice, **215–16**
basic recipe, **215**
with shiitake mushrooms, 69, **215–16**
with tri-color peppers, 69, 95, 106, **216**
Winter/summer fruit compote, 105, **134–35**

Y

Yam and apple salad, Ruth and Hilary Baum's, 67, **280**
Yellow split pea(s):
dahl with scallions, tomatoes, and lemon, 69, **234**
loaf with vegetables, cheese, or tofu, 15, 69, **231–32**
soup with vegetables, mellow, 166, **174–75**
Yellow squash:
kasha with crisp green and yellow vegetables, 69, **222**
skewered scallops with zucchini and, **148–49**
Yogurt:
cheese, **122–23**
cilantro sauce with green chiles and, **124**
and cucumbers in the Middle Eastern style, 65, 101, **277**
horseradish cheese spread with strawberries, **123**

Z

Ziti:
with chicken Moroccan and cilantro sauce, 68, **329**
with red cabbage and pimiento-stuffed olives, 68, **260**
Zucchini:
apple soup, Nene's, 41, 166, **167–68**
Italienne, 35, 37, 41, **200**
lasagna, 105, **238–39**
ratatouille, 68, 79, **188–89**
skewered scallops with summer squash and, **148–49**